# OHIO Real Estate

# Finance

7TH EDITION

HONDROS LEARNING™

4140 Executive Parkway

Westerville, Ohio 43081

www.hondroslearning.com

© 2015 by Hondros Learning™. All rights reserved

Published 2015. Printed in the United States of America

18  17  16    2  3  4

ISBN:  978-1-59844-259-5

*For more information on or to purchase our products, please visit www.hondroslearning.com.*

# Suggested Syllabus

## OHIO REAL ESTATE FINANCE—DAY CLASSES

**COURSE DESCRIPTION:** The course is designed to provide students with a basic understanding of the instruments, procedures, methods, institutions, and markets involved in real estate financing.

**COURSE OBJECTIVES:** On completion of this course, students will be able to:
1. Demonstrate a basic knowledge of Ohio real estate finance.
2. Demonstrate a basic knowledge of real estate finance terminology and principles.
3. Recognize finance instruments and procedures used in real estate practice.

**COURSE TEXTBOOK:** *Ohio Real Estate Finance*, 7th edition, ©2015 Hondros Learning™

**COURSE NUMBER:** RE130

**COURSE CREDIT HOURS:** 20 clock hours or 2 credit hours awarded on successful course completion.

**PREREQUISITES:** None

**INSTRUCTION METHOD:** Lecture

| | |
|---|---|
| **MODULE 1** (a.m.) | Introduction and Overview |
| | Chapter 1 Housing Cycles, Money Supply, and Government Regulation |
| | Chapter 2 Types of Finance Instruments |
| **MODULE 2** (p.m.) | Chapter 3 Primary and Secondary Markets |
| | Chapter 4 Conventional Financing |
| **MODULE 3** (a.m.) | Chapter 5 Government Financing (FHA and VA) |
| | Chapter 6 Nontraditional Financing Tools |
| **MODULE 4** (p.m.) | Chapter 6 Nontraditional Financing Tools (*continued*) |
| | Chapter 7 Qualifying the Buyer |
| | Review |
| | Final Examination |
| | Evaluations |
| | Review of Final Examination |
| | Certificate Distribution |

**CLASSROOM HOURS ALL CAMPUSES:** 8:00 a.m. - 5:35 p.m.
Module (a.m.): 8:00 a.m. - 12:35 p.m.
Lunch Break: 12:35 p.m. - 1:05 p.m.
Module (p.m.): 1:05 p.m. - 5:35 p.m.

**ATTENDANCE:** Attendance is mandatory to receive course credit.

**GRADING:** Final grade is based 25% on classroom participation and attendance, and 75% on Final Exam and Quiz grades.

**NOTES:** Recording devices are not permitted during class lecture sessions.

# OHIO REAL ESTATE FINANCE—NIGHT CLASSES

**COURSE DESCRIPTION:** The course is designed to provide students with a basic understanding of the instruments, procedures, methods, institutions, and markets involved in real estate financing.

**COURSE OBJECTIVES:** On completion of this course, students will be able to:
1. Demonstrate a basic knowledge of Ohio real estate finance.
2. Demonstrate a basic knowledge of real estate finance terminology and principles.
3. Recognize finance instruments and procedures used in real estate practice.

**COURSE TEXTBOOK:** *Ohio Real Estate Finance*, 7th edition, ©2015 Hondros Learning™

**COURSE NUMBER:** RE130

**COURSE CREDIT HOURS:** 20 clock hours or 2 credit hours awarded upon successful course completion.

**PREREQUISITES:** None

**INSTRUCTION METHOD:** Lecture

| | |
|---|---|
| **MODULE 1** | Introduction and Overview |
| | Chapter 1  Housing Cycles, Money Supply, and Government Regulation |
| | Chapter 2  Types of Finance Instruments |
| **MODULE 2** | Chapter 3  Primary and Secondary Markets |
| | Chapter 4  Conventional Financing |
| **MODULE 3** | Chapter 5  Government Financing (FHA and VA) |
| | Chapter 6  Nontraditional Financing Tools |
| **MODULE 4** | Chapter 6  Nontraditional Financing Tools (*continued*) |
| | Chapter 7  Qualifying the Buyer |
| | Review |
| | Final Examination |
| | Evaluations |
| | Review of Final Examination |
| | Certificate Distribution |

**CLASSROOM HOURS:** 6:00 p.m. - 10:30 p.m.

**ATTENDANCE:** Attendance is mandatory to receive course credit.

**GRADING:** Final grade is based 25% on classroom participation and attendance, and 75% on Final Exam and Quiz grades.

**NOTES:** Recording devices are not permitted during class lecture sessions.

*rev. 06.15.15*

# Table of Contents

Suggested Syllabus . . . . . . . . . . . . . . . . . . . . . . . . . .iii

Preface. . . . . . . . . . . . . . . . . . . . . . . . . . . . . . . . . . . . .ix

## Chapter 1: Housing Cycles, Money Supply, and Government Regulations . . . . . . . . . 1

Real Estate Finance . . . . . . . . . . . . . . . . . . . . . . . . . . . 2

Housing Cycles . . . . . . . . . . . . . . . . . . . . . . . . . . . . . . . 2

Broad Forces Influencing Real Estate Cycles . . . . . . . . . . . . . . 3

Money Supply . . . . . . . . . . . . . . . . . . . . . . . . . . . . . . . . 5

Fiscal Policy and the United States Treasury Department . . . 5

American Recovery Reinvestment Act of 2009. . . . . . . . . . . 8

Monetary Policy and the Federal Reserve Board . . . . . . . . . 8

Government Influence via Regulations . . . . . . . . . . . . . . . . . 14

Laws Prohibiting Discrimination in the Financing of Homes. . . . . . . . . . . . . . . . . . . . . . . . . . . . . . . . . . . . 14

Laws Requiring Financial Disclosures . . . . . . . . . . . . . . . . . 14

Loan Estimate Form . . . . . . . . . . . . . . . . . . . . . . . . . . . . . 19

Sections of the Loan Estimate Form. . . . . . . . . . . . . . . . . . . 19

**Loan Estimate Page 2 . . . . . . . . . . . . . . . .19**

Completed Application . . . . . . . . . . . . . . . . . . . . . . . . . . 20

Ability to Repay Rule . . . . . . . . . . . . . . . . . . . . . . . . . . . 20

Closing Disclosure Form. . . . . . . . . . . . . . . . . . . . . . . . . . 24

Sections of the Closing Disclosure Form . . . . . . . . . . . . . . . 24

Preparing the Disclosure . . . . . . . . . . . . . . . . . . . . . . . . . 33

Other Disclosures . . . . . . . . . . . . . . . . . . . . . . . . . . . . . . 33

Summary. . . . . . . . . . . . . . . . . . . . . . . . . . . . . . . . . . . . . 35

Quiz . . . . . . . . . . . . . . . . . . . . . . . . . . . . . . . . . . . . . . . . 36

## Chapter 2: Types of Finance Instruments. . . . . . 39

Real Estate Finance Instruments . . . . . . . . . . . . . . . . . . . . 40

Promissory Notes . . . . . . . . . . . . . . . . . . . . . . . . . . . . . . 40

Negotiable Instruments . . . . . . . . . . . . . . . . . . . . . . . . . 44

Security Instruments . . . . . . . . . . . . . . . . . . . . . . . . . . . 45

Trust Deeds . . . . . . . . . . . . . . . . . . . . . . . . . . . . . . . . . . . 45

Advantages and Disadvantages of Trust Deeds . . . . . . . . . . 46

Mortgages. . . . . . . . . . . . . . . . . . . . . . . . . . . . . . . . . . . . 46

Judicial Foreclosure Procedure . . . . . . . . . . . . . . . . . . . . . 46

Short Sales. . . . . . . . . . . . . . . . . . . . . . . . . . . . . . . . . . . 48

Advantages and Disadvantages of Mortgages. . . . . . . . . . . 49

Typical Clauses in Finance Instruments . . . . . . . . . . . . . . . 49

Acceleration Clause . . . . . . . . . . . . . . . . . . . . . . . . . . . . 49

Alienation Clause . . . . . . . . . . . . . . . . . . . . . . . . . . . . . . 49

Defeasance Clause . . . . . . . . . . . . . . . . . . . . . . . . . . . . . 50

Partial Release, Satisfaction, or Conveyance Clause . . . . . . . 50

Prepayment Clause . . . . . . . . . . . . . . . . . . . . . . . . . . . . . 51

Subordination Clause. . . . . . . . . . . . . . . . . . . . . . . . . . . . 51

Other Mortgage Clauses and Covenants . . . . . . . . . . . . . . . 51

Types and Features of Mortgages . . . . . . . . . . . . . . . . . . . 52

First Mortgage . . . . . . . . . . . . . . . . . . . . . . . . . . . . . . . . 52

Second Mortgage . . . . . . . . . . . . . . . . . . . . . . . . . . . . . . 53

Purchase Money Mortgage . . . . . . . . . . . . . . . . . . . . . . . . 53

Cash-Out Refinance Mortgage . . . . . . . . . . . . . . . . . . . . . 53

Refinance Mortgage. . . . . . . . . . . . . . . . . . . . . . . . . . . . . 53

Home Equity Loan, Home Equity Line of Credit . . . . . . . . . . 54

Blanket Mortgage . . . . . . . . . . . . . . . . . . . . . . . . . . . . . . 54

Bridge Mortgage . . . . . . . . . . . . . . . . . . . . . . . . . . . . . . . 54

Budget Mortgage . . . . . . . . . . . . . . . . . . . . . . . . . . . . . . 54

Package Mortgage . . . . . . . . . . . . . . . . . . . . . . . . . . . . . . 54

Reverse Mortgage . . . . . . . . . . . . . . . . . . . . . . . . . . . . . . 55

Wraparound Mortgage . . . . . . . . . . . . . . . . . . . . . . . . . . . 55

Adjustable (or Variable) Rate Mortgage . . . . . . . . . . . . . . . 55

Option ARM; Pick a Payment. . . . . . . . . . . . . . . . . . . . . . . 56

Lot Loans . . . . . . . . . . . . . . . . . . . . . . . . . . . . . . . . . . . . 56

Interest-only Loans . . . . . . . . . . . . . . . . . . . . . . . . . . . . . 56

Construction Mortgage . . . . . . . . . . . . . . . . . . . . . . . . . . 56

Advantages and Disadvantages of Land Contracts . . . . . . . . 58

Ohio Division of Real Estate. . . . . . . . . . . . . . . . . . . . . . . 58

Summary. . . . . . . . . . . . . . . . . . . . . . . . . . . . . . . . . . . . . 59

Quiz . . . . . . . . . . . . . . . . . . . . . . . . . . . . . . . . . . . . . . . . 60

## Chapter 3: Primary and Secondary Markets. . . . 61

Primary Mortgage Market Lenders . . . . . . . . . . . . . . . . . . . 62

Commercial Banks . . . . . . . . . . . . . . . . . . . . . . . . . . . . . 62

Savings and Loan Associations . . . . . . . . . . . . . . . . . . . . . 62

Mortgage Companies. . . . . . . . . . . . . . . . . . . . . . . . . . . . 63

Other Primary Mortgage Market Lenders for Residential Real Estate . . . . . . . . . . . . . . . . . . . . . . . . . . . 64

Commercial Real Estate Lenders . . . . . . . . . . . . . . . . . . . . 65

Insurance Companies. . . . . . . . . . . . . . . . . . . . . . . . . . . . 65

Pension Funds. . . . . . . . . . . . . . . . . . . . . . . . . . . . . . . . 66

Real Estate Investment Trusts. . . . . . . . . . . . . . . . . . . . . . 66

Private Lending . . . . . . . . . . . . . . . . . . . . . . . . . . . . . . . 67

Sellers. . . . . . . . . . . . . . . . . . . . . . . . . . . . . . . . . . . . . . 67

Subprime Lending . . . . . . . . . . . . . . . . . . . . . . . . . . . . . . 67

Predatory Lending Practices. . . . . . . . . . . . . . . . . . . . . . . 67

Secondary Mortgage Markets . . . . . . . . . . . . . . . . . . . . . . 68

Function of Secondary Markets . . . . . . . . . . . . . . . . . . . . . 68

Fannie Mae—Federal National Mortgage Association..... 70

Ginnie Mae—Government National Mortgage
Association ......................................... 70

Freddie Mac—Federal Home Loan Mortgage
Corporation. ....................................... 71

Secondary Market Quality Control ................... 71

Other Secondary Mortgage Players .................. 72

**Present Day Mortgage Lending (As of this writing)** ....... 72

**Summary**.............................................. 73

**Quiz** ................................................. 74

**CHAPTER 4: Conventional Financing**........... **75**

**Conventional Financing** ............................. 76

Traditional Conventional Loans ...................... 76

15-Year Mortgage Loans ............................. 77

40-Year Mortgage Loans ............................. 78

Conforming Versus Nonconforming Loans ............. 78

**Conventional Loan Products**........................ 79

80% Conventional Loan.............................. 79

90% Conventional Loan.............................. 79

95% Conventional Loan.............................. 80

Other Conventional Loan Products................... 80

**Conventional Loans with Less than
a 20% Down Payment** ............................. 81

Private Mortgage Insurance (PMI) .................... 81

Secondary Financing ................................ 85

**Prepayment Penalties**............................... 89

**Fannie Mae and Freddie Mac Underwriting Standards** .... 90

Income Qualifying Standards......................... 90

**Summary**.............................................. 93

**Quiz** ................................................. 94

**CHAPTER 5: Government Financing**............ **95**

**FHA-Insured Loans** .................................. 96

**FHA Loan Guidelines** ................................ 96

FHA Loan Borrower Guidelines ...................... 96

Property Guidelines for FHA Loans................... 97

FHA Loan Regulations ............................... 98

**FHA Loan Programs** ................................ 102

Home Equity Conversion Mortgage ................. 104

Other Special FHA Loan Programs ................... 105

Manufactured Housing .............................. 106

**VA-Guaranteed Home Loans**....................... 107

**VA Loan Guidelines**................................ 108

Borrower Guidelines for VA Loans ................... 108

Property Guidelines for VA Loans ................... 112

VA Loan Regulations ................................ 113

**VA Loan Programs** ................................. 115

**USDA Rural Development Housing Programs**.......... 117

**Summary**............................................ 119

**Quiz** ............................................... 120

**CHAPTER 6: Nontraditional Financing Tools** .... **123**

**Purpose of Nontraditional Financing Tools** ............. 124

**Types of Financing Tools** ........................... 124

**Buydowns** .......................................... 125

Discount Points..................................... 125

Buydown Plans ..................................... 126

Permanent Buydown ................................ 127

Temporary Buydown ................................ 128

Limits on Seller-Paid Points ......................... 128

**Adjustable Rate Mortgages (ARMs)**.................. 129

How ARMs Work .................................... 130

Elements of ARM Loans ............................. 132

ARM Loan-to-Value Ratios .......................... 134

ARM Disclosures ................................... 135

**Other Structured Mortgages** ....................... 136

Bi-weekly Mortgage................................. 136

Reverse Mortgage .................................. 137

Shared Appreciation Mortgage (SAM) ................ 137

Graduated Payment Mortgage (GPM) ................ 137

Interest Only Mortgage ............................. 137

Hybrid ARMs ...................................... 138

**Structured Mortgages That are No Longer Available** ..... 138

Growth Equity Mortgage ........................... 138

Low Doc or No Doc Loans ........................... 138

Option or Payment Option ARMs. ................... 138

Subprime Loans (B/C Loans) ........................ 139

**Homebuyer Assistance Programs**..................... 140

Ohio Housing Finance Agency....................... 141

Community Reinvestment Act (CRA) ................. 141

**Seller Financing** .................................... 142

Purchase Money Mortgage .......................... 142

Purchase Money Second Mortgage .................. 143

Land Contract ...................................... 144

Lease/Options ..................................... 144

Lease/Purchase .................................... 146

Equity Exchange ................................... 147

Participation Plan................................... 148

Selecting and Executing Seller Financing ............. 148

**Summary**............................................ 150

**Quiz** ............................................... 151

**Chapter 7: Qualifying the Buyer** . . . . . . . . . . . . . **153**

  **Getting a Buyer Approved** . . . . . . . . . . . . . . . . . . . . . . . . . 154

    Pre-Qualification . . . . . . . . . . . . . . . . . . . . . . . . . . . . . . . . 154

    Pre-Approval . . . . . . . . . . . . . . . . . . . . . . . . . . . . . . . . . . . 154

  **The Loan Approval Process** . . . . . . . . . . . . . . . . . . . . . . . . 155

  **Consulting with the Lender** . . . . . . . . . . . . . . . . . . . . . . . 155

    Common Fees Associated with Real Estate Loans . . . . . . . 156

  **Completing the Loan Application** . . . . . . . . . . . . . . . . . . . 157

    The Loan Application . . . . . . . . . . . . . . . . . . . . . . . . . . . . . 158

  **Processing and Analyzing the Borrower and Property** . . . . 159

  **Underwriting and Approving the Loan Application** . . . . . . 165

  **Automated Underwriting** . . . . . . . . . . . . . . . . . . . . . . . . . 165

  **The Art of Qualifying a Buyer** . . . . . . . . . . . . . . . . . . . . . . 166

  **Fannie Mae and Freddie Mac Underwriting Standards** . . . 167

    Income Qualifying Standards . . . . . . . . . . . . . . . . . . . . . . . 167

    Credit History . . . . . . . . . . . . . . . . . . . . . . . . . . . . . . . . . . 172

    Net Worth . . . . . . . . . . . . . . . . . . . . . . . . . . . . . . . . . . . . . 176

    Summary of Qualifying the Buyer . . . . . . . . . . . . . . . . . . . 178

  **FHA Underwriting Standards** . . . . . . . . . . . . . . . . . . . . . . . 180

    Income Qualifying Standards . . . . . . . . . . . . . . . . . . . . . . . 180

  **VA Underwriting Standards** . . . . . . . . . . . . . . . . . . . . . . . . 181

    Income Qualifying Standards . . . . . . . . . . . . . . . . . . . . . . . 181

  **Review of Qualifying Standards** . . . . . . . . . . . . . . . . . . . . 182

    Other Factors Considered . . . . . . . . . . . . . . . . . . . . . . . . . 183

  **Closing the Loan** . . . . . . . . . . . . . . . . . . . . . . . . . . . . . . . . 183

    Closing Procedure . . . . . . . . . . . . . . . . . . . . . . . . . . . . . . . 184

  **Summary** . . . . . . . . . . . . . . . . . . . . . . . . . . . . . . . . . . . . . . 187

  **Quiz** . . . . . . . . . . . . . . . . . . . . . . . . . . . . . . . . . . . . . . . . . . 188

**Final Exams** . . . . . . . . . . . . . . . . . . . . . . . . . . . . . **191**

  **Final Exam 1** . . . . . . . . . . . . . . . . . . . . . . . . . . . . . . . . . . . 191

  **Final Exam 2** . . . . . . . . . . . . . . . . . . . . . . . . . . . . . . . . . . . 195

  **Final Exam 1 Answer Key** . . . . . . . . . . . . . . . . . . . . . . . . . 199

  **Final Exam 2 Answer Key** . . . . . . . . . . . . . . . . . . . . . . . . . 200

**Appendix** . . . . . . . . . . . . . . . . . . . . . . . . . . . . . . . **201**

  **Chapter Answer key** . . . . . . . . . . . . . . . . . . . . . . . . . . . . . 201

    Federal Regulations/Loan Programs . . . . . . . . . . . . . . . . . 210

    Secondary Markets . . . . . . . . . . . . . . . . . . . . . . . . . . . . . . . 210

    Miscellaneous . . . . . . . . . . . . . . . . . . . . . . . . . . . . . . . . . . 210

**Glossary** . . . . . . . . . . . . . . . . . . . . . . . . . . . . . . . . **211**

**Index** . . . . . . . . . . . . . . . . . . . . . . . . . . . . . . . . . . . **231**

# *Preface*

An important part of a real estate agent's job is understanding the specifics of real estate finance. Whether your specialty is residential or commercial real estate, buyers will count on you to know the in's and out's of financing the transaction. You will need to understand the government's influence on real estate finance, as well as the types of financing available as these often influence what type of home or property a buyer will purchase.

Real estate is a growing field. The attractive salary potential combined with the ability to be your own boss makes it easy to see why the industry continues to expand. In addition, the rate of home ownership continues to grow in the U.S.—and that means the job outlook for real estate agents is promising.

As a real estate professional, you will help clients make their dreams and financial goals come true. Whether helping a newly married couple acquire their first home or an investor purchase rental property, you will evaluate property, determine a fair sale or purchase price, and work through the details of contracts and negotiations. You will also assist in explaining financing options, which is the reason for this textbook.

## How to Use this Text

This textbook is designed to give you the information you need to understand the ever-evolving and sometimes confusing world of real estate finance. You will learn the fundamentals of real estate finance including housing cycles, different types of finance instruments, how lenders qualify buyers, types of loans available, and more.

Whether in the classroom or studying on your own, you will find the information presented in a clear and concise manner. The text provides **key terms**, **examples**, finance exercises, **chapter summaries**, **chapter quizzes,** and a thorough **glossary** to reinforce the concepts presented throughout.

To get the most out of your coursework, read each chapter in its entirety, paying close attention to key terms. After reading, be sure to take the chapter quizzes because they will help prepare you for the licensing exam. And, once you have completed your course of study, keep this book handy as a valuable reference tool as you begin your real estate career.

## Hondros Learning™

Hondros Learning is the leading provider of classroom materials for real estate prelicensing and continuing education. Together with Hondros College of Business, we have provided training and educational products to more than one million students.

Successful completion of this course is essential to your career. To help you with that—and passing your licensing exam the first time— these additional real estate products are available from Hondros Learning:

Ohio Real Estate Salesperson CompuCram® Online Exam Prep

Real Estate Vocab Crammer™ Flashcards

Real Estate Vocab Crammer™ Audio CD and Dictionary Set

*Ohio Real Estate Principles & Practices* textbook

*Ohio Real Estate Appraisal* textbook

*Ohio Real Estate Law* textbook

*Real Estate National Sales Review Crammer™* textbook

*Ohio Real Estate State-Specific Sales Review Crammer™* textbook

## Recognitions: Reviewer Acknowledgments

Hondros Learning™ would like to thank the following expert reviewers for their comments and suggestions:

**Al Batteiger**

**Rod Farthing**

**Kim Kovacs**

**Mike Prozy**

**Rob Streicher**

# Housing Cycles, Money Supply, and Government Regulations

Housing cycles are influenced by many factors. Real estate markets and real estate finance are interrelated: Real estate can be helped or hurt by interest rates; interest rates depend on supply and demand for money; loan activity depends on availability of money; property values depend on the health of the economy. We'll look at the four broad forces influencing real estate cycles, then focus on government influences on real estate finance through fiscal policy, monetary policy, government programs, and regulations.

There are several laws, both federal and state, that regulate various aspects of the real estate financing process. These include laws prohibiting discrimination and requiring certain financial disclosures in real estate transactions. You must be knowledgeable about these laws for your real estate practice and for the state licensing exams.

**Annual Percentage Rate (APR)** Relationship between the cost of borrowing and the total amount financed, represented as a percentage.

**Equal Credit Opportunity Act (ECOA)** Federal law that prohibits discrimination in granting credit to people based on sex, age, marital status, race, color, religion, national origin, or receipt of public assistance.

**Fed Funds Rate** The Federal Reserve's target for short-term interest rates.

**Federal Reserve Board (the Fed)** The body responsible for U.S. monetary policy, maintaining economic stability, and regulating commercial banks. Also referred to as the **Board of Governors**, but most commonly called **the Fed**.

**Fiscal Policy** The government's plan for spending, taxation, and debt management.

**Interest Rate** The rate which is charged or paid for the use of money, generally expressed as a percentage of the principal.

**Monetary Policy** Means by which the government exerts control over the supply and cost of money.

**Real Estate Settlement Procedures Act (RESPA)** Federal law dealing with real estate closings that provides specific procedures and guidelines for the disclosure of settlement costs.

**Truth in Lending Act (TILA)** Act that requires lenders to disclose credit costs in order to promote informed use of consumer credit.

**Key Terms**

# Real Estate Finance

To be a successful real estate professional, you need to know the intricacies of real estate finance. When working for sellers, understanding real estate finance helps you bring qualified buyers to them—and more knowledge means finding more ways to get buyers qualified. Plus, sellers compete against builders who have many creative financing options, so knowledge of real estate finance can help your listing compete in the market.

When working with buyers, knowing about financing options helps you find the best program for their situation rather than relying on one program offered by a mortgage broker or banker. Plus, finance knowledge can give you an advantage in negotiations.

Whether you work with sellers or buyers, getting a buyer approved for a loan is essential to close a real estate transaction. Of course, you can rely on mortgage or bank professionals to answer detailed questions, but you still must understand financing, interest rates, and how both of these are affected by real estate cycles and government influences. You will be asked questions about financing by clients and on the state exam.

# Housing Cycles

**Housing cycles** are *general swings in real estate activity*, resulting in increasing or decreasing activity and property values during different phases of the cycle. Cycle lengths vary. Economic theory says supply and demand always seek to balance each other and thus, the market responds. When demand for a product (such as housing) exceeds supply, the price for that product will rise, thereby stimulating more production. This is commonly referred to as a **seller's market**. How can you tell when it's a seller's market? Some signs include:

- A limited supply or no homes for sale in an area
- Homes sell quickly—some may not even make it on the market before they are sold
- Selling prices rapidly increase
- Multiple buyers compete for a particular home or property for sale
- Homes may sell for more than the asking price

As production increases, or more homeowners decide to sell, more demand is satisfied until eventually the supply outstrips demand creating a higher inventory of unsold home and a **buyer's market** is created. The absorption rate slows (the number of sales on a monthly basis compared to the number of homes available to be sold), prices fall, production and sales slow until demand catches up with supply, and the cycle starts over. Other indicators of a buyer's market include:

- Homes are on the market longer (days on market) due to high supply and low demand
- Home values go down
- Buyers become price sensitive and fear paying too much for a home
- Sellers and homebuilders may provide incentives to buyers to purchase their homes which may include offering better loan rates, no closing costs, bonuses, free options, etc.

In a healthy economy, supply and demand are more or less in balance, also known as *equilibrium*. The forces affecting supply and demand are constantly changing, thereby shifting the balance.

There are two factors that separate the housing market from other supply and demand models:

1. Lag time needed for the construction industry to respond to perceived changes in supply and demand. Because of this, real estate cycles generally take longer to respond to upswings and downswings than other businesses.

2. The limit to the supply of land with all utilities (gas, electric, water, public sewer) in a given area.

## Broad Forces Influencing Real Estate Cycles

Imbalances in supply and demand may be short-term or long-term, depending on their causes, including such factors as:

- Consumer confidence
- Supply of land
- Inflation
- Cost of money
- Availability of credit
- Construction costs
- Health of the economy
- Demographics
- Population shifts
- Population growth
- Fiscal policy

All of these factors can be divided into the *four broad forces that affect real estate* (remembered easily as **P-E-G-S**):

- **Physical**
- **Economic**
- **Governmental**
- **Social**

### Physical

Physical forces that affect real estate cycles can be *on* a property or *external* to a property, *natural* or *man-made*. Physical forces can include **location** and **popularity**, as areas go in and out of favor with the public because of location, jobs, climate, or other reasons. Land availability and desirability are important factors in real estate cycles, as well as overall supply and demand. The **environment** can also impact real estate cycles; a natural waterway or man-made lake is a positive environmental factor where pollution that affects an entire area is obviously a negative. Think of it this way: Some homes, neighborhoods, and styles of homes simply wear out.

_For Example_

Think of the home you grew up in, or your grandparent's home. Would either style of home and number of bathrooms be in demand today? What about your old neighborhood? Has it declined?

## Economic

Local economic trends have a big impact on real estate cycles. The **economic base** of an area is the *main business or industry a community uses to support and sustain itself.* While the presence of a good economic base is important for all businesses in an area, it's critical to maintain home values in real estate markets. This is due to the immobility of real estate and customers. Houses can't be relocated to where buyers are, and usually buyers can't move their jobs to where a specific house is located.

The economic base of an area is a primary factor when determining the supply of housing. In prosperous areas, there should be funds available to finance the purchase and construction of housing and, in theory, the marketplace will function smoothly.

National economic factors are increasingly important, as was demonstrated in 2008 and 2009. Although local economic health continued to be a major factor, it was influenced more and more by the national economic picture where inflation, interest rates, and the availability of credit were also a consideration. In fact, one of the **most important factors** in determining demand in the real estate market is *interest rates*. When interest rates are low, the demand for housing increases; when they are high, there's a decrease in demand. (All things being equal, a drop in interest rates can spur housing market activity—for either home purchases or refinancing.) Furthermore, interest rates determine whether money flows into savings accounts, thus increasing the available pool of money for home loans, or flows to other higher-yield investments.

Some examples of economic factors that affect the real estate market in a particular area are the availability of jobs, tax rates, and local policies.

### For Example

If there is an increase in available jobs, there will likely be an influx of money in the community. Conversely, if employers are scaling back and jobs are scarce, it will have a negative effect on housing.

## Governmental

Government activities affecting real estate can be divided **nationally** and **locally**. *National government influences* include taxation, fiscal and monetary policies, secondary markets, government financing programs, and federal regulations. The federal government also influences interest rates via the Federal Reserve Board. Since the federal government is the largest borrower in the country, its spending has a huge influence on the national economy. Things like international conflict and war also have an effect on the economy and real estate market because worried consumers are less likely to make large purchases.

*Local government activities* affect the real estate market. State and local governments have two types of laws that influence real estate:

- **Revenue generating laws** deal with taxes, and although they're passed primarily to raise revenue, they can have other effects on real estate.

- **Right to regulate laws** deal with government police powers. These laws can take the form of land use controls, zoning laws, environmental protection laws, eminent domain, and escheat—all of which can limit land use.

Furthermore, in many areas of the U.S., overcrowded cities are beginning to enact **no-growth** policies that limit the number of new homes built. If no-growth becomes widespread, the housing supply will be squeezed more, leading to price increases.

## Social

Social forces also have an interrelated effect on real estate cycles. These factors include *demographics, migrations, size of families, population shifts, growth, and age.* As populations grow and change, so do their housing needs.

Social behavior patterns and population distribution can have major effects on supply and demand in the real estate market.

### For Example

When the number of people in their prime home buying years increases, it increases housing prices and supply. Smaller families, high divorce rates, and a trend toward marriages later in life also stimulate demand due to fewer people per household. Finally, a general aging of the population indicates more changes on the horizon.

Migration of the population is also a powerful force. This social factor may actually be the result of an economic factor (e.g., a factory moving into or out of an area) or a governmental factor (e.g., higher or lower state/local tax rates). Housing values can benefit from an influx of people, or be devastated by an exodus.

Think of social factors that cause the buying and selling of houses: Divorce, marriage, school quality, and housing styles. What was a popular area ten years ago may not be as popular today. As the country ages, features like first-floor master suites, three- and four-car garages, and the addition of mother-in-law suites have increased.

# Money Supply

There **are several ways the federal government can influence housing cycles and real estate finance. We will first look at the federal government's use of fiscal policy,** through the U.S. Treasury Department, including taxation. We will also discuss use of **monetary policy,** through the Federal Reserve Board, which affects interest rates. Fiscal and monetary policies have direct and indirect influences on real estate, including interest rates charged by lenders for all types of loans. To a large degree, the supply of money in the United States is controlled by the federal government, whereas interest rates, similar to the cost of most things in a market economy, are controlled primarily by the **law of supply and demand**.

The **law of supply and demand** says that *for all products, goods, and services, when supply exceeds demand, prices will fall and when demand exceeds supply, prices will rise.* This is true for real estate, houses, and money itself. If the supply of something is large—in this case, a large amount of money in circulation—the price will fall, so interest rates tend to decrease.

Falling interest rates tend to increase activities in the areas of real estate sales and borrowing. Conversely, if the supply of money is small, the price of borrowing money tends to rise and is reflected in higher interest rates. Of course, there are other factors that affect interest rates, but the forces of supply and demand have the greatest effect.

## Fiscal Policy and the United States Treasury Department

**Fiscal policy** is *the government's plan for spending, taxation, and debt management.* The legislative and executive branches of government enact fiscal policy by passing legislation, which sets the government's priorities for how much money will be collected, from whom, and how it will be spent. The ultimate goals of fiscal and monetary policies are economic growth, full employment, and international balance of payments. Unfortunately, there's much debate over which policies actually promote these results. Worse yet, the government's fiscal policy is subject to tremendous political pressure.

The **United States Treasury Department** is *part of the executive branch of the federal government*. The Treasury Department, as fiscal manager of the nation, is responsible for carrying out the nation's fiscal policy by doing the actual spending, taxing, and debt financing through an account it keeps with the Federal Reserve. Treasury funds come from a number of sources, but the largest source is personal and business income taxes.

The **Internal Revenue Service** (**IRS**), *a branch of the Treasury Department, collects taxes and enforces tax laws, and issues interest-bearing notes (called securities) to cover any spending deficits*. **Deficit spending** and **taxation** are the two main policy tools the Treasury Department uses to implement fiscal policy. Both are a means of controlling the supply of money in circulation and thus indirectly affect interest rates.

## Deficit Spending

The first tool is **deficit spending**—*when the government spends more money than it takes in* from tax revenue. When federal income is less than federal expenditures, a shortfall called a **federal budget deficit** results. Since the Great Depression, most years have experienced a deficit. When this happens, the Treasury obtains funds to cover the shortfall by issuing interest-bearing securities to investors. These securities are referred to as **Treasury Bills** or **T-Bills** (less than one-year term), **Treasury Notes** (one- to five-year term) or **Treasury Certificates** (five- to ten-year term). In issuing these securities, the federal government borrows from the private sector and accumulates debt. When the government borrows money to cover deficits or debt, less money is available for private borrowers.

While some economists believe federal deficits and debt have little impact on interest rates, others believe large-scale federal borrowing can have a dramatic effect on interest rates, as private borrowers compete for limited remaining funds. Although there were surpluses in the '90s, for example, the government still had to maintain fiscal discipline to pay down the national debt as future budget projections are influenced by economic conditions and other factors.

Government borrowing (whether through deficits or debt) is the single largest drain on the supply of mortgage loan funds. The amount of money the government spends directly affects the amount of money available on an individual basis to purchase real estate. If the government spends more than what is brought in through taxes, less money is available for people to borrow—which could increase interest rates. If the goal of Congress, the President, and others in government is to balance the budget and pay down the national debt, this should have a positive effect on the real estate market.

## Taxation

The second tool of fiscal policy is *taxation*. Taxes directly impact spending habits of most businesses and individuals. When tax rates are low, banks have more money to lend and consumers have more to invest. Conversely, higher taxes result in fewer funds to lend and invest. And if consumers are investing, it is often in tax-exempt securities instead of taxable investments, like mortgages. While some would argue government spending is necessary and has the same net result on economic activity, the bottom line is higher taxes resulting in consumers having less money with which to buy homes.

Taxation can also have direct and deliberate secondary effects on real estate and mortgage financing. Along with raising revenue, tax provisions are used to implement social policies by encouraging or discouraging certain behaviors or activities. This is done through tax deductions and exemptions.

### For Example

The deduction for mortgage interest from taxable income effectively stimulates housing and encourages home ownership. Beginning in 1988, tax code changes limited the deductibility of home mortgage interest, which was previously fully deductible. If money is used to buy or improve a primary residence, then mortgage interest is deductible for loans up to $1,000,000 ($500,000 or less if married filing separately). Interest on home loans for purposes other than buying or improving a home is deductible to a much lesser extent, depending on filing status.

Provisions of the Tax Reform Act of 1986 also limited or eliminated tax benefits previously available for real property owners. Eliminated were the capital gains exclusion for long-term capital gains and accelerated cost recovery methods, while straight-line cost recovery periods for income and investment property were increased. The ability to offset losses from income property (termed "passive losses") against income from wages and salaries was restricted for many taxpayers. All of these factors served to make real estate investing less attractive.

Still, investors can deduct expenses and depreciation for *commercial and investment properties*. **Depreciation** is *the expensing of the cost of business or investment property over a set number of years, determined by the IRS to be the asset's useful life*.

### For Example

The cost of a residential building is divided by a depreciation life of 27.5 years, whereas the cost of a commercial building is divided by a depreciation life of 39 years.

For a commercial property to be depreciable, it must be used in a trade or business. Thus, a house rented to tenants is a depreciable asset, whereas a personal residence is not (unless part of it is used for a home office and even in this situation, the laws are very limiting.) Only capital assets (buildings and improvements) are depreciable; land is not. Repairs are expensed in the year they are incurred. Rules are complicated, though, so professional tax advice is always encouraged.

The **Taxpayer Relief Act of 1997** added benefits for homeowners by adding a new tax exclusion on the sale of a principal residence. The exclusion is $500,000 in profits for married couples filing jointly and $250,000 in profits for single taxpayers. Anyone selling a home can claim the exclusion as often as every two years—without having to buy another home of equal or greater value—as long as **three conditions** are met, including:

1.  The seller must have owned the home for at least two of the five years preceding the sale.
2.  The seller must have used the property as a principal residence for at least two of the five years preceding the sale.
3.  The seller must not have used the exclusion for a sale during the prior two years.

The IRS clarified these rules such that, in certain circumstances (such as a job relocation), if the person did not own or use the home for the entire two-year period, the exclusion amount may be prorated.

√ **Note:** These tax laws are mentioned here to make you aware that fiscal policy and tax laws can affect real estate but, as a real estate professional, you should never give tax advice to anyone. Advise clients to seek counsel from tax professionals as tax laws are complicated and change often.

## American Recovery Reinvestment Act of 2009

Other tax-related programs come and go. For example, with the **American Recovery and Reinvestment Act of 2009**, Congress authorized a tax credit of up to $8,000 for qualified first-time homebuyers purchasing homes on or after January 1, 2009 and before December 1, 2009.

### Worker, Homeownership and Business Assistance Act of 2009

The **Worker, Homeownership and Business Assistance Act of 2009** extended the deadline—taxpayers who had a binding contract to purchase a home before April 30, 2010 were eligible for the credit. Buyers had to close on the home before June 30, 2010.

For homes purchased in 2009, the credit did not have to be paid back unless the home ceased to be the taxpayer's main residence within a three-year period following the purchase.

Additionally, this new law provided a move-up or "long-time existing resident" credit of up to $6,500 to others who did not qualify as "first-time homebuyers." To qualify for this credit, a buyer must have owned and used the same home as her principal or primary residence for at least five consecutive years of the eight-year period ending on the date of purchase of a new home as a primary residence.

## Monetary Policy and the Federal Reserve Board

**Monetary policy** is *the government's mechanism through which it exerts control over the supply and cost of money*. Monetary policy also has the goals of economic growth, full employment, and international balance of payments. Additionally, monetary policy tries to maintain stability in prices, interest rates, and financial markets.

The **Federal Reserve Board** (also called **the Fed**) *is responsible for U.S. monetary policy, maintaining economic stability, and regulating commercial banks*. The Fed consists of appointees whose terms do not coincide with those of politicians. Theoretically, this insulates the agency from making politically-based decisions. In reality, politics can still play a part in the Fed's decisions.

President Woodrow Wilson introduced the Federal Reserve Act of 1913, which established a Federal Reserve System with 12 regional Federal Reserve Banks. Woodrow's Act created a decentralized national banking system that became the lender of last resort and provided funds to banks to avoid bank runs common in the late 1800s and early 1900s.

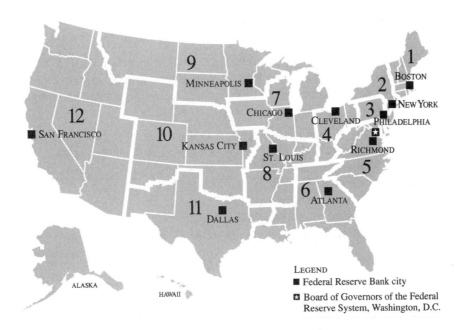

*Federal Reserve Map of The United States*

The Fed's structure distributes power three different ways:

- Geographically
- Between private and government sectors
- Among bankers, businesses, and the public

The Federal Reserve System is comprised of the Board of Governors (Federal Reserve Board), Federal Open Market Committee (FOMC), Federal Advisory Council, Federal Reserve Banks, and more than 5,000 member banks.

The **Board of Governors**, called the **Federal Reserve Board**, is a seven-member committee that controls the Federal Reserve System. The governors are appointed by the President and confirmed by the Senate for 14-year terms. The chairman serves a four-year, renewable term as part of his 14-year, non-renewable appointment to the Federal Reserve Board. The Board members control the Fed's monetary policy by implementing various policy tools, which we'll discuss shortly. The Board also has substantial control over regulations affecting the activities of commercial banks and bank holding companies. The Federal Reserve Board also oversees federal regulations dealing with money.

The **Federal Open Market Committee (FOMC)** controls the Fed's open market operations—the sale and purchase of government securities. The FOMC consists of the seven members of the Federal Reserve Board, plus the President of the Federal Reserve Bank of New York, and four other Federal Reserve Bank presidents. FOMC actions are a very important way of controlling the money supply.

The **Federal Advisory Council** consists of 12 members, elected one each by the 12 Federal Reserve Banks, who act as district representatives. They meet quarterly with the Board of Governors to discuss business conditions and make policy recommendations.

**Federal Reserve Banks** have one main office located in each of the 12 Federal Reserve districts. In addition to the 12 Federal Reserve Banks, there are 25 branches and 12 offices. Federal Reserve Banks provide services to financial institutions, such as check clearing. All nationally chartered commercial banks are required to join the Federal Reserve and purchase stock in its Federal Reserve District, technically making each a Federal Reserve

Bank owned by the member commercial banks in that district. Each Reserve Bank has a nine-member board of directors.

**Member banks** include more than 5,000 commercial banks across the U.S. Each has some input into the Fed's policies via the election of six directors to its district Federal Reserve Bank. All commercial banks are subject to the rules and policies implemented by the Fed, such as maintaining required reserves of depositors' funds.

The **Federal Housing Finance Agency** (**FHFA**) was created in 2008 under the Housing and Economic Recovery Act of 2008. The FHFA has oversight of Fannie Mae, Freddie Mac, and the Federal Home Loan Banks. This law combined the staff of the Office of Federal Housing Enterprise Oversight (OFHEO), the Federal Housing Finance Board (FHFB), and the GSE mission office at the Department of Housing and Urban Development (HUD). With the initial creation of the FHFA, it was not clear whether there would be any changes to the organization of the Federal Reserve System.

## Monetary Policy

Through monetary policy, the Fed can control the amount of money available for banks to lend, in effect, raising or lowering interest rates for the banks' customers. As explained earlier in this chapter, higher interest rates mean tougher credit and lower interest rates mean easier credit. Making credit easier or more difficult to obtain allows the Fed to also control the quality of credit.

There are four tools used by the Fed to implement monetary policy (remembered easily as **D-O-R-M**):

- **D**iscount rates
- **O**pen market operations
- **R**eserve requirements
- **M**oral suasion

Let's look at how these tools of monetary policy influence the supply and cost of money.

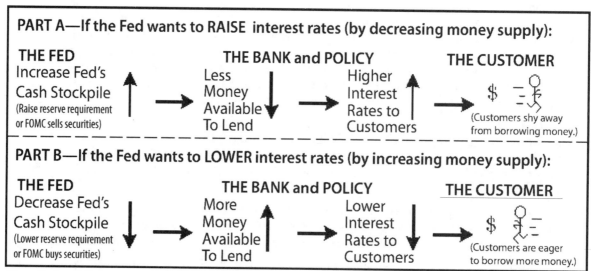

*How Federal Reserve actions affect interest rates.*

## Discount Rates

**Discount rates** or **federal discount rates** are *the interest rates charged by Federal Reserve Banks on loans to member commercial banks.* If Federal Reserve Banks charge higher discount rates for loans to commercial banks, the banks will pass those higher costs to customers in the form of higher interest rates. A cut in the discount rate also filters down to loans banks make to their customers (but usually not as fast). So, an increase in the discount rate usually equals an increase in interest rates to customers; a decrease in the discount rate usually equals a decrease in interest rates to customers.

Currently, the discount rate is a policy tool used less often. The Fed discourages banks from borrowing funds directly from them, unless they are in financial trouble and not able to borrow from other banks on the open funds market. The discount rate is still important, because money managers watch the discount rate. When the Fed adjusts the discount rate in line with the funds rate, it is seen as confirmation of their long-term outlook on interest rates and the economy. It is also seen as an indication of the Fed's bias for future monetary policy decisions. While the adjustment of these rates between the Fed and the member banks does not directly affect you, it normally causes member banks to raise the rate for consumer loans to stay in line with the increased cost of money to them.

## Open Market Operations

**Open market operations** are *when the Fed sells or buys government securities (bonds) as a means of controlling the supply of, and demand for, money.* Interest rates are affected by this activity because when the Fed buys and sells securities, it makes more or less money available for banks to lend.

The Federal Open Market Committee (FOMC) meets regularly to discuss the present and future state of the economy, including where interest rates should ideally be to accomplish the Fed's long-term objectives of economic growth and stability with minimal inflation. At its FOMC meeting, the Fed tries to exert indirect influence over long-term interest rates by establishing a target **Fed funds rate**. The **Fed funds rate** affects the short-term interest rate banks charge when borrowing money in the Fed funds market (usually very short-term loans for a day or two to help banks cover reserve requirements caused by the normal daily fluctuations in deposits).

To hit its target Fed funds rate, the Fed sells or buys securities (called bonds). When the Fed sells Fed fund securities, it increases its stockpile of cash and takes money out of circulation. Since the banks have less money available to lend, interest rates rise. Conversely, when the Fed buys securities, it decreases its stockpile of cash and puts more money into circulation. Since the banks that sold the security (or the banks of the customers that sold the security) have more money available, they want to quickly re-lend the money elsewhere to earn interest instead of just letting the money sit in their banks. Since banks have more money to lend, they will lower interest rates.

Keep in mind that other factors, such as inflation, may be applying upward pressure on interest rates at the same time that an increase in money supply is exerting downward pressure. And the Fed can exert influence only on short-term Fed funds interest rates. **The Fed does not set the prime rate (the rate that banks charge their best customers) and the Fed's actions have no direct effect on the prime rate**, but long-term rates usually follow the lead established by the Fed funds rate movement. However, there are times when long-term interest rates don't follow this lead; this may occur if there are other perceived long-term risks, such as fear of future inflation.

The Fed can also buy and sell U.S. dollars as part of its open market operations if there's an imbalance in international supply and demand for U.S. dollars. Although this can also affect inflation and interest rates, it is beyond the scope of this text.

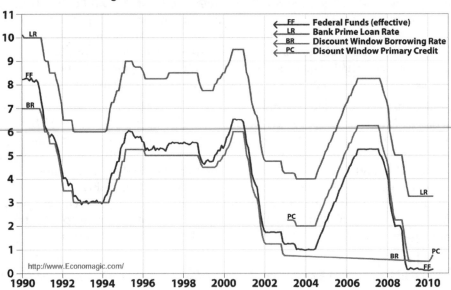

**Monthly Fed Funds, Prime, and Discount Rate**

FF — Federal Funds (effective)
LR — Bank Prime Loan Rate
BR — Discount Window Borrowing Rate
PC — Disount Window Primary Credit

http://www.Economagic.com/

## Reserve Requirements

**Reserve requirements** are *the percentage of deposits commercial banks are required to keep on deposit*, either on hand at the bank or in the bank's own accounts—in other words, money the bank *cannot* lend to customers. The original purpose of reserve requirements was to help avert financial panic by giving depositors some confidence that their deposits were safe and accessible. Reserve requirements, however, have also become a policy tool.

By raising or lowering reserve requirements, the Fed controls the supply and cost of money, and the quality of credit. If you wanted to raise interest rates, make credit tougher to get, and/or improve the quality of credit, you'd raise the reserve requirements to decrease the money supply available for banks to loan. When there's a smaller supply of money, you can be more selective about who borrows it and thus, improve the quality of loans (and hopefully have less loss due to bad debt). When there's a smaller supply of something, you want to decrease demand—and higher interest rates usually decrease demand!

Conversely, if you wanted to lower interest rates or make credit easier to get, you'd lower the reserve requirements. Lowering the reserve requirements increases the money supply available for banks to loan. When there's a larger supply of money, you can be less selective about who borrows it. You also want to increase demand—and lower interest rates should do that.

Using reserve requirements to adjust interest rates and control inflation has become a less important near-term Fed tool. Instead, reserve requirement changes are used in the face of a severe recession or severe inflation. This is because changing reserve requirements has a great impact on the money supply since it affects all deposit assets of banks. The Fed is able to have a similar effect but on a smaller, more manageable scale with FOMC open market operations.

Moral Suasion

**Moral suasion** is *using persuasive influences on the public and financial markets so they perceive credit in a specific way.*

### For Example

The Chairman of the Federal Reserve Board may make a speech stating the Fed is concerned about rising stock prices fueling inflation. Even though the Fed does not intend to actually raise interest rates, the Chairman's statement may still produce the desired effect of having the public and financial markets do less speculating in the market.

A new factor growing in influence is the exchange rate between countries. Because we are evolving into a global economy, the trading power of the dollar also has an effect on our economy. The Fed is highly involved in monetary issues with our main trading partners to stabilize the dollar in other marketplaces, making our products viable in other countries.

Recent Monetary Policy

The balancing efforts of the Fed are directed to managing the growth of the money supply to allow adequate growth of the economy at reasonable interest rates, without fueling inflation or fears of inflation, which could lead to higher interest rates. Prior to 1979, the Federal Reserve attempted to moderate interest rates by increasing the money supply when interest rates started to rise, thereby hoping to cause rates to fall. This policy led to high inflation as more and more money was pumped into the economy to satisfy the borrowers' demands.

In October 1979, the Fed adopted a different approach. Rather than try to control interest rates by adjusting the money supply, the Fed instituted a policy of controlling the money supply (and inflation) by adjusting interest rates. The discount rate reached as high as 14% in 1981. The result was a much tighter credit market, since the only way to slow the rampant growth of the money supply was to discourage borrowing by raising interest rates. As inflation was brought under control, the Fed was able to lower the discount rate.

√ **Note:** According to the Bureau of Labor Statistics, since 2000, the Consumer Price Index has reached manageable proportions, ranging from a high of 3.8% in 2008 to a low of -0.04% in 2009. At the beginning of 2010, the current discount rate ranged from 0.00% to 0.25%.

Part of the Fed's role in managing interest rates is to deal not only with actual inflation, but also with *anticipated* inflation. The Fed has adopted a policy of trying to anticipate future economic conditions rather than simply reacting to them, as in the past. This has also meant trying to reduce further the size and impact of swings in the business cycle. Most economists and businesses watch the Fed's actions when the FOMC meets to see if they will raise interest rates to reduce growth and head off inflation, or lower rates in an effort to spur economic growth and head off recession. Although many believe inflation is less of a threat in our current global economy, the Fed still plays an important role in managing economic growth and interest rates.

# Government Influence via Regulations

**Government regulations** that affect the real estate market and real estate finance include *tax laws, environmental laws, anti-discrimination laws, financial disclosure laws*, and many others. Compliance with some of these laws—**Truth in Lending**, **Equal Credit Opportunity**, and **Home Mortgage Disclosure**—are monitored and implemented through the Federal Reserve. Many of these laws were designed specifically to protect homeowners and consumers.

## Laws Prohibiting Discrimination in the Financing of Homes

Although real estate agents aren't directly involved in the lending process, it's a good idea for all agents to be familiar with laws regarding financing.

### Equal Credit Opportunity Act (ECOA)

The **Equal Credit Opportunity Act (ECOA)** is a federal law that *prohibits discrimination in granting credit to people based on **sex**, **age**, **marital status**, **race**, **color**, **religion**, **national origin**, **receipt of public assistance**, or exercised rights under the Consumer Credit Protection Act*.

The law was originally passed in 1974 to prohibit discrimination on the basis of sex or marital status. This law led to, among other things, the requirement that credit bureaus maintain separate credit files on married spouses, if so requested. The law was also intended to ensure that women received the same consideration by lenders as their male counterparts when applying for credit. The law was expanded in 1976 to include all the protected classes listed previously. Most notable among the law's revisions is prohibiting discrimination against a potential borrower *on public assistance*. If the income is permanent, the law says a lender must consider it as valid income—*only sufficiency* of income may be considered by the lender, not the income's source.

The law protects a borrower against any creditor who regularly extends credit, including banks, small loan and finance companies, retail and department stores, credit card companies, and credit unions. Anyone involved in granting credit (e.g., real estate brokers and mortgage brokers who arrange financing) are covered by the laws. Businesses applying for credit are also protected by the law.

How this affects someone looking for a home loan is monumental. Due to the ECOA, many more people have the potential to buy a home. If someone is on disability or receives child support, retirement benefits, Social Security income, or even public assistance or welfare/ADC, that person may be able to buy a home. Understand, however, the amount of the income may not be sufficient to buy a particular home.

## Laws Requiring Financial Disclosures

Real estate agents must be aware of the various disclosure requirements in their field and must make some of the disclosures themselves.

### For Example

Agents must disclose whether they have any relationship with service companies they suggest to buyers or sellers, and if any compensation will be paid. Even more disclosures must be made by the lender, such as total costs involved in the transaction.

Some disclosures are imposed by federal or state law, and others are imposed by the licensee's responsibilities as an agent. Here, we focus on disclosure requirements under federal law relating to real estate finance and real estate closings. The two most pertinent laws are **Regulation Z** of the **Truth in Lending Act (TILA)** and the **Real Estate Settlement Procedures Act (RESPA)**.

## Truth in Lending Act

Enacted in 1969, the **Truth in Lending Act (TILA)** requires lenders to disclose consumer credit costs to promote informed use of consumer credit. The purpose of TILA is to provide standard disclosure procedures all lenders must follow. The disclosures are required so consumers will know exactly what they're paying for credit; enabling them to compare costs and shop for the best terms. The Act is implemented by **Regulation Z**.

## Regulation Z

While **Regulation Z** does not set limits on interest rates or other finance charges imposed by lenders, *it does regulate the disclosure of these items in written disclosures concerning all finance charges and related aspects of credit transaction*.

### Coverage of the Act

The provisions of the Act apply to each lender who offers or extends credit to consumers (people, not companies) in the ordinary course of business; primarily for personal, family, or household purposes. The credit offered must be subject to a finance charge or payable in more than four installments. Under the Act, the definition of credit includes *all* real estate loans made to consumers, no matter what the amount, if the loan is for something other than business or commercial purposes.

√ **Note:** One exemption from coverage of the Act is credit of more than $25,000, which is *not* secured by real property.

### Disclosures

Lenders who offer credit, including real estate credit, must make certain disclosures to the consumer before the transaction is consummated. Lenders of residential mortgages must make required TILA disclosures no later than **three business days** after the lender receives the buyer's written application. Most lenders give the applicant the disclosure statement when applying for a real estate loan. If any of the estimated figures change over the course of the transaction, new disclosures must be made before settlement.

Once the initial disclosures are delivered, the **Mortgage Disclosure Improvement Act** requires the following timeframes before closing a home loan:

- Creditors must wait **seven business days** after they provide the early disclosures before closing the loan.

- Creditors must provide new disclosures with a revised annual percentage rate (APR), and wait an additional **four business days** before closing the loan, if a change occurs that makes the APR in the early disclosures inaccurate beyond a specified tolerance.

The rules would permit a consumer to expedite the closing to address a personal financial emergency, such as a foreclosure. Real estate agents need to be mindful of these times frames when scheduling a closing date.

Disclosures are required in two general areas:

- **When lenders offer credit but before the transaction is consummated.** TILA requires disclosures be made clearly, conspicuously, in writing, and in a form the consumer may keep and read prior to the loan closing. If the disclosures are incorporated into the loan agreement, they must be separated from all other loan details (e.g., in a boxed section on the form or separated by bold print dividing lines).

- **When credit terms are advertised to potential customers.** The Act also requires advertisers of consumer credit to clearly and conspicuously provide certain information if they use specific triggering terms in their credit ads. The Act requires that the credit terms advertised actually be available.

The following are the specific disclosures required by TILA:

- Annual Percentage Rate (APR)

- Consumer Handbook on Adjustable Rate Mortgages (CHARM booklet) *only for all ARM loans*

- ARM Disclosure *(if applicable)*

- Balloon Disclosure *(if applicable)*

- Prepayment Disclosure

- Notice of Right to Rescind

- When Your Home is on the Line Disclosure *for home equity loans such as home equity lines of credit (HELOCs)*

A lender must retain evidence of compliance with these disclosure requirements for at least two years after the disclosures were required to be made.

### Annual Percentage Rate (APR) Disclosure

For residential mortgages, the most important disclosure required is the **annual percentage rate (APR)**. The **APR** is *the relationship between the cost of borrowing money and the total amount financed, represented as a percentage*. The APR tells a borrower the total cost of financing the loan in percentage terms. Finance charges are more than just interest, or the **note rate** that appears in the promissory note. They include any points required by the lender for any reason—discount points, loan origination fees, etc. When the buyer must pay points or a loan fee, the APR will be higher than just the interest rate.

### For Example

A mortgage loan with a 6% interest rate may have an APR of 6.5%, representing the total cost of the loan, including all finance charges spread over the life of the loan.

Even though different interest rates may apply during the loan term (as with ARMs or buydowns), a loan still has only one initial APR. Additionally, *not all* closing costs are calculated into the APR.

Many borrowers are confused by the apparent contradiction of the loan documents showing more than one interest rate—particularly when they thought they were getting a fixed-rate loan at a particular interest rate. It would be helpful at this point for the real estate agent to explain to the borrower that the interest rate paid on the mortgage loan and the APR are two different items. The APR includes not just the interest rate, but also the total cost of the loan, including all finance charges spread over the life of the loan, represented as a single number.

### Right to Rescind

Under the Truth in Lending Act, consumers have the right to **rescind** any credit transaction where a *security interest* (usually a mortgage) *is given in their principal residence*, except for the initial purchase or construction of a home. **Rescind** means *to take back* *or withdraw an offer or contract*. The right to rescind a credit transaction extends until midnight of the third business day *after* a transaction closes.

Note one major exception to the right to rescind: *Consumers may not rescind a residential mortgage transaction that is used to finance the purchase or construction of a residence*. This protects builders who may have performed services based on the buyers' commitment, and sellers who may have entered into another contract or purchased a home contingent on the buyers purchasing their present home. Since the exception covers the typical mortgage transaction, consumers have the right to rescind only home equity loans, home improvement loans, refinances, etc.

Lenders must inform consumers of their right to rescind. The notice of the right to rescind must be in a separate document from the sale or credit document, and must describe the acquisition of the security interest, how the right to rescind can be exercised, the effects of rescinding the transaction, and the date and time the right to rescind expires. Due to the three-day window the consumer has to rescind, many lenders will not refinance a loan on the last day of the month. However, borrowers who have a bona fide financial emergency may be able to waive the rescission period.

### Advertisement

The Truth in Lending Act also contains provisions that apply to advertising. Prior to the passage of the Act, an advertiser might have disclosed only the most attractive credit terms, thus distorting the true cost of financing.

## For Example

The ad could have included the low monthly payments (e.g., $75 a month) without indicating the large down payment necessary to qualify for that payment level. Advertisers did not have to disclose the APR or whether the transaction was a credit sale or lease. The Act now requires the advertiser to tell the whole story.

Anyone placing a consumer credit or lease advertisement must comply with the Act. **This includes real estate agents who advertise private homes for sale.**

If an advertisement contains any one of the terms specified in the Act, that advertisement must also include the required disclosures. The idea is that a lender can't simply state a low interest rate, or payment amount, or other specific attractive features of a loan without telling the borrower all the provisions. If an ad uses a trigger phrase detailing some aspect of the loan, disclosures are needed to tell everything about the loan; if an ad doesn't use a trigger, no disclosures are needed. The triggering terms for real estate advertisements include:

- Amount of the down payment (e.g., "20% down")
- Amount of any payment (e.g., "Pay less than $700 per month")
- Number of payments (e.g., "Only 360 monthly payments")
- Period of repayment (e.g., "30-year financing available")
- Amount of any finance charge (e.g., "1% finance charge")

Some examples of terms that do *not* trigger the required disclosures are:

- "No down payment"
- "7% Annual Percentage Rate loan available here"
- "Easy monthly payments"
- "VA and FHA financing available" or "100% VA financing available"
- "Terms to fit your budget"

If any triggering terms are used in an ad, *all* of these disclosures must be made:

- Amount or percentage of down payment
- Terms of repayment
- Annual percentage rate, using that term spelled out in full, and whether rate may increase (e.g., for ARMs)

If an ad discloses only the APR, the additional disclosures are not required.

## For Example

An ad may simply say, "Assume a 7% annual percentage rate mortgage." If an adjustable rate mortgage is being advertised, it should be described as "7% annual percentage rate, subject to increase after settlement."

Fixed-rate buydowns are not adjustable rate mortgages and cannot be described as such. The buydown involves different interest rates in effect during the life of the loan, but all the rates are known at the time of settlement. When more than one simple interest rate is applied to the transaction, these rates may be advertised if all the interest rates and the terms during which the rates apply are disclosed, and the annual percentage rate is stated. Remember, though, that even though different interest rates may apply during the loan term, the loan has only one annual percentage rate (APR). Due to the complexity of this law and the required disclosures, most real estate agents do not quote payments in their advertisements.

## Real Estate Settlement Procedures Act (RESPA)

The **Real Estate Settlement Procedures Act (RESPA)** is *a federal law dealing with real estate closings that sets forth specific procedures and guidelines for disclosure of settlement costs.* RESPA laws apply to most sales of one- to four-unit residential properties (including condos, co-ops, and mobile homes) where the purchase loan is secured by a first mortgage on the property.

The Act does not apply to loans used to finance the purchase of 25 acres or more, loans for the purchase of vacant land, or transactions where the buyer assumes, or takes subject to, an existing first lien loan.

RESPA rules and compliance are administered by the Consumer Financial Protection Bureau (CFPB). CFPB's purpose is to regulate settlement and closing procedures and practices. RESPA laws call for disclosure of all settlement costs, using standardized settlement statements given to borrowers.

RESPA standardizes real estate closings by:

- Requiring lenders to provide a **Loan Estimate** that includes a "good faith" estimate of settlement costs no later than three business days following the date of a completed mortgage loan application.
- Requiring lenders to provide a **booklet explaining settlement costs**.
- Requiring the use of a **standardized Closing Disclosure** form that must be completed and provided to the borrower at least three business days prior to closing.

# Loan Estimate Form

For many years, the disclosure requirements of RESPA and TILA associated with a completed loan application have been accomplished with two separate documents:

- A Good Faith Estimate that lists the approximate closing costs
- A Truth in Lending Statement that indicates the annual percentage rate

Under provisions of the **Dodd-Frank Wall Street Reform and Consumer Protection Act of 2010**, these separate statements have been integrated into a single loan application disclosure document called the **Loan Estimate** form. It includes:

- Estimated closing costs
- Projected monthly payments
- True cost of credit as an annual percentage rate

This disclosure allows consumers to more easily compare terms of different loan options.

The timing of the Loan Estimate is similar as for current disclosures: The loan originator must provide the Loan Estimate within **three business days** of receiving a completed loan application and at least **seven business days** before loan consummation. Revised Loan Estimates must be provided at least **four business days** before loan consummation.

√ **Note:** This disclosure form is required for all RESPA-related transactions that close on **October 1, 2015,** and beyond.

## Sections of the Loan Estimate Form

The Loan Estimate form has sections on each page that must be completed.

### Loan Estimate Page 1

Page 1 of the **Loan Estimate** includes:

- General information, such as the name of the applicants, the property address, and the sale price of the property
- The purpose of the loan, for example, purchase, refinance, construction
- A description of the loan, including whether it has a payment feature that could change
- Any rate lock, including the date and time the rate lock ends
- A **Loan Terms** table that discloses the initial interest rate, the monthly principal and interest, any prepayment penalty or balloon payment
- A **Projected Payments** table calculating the entire monthly PITI obligation
- A **Costs at Closing** table indicating the estimated closing costs and the estimated amount of cash needed to close the loan

### Loan Estimate Page 2

Page 2 of the Loan Estimate provides a good faith itemization of the costs of obtaining the loan. The items associated with the mortgage are broken down into two general types:

- **Loan Costs** are those costs paid by the consumer to the creditor and third-party providers of services the creditor requires to be obtained by the consumer during the origination of the loan. These costs are categorized as origination charges, services the borrower cannot shop for such as an appraisal fee or credit report fee, and services the borrower can shop for, such as fees for pest inspections and title insurance.

- **Other Costs** include taxes, governmental recording fees, and certain other payments involved in the real estate closing process, for example, initial escrow payments and prepaid fees such as insurance.

The **Calculating Cash to Close** table then shows how the amount of cash needed at closing is calculated, taking the down payment, earnest money deposit, and other credits into consideration.

### Loan Estimate Page 3

The last page of the Loan Estimate provides additional information about the loan, as well as contact information.

The **Comparisons** table discloses the critical **annual percentage rate (APR)**, which expresses the full cost of obtaining the loan as a rate. This is NOT the interest rate negotiated between the borrower and lender. This table also shows the borrower how much he or she will have paid in interest and principal at the end of given years. The Comparison Table is intended to help a borrower easily compare loans terms offered by other various lenders.

Finally, any **Other Considerations** related to the loan are indicated. A borrower is NOT required to sign the Loan Disclosure, although the lender may ask for a signature as proof of receipt. Signing the Loan Disclosure does not obligate the borrower to continue with the loan process.

## Completed Application

Lenders are required to provide borrowers with the Loan Estimate within **three business days** of a completed loan application. A **completed application** means that lender has the items from the prospective borrower necessary to make a credit decision:

- Name(s) of borrower
- Social Security number for each borrower
- Gross monthly income of borrower(s)
- Loan amount sought
- Address of subject property
- Estimate of property value

A loan originator may *not* obtain a credit/debit card number to pay for appraisal fees, application fees, or any other fee until the Loan Estimate has been delivered to the borrowers and the borrowers acknowledge their intent to proceed with the mortgage loan.

## Ability to Repay Rule

Also under provisions of the **Dodd-Frank Act**, lenders may **not** grant loans solely based on the collateral value of the borrower's property without regard to the borrower's **ability to repay** the loan, including the borrower's current and reasonably expected income, employment status, assets other than the collateral, current obligations, and mortgage-related obligations, which include expected property taxes, premiums for mortgage-related insurance required by the lender, and similar expenses. Lenders must verify the information an applicant provides using reliable documents such as a W-2 or a pay stub.

A lender is presumed to have met the ability-to-repay requirements by making a "**qualified mortgage**" that does not include certain risky features, for example, a period where the borrower pays only interest on the loan, the need for a lump sum payment at the end of the loan term, or a loan term that exceeds 30 years.

# FICUS BANK

4321 Random Boulevard • Somecity, ST 12340

*Save this Loan Estimate to compare with your Closing Disclosure.*

## Loan Estimate

| | |
|---|---|
| **DATE ISSUED** | 2/15/2013 |
| **APPLICANTS** | Michael Jones and Mary Stone<br>123 Anywhere Street<br>Anytown, ST 12345 |
| **PROPERTY** | 456 Somewhere Avenue<br>Anytown, ST 12345 |
| **SALE PRICE** | $180,000 |

| | |
|---|---|
| **LOAN TERM** | 30 years |
| **PURPOSE** | Purchase |
| **PRODUCT** | Fixed Rate |
| **LOAN TYPE** | ☒ Conventional ☐ FHA ☐ VA ☐ _____ |
| **LOAN ID #** | 123456789 |
| **RATE LOCK** | ☐ NO ☒ YES, until 4/16/2013 at 5:00 p.m. EDT |

*Before closing, your interest rate, points, and lender credits can change unless you lock the interest rate. All other estimated closing costs expire on **3/4/2013** at 5:00 p.m. EDT*

## Loan Terms

| | | Can this amount increase after closing? |
|---|---|---|
| **Loan Amount** | $162,000 | **NO** |
| **Interest Rate** | 3.875% | **NO** |
| **Monthly Principal & Interest**<br>*See Projected Payments below for your Estimated Total Monthly Payment* | $761.78 | **NO** |
| | | **Does the loan have these features?** |
| **Prepayment Penalty** | | **YES** • **As high as $3,240** if you pay off the loan during the first 2 years |
| **Balloon Payment** | | **NO** |

## Projected Payments

| Payment Calculation | Years 1-7 | Years 8-30 |
|---|---|---|
| Principal & Interest | $761.78 | $761.78 |
| Mortgage Insurance | + 82 | + — |
| Estimated Escrow<br>*Amount can increase over time* | + 206 | + 206 |
| **Estimated Total Monthly Payment** | $1,050 | $968 |

| | | This estimate includes | In escrow? |
|---|---|---|---|
| **Estimated Taxes, Insurance & Assessments**<br>*Amount can increase over time* | **$206**<br>a month | ☒ Property Taxes<br>☒ Homeowner's Insurance<br>☐ Other:<br>*See Section G on page 2 for escrowed property costs. You must pay for other property costs separately.* | **YES**<br>**YES** |

## Costs at Closing

| | | |
|---|---|---|
| **Estimated Closing Costs** | $8,054 | Includes $5,672 in Loan Costs + $2,382 in Other Costs – $0 in Lender Credits. *See page 2 for details.* |
| **Estimated Cash to Close** | $16,054 | Includes Closing Costs. *See Calculating Cash to Close on page 2 for details.* |

Visit **www.consumerfinance.gov/mortgage-estimate** for general information and tools.

## Closing Cost Details

### Loan Costs

| A. Origination Charges | $1,802 |
|---|---|
| .25 % of Loan Amount (Points) | $405 |
| Application Fee | $300 |
| Underwriting Fee | $1,097 |

| B. Services You Cannot Shop For | $672 |
|---|---|
| Appraisal Fee | $405 |
| Credit Report Fee | $30 |
| Flood Determination Fee | $20 |
| Flood Monitoring Fee | $32 |
| Tax Monitoring Fee | $75 |
| Tax Status Research Fee | $110 |

| C. Services You Can Shop For | $3,198 |
|---|---|
| Pest Inspection Fee | $135 |
| Survey Fee | $65 |
| Title – Insurance Binder | $700 |
| Title – Lender's Title Policy | $535 |
| Title – Settlement Agent Fee | $502 |
| Title – Title Search | $1,261 |

| D. TOTAL LOAN COSTS (A + B + C) | $5,672 |
|---|---|

### Other Costs

| E. Taxes and Other Government Fees | $85 |
|---|---|
| Recording Fees and Other Taxes | $85 |
| Transfer Taxes | |

| F. Prepaids | $867 |
|---|---|
| Homeowner's Insurance Premium ( 6 months) | $605 |
| Mortgage Insurance Premium ( months) | |
| Prepaid Interest ( $17.44 per day for 15 days @ 3.875%) | $262 |
| Property Taxes ( months) | |

| G. Initial Escrow Payment at Closing | $413 |
|---|---|
| Homeowner's Insurance $100.83 per month for 2 mo. | $202 |
| Mortgage Insurance per month for mo. | |
| Property Taxes $105.30 per month for 2 mo. | $211 |

| H. Other | $1,017 |
|---|---|
| Title – Owner's Title Policy (optional) | $1,017 |

| I. TOTAL OTHER COSTS (E + F + G + H) | $2,382 |
|---|---|

| J. TOTAL CLOSING COSTS | $8,054 |
|---|---|
| D + I | $8,054 |
| Lender Credits | |

### Calculating Cash to Close

| Total Closing Costs (J) | $8,054 |
|---|---|
| Closing Costs Financed (Paid from your Loan Amount) | $0 |
| Down Payment/Funds from Borrower | $18,000 |
| Deposit | – $10,000 |
| Funds for Borrower | $0 |
| Seller Credits | $0 |
| Adjustments and Other Credits | $0 |
| Estimated Cash to Close | $16,054 |

## Additional Information About This Loan

| | | | |
|---|---|---|---|
| **LENDER** | Ficus Bank | **MORTGAGE BROKER** | |
| **NMLS/__ LICENSE ID** | | **NMLS/__ LICENSE ID** | |
| **LOAN OFFICER** | Joe Smith | **LOAN OFFICER** | |
| **NMLS/__ LICENSE ID** | 12345 | **NMLS/__ LICENSE ID** | |
| **EMAIL** | joesmith@ficusbank.com | **EMAIL** | |
| **PHONE** | 123-456-7890 | **PHONE** | |

| **Comparisons** | Use these measures to compare this loan with other loans. | |
|---|---|---|
| **In 5 Years** | $56,582 | Total you will have paid in principal, interest, mortgage insurance, and loan costs. |
| | $15,773 | Principal you will have paid off. |
| **Annual Percentage Rate (APR)** | 4.274% | Your costs over the loan term expressed as a rate. This is not your interest rate. |
| **Total Interest Percentage (TIP)** | 69.45% | The total amount of interest that you will pay over the loan term as a percentage of your loan amount. |

### Other Considerations

| | |
|---|---|
| **Appraisal** | We may order an appraisal to determine the property's value and charge you for this appraisal. We will promptly give you a copy of any appraisal, even if your loan does not close. You can pay for an additional appraisal for your own use at your own cost. |
| **Assumption** | If you sell or transfer this property to another person, we<br>☐ will allow, under certain conditions, this person to assume this loan on the original terms.<br>☒ will not allow assumption of this loan on the original terms. |
| **Homeowner's Insurance** | This loan requires homeowner's insurance on the property, which you may obtain from a company of your choice that we find acceptable. |
| **Late Payment** | If your payment is more than *15* days late, we will charge a late fee of *5% of the monthly principal and interest payment.* |
| **Refinance** | Refinancing this loan will depend on your future financial situation, the property value, and market conditions. You may not be able to refinance this loan. |
| **Servicing** | We intend<br>☐ to service your loan. If so, you will make your payments to us.<br>☒ to transfer servicing of your loan. |

### Confirm Receipt

By signing, you are only confirming that you have received this form. You do not have to accept this loan because you have signed or received this form.

| | | | |
|---|---|---|---|
| _____ | _____ | _____ | _____ |
| Applicant Signature | Date | Co-Applicant Signature | Date |

LOAN ESTIMATE

# Closing Disclosure Form

The standardized **Closing Disclosure** form is a five-page document that must be used in all RESPA transactions that include one- to four-family residential properties and are financed by a federally regulated lender. The creditor must provide the Closing Disclosure to the borrower at least **three business days** prior to loan consummation.

The Closing Disclosure **replaces the HUD-1 Settlement Statement** that had been the standard closing document used in residential real estate for many years as mandated by Real Estate Settlement Procedures Act. Under provisions of the Dodd-Frank Act, the Closing Disclosure is required for RESPA-related transactions that close on **October 1, 2015,** and beyond.

The Closing Disclosure may be prepared by the lender or by the closing or settlement agent with input from the lender. Ultimately, however, it is the lender's responsibility to ensure the accuracy and timely delivery of the Closing Disclosure.

## Sections of the Closing Disclosure Form

The Closing Disclosure form has separate sections that provide specific information about the transaction.

### Page 1: Transaction Details

The data on **Page 1** of the Closing Disclosure begins with the basic details of the transaction, including:

- Closing information, such as the date, settlement agent, address of the property serving as collateral for the loan, and sale price
- Transaction information, such as the names and addresses of the borrower(s), seller(s), and lender
- Loan information, including the term, purpose, product, type, loan ID number, and, if applicable, the MIC #, which is the mortgage insurance case number

### Page 1: Loan Terms

The terms of the loan indicated here disclose the same details as found on the **Loan Estimate**, the disclosure that lenders are required to provide within three business days of a completed loan application. Loan terms should be updated to reflect the borrower's legal obligation and include:

- Loan amount
- Interest rate (the note rate, not the annual percentage rate)
- Monthly principal and interest payments

It also indicates whether there is a prepayment penalty or a required balloon payment.

### Page 1: Projected Payments

The data in the Projected Payments section also discloses the same data that was in the Loan Estimate disclosure and includes:

- P&I in years 1-7 and 8-30 of the loan
- Mortgage insurance in years 1-7 and 8-30 of the loan
- Estimated escrow in years 1-7 and 8-30 of the loan
- Estimated total monthly payment in years 1-7 and 8-30 of the loan

To provide a complete picture of the borrower's **total monthly obligations**, this section also includes an estimate of property taxes, homeowner's insurance, and homeowner's association fees, and whether these costs are held in escrow.

# Closing Disclosure

*This form is a statement of final loan terms and closing costs. Compare this document with your Loan Estimate.*

| Closing Information | | Transaction Information | | Loan Information | |
|---|---|---|---|---|---|
| Date Issued | 4/14/2016 | Borrower | Michael Jones and Mary Stone | Loan Term | 30 years |
| Closing Date | 4/14/2016 | | 123 Anywhere Street | Purpose | Purchase |
| Disbursement Date | 4/14/2016 | | Anytown, ST 12345 | Product | Fixed Rate |
| Settlement Agent | Epsilon Title Co. | Seller | Steve Cole and Amy Doe | | |
| File # | 12-3456 | | 321 Somewhere Drive | Loan Type | ☒ Conventional ☐ FHA |
| Property | 456 Somewhere Ave | | Anytown, ST 12345 | | ☐ VA ☐ _____ |
| | Anytown, ST 12345 | Lender | Ficus Bank | Loan ID # | 123456789 |
| Sale Price | $180,000 | | | MIC # | 000654321 |

## Loan Terms

| | | Can this amount increase after closing? |
|---|---|---|
| **Loan Amount** | $162,000 | **NO** |
| **Interest Rate** | 3.875% | **NO** |
| **Monthly Principal & Interest** *See Projected Payments below for your Estimated Total Monthly Payment* | $761.78 | **NO** |
| | | **Does the loan have these features?** |
| **Prepayment Penalty** | **YES** | • **As high as $3,240** if you pay off the loan during the first 2 years |
| **Balloon Payment** | **NO** | |

## Projected Payments

| Payment Calculation | | Years 1-7 | | Years 8-30 |
|---|---|---|---|---|
| Principal & Interest | | $761.78 | | $761.78 |
| Mortgage Insurance | + | 82.35 | + | — |
| Estimated Escrow *Amount can increase over time* | + | 206.13 | + | 206.13 |
| **Estimated Total Monthly Payment** | | **$1,050.26** | | **$967.91** |

| Estimated Taxes, Insurance & Assessments *Amount can increase over time* *See page 4 for details* | $356.13 a month | This estimate includes | In escrow? |
|---|---|---|---|
| | | ☒ Property Taxes | YES |
| | | ☒ Homeowner's Insurance | YES |
| | | ☒ Other: Homeowner's Association Dues | NO |
| | | *See Escrow Account on page 4 for details. You must pay for other property costs separately.* | |

## Costs at Closing

| **Closing Costs** | $9,712.10 | Includes $4,694.05 in Loan Costs + $5,018.05 in Other Costs – $0 in Lender Credits. *See page 2 for details.* |
|---|---|---|
| **Cash to Close** | $14,147.26 | Includes Closing Costs. *See Calculating Cash to Close on page 3 for details.* |

# Closing Cost Details

| Loan Costs | | Borrower-Paid | | Seller-Paid | | Paid by Others |
|---|---|---|---|---|---|---|
| | | At Closing | Before Closing | At Closing | Before Closing | |
| **A. Origination Charges** | | **$1,802.00** | | | | |
| 01  0.25 % of Loan Amount (Points) | | $405.00 | | | | |
| 02  Application Fee | | $300.00 | | | | |
| 03  Underwriting Fee | | $1,097.00 | | | | |
| 04 | | | | | | |
| 05 | | | | | | |
| 06 | | | | | | |
| 07 | | | | | | |
| 08 | | | | | | |
| **B. Services Borrower Did Not Shop For** | | **$236.55** | | | | |
| 01  Appraisal Fee | to John Smith Appraisers Inc. | | | | | $405.00 |
| 02  Credit Report Fee | to Information Inc. | | $29.80 | | | |
| 03  Flood Determination Fee | to Info Co. | $20.00 | | | | |
| 04  Flood Monitoring Fee | to Info Co. | $31.75 | | | | |
| 05  Tax Monitoring Fee | to Info Co. | $75.00 | | | | |
| 06  Tax Status Research Fee | to Info Co. | $80.00 | | | | |
| 07 | | | | | | |
| 08 | | | | | | |
| 09 | | | | | | |
| 10 | | | | | | |
| **C. Services Borrower Did Shop For** | | **$2,655.50** | | | | |
| 01  Pest Inspection Fee | to Pests Co. | $120.50 | | | | |
| 02  Survey Fee | to Surveys Co. | $85.00 | | | | |
| 03  Title – Insurance Binder | to Epsilon Title Co. | $650.00 | | | | |
| 04  Title – Lender's Title Insurance | to Epsilon Title Co. | $500.00 | | | | |
| 05  Title – Settlement Agent Fee | to Epsilon Title Co. | $500.00 | | | | |
| 06  Title – Title Search | to Epsilon Title Co. | $800.00 | | | | |
| 07 | | | | | | |
| 08 | | | | | | |
| **D. TOTAL LOAN COSTS (Borrower-Paid)** | | **$4,694.05** | | | | |
| Loan Costs Subtotals (A + B + C) | | $4,664.25 | $29.80 | | | |

| Other Costs | | | | | | |
|---|---|---|---|---|---|---|
| **E. Taxes and Other Government Fees** | | **$85.00** | | | | |
| 01  Recording Fees | Deed: $40.00   Mortgage: $45.00 | $85.00 | | | | |
| 02  Transfer Tax | to Any State | | | $950.00 | | |
| **F. Prepaids** | | **$2,120.80** | | | | |
| 01  Homeowner's Insurance Premium ( 12 mo.) to Insurance Co. | | $1,209.96 | | | | |
| 02  Mortgage Insurance Premium (    mo.) | | | | | | |
| 03  Prepaid Interest ( $17.44 per day from 4/15/13 to 5/1/13 ) | | $279.04 | | | | |
| 04  Property Taxes ( 6 mo.) to Any County USA | | $631.80 | | | | |
| 05 | | | | | | |
| **G. Initial Escrow Payment at Closing** | | **$412.25** | | | | |
| 01  Homeowner's Insurance $100.83 per month for 2 mo. | | $201.66 | | | | |
| 02  Mortgage Insurance           per month for    mo. | | | | | | |
| 03  Property Taxes      $105.30 per month for 2 mo. | | $210.60 | | | | |
| 04 | | | | | | |
| 05 | | | | | | |
| 06 | | | | | | |
| 07 | | | | | | |
| 08  Aggregate Adjustment | | – 0.01 | | | | |
| **H. Other** | | **$2,400.00** | | | | |
| 01  HOA Capital Contribution | to HOA Acre Inc. | $500.00 | | | | |
| 02  HOA Processing Fee | to HOA Acre Inc. | $150.00 | | | | |
| 03  Home Inspection Fee | to Engineers Inc. | $750.00 | | | $750.00 | |
| 04  Home Warranty Fee | to XYZ Warranty Inc. | | | $450.00 | | |
| 05  Real Estate Commission | to Alpha Real Estate Broker | | | $5,700.00 | | |
| 06  Real Estate Commission | to Omega Real Estate Broker | | | $5,700.00 | | |
| 07  Title – Owner's Title Insurance (optional)   to Epsilon Title Co. | | $1,000.00 | | | | |
| 08 | | | | | | |
| **I. TOTAL OTHER COSTS (Borrower-Paid)** | | **$5,018.05** | | | | |
| Other Costs Subtotals (E + F + G + H) | | $5,018.05 | | | | |
| **J. TOTAL CLOSING COSTS (Borrower-Paid)** | | **$9,712.10** | | | | |
| Closing Costs Subtotals (D + I) | | $9,682.30 | $29.80 | $12,800.00 | $750.00 | $405.00 |
| Lender Credits | | | | | | |

Housing Cycles, Money Supply, and Government Regulations 1

## Calculating Cash to Close

**Use this table to see what has changed from your Loan Estimate.**

| | Loan Estimate | Final | Did this change? |
|---|---|---|---|
| Total Closing Costs (J) | $8,054.00 | $9,712.10 | **YES** • See **Total Loan Costs (D)** and **Total Other Costs (I)** |
| Closing Costs Paid Before Closing | $0 | − $29.80 | **YES** • You paid these Closing Costs **before closing** |
| Closing Costs Financed (Paid from your Loan Amount) | $0 | $0 | **NO** |
| Down Payment/Funds from Borrower | $18,000.00 | $18,000.00 | **NO** |
| Deposit | − $10,000.00 | − $10,000.00 | **NO** |
| Funds for Borrower | $0 | $0 | **NO** |
| Seller Credits | $0 | − $2,500.00 | **YES** • See Seller Credits in **Section L** |
| Adjustments and Other Credits | $0 | − $1,035.04 | **YES** • See details in **Sections K and L** |
| **Cash to Close** | $16,054.00 | $14,147.26 | |

## Summaries of Transactions

**Use this table to see a summary of your transaction.**

**BORROWER'S TRANSACTION**

| K. Due from Borrower at Closing | $189,762.30 |
|---|---|
| 01 Sale Price of Property | $180,000.00 |
| 02 Sale Price of Any Personal Property Included in Sale | |
| 03 Closing Costs Paid at Closing (J) | $9,682.30 |
| 04 | |
| **Adjustments** | |
| 05 | |
| 06 | |
| 07 | |
| **Adjustments for Items Paid by Seller in Advance** | |
| 08 City/Town Taxes to | |
| 09 County Taxes to | |
| 10 Assessments to | |
| 11 HOA Dues 4/14/16 to 4/30/16 | $80.00 |
| 12 | |
| 13 | |
| 14 | |
| 15 | |

| L. Paid Already by or on Behalf of Borrower at Closing | $175,615.04 |
|---|---|
| 01 Deposit | $10,000.00 |
| 02 Loan Amount | $162,000.00 |
| 03 Existing Loan(s) Assumed or Taken Subject to | |
| 04 | |
| 05 Seller Credit | $2,500.00 |
| **Other Credits** | |
| 06 Rebate from Epsilon Title Co. | $750.00 |
| 07 | |
| **Adjustments** | |
| 08 | |
| 09 | |
| 10 | |
| 11 | |
| **Adjustments for Items Unpaid by Seller** | |
| 12 City/Town Taxes 1/1/16 to 4/14/16 | $365.04 |
| 13 County Taxes to | |
| 14 Assessments to | |
| 15 | |
| 16 | |
| 17 | |

| CALCULATION | |
|---|---|
| Total Due from Borrower at Closing (K) | $189,762.30 |
| Total Paid Already by or on Behalf of Borrower at Closing (L) | − $175,615.04 |
| **Cash to Close** ☒ **From** ☐ **To Borrower** | **$14,147.26** |

**SELLER'S TRANSACTION**

| M. Due to Seller at Closing | $180,080.00 |
|---|---|
| 01 Sale Price of Property | $180,000.00 |
| 02 Sale Price of Any Personal Property Included in Sale | |
| 03 | |
| 04 | |
| 05 | |
| 06 | |
| 07 | |
| 08 | |
| **Adjustments for Items Paid by Seller in Advance** | |
| 09 City/Town Taxes to | |
| 10 County Taxes to | |
| 11 Assessments to | |
| 12 HOA Dues 4/14/16 to 4/30/16 | $80.00 |
| 13 | |
| 14 | |
| 15 | |
| 16 | |

| N. Due from Seller at Closing | $115,665.04 |
|---|---|
| 01 Excess Deposit | |
| 02 Closing Costs Paid at Closing (J) | $12,800.00 |
| 03 Existing Loan(s) Assumed or Taken Subject to | |
| 04 Payoff of First Mortgage Loan | $100,000.00 |
| 05 Payoff of Second Mortgage Loan | |
| 06 | |
| 07 | |
| 08 Seller Credit | $2,500.00 |
| 09 | |
| 10 | |
| 11 | |
| 12 | |
| 13 | |
| **Adjustments for Items Unpaid by Seller** | |
| 14 City/Town Taxes 1/1/16 to 4/14/16 | $365.04 |
| 15 County Taxes to | |
| 16 Assessments to | |
| 17 | |
| 18 | |
| 19 | |

| CALCULATION | |
|---|---|
| Total Due to Seller at Closing (M) | $180,080.00 |
| Total Due from Seller at Closing (N) | − $115,665.04 |
| **Cash** ☐ **From** ☒ **To Seller** | **$64,414.96** |

CLOSING DISCLOSURE

# Additional Information About This Loan

## Loan Disclosures

### Assumption

If you sell or transfer this property to another person, your lender

☐ will allow, under certain conditions, this person to assume this loan on the original terms.

☒ will not allow assumption of this loan on the original terms.

### Demand Feature

Your loan

☐ has a demand feature, which permits your lender to require early repayment of the loan. You should review your note for details.

☒ does not have a demand feature.

### Late Payment

If your payment is more than *15 days* late, your lender will charge a late fee of *5% of the monthly principal and interest payment.*

### Negative Amortization (Increase in Loan Amount)

Under your loan terms, you

☐ are scheduled to make monthly payments that do not pay all of the interest due that month. As a result, your loan amount will increase (negatively amortize), and your loan amount will likely become larger than your original loan amount. Increases in your loan amount lower the equity you have in this property.

☐ may have monthly payments that do not pay all of the interest due that month. If you do, your loan amount will increase (negatively amortize), and, as a result, your loan amount may become larger than your original loan amount. Increases in your loan amount lower the equity you have in this property.

☒ do not have a negative amortization feature.

### Partial Payments

Your lender

☒ may accept payments that are less than the full amount due (partial payments) and apply them to your loan.

☐ may hold them in a separate account until you pay the rest of the payment, and then apply the full payment to your loan.

☐ does not accept any partial payments.

If this loan is sold, your new lender may have a different policy.

### Security Interest

You are granting a security interest in
*456 Somewhere Ave., Anytown, ST 12345*

You may lose this property if you do not make your payments or satisfy other obligations for this loan.

### Escrow Account

*For now,* your loan

☒ will have an escrow account (also called an "impound" or "trust" account) to pay the property costs listed below. Without an escrow account, you would pay them directly, possibly in one or two large payments a year. Your lender may be liable for penalties and interest for failing to make a payment.

| Escrow | | |
|---|---|---|
| Escrowed Property Costs over Year 1 | $2,473.56 | Estimated total amount over year 1 for your escrowed property costs: *Homeowner's Insurance Property Taxes* |
| Non-Escrowed Property Costs over Year 1 | $1,800.00 | Estimated total amount over year 1 for your non-escrowed property costs: *Homeowner's Association Dues* <br><br> You may have other property costs. |
| Initial Escrow Payment | $412.25 | A cushion for the escrow account you pay at closing. See Section G on page 2. |
| Monthly Escrow Payment | $206.13 | The amount included in your total monthly payment. |

☐ will not have an escrow account because ☐ you declined it ☐ your lender does not offer one. You must directly pay your property costs, such as taxes and homeowner's insurance. Contact your lender to ask if your loan can have an escrow account.

| No Escrow | |
|---|---|
| Estimated Property Costs over Year 1 | Estimated total amount over year 1. You must pay these costs directly, possibly in one or two large payments a year. |
| Escrow Waiver Fee | |

### In the future,

Your property costs may change and, as a result, your escrow payment may change. You may be able to cancel your escrow account, but if you do, you must pay your property costs directly. If you fail to pay your property taxes, your state or local government may (1) impose fines and penalties or (2) place a tax lien on this property. If you fail to pay any of your property costs, your lender may (1) add the amounts to your loan balance, (2) add an escrow account to your loan, or (3) require you to pay for property insurance that the lender buys on your behalf, which likely would cost more and provide fewer benefits than what you could buy on your own.

## Loan Calculations

| | |
|---|---|
| **Total of Payments.** Total you will have paid after you make all payments of principal, interest, mortgage insurance, and loan costs, as scheduled. | $285,803.36 |
| **Finance Charge.** The dollar amount the loan will cost you. | $118,830.27 |
| **Amount Financed.** The loan amount available after paying your upfront finance charge. | $162,000.00 |
| **Annual Percentage Rate (APR).** Your costs over the loan term expressed as a rate. This is not your interest rate. | 4.174% |
| **Total Interest Percentage (TIP).** The total amount of interest that you will pay over the loan term as a percentage of your loan amount. | 69.46% |

**? Questions?** If you have questions about the loan terms or costs on this form, use the contact information below. To get more information or make a complaint, contact the Consumer Financial Protection Bureau at **www.consumerfinance.gov/mortgage-closing**

## Other Disclosures

**Appraisal**

If the property was appraised for your loan, your lender is required to give you a copy at no additional cost at least 3 days before closing. If you have not yet received it, please contact your lender at the information listed below.

**Contract Details**

See your note and security instrument for information about
- what happens if you fail to make your payments,
- what is a default on the loan,
- situations in which your lender can require early repayment of the loan, and
- the rules for making payments before they are due.

**Liability after Foreclosure**

If your lender forecloses on this property and the foreclosure does not cover the amount of unpaid balance on this loan,

☒ state law may protect you from liability for the unpaid balance. If you refinance or take on any additional debt on this property, you may lose this protection and have to pay any debt remaining even after foreclosure. You may want to consult a lawyer for more information.

☐ state law does not protect you from liability for the unpaid balance.

**Refinance**

Refinancing this loan will depend on your future financial situation, the property value, and market conditions. You may not be able to refinance this loan.

**Tax Deductions**

If you borrow more than this property is worth, the interest on the loan amount above this property's fair market value is not deductible from your federal income taxes. You should consult a tax advisor for more information.

## Contact Information

| | Lender | Mortgage Broker | Real Estate Broker (B) | Real Estate Broker (S) | Settlement Agent |
|---|---|---|---|---|---|
| **Name** | Ficus Bank | | Omega Real Estate Broker Inc. | Alpha Real Estate Broker Co. | Epsilon Title Co. |
| **Address** | 4321 Random Blvd. Somecity, ST 12340 | | 789 Local Lane Sometown, ST 12345 | 987 Suburb Ct. Someplace, ST 12340 | 123 Commerce Pl. Somecity, ST 12344 |
| **NMLS ID** | | | | | |
| **ST License ID** | | | Z765416 | Z61456 | Z61616 |
| **Contact** | Joe Smith | | Samuel Green | Joseph Cain | Sarah Arnold |
| **Contact NMLS ID** | 12345 | | | | |
| **Contact ST License ID** | | | P16415 | P51461 | PT1234 |
| **Email** | joesmith@ ficusbank.com | | sam@omegare.biz | joe@alphare.biz | sarah@ epsilontitle.com |
| **Phone** | 123-456-7890 | | 123-555-1717 | 321-555-7171 | 987-555-4321 |

## Confirm Receipt

By signing, you are only confirming that you have received this form. You do not have to accept this loan because you have signed or received this form.

_____    _____
Applicant Signature      Date

_____    _____
Co-Applicant Signature      Date

CLOSING DISCLOSURE

## Page 1: Costs at Closing

The total **closing costs** are summarized on Page 1, reflecting a detailed breakdown of costs found on Page 2 of the Closing Disclosure.

Similarly, the total amount of **cash** that the borrower must bring to closing is summarized, reflecting the calculations found on Page 3 of the Closing Disclosure.

## Page 2: Closing Cost Details

Page 2 of the Closing Disclosure itemizes the closing costs paid by the **borrower**, the **seller** or by **others**. The columns for Borrower-Paid items and Seller-Paid items are divided into two parts:

- Items paid **at closing**. These items figure into the total costs owed by the buyer and seller on the day of closing.

- Items paid **before closing**. These items are noted here for both buyer and seller. Items the buyer paid before closing are part of the buyer's cash to close calculation on Page 3. Items paid before closing are **not** included in the summaries of transactions for either buyer or seller, however.

## Page 2: Loan Costs

The **Loan Costs** section itemizes the fees required by the lender in order to **make the loan**, such as:

**A. Origination Charges.** This is for bank fees, including application and underwriting fees, as well as any points the borrower may be paying

**B. Services Borrower Did Not Shop For.** When a borrower chooses a provider from the lender's list in the Loan Estimate, those fees are listed here, for example, appraisal and flood zone determination fees.

**C. Services Borrower Did Shop For.** Items that the borrower could have shopped for but may not have will appear here, for example, fees for a pest inspection or title-related fees.

The total of blocks A+B+C can be found in block **D. Total Loan Costs (Borrower-Paid).**

## Page 2: Other Costs

**Other Costs** incurred by the buyer and seller in order to close this transaction are also itemized on Page 2 of the Closing Disclosure. Such costs were **not** required to be disclosed on the Loan Estimate. Recall that payment of some of these costs is the result of negotiation between buyer and seller or a reflection of local custom.

**E. Taxes and Other Government Fees.** Indicates fees for recording the deed and mortgage in the public record, as well as the taxes that are required when property transfers ownership. We'll look at how to calculate such taxes in the next unit.

**F. Prepaids.** Lenders often require borrowers to prepay a portion of their homeowner's insurance, mortgage insurance (if any), and property taxes.

**G. Initial Escrow Payment at Closing.** Recall that lenders generally require borrowers to establish an **escrow account** into which the borrower makes periodic payments to cover **property taxes** and **property insurance**. With an escrow account, the lender ensures that the property taxes are being paid, protecting their interests in the event of default. And ensuring payment of property insurance protects the collateral in the event of some covered hazard such as fire. If such an account is established, borrowers may be required to prepay a certain number of months.

**H. Other.** This general category may be used for expenses such as homeowner association fees, home inspection fees, or mortgagor (borrower) title insurance. This category is also where any **commission** due is itemized. In this sample, the seller is paying both the listing broker and the selling broker.

The total of blocks E+F+G+H is shown in block **I. Total Other Costs (Borrower-Paid).**

## Page 2: Total Closing Costs

The total closing costs to the borrower, Loan and Other, are found in block **J. Total Closing Costs (Borrower-Paid)**. It's this number that is indicated as **Closing Costs** on **Page 1** of the Closing Disclosure. This number is also carried forward to **Page 3** of the Closing Disclosure and used to calculate the borrower's **cash to close**. The Closing Costs Subtotal (At Closing) will carry forward to the Borrower's Transaction column on Page 3 of the Closing Disclosure when calculating the Due from Borrower at Closing amount.

Similarly, the Closing Costs Subtotal on Page 2 from the **Seller-Paid** (At Closing) column will carry forward to Seller's Transaction column on Page 3 of the Closing Disclosure to be used when calculating the Due from Seller at Closing amount.

## Page 3: Calculating Cash to Close

This section of Page 3 has columns to compare items from the **Loan Estimate** to the **Final** amount to arrive at **Cash to Close,** which is the amount the borrower must bring to closing:

*   Total Closing Costs (J) = Total Loan Costs (D) + Total Other Costs (I)
*   Closing Costs Paid Before Closing
*   Closing Costs Financed (Paid from your Loan Amount)
*   Down Payment/Funds from Borrower
*   Deposit (note that earnest money held on behalf of the buyer is subtracted here)
*   Funds for Borrower
*   Seller Credits (itemized in block L on Page 3)
*   Adjustments and Other Credits (noted in blocks K and L on Page 3)

These items also require an answer to the question **Did this change?** Lenders may be required to pay a credit if changes between the original Loan Estimate and the final numbers exceed allowable tolerances.

## Page 3: Summaries of Transactions

These tables itemize the amounts associated with the real estate purchase transaction between the buyer and seller, together with closing costs, in order to disclose the amounts **due from the borrower** or **due to the seller** at closing as applicable.

The borrower's transaction details are on the left side of the page; the seller's transaction details are on the right side of the page.

## Page 3: Blocks K and M

In block **K. Due from Borrower at Closing**, the borrower's **debits** are totaled. In block **M. Due to Seller at Closing**, the seller's **credits** are totaled.

Here we find the **sale price** of the property and the sale price of any **personal property** included in the sale. This could be, for example, carpets, draperies, appliances, lawn mowers, etc.

This is an example of a **double entry** where the amount is a **debit to the borrower** and a corresponding **credit to the seller.** Similarly, any **Adjustments for Items Paid by the Seller in Advance** would be shown as a debit to the borrower and a credit to the seller.

## Page 3: Blocks L and N

On the borrower's side in block **L. Paid Already by or on Behalf of Borrower at Closing**, we see an accounting of the borrower's **credits**. For example, any earnest money deposit the borrower made is a credit, as is the loan amount, since it's the lender who brings that amount to closing.

On the seller's side, block **N. Due from Seller at Closing** indicates all of the seller's **debits**. This includes the seller's closing costs, as well as the amount of any outstanding mortgage(s) that must be paid from the proceeds of the sale.

**Credits** from the seller to the buyer are shown in blocks L. and M. as well, for example, any amount paid by the seller to address any outstanding issues identified during the final walk-though of the property.

These blocks also indicate any **Adjustments for Items Unpaid by the Seller**, for example, real estate taxes, which are paid in arrears.

## Page 3: Calculation

The Borrower's Transaction debits and credits and the Seller's Transaction debits and credits are reconciled, with the **final calculations** indicated at the bottom of Page 3.

Notice that the settlement agent must select a box indicating whether cash is going from or to the borrower, and from or to the seller. There are certainly instances where a seller has to bring cash to the closing table, for example, if the seller has outstanding mortgage debts that cannot be repaid from the sale of the property after all closing costs are paid.

## Page 4: Additional Information About This Loan

Critical characteristics of the loan are noted on Page 4 of the Closing Disclosure:

- Information about future **assumption** of the loan by a subsequent purchaser
- Whether the loan contains a **demand feature** such as an acceleration clause or due on sale clause that can require early repayment of the loan
- Any obligation for borrower to pay a **late fee**
- Whether there could be **negative amortization**
- Whether the lender will allow **partial payments**
- A statement indicating that the borrower is granting a **security interest** in the property
- Details about any **escrow account** held by the lender or loan servicer

> √ **NOTE:** Additional information would be found on this page for other types of loans. For example, if it's an adjustable rate mortgage, a table showing details about the index, margin, change frequency, and payment caps would be included.

## Page 5 Sections

Page 5 includes four sections:

- **Loan Calculations.** Details about the payments made by the borrower.
- **Other Disclosures.** Miscellaneous disclosures to the borrower about their ongoing rights and responsibilities.

- **Contact Information.** Includes lender, mortgage broker, real estate broker(s), and settlement agent as applicable.
- **Confirm Receipt.** The signature(s) of the borrower(s)

### Page 5: Loan Calculations

Let's quickly look at the information contained in the **Loan Calculations** section. This is likely to be the scariest section of the entire Closing Disclosure to a borrower—even more so than the amount of cash needed at closing. This section indicates the:

- **Total of Payments.** The amount that would be paid to the lender upon repayment (principal plus all loan costs).
- **Finance Charge.** The total amount of interest the borrower will pay.
- **Amount Financed.** The principal amount of the loan.
- **Annual Percentage Rate (APR).** The costs over the loan term expressed as a rate, taking the note rate and other loan costs into consideration.
- **Total Interest Percentage (TIP).** The ratio of principal and total interest paid over the life of the loan.

## Preparing the Disclosure

Although the standardized **Closing Disclosure** is required to be used in closings that fall under RESPA requirements, note that the closing statement for some transactions may not follow precisely the line numbering of our sample, perhaps needing more space for debits, credits, and adjustments, for instance. The complexity of some transactions, the software programs used by some title companies, attorneys, and requirements of various lenders may result in entries on lines other than those in our sample.

Privately financed transactions and cash sales do not fall under RESPA, and so this Closing Disclosure is not required, although it may be used as a convenience.

## Other Disclosures

The terms "settlement" and "closing" can be used interchangeably. An **Affiliated Business Arrangement Disclosure (AfBA)** is required whenever a settlement service provider involved in a RESPA-covered transaction refers the consumer to a provider with whom the referring party has an ownership or other beneficial interest.

The **Initial Escrow Statement** itemizes the estimated taxes, insurance premiums, and other charges anticipated to be paid from the escrow account during the first 12 months of the loan. It lists the escrow payment amount and any required cushion. Although the statement is usually given at settlement, the lender has 45 days from settlement to deliver it.

Loan servicers must deliver to borrowers an **Annual Escrow Statement** once a year. The annual escrow account statement summarizes all escrow account deposits and payments during the servicer's 12-month computation year. It also notifies the borrower of any shortages or surpluses in the account and advises the borrower about the course of action being taken.

A **Servicing Transfer Statement** is required if the loan servicer sells or assigns the servicing rights to a borrower's loan to another loan servicer. Generally, the loan servicer must notify the borrower 15 days before the effective date of the loan transfer. As long as the borrower makes a timely payment to the old servicer within 60 days of the loan transfer, the borrower cannot be penalized. The notice must include the name and address of the new servicer, toll-free telephone numbers, and the date the new servicer will begin accepting payment.

### Kickbacks

**Section 8** of RESPA prohibits anyone from giving or accepting a fee, kickback, or anything of value in exchange for referrals of settlement service business involving a federally related mortgage loan. In addition, RESPA prohibits fee splitting and receiving unearned fees for services not actually performed.

## For Example

If a lender gives a real estate agent a fee for referring a client, it would be a violation.

According to HUD and FHA loans, and the Ohio Department of Commerce Department of Financial Institutions for any loan type, a real estate agent who is also a mortgage broker may *not* be involved in the same transaction.

What is *not* a kickback is if a real estate agent owns a share of a company, the agent can share in its profits.

## For Example

If you buy stock in a bank and that bank has a profitable year, it can pay a dividend based on the profit.

This provision does not apply to referral fees paid between real estate brokers, but applies to any other fees received, other than the commission. Also, the sale of a property may *not* be conditioned on the use of a particular title insurer or escrow company chosen by the seller. You are likely to encounter other relevant aspects of RESPA as you practice real estate.

Be aware that it is *against the law to defraud a lender by supplying falsified and/or inflated settlement statements.* One popular mortgage fraud scam involved inflated sale prices using second mortgages.

## For Example

A property was for sale for $100,000. A buyer was willing to pay $120,000, with a $100,000 first mortgage and a $20,000 second mortgage, which disappeared after closing. The lender who bought the mortgage thought it was a $120,000 house with a $20,000 down payment when in fact it was a $100,000 house with zero down.

## Best Practices

It is easy for a new agent to become overwhelmed with the many rules and regulations associated with real estate finance. If you feel you are being asked to participate in a program or idea where money is being refunded, documents are being altered or misplaced, or you have been offered money or something of value for referring business, you need to consult with your broker or manager for guidance.

## Summary

1. **Housing cycles** are the response of the real estate and mortgage markets to the forces of supply and demand. Two things that separate the housing markets from other supply and demand models are the *lag time for construction* industry response and the fact that *land (with all utilities) is limited* in a given area.

2. **Physical, economic, government,** and **social forces (P-E-G-S)** affect the real estate cycle. *Physical*: Location, popularity, climate, and environment; internal or external. *Economic*: Economic base of an area (critical for home values) and cost of money. *Government (federal)*: Fiscal policy (taxes), monetary policy (interest rates), and regulation. *Government (state/local)*: Revenue generating (taxes) and regulation (police power including land use controls, zoning, environmental, eminent domain, and escheat). *Social*: Demographics, migration, family size, population shift, growth, and age.

3. **Fiscal policy** is the government's plan for spending, taxing, and managing debt. The Treasury department carries out fiscal policy: Issues checks, collects taxes, and issues notes to cover deficits. Tools of fiscal policy are *deficit spending* and *taxation*. Deficit spending is when expenditures exceed revenues. Taxation is a way to collect revenue and implement social policies, such as giving tax deductions for mortgage interest to promote home ownership.

4. **Monetary policy** is the government's way to control the supply and cost of money. The Federal Reserve Board (the Fed) is responsible for monetary policy, maintaining economic stability, and regulating commercial banks. Policy tools (**D-O-R-M**): *Discount rate* (interest rate charged to member banks on overnight loans), *open market operation* (Fed sells/buys bonds to adjust money supply and demand), *reserve requirement* (banks must keep money on deposit—can't lend), and *moral suasion* (using persuasive influences on public and financial markets). Laws prohibiting discrimination: **Equal Credit Opportunity Act** prohibits discrimination based on sex, age, marital status, race, color, religion, national origin, receipt of public assistance, or exercised rights under the Consumer Credit Protection Act. **The Ohio Civil Rights Law** prohibits discrimination based on race, color, religion, sex, ancestry, national origin, disability, military status, and familial status (applies to vacant land).

5. Laws requiring financial disclosure: **Truth in Lending Act (TILA)** is implemented by **Regulation Z**. It doesn't limit rates, but requires lender to disclose credit cost. TIL disclosure statement, APR of loan, right to rescind, and advertising rules all fall under disclosure. **Annual Percentage Rate (APR)** is the total cost of financing, including the interest rate and all fees. The **right to rescind** lasts until three days after closing, but applies only to home equity loans, refinances, etc. Ads with finance details must tell all—down payment, terms, and APR spelled out. The **Real Estate Settlement Procedures Act (RESPA)** prohibits kickbacks, limits escrow reserves, requires giving HUD booklet to buyer, requires the lender to provide a **Loan Estimate** that includes a "good faith" estimate of settlement costs no later than three business days following the date of a completed mortgage loan application, use of a standardized **Closing Disclosure** form at least three business days before closing, and requires disclosure of multiple relationships. RESPA prevents mandatory use of service providers and requires lenders to disclose business relationships and how often loans are sold.

# Quiz

1. **When there are more home buyers than there are homes for sale, it is a**
   a. buyer's market.
   b. conveyance of deed.
   c. equal market.
   d. seller's market.

2. **_____ factors are NOT a force influencing housing cycles.**
   a. Economic
   b. Social
   c. Structure
   d. Supply

3. **The federal government influences the money supply through**
   a. fiscal and monetary policy.
   b. physical and social factors.
   c. rules of equilibrium.
   d. supply and demand.

4. **The Treasury Department is responsible for**
   a. federal spending.
   b. managing the federal deficit.
   c. tax collection.
   d. all of the above

5. **Under the Truth in Lending Act, a consumer refinancing a home has ____ day(s) to change his mind after closing.**
   a. 0
   b. 1
   c. 3
   d. 5

6. **How many Federal Reserve Banks are there?**
   a. 6
   b. 8
   c. 12
   d. 14

7. **Tools used by the Fed to implement monetary policy include**
   a. Congressional Acts.
   b. discount rates and reserve requirements.
   c. fiscal assertiveness.
   d. prime rates and subprime rates.

8. **The federal regulation prohibiting discrimination in the lending process is**
   a. the Equal Credit Opportunity Act.
   b. the Fair Housing Act.
   c. redlining.
   d. the Truth in Lending Act.

9. **The Real Estate Settlement and Procedures Act (RESPA) covers buying a**
   a. first home.
   b. share of a shopping center.
   c. small restaurant.
   d. storage warehouse.

10. **Under the Truth in Lending Act, a consumer selling a home and buying another to live in has ____ day(s) to change her mind.**
    a. 0
    b. 1
    c. 3
    d. 5

11. **The document given to the buyer within three business days after completing a loan application is the**
    a. disclosure of APR.
    b. Good Faith Agreement.
    c. Loan Estimate.
    d. Truth in Lending disclosure.

12. **The process of inflating the sale price of a property with a fraudulent second mortgage is considered**
    a. customer service.
    b. good selling skills.
    c. mortgage fraud.
    d. a way to increase your commission.

13. **Selling your home due to a death in your immediate household most likely is a(n) _____ factor.**
    a. economic
    b. governmental
    c. physical
    d. social

14. **The U.S. Treasury is responsible for _____ policy.**

    a. economic
    b. fiscal
    c. monetary
    d. social

15. **Receiving a cash incentive for referring a buyer to a lender is a violation of**

    a. the Fair Housing Act.
    b. Regulation Z.
    c. RESPA.
    d. the Truth in Lending Act.

16. **The amount a commercial bank must keep on deposit is known as**

    a. equilibrium.
    b. monetary policy.
    c. reserve requirements.
    d. supply and demand.

17. **The relationship between the cost of money and the total amount financed is the**

    a. APR.
    b. cost of goods sold.
    c. interest rate.
    d. prime rate.

18. **Which is FALSE under the Equal Credit Opportunity Act?**

    a. All income declared can count towards buying a home.
    b. Homebuyers may not be discriminated against due to sex.
    c. Homebuyers receiving public assistance may qualify for a loan.
    d. Lenders cannot deny a homebuyer's application when income is not ongoing and/or verifiable.

19. **When housing prices fall due to the relocation of a major employer, it is an example of a(n) _____ factor.**

    a. economic
    b. governmental
    c. physical
    d. social

20. **Members of the Federal Reserve Board of Governors are appointed for terms of**

    a. 1 year.
    b. 4 years.
    c. 10 years.
    d. 14 years.

# Types of Finance Instruments

The "instruments" discussed in this chapter are written documents. Any legal form is an integral part of most real estate financing transactions. This chapter discusses promissory notes, trust deeds, mortgages, types and features of mortgages, and land contracts. We also look at typical clauses found in those documents.

## Key Terms

**Acceleration Clause** A contract clause that gives the lender the right to declare the entire loan amount due immediately because of borrower's default, or other reasons as stated in the contract.

**Alienation Clause** A contract clause that gives the lender certain stated rights when there's a transfer of ownership in property. (Often called a **due-on-sale clause**.)

**Equitable Right of Redemption** The right of a debtor to redeem property from foreclosure proceedings prior to confirmation of sale.

**Hypothecate** To pledge property as security for a loan without giving up possession of it, as with a mortgage.

**Land Contract** A real estate installment agreement where a buyer makes payment to a seller in exchange for the right to occupy and use property, but no deed or title transfers until all, or a specified portion of, payments have been made.

**Mortgage** An instrument that creates a voluntary lien on real property to secure repayment of a debt. The parties to a mortgage are the mortgagor (borrower) and mortgagee (lender).

**Negotiable Instrument** Promissory note or other finance instrument that is freely transferable.

(continued on page 40)

# Real Estate Finance Instruments

In our discussion of real estate finance instruments, we focus on the more common written documents encountered in real estate transactions for buyers and sellers. These instruments include **promissory notes**, **trust deeds**, **mortgages**, and **land contracts**. Also covered are types and features of mortgages, as well as typical clauses found in these instruments.

**Instruments** are simply *written legal documents that establish the rights and duties of the parties involved in a transaction*. It's important to note that this chapter is intended to be an overview—*not* the basis for personal action nor as a substitute for competent professional or legal advice. You should *not* advise clients regarding the operation of any of these documents as that could be considered unauthorized practice of law. Ask your broker about her policies in this area. And always consult an attorney for current, local legal advice.

# Promissory Notes

**Promissory notes** are *instruments that evidence a promise to pay a specific amount of money to a specific person within a specific time frame*. Simply stated, a promissory note is a written promise to pay money. Before a lender will finance the purchase of a house, the borrower must promise to repay the funds. *The one promising to pay the money* is the **maker** of the note (usually the homebuyer). *The one to whom payment is promised* is the **payee** (usually the lender, which in some cases can also be the seller).

Promissory notes are basic evidence of debt, showing who owes how much to whom. They're usually simple documents, often less than a page long. A typical promissory note includes:

- The date
- Names of the parties involved
- Amount of the debt
- How and when the money is to be repaid
- What happens in the event of default
- Maker's signature

**Key Terms**

**Promissory Note** An instrument that evidences a promise to pay a specific amount of money to a specific person within a specific time frame. A written, legally binding promise to repay a debt.

**Security Instrument** An instrument that gives a creditor the right to sell collateral to satisfy a debt if the debtor fails to pay according to the terms of the agreement.

**Subordination Clause** A contract clause that gives a mortgage recorded at a later date the right to take priority over an earlier recorded mortgage.

**Trust Deed** An instrument held by a third party as security for the payment of a note. Like a mortgage, it creates a voluntary lien on real property to secure repayment of a debt. Parties to a trust deed are grantor or trustor (borrower), beneficiary (lender), and trustee (neutral third party). Unlike a mortgage, a trust deed has a power of sale, allowing trustee to foreclose non-judicially. Also called a **Deed of Trust**.

# NOTE

_____, _____          _____, _____
          [Date]                                                    [City]                    [State]

_____
                             [Property Address]

## 1. BORROWER'S PROMISE TO PAY

In return for a loan that I have received, I promise to pay U.S. $_____ (this amount is called "Principal"), plus interest, to the order of the Lender. The Lender is _____. I will make all payments under this Note in the form of cash, check or money order.

I understand that the Lender may transfer this Note. The Lender or anyone who takes this Note by transfer and who is entitled to receive payments under this Note is called the "Note Holder."

## 2. INTEREST

Interest will be charged on unpaid principal until the full amount of Principal has been paid. I will pay interest at a yearly rate of _____%.

The interest rate required by this Section 2 is the rate I will pay both before and after any default described in Section 6(B) of this Note.

## 3. PAYMENTS

### (A) Time and Place of Payments

I will pay principal and interest by making a payment every month.

I will make my monthly payment on the _____ day of each month beginning on _____, _____. I will make these payments every month until I have paid all of the principal and interest and any other charges described below that I may owe under this Note. Each monthly payment will be applied as of its scheduled due date and will be applied to interest before Principal. If, on _____, 20____, I still owe amounts under this Note, I will pay those amounts in full on that date, which is called the "Maturity Date."

I will make my monthly payments at _____ _____ or at a different place if required by the Note Holder.

### (B) Amount of Monthly Payments

My monthly payment will be in the amount of U.S. $_____.

## 4. BORROWER'S RIGHT TO PREPAY

I have the right to make payments of Principal at any time before they are due. A payment of Principal only is known as a "Prepayment." When I make a Prepayment, I will tell the Note Holder in writing that I am doing so. I may not designate a payment as a Prepayment if I have not made all the monthly payments due under the Note.

I may make a full Prepayment or partial Prepayments without paying a Prepayment charge. The Note Holder will use my Prepayments to reduce the amount of Principal that I owe under this Note. However, the Note Holder may apply my Prepayment to the accrued and unpaid interest on the Prepayment amount, before applying my Prepayment to reduce the Principal amount of the Note. If I make a partial Prepayment, there will be no changes in the due date or in the amount of my monthly payment unless the Note Holder agrees in writing to those changes.

## 5. LOAN CHARGES

If a law, which applies to this loan and which sets maximum loan charges, is finally interpreted so that the interest or other loan charges collected or to be collected in connection with this loan exceed the permitted limits, then: (a) any such loan charge shall be reduced by the amount necessary to reduce the charge to the permitted limit; and (b) any sums already collected from me which exceeded permitted limits will be refunded to me. The Note Holder may choose to make this refund by reducing the Principal I owe under this Note or by making a direct payment to me. If a refund reduces Principal, the reduction will be treated as a partial Prepayment.

**6. BORROWER'S FAILURE TO PAY AS REQUIRED**

**(A) Late Charge for Overdue Payments**

If the Note Holder has not received the full amount of any monthly payment by the end of _____ calendar days after the date it is due, I will pay a late charge to the Note Holder. The amount of the charge will be _____ % of my overdue payment of principal and interest. I will pay this late charge promptly but only once on each late payment.

**(B) Default**

If I do not pay the full amount of each monthly payment on the date it is due, I will be in default.

**(C) Notice of Default**

If I am in default, the Note Holder may send me a written notice telling me that if I do not pay the overdue amount by a certain date, the Note Holder may require me to pay immediately the full amount of Principal which has not been paid and all the interest that I owe on that amount. That date must be at least 30 days after the date on which the notice is mailed to me or delivered by other means.

**(D) No Waiver By Note Holder**

Even if, at a time when I am in default, the Note Holder does not require me to pay immediately in full as described above, the Note Holder will still have the right to do so if I am in default at a later time.

**(E) Payment of Note Holder's Costs and Expenses**

If the Note Holder has required me to pay immediately in full as described above, the Note Holder will have the right to be paid back by me for all of its costs and expenses in enforcing this Note to the extent not prohibited by applicable law. Those expenses include, for example, reasonable attorneys' fees.

**7. GIVING OF NOTICES**

Unless applicable law requires a different method, any notice that must be given to me under this Note will be given by delivering it or by mailing it by first class mail to me at the Property Address above or at a different address if I give the Note Holder a notice of my different address.

Any notice that must be given to the Note Holder under this Note will be given by delivering it or by mailing it by first class mail to the Note Holder at the address stated in Section 3(A) above or at a different address if I am given a notice of that different address.

**8. OBLIGATIONS OF PERSONS UNDER THIS NOTE**

If more than one person signs this Note, each person is fully and personally obligated to keep all of the promises made in this Note, including the promise to pay the full amount owed. Any person who is a guarantor, surety or endorser of this Note is also obligated to do these things. Any person who takes over these obligations, including the obligations of a guarantor, surety or endorser of this Note, is also obligated to keep all of the promises made in this Note. The Note Holder may enforce its rights under this Note against each person individually or against all of us together. This means that any one of us may be required to pay all of the amounts owed under this Note.

**9. WAIVERS**

I and any other person who has obligations under this Note waive the rights of Presentment and Notice of Dishonor. "Presentment" means the right to require the Note Holder to demand payment of amounts due. "Notice of Dishonor" means the right to require the Note Holder to give notice to other persons that amounts due have not been paid.

**10. UNIFORM SECURED NOTE**

This Note is a uniform instrument with limited variations in some jurisdictions. In addition to the protections given to the Note Holder under this Note, a Mortgage, Deed of Trust, or Security Deed (the "Security Instrument"), dated the same date as this Note, protects the Note Holder from possible losses which might result if I do not keep the promises which I make in this Note. That Security Instrument describes how and under what conditions I may be required to make immediate payment in full of all amounts I owe under this Note. Some of those conditions are described as follows:

If all or any part of the Property or any Interest in the Property is sold or transferred (or if Borrower is not a natural person and a beneficial interest in Borrower is sold or transferred) without Lender's prior written consent, Lender may require immediate payment in full of all sums secured by this Security Instrument. However, this option shall not be exercised by Lender if such exercise is prohibited by Applicable Law.

 MULTISTATE FIXED RATE NOTE—Single Family—Fannie Mae/Freddie Mac UNIFORM INSTRUMENT          Form 3200   1/01 *(page 2 of 3 pages)*

If Lender exercises this option, Lender shall give Borrower notice of acceleration. The notice shall provide a period of not less than 30 days from the date the notice is given in accordance with Section 15 within which Borrower must pay all sums secured by this Security Instrument. If Borrower fails to pay these sums prior to the expiration of this period, Lender may invoke any remedies permitted by this Security Instrument without further notice or demand on Borrower.

WITNESS THE HAND(S) AND SEAL(S) OF THE UNDERSIGNED.

_____(Seal)
                                    - Borrower

_____(Seal)
                                    - Borrower

_____(Seal)
                                    - Borrower

*[Sign Original Only]*

**MULTISTATE FIXED RATE NOTE**—Single Family—**Fannie Mae/Freddie Mac UNIFORM INSTRUMENT**          Form 3200   1/01  *(page 3 of 3 pages)*

43

## Negotiable Instruments

**Negotiable instruments** are *promissory notes or other finance instruments that are freely transferable from one party to another*. Most promissory notes used in real estate are negotiable instruments. When a note is **freely transferable**, the lender or other creditor can *obtain immediate cash by selling the note*, such as when real estate notes are sold to the secondary market. The sale is usually at a discount, meaning the note is sold for a cash amount less than the note's face value.

Two types of notes most commonly used in real estate transactions, such as buying or refinancing a home, are:

1. **Straight note**—*Calls for payments of interest only during the term of the note, with a balloon payment at the end of the loan term to pay off the principal amount.* A **balloon payment** is *a large payment due at a specific point in time, usually at the end of the loan to pay off the entire remaining balance.*

### For Example

If money is borrowed for a three-year period with a balloon payment at the end of the third year, the total remaining balance would be due at that time.

2. **Amortized installment note**—*Calls for regular payment of principal and interest, calculated to pay off the entire balance by the end of the loan term.* A portion of each payment goes toward paying off the loan, and the rest toward interest paid to the lender; these amounts will fluctuate based on the length of the loan. When a loan is "fully amortized," it will end in a zero balance. When a loan is "partially amortized," the balance due at the end will be in the form of a balloon payment. The borrower may have to obtain another loan to refinance the balance if he does not have the cash to pay it off.

### DO THE MATH!

Most people buying a house want to know the monthly payment amount, not necessarily the total cost of the house. **It is important to remember when calculating house payments that interest is paid only on the loan amount, not the purchase price!** Simply subtract the down payment from the purchase price to get the loan amount.

Let's take a quick look at how to figure the payments on two common types of notes.

**Straight Note**

Since a straight note offers interest only with no money towards the principal, the formula is fairly simple:

**Loan Amount x Annual Interest Rate = Annual Interest Payment**

When the lender requires payment monthly (this is very common), the formula is:

**Loan Amount x Annual Rate of Interest ÷ 12 (Months in a Year) = Monthly Payment**

**Let's Try One!**

Mary wants to purchase a house and the lender offers her a loan at 6% fixed for 15 years on a straight note. If the house costs $150,000 and Mary is putting no money down, what will her monthly payment be? Will Mary owe any money at the end of the loan?

## Security Instruments

**Security instruments** *give a creditor the right to sell collateral* (in real estate, usually the house) *to satisfy the debt,* if the debtor fails to pay according to the terms of the agreement. Keep in mind, though, a security instrument just describes the collateral for a note. **Even without a security instrument, the debtor is still obligated to pay the note.**

In almost all real estate financing transactions, a promissory note is accompanied by a security instrument. A security instrument allows a debtor to *hypothecate* property. **Hypothecate** means *a debtor can pledge property as security for a debt without giving up possession of it.* The property serves as security for the creditor and motivation for the debtor to make sure the terms of the note are fulfilled and the note is repaid as agreed. Failure to do so could result in loss of possession.

The two main types of security instruments used in real estate transactions are **trust deeds** and **mortgages**. (Our discussion of trust deeds will be brief as they are rarely used in Ohio.)

## Trust Deeds

**Trust deeds** (also called **deeds of trust**) are *instruments held by a third party as security for the payment of a note.* Trust deeds are three-party devices:

- The *borrower* is the **trustor**
- The *lender* is the **beneficiary**
- An *independent third party* is the **trustee**

*Ohio is considered a **lien theory** state*, so trust deeds create a lien against property in favor of the beneficiary. This lien gives the creditor the right to force the sale of the property if the debtor defaults on payments under the note or trust deed.

---

Here's the formula:

**$150,000 x 6% (0.06) ÷ 12 = $750 Per Month**

Because Mary has a straight note, she will have a balance due of $150,000 at the end of 15 years.

**Amortized Note**

Calculating payments on an amortized note is a little more complicated. Each payment includes some principal and some interest and pays off, or amortizes, the mortgage balance. It is helpful to have a mortgage calculator, a computer, or a factor chart to calculate monthly payments (there is a factor chart in the Appendix). Here is the formula:

**Loan Amount ÷ 1,000 x Factor = Monthly Payment**

**Let's Try One!**

Bill wants to buy a house and the lender offers him a loan at 6.5% fixed for 30 years on an amortized note. If the house costs $200,000 and Bill is putting 10% down, what will his monthly payment be? Will Bill owe any money at the end of the loan?

**(180,000) ÷ (1,000) x (6.32) = $ 1,137.60 Per Month**

No balance will be due at the end of 30 years.

The distinguishing characteristic of trust deeds is that when the debtor defaults on loan payments, the creditor may begin a **non-judicial foreclosure** action. This non-judicial action is authorized by a **power of sale clause** in the note or trust deed, which *allows the trustee to sell the property without court supervision*. The entire process of foreclosing and selling property through the power of sale clause may be concluded in well under a year, without the expense involved for court proceedings.

## Advantages and Disadvantages of Trust Deeds

| Party | Advantages | Disadvantages |
|---|---|---|
| Borrower (trustor) | Right to stop the sale and reinstate the loan by making up back payments (plus interest, trustee's fees, and attorneys' fees) | A debtor can often stop the sale by making up back payments (plus interest and fees) until just a few days before the sale |
| Lender (beneficiary) | A quick and inexpensive non-judicial sale process | The speed of the process, lack of judicial supervision, and the lack of redemption rights following the trustee's sale |

*Trust deeds are rarely used in Ohio* because the foreclosure is not backed by a judicial decree. Thus, questions regarding the validity of the sale can be raised by the debtor. The sale could be attacked for many defects, such as failure to notify all parties or lack of competition among bidders at the foreclosure sale. Lenders feel more secure foreclosing by judicial sale (which is the case with mortgages).

# Mortgages

**Mortgages** are *instruments that create a lien against real property as security for the payment of a note*. A mortgage is a type of security instrument, where the *borrower* (the **mortgagor**) pledges property to the *lender* (the **mortgagee**) as collateral for the debt. Most people think they get a mortgage from a lender when, in fact, *the borrower actually gives the mortgage to the lender*. A promissory note is almost always accompanied by a security instrument to give the creditor some leverage against the debtor, and the debtor an extra incentive to pay. With a mortgage as security, the collateral is real estate. And, with a mortgage, the procedure in the event of default is *judicial foreclosure*. **Judicial foreclosure** under a mortgage *requires a court-ordered sheriff's sale of the property to repay the debt*.

## Judicial Foreclosure Procedure

When a borrower is in default, the lender *accelerates* the due date of the debt to the present and gives the debtor **notice of default,** *demanding the full loan balance be paid at once*. If the debtor fails to do so, the lender files *a lawsuit*, called a **foreclosure action**, in Common Pleas Court where the land is located.

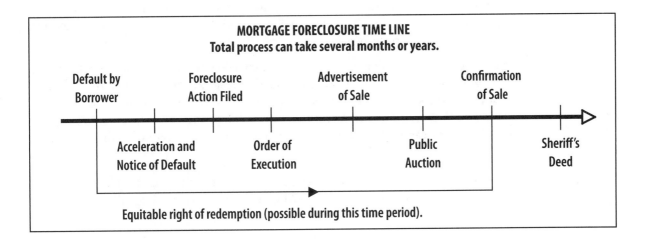

**MORTGAGE FORECLOSURE TIME LINE**
**Total process can take several months or years.**

Default by Borrower — Acceleration and Notice of Default — Foreclosure Action Filed — Order of Execution — Advertisement of Sale — Public Auction — Confirmation of Sale — Sheriff's Deed

Equitable right of redemption (possible during this time period).

Under a foreclosure action:

1. The court determines if the lender is rightfully owed the money.

2. If the court finds in favor of the creditor, a judge will issue an **order of execution** *directing an officer of the court, usually the county sheriff, to seize and sell the property*.

3. The public is notified of the place and date of the sale via *advertising* that runs for three consecutive weeks in a newspaper circulated in the county.

4. On the sale date, a **public auction** is *held at the courthouse where anyone can bid on the property*. The minimum bid is two-thirds of the appraised value, as determined by three disinterested appraisers who live in the county. (The minimum two-thirds bid requirement protects whatever equity the debtor may have in the property, so a bidder can't simply get a "good deal" by paying just the mortgage balance.)

5. The property is sold to the highest bidder, with proceeds used to pay costs of the sale and to pay off the mortgages and liens. Any surplus funds (left over after all debts, liens, expenses, and costs related to the property are paid) go to the debtor.

6. After the sale, a document called a **confirmation of sale** is *filed to finalize the sale*. A **sheriff's deed** is then *issued to the purchaser of the property, which is executed, acknowledged, and recorded just like any other deed*.

7. If the property does not sell for enough money at the foreclosure sale to pay off the mortgage, the creditor may be able to obtain a **deficiency judgment** against the debtor *for the remaining debt*. A deficiency judgment requires a *separate* court action.

   √ **Note:** This was a simple explanation. In today's marketplace, foreclosure procedures are undergoing challenges and modifications by both state governments and federal agencies. Make sure you stay current with the practices and legal issues in the jurisdictions where you do business.

## Redemption

The debtor can *redeem* (save) the property *from the time the foreclosure action is brought up until the confirmation of the foreclosure sale*. This is done by paying the court what is due, which may include court costs and attorneys' fees. This right to save or redeem the property prior to the confirmation of sale is called the **equitable right of redemption.** Once the redemption is made, the court will set aside the sale, pay the parties, and the debtor gets title to the property again.

Another option is for a debtor to make a **voluntary conveyance** of property (also called **deed in lieu of foreclosure**). Here, *debtors still lose the property but by returning it **voluntarily** to the lender before the court action is final, they can avoid having a foreclosure on their credit report.* After the confirmation of sale, the transfer of the property is final. The debtor can no longer redeem the property or do a voluntary conveyance.

√ **Note:** A lender does not have to accept a deed in lieu of foreclosure as full satisfaction of the debt and could still pursue a deficiency judgment.

## Short Sales

A **short sale** is *a lender-approved sale in which the proceeds are not sufficient to cover the mortgage amount(s).* Short sales are typically done to avoid foreclosure and its inherent costs. For a short sale to occur, the lender(s) must agree to take less than what is owed against the property and to satisfy the lien(s) against the property so that clear title can be conveyed.

Homeowners can benefit from a short sale, if the lender will agree to one, because there is less of an impact on their credit report as compared to a foreclosure, and the mortgage debt is fully discharged. Lenders benefit from short sales because they avoid foreclosure which is very time consuming (short sales are generally faster than a foreclosure) and costly.

### Home Mortgage Affordability Program (HAMP)

In 2009, the U.S. Treasury unveiled the **Home Mortgage Affordability Program (HAMP).** A Dec. 10, 2009 U.S. Treasury report stated that 85% of all outstanding mortgage loans may be covered under HAMP. This program allows certain borrowers to apply for mortgage modifications through their lender that may enable them to stay in their home. Selected applicants are placed in a "trial modification" and, upon meeting certain criteria, these homeowners qualify for permanent modifications of their loans.

### Home Affordable Foreclosure Alternatives (HAFA)

The **Home Affordable Foreclosure Alternatives Program (HAFA)** took effect on April 5, 2010. This program sets out criteria for lenders and borrowers that may make a short sale or deed in lieu of foreclosure a viable option to help homeowners avoid foreclosure. Most lenders are required to meet HAFA guidelines.

## Advantages and Disadvantages of Mortgages

| Party | Advantages | Disadvantages |
|---|---|---|
| Borrower (trustor) | Usually has ample time to get money together due to lengthy court proceedings | A buyer who misses one or two payments may have to pay off the entire debt to save the house |
| Lender (beneficiary) | Right to accelerate the entire debt in the event of default<br><br>Authority of the court for judicial foreclosure | Time and expense involved with judicial foreclosure. Legal fees and court costs can be several thousand dollars, which the lender may or may not recover from the sale, and the entire process can take several months or years to complete |

# Typical Clauses in Finance Instruments

We'll now look at some typical clauses used in real estate finance instruments. Many of these can be found in the promissory note or security instrument—and often these clauses appear in both.

## Acceleration Clause

An **acceleration clause** in a contract *gives the lender the right to declare the entire loan balance due immediately because of borrower default, or for violation of other contract provisions.* Most notes, mortgages, trust deeds, and even land contracts contain an acceleration clause. This is important to lenders because, upon default, they want to be able to make *all* payments due—without having to file a separate action for each missed payment. The actions that constitute default are defined in the contract. A debtor who misses one payment may discover that not just two payments are due next month but rather, the contract may state the entire loan balance is due as a result of the missed payment. Most lenders will wait until payments are at least 90 days delinquent before enforcing an acceleration clause that appears in the mortgage or note—although buyers should never take this for granted.

## Alienation Clause

An **alienation clause** in a contract *gives the lender certain stated rights when there's a transfer of ownership in the property.* This is designed to *limit the debtor's right to transfer property without the creditor's permission.* Depending on the actual clause wording (that's why lawyers are important), alienation may be triggered by a transfer of title or simply by transfer of a significant interest in the property. Transfer of a "significant interest" can be construed as an obvious long-term lease, but often is also interpreted to cover a lease with an option to buy or a land contract.

Upon sale or transfer of a significant interest in the property, *the lender will often have the right to accelerate the debt* (called a **due on sale clause**), *change the interest rate, or charge a hefty assumption fee.* ARM loans seldom have an alienation clause that calls for an interest rate change since the rate can already be adjusted under the original contract. But an ARM loan may have other alienation provisions, such as an assumption fee. The lender may choose which, if any, options stated in the contract to enforce. This is true for most conventional loans. Although FHA and VA loans cannot technically have alienation clauses, they still attempt to restrict transfers in other ways, such as by reserving the right to approve a new debtor who will take over an FHA or VA loan.

For conventional loans, states tried to restrict enforcement of due on sale clauses. But in the 1982 landmark case, *Fidelity Savings and Loan v. De La Cuesta, et. al.*, the U.S. Supreme Court ruled that federally chartered S&Ls could follow the Federal Office of Thrift Supervision rules allowing due on sale clauses instead of following state laws that attempted to limit this right. Later that same year, the U.S. Congress passed the **Deposit Insurance Flexibility Act (Garn-St. Germain Act)** extending this right of preemption of state laws limiting due on sale clauses. As a result, *all lenders* can now enforce due on sale clauses.

This law has led to a new problem yet to be addressed adequately, as of this writing. Lenders often have alienation clauses *and* prepayment penalty clauses in contracts. Essentially, the lender could collect additional fees or penalties *twice*—once under the provisions of each clause. Several rules or regulations have been proposed that would eliminate this problem by forcing lenders to choose to enforce one or the other, but no new rules have been enacted as of this writing. Of course, with increased competition in the home mortgage market, lenders do not have free reign on charging exorbitant fees. It's important, nevertheless, for buyers and sellers (and agents) to be aware this situation may exist.

## Defeasance Clause

A **defeasance clause** is *used to defeat or cancel a certain right on the occurrence of a specific event.* This clause can appear in contracts or mortgages. A defeasance clause can also give a borrower the right to redeem real estate after default on a note by paying the full amount owed plus fees and court costs incurred in pursuing the defaulting party. The defeasance clause will outline the circumstances, procedures, and rules for the redemption to be successful.

### For Example

A debtor fails to make a balloon payment when due. The debtor can make the payment in full within the time frame specified in the defeasance clause and regain title to the property, thus overriding another clause in the contract that transferred the property title to the creditor upon default.

## Partial Release, Satisfaction, or Conveyance Clause

A **partial release, satisfaction,** or **conveyance clause** in a contract *obligates the creditor to release part of the property from lien and convey title to that part back to the debtor once certain provisions of the note or mortgage have been satisfied.* Usually, this occurs after a certain percentage of the mortgage balance has been paid. This is an important clause that appears in many blanket mortgages and some construction mortgages so the developer or builder can sell off completed houses with clear title before having to pay back the entire amount borrowed for the development project. Also, if the land is bought with a mortgage, later construction financing is much easier to obtain when the builder owns part of the land free of liens.

### For Example

A builder bought five acres of land with a contract that had a partial release clause. Per the contract, one acre of land would be released with clear title to the builder for each 20% of the note amount paid. This allows the builder to build a house on this one-acre parcel and sell it free and clear.

## Prepayment Clause

A **prepayment clause** in a contract *gives the lender the right to charge the borrower a penalty for paying off the loan early.* While the time period and amount of the penalty may vary considerably, the basic effect of a prepayment clause is to charge the debtor extra money to make up for the interest income the lender loses when a debtor pays off a loan early. For example, a prepayment clause may call for the debtor to pay an additional 3% of the loan amount if more than 20% of the principal is repaid during the first five years of the loan. This type of clause *may* be seen in a conventional loan, but is *prohibited in FHA or VA loans.*

### Best Practices

Be careful when a buyer asks you about making extra payments on a home loan to pay it off early. Always advise the buyer to check the mortgage and note to make sure there are no prepayment penalties. This may also be a problem when a person wants to sell a home after being in it for just a few years.

## Subordination Clause

A **subordination clause** in a contract *gives a mortgage recorded at a later date the right to take priority over one recorded earlier.* Normally with mortgages, trust deeds, and other real estate contracts, the first instrument or document recorded gets *lien priority.* **Lien priority** is *the order in which liens are paid off out of the proceeds of a foreclosure sale.* This is important because the lien with the highest priority gets paid first, as follows:

1.  Liens for real estate taxes always have the highest priority.
2.  The first recorded lien gets paid.
3.  If there's money left, the second lien gets paid, and so on.
4.  When the funds are exhausted, liens in a later position get nothing.

In some situations, however, the parties may desire that a later recorded instrument have priority over an earlier recorded instrument. This is very common in construction financing. Because of the high-risk nature of construction loans, construction lenders frequently refuse to lend any money unless they can be assured of a first lien position. Since the developer in many cases has already purchased the land on some sort of deferred payment plan, there is often a security instrument (mortgage, trust deed, or contract) already recorded. For the later construction loan mortgage to take priority over the earlier recorded mortgage instrument on the land, that earlier instrument must contain a *subordination clause.*

The subordination clause usually states that the instrument containing the clause will be subordinate (junior) to another loan lien (mortgage or trust deed) to be recorded later. The inclusion of a subordination clause must be negotiated at the time the earlier transaction is being entered into. Once the first instrument is recorded, it's usually too late to make this kind of arrangement with the lender. Subordination clauses are also common in home equity loans or lines of credit, where the holder of the junior "second mortgage" agrees to a subordinate position even if the homeowner later refinances the first mortgage.

## Other Mortgage Clauses and Covenants

In addition to the typical clauses discussed, there are also a number of other *covenants* to consider. **Covenants** are simply *promises.* Covenants can appear in deeds, mortgages, or any other document. Typical covenants can compel or prevent certain actions by the property owner or uses for the property.

Typical covenants the property owner must sign that appear in mortgages include provisions protecting the lender's security interests in the property. These covenants include having the property owner promise to keep the property in good condition and repair, to not damage or diminish the value of the property in any way, to keep fire and hazard insurance on the property in force, and to pay taxes and other assessments on time. Failure to keep any of these promises or covenants can be cited in the mortgage or note as causes for default.

There are a number of other clauses and covenants important to typical mortgages. Buyers should make sure they understand all of them, and should be encouraged to consult legal counsel before entering into a mortgage. Some of these clauses and covenants are very specific, and your broker or an attorney should be consulted if you think they may have an impact on your real estate transaction.

## Types and Features of Mortgages

Although mortgages are primarily security devices used to collateralize real estate loans, the word "mortgage" is often prefaced with adjectives that describe the particular function it is serving, or the nature of the circumstances surrounding its use.

### For Example

A "construction mortgage" is a mortgage used to secure a construction loan; a "blanket mortgage" is a mortgage that secures a loan with two or more parcels of land as collateral.

It's also important to note that some mortgage loans can be more than one type of mortgage loan at the same time, plus some share many different mortgage features.

### For Example

A buyer can have a conventional mortgage loan that is a first mortgage (and thus a senior mortgage). This same mortgage can also be an adjustable rate mortgage that is a budget mortgage.

Of course, some mortgage types and features are mutually exclusive—a construction mortgage can't also be a reverse equity mortgage. Don't worry if you don't know all these terms yet—you will.

## First Mortgage

A **first mortgage** is *a security instrument with a first lien position*. As such, a first mortgage always has priority over all other mortgages, meaning the first mortgage holder is paid first in the event of foreclosure. When a first mortgage is recorded first, the only lien that preempts it is a real estate tax lien.

## Senior Mortgage

A **senior mortgage** is *any mortgage with a higher lien position than another*. Thus, a first mortgage is always in a senior mortgage position.

As we just learned, lien status is important in the event of foreclosure, because the proceeds from a foreclosure sale pay the first lien in its entirety; if any money remains, the second lien is paid; then the third, and so on until the money is gone. Obviously, it's best to have a first lien.

## Second Mortgage

A **second mortgage** is *a security instrument in a second lien position*. Although property is still used as security, the second mortgage lender is in a riskier position because a first mortgage gets paid first out of foreclosure proceedings—if there's nothing left, the second mortgage holder gets nothing. A second mortgage may be used to help buy the property (e.g., small loan from the seller) or a second mortgage might be taken out later to generate additional funds from the owner's equity in the property (e.g., home equity loan to be used for repairs, to send a child to college, or for some other purpose).

## Junior Mortgage

A **junior mortgage** is *any mortgage with a lower lien position than another*. Thus, a second mortgage is a junior mortgage to a first mortgage, but a second mortgage is a senior mortgage to a third mortgage.

## Purchase Money Mortgage

A **purchase money mortgage** is *a mortgage given by a buyer to a lender or a seller to secure part or all of the money borrowed to purchase property*. A seller may take part of the purchase price as a mortgage to help the sale. *If given to a seller*, a purchase money mortgage can be called a **soft money mortgage**, *because the borrower receives credit instead of actual cash*. Also, note that a purchase money mortgage can be a first mortgage or a junior mortgage, depending on its lien priority.

### For Example

The sale price of a house is $100,000. The buyer pays $20,000 to the seller as a down payment and signs a note and a purchase money mortgage, in favor of the seller, for the remaining $80,000 to be paid at 10% interest over the next 30 years.

## Cash-Out Refinance Mortgage

A **cash-out refinance mortgage** is *a mortgage that a borrower gives to a lender to get cash for the equity in a property*. An example of a cash-out mortgage is when a property owner takes out a portion of the equity in his home for some purpose (e.g. to pay off credit cards, car loans, or student loans). This way, an owner can utilize the equity in the property but still retain ownership. The existing first mortgage is paid off and a new first mortgage (with the cash-out amount included) is created. A cash-out mortgage is sometimes referred to as a **hard money mortgage**, because *the borrower receives actual cash for the mortgage*.

## Refinance Mortgage

A **refinance mortgage** is *a mortgage that a borrower gives to a lender so the borrower can redo or change her interest rate, term (number of years), or both, creating a new first mortgage on her property*. For years, borrowers were told it was beneficial to refinance only if the interest rate on their current loan was 2% higher than what they could negotiate. Depending on the length of time a borrower might live in a home, it can be advantageous to refinance when there is a 1% difference in rates. Additionally, it may be possible for homeowners, in some cases, to reduce their term and shave years off their mortgage.

### Home Equity Loan, Home Equity Line of Credit

A **home equity loan** or **home equity line of credit,** sometimes known as a **HELOC loan**, *is secured by a mortgage on one's principal residence.* These are often used for non-housing expenditures. The difference between the two is that a **home equity loan** is *usually a one-time loan for a specific amount of money* (and often a specific purpose), whereas a **home equity line of credit** is *money available to the homeowner to be borrowed as expenses arise* (an open-end loan in which a borrower is granted a specific limit from which he can draw and pay back over time). Both of these financing vehicles take advantage of the equity in the property (and the fact that the IRS allows interest on a home mortgage to be tax deductible) by attaching a junior mortgage to it (unless the property is free and clear).

## Blanket Mortgage

A **blanket mortgage** *covers more than one parcel of land or lot,* and is usually used to finance subdivision developments. These loans usually have a partial release clause, allowing the borrower to pay a certain amount to release some lots with the mortgage continuing to cover the other lots.

### For Example

In a subdivision scenario, a builder may initially have one mortgage covering the entire acreage, but by paying down a certain percentage of the loan, the builder can sell off completed home lots.

## Bridge Mortgage

A **bridge mortgage** is *a mortgage that occurs between the termination of one mortgage and the beginning of the next.* The bridge mortgage is commonly used by a buyer who is able to purchase a new home before selling the existing home. The lender advances the mortgage for the new home and then "recasts" this loan when the existing home is sold and money is put down on the new home. Bridge mortgages are designed to be temporary and are used for the purchase of resale homes and for new construction.

## Budget Mortgage

A **budget mortgage** *has payments that include principal, interest, taxes, and insurance on the loan.* The all-inclusive payment of a budget mortgage is often referred to as **PITI** (Principal, Interest, Taxes, and Insurance). One-twelfth of the year's property taxes and hazard insurance premiums are collected each month and deposited into a separate escrow account by the lender so these expenses can be paid when they come due. Most home loans are secured by budget mortgages, because it's the best way for a lender to ensure that property taxes and insurance are paid on time.

√ **Remember:** A budget mortgage can also be a first mortgage, a senior mortgage, etc.

## Package Mortgage

A **package mortgage** *includes personal property, like appliances, in a property sale and all are financed together with one contract.* With package mortgages, the personal property also serves as collateral for the loan. A common use for this type of mortgage is when a person buys a furnished condominium, where the loan and mortgage documents may also recite appliances and/or furniture as part of the transaction.

### Best Practices

Buyers need to be careful when attempting to add personal property, such as furniture, tools, pools, or hot tubs to a residential sale. The lender may not want to lend on the personal property due to the value. It might be wise for the buyer and seller to negotiate the sale of personal property in a separate document.

## Reverse Mortgage

A **reverse mortgage** is *when a qualified senior citizen (age 62 and older) mortgages his home and, in return, receives a lump sum of cash, sets up an equity line, or receives a monthly check from the lender.* The borrower must have a substantial amount of equity in the home to make this option viable. (This works well if a home is owned free and clear.) The mortgage is repaid when the home is sold, the borrower has been out of the home for more than one year, or the borrower dies. The bank does not own the home so the homeowner is still responsible for taxes, insurance, and maintenance on the property. Reverse mortgages can also be used by senior citizens to move from one property to another. This type of mortgage is also called a **reverse annuity mortgage**, **reverse equity mortgage**, or **home equity conversion mortgage**.

## Wraparound Mortgage

A **wraparound mortgage** is *when an existing loan on a property is combined with a new loan.*

### For Example

This arrangement could be used in lieu of traditional refinancing where a lender makes a second loan to a borrower, leaving the first loan intact. The borrower pays the wraparound lender a single payment on the combined principal. If the wraparound lender is not the original lender, the wraparound lender makes payments on the original mortgage to the first mortgage lender.

This type of arrangement gives a borrower more favorable terms than a typical refinance, since the wraparound lender is advancing only the difference between the unpaid first mortgage and the combined principal on both loans. Less commonly, a wraparound mortgage could be used as a form of seller financing. The buyer makes full payment to the holder of the wraparound mortgage (the seller), who in turn makes payments on the original mortgage. Essentially, the buyer pays the seller who, in turn, pays the original lender. This is often done when a buyer can't, or won't, assume the loan. For this arrangement to be proper and legal, there must be an assumable first mortgage with bank approval for the wraparound loan. Otherwise, the seller may be violating any due on sale clause.

## Adjustable (or Variable) Rate Mortgage

An **adjustable rate mortgage (ARM)** is *a loan with interest rates that rise and fall based on fluctuations in the cost of money.* This type of mortgage may also be called a **variable rate mortgage**. These are fairly common loans and will be discussed more thoroughly in Chapter 6.

## Option ARM; Pick a Payment

Before the mortgage crisis of 2007, **option ARMs** or **pick a payment loans** were probably the most complex to understand due to the many variations available to a buyer. These loans are no longer available and are expected to add significantly to the national foreclosure and short sales balance of 2010 and 2011.

These loans were *ARMs for which the interest rate and payments can be adjusted every 30 days*. One of the reasons for their popularity with buyers was the "teaser rate" that was usually 2% or less. This low initial rate allowed a buyer, especially in high-cost areas of the country, to purchase a home. These ARMs had four payment options:

1. The minimum payment, with the rest of the interest added to the mortgage creating "negative amortization" (the loan amount on the home increased, not decreased)

2. An interest-only loan with no principal reduction—the loan balance stayed the same

3. A 15-year fully amortized loan

4. A 30-year fully amortized loan

Option ARMs should have been used *only* by buyers who were well educated on the pros and cons of this type of mortgage.

# Lot Loans

Most **lot loans** are *made to buyers with the intention of building a home in the future*. These loans are usually done as ARM loans. The lot can range in size from a small parcel to 50 acres or more, depending on the mortgage investor.

# Interest-only Loans

As the name implies, an **interest-only loan** *includes a period of time a buyer is paying only the interest on the loan*; nothing is applied to reduce the principal balance unless the buyer adds extra money to the payment. These loans are available in both fixed-rate loans as well as ARMs.

### For Example

A 30-year loan may have interest-only paid for the first 10-15 years, and then the loan is recalculated to pay off the balance in the remaining term.

# Construction Mortgage

A **construction mortgage** is *a temporary loan used to finance the construction of improvements and buildings on land*. This may also be called an **interim loan**. Buyers wanting to buy or build a new home will find several financing options. A buyer wanting to purchase an existing newly built home is looking for new construction financing and is much like a buyer purchasing an existing home. In many cases, the builder utilizes their own personal credit line to "tract" build homes—homes often built as speculation properties.

## Permanent Construction Loan

A **permanent construction loan** is *for the buyer who wants to build a custom home*. The home could be a personal residence, a second or vacation home, investment, log home, modular home, or, in some instances, a condominium. In this case, many builders will not use their credit line to build the home, but will instead use the buyer's money from a "draw" system to fund the home at different stages of completion. Draws are monetary advances to the builder to pay sub-contactors. Three to ten draws are usually acceptable, with five or six being an average depending on the complexity of the project.

## For Example

The loan agreement may state that the lender will release only 10% of the funds when the project is 20% complete, with future draws of 20% each time construction progresses 20% more toward completion.

| First Release/Draw | 10% of Loan | Project 20% complete |
| --- | --- | --- |
| Second Release/Draw | 20% of Loan | Project 40% complete |
| Third Release/Draw | 20% of Loan | Project 60% complete |
| Fourth Release/Draw | 20% of Loan | Project 80% complete |
| Fifth Release/Draw | 20% of Loan | Project 100% complete |

Lenders often hold the final 10% (or more) of the loan proceeds until the lien period has expired to protect against unpaid mechanic's liens, which could affect the marketability of the property. If a valid mechanic's lien is recorded, the construction loan agreement usually allows lenders to pay it from the part of the loan not disbursed.

There are variations on this type of loan:

- A buyer seeks financing from one lender for the construction phase of the new build and another lender to do permanent financing upon completion. This can be time consuming for a buyer, and looking for two lenders can be cumbersome as well as costly because of two sets of closing costs.

- More popular is the "*one time close*." In this instance, the buyer goes to one closing and has financing in place for the construction phase, the land it will be built on, as well as the permanent phase/completion. These loans can be set up for construction periods from 6 months to 24 months, again depending on the complexity of the project and/or part of the country (e.g., weather could be an issue). Some lenders will finance the construction phase as an ARM since monies needed are for a short period of time. In the permanent phase, there is the option of rolling the completed house into a fixed rate or an ARM.

## Land Contracts

**Land contracts** are *real estate installment agreements where the buyer makes payments to the seller in exchange for the right to occupy and use the property, but no deed or title is transferred until all, or a specified portion of, payments have been made.* Land contracts are another instrument used to finance the purchase of real estate. They are also called **land installment contracts**, **installment sales contracts**, **land sales contracts**, **real estate contract**, among other names.

Land contracts are much different than mortgages or trust deeds. With both of these, the debtor actually takes title to the property, with the creditor holding a mortgage or trust deed as a security lien against the property. But under a **land contract**, *the seller (vendor) actually holds title to the property as security, not just a mortgage lien*. The debtor (vendee) has the right to possess and enjoy the land, but is not the legal owner. The seller retains legal title to the subject property—the buyer only becomes an owner in fact, having possession and *equitable title*, but no actual title and no deed. **Equitable title** is *an interest in real property created upon execution of a valid sales contract whereby* *actual title will be transferred by deed at a future date*. Even though actual title won't be transferred until a future date, the person who holds equitable title still enjoys certain rights and privileges (e.g., the benefit of minerals found on land after a valid sales contract was signed and entered into, but before the passage of actual title to the new owner).

## Advantages and Disadvantages of Land Contracts

| Party | Advantages | Disadvantages |
|-------|-----------|---------------|
| Seller | Right to hold title as security, since the buyer does not receive a deed to the property until all or a specified portion of the contract purchase price is paid | Expense and time required for foreclosure after the five-year period |
| Buyer | Typically easier to qualify for than a conventional loan | Lack of ownership, making it difficult for the borrower to obtain financing for the equity or improvements, since banks are reluctant to lend to a person without actual legal title to the property |

Because the seller retains title to the property, there's some risk that the seller could mortgage the property for an amount greater than his interest in the property. Under most state laws, the seller can't mortgage the property for more than the balance due under the land contract without the buyer's consent. This protects the buyer's interest in the property. The seller must also give the buyer a statement, at least once a year or as requested, showing the amount of payments that have been credited to principal and interest, and the balance due under the contract.

## Ohio Division of Real Estate

The Ohio Division of Real Estate's position on listing properties sold by land contract is to remind the licensee to exercise extreme caution. It is a violation of Ohio license law to list property owned on land contract without the permission of the deed holder (not just the person who holds the land contract). Furthermore, a licensee cannot give legal advice on any questions regarding validity of title, maximum permitted interest rate that may be charged for a land contract under state usury laws, nor any other legal issues that may arise from listing or selling property with a land contract. An attorney should always be consulted by all parties involved, and a licensee must never draft any documents relating to this, or any other, real estate transaction. Such actions can be grounds for license suspension or revocation.

# Summary

1.  **Finance instruments** are written documents establishing rights and duties of the parties involved in a transaction. **Promissory notes** are written promises to pay money. They're negotiable instruments and freely transferable so the creditor can sell for cash. The two note types are *straight* and *amortized*.

2.  **Security instruments** give creditors the right to sell collateral to satisfy the debt if the debtor doesn't pay as agreed. A security instrument gives a debtor the right to *hypothecate* (pledge) property as collateral without giving up possession. Two types are *trust deeds* and *mortgages*. **Trust deeds** are three-party instruments with non-judicial foreclosure via power of sale clause in the event of default. Trust deeds are rarely used in Ohio because of non-judicial foreclosure.

3.  A **mortgage** creates a lien against property as security for debt. If in default, *judicial foreclosure* ensues: Notice of default, foreclosure action filed, order of execution has sheriff sell property, advertising for three weeks, public auction—at least 2/3 bid of appraised value, confirmation of sale to highest bidder, and sheriff's deed issued. Debtor has *equitable right of redemption* to regain property until confirmation of sale. Process is slow and expensive, but has court authority.

4.  Many clauses are common in real estate contracts. An **acceleration clause** lets the lender call loan balance due if in default. A **prepayment clause** lets the lender charge a penalty for paying off loan early. An **alienation clause** gives the lender some stated rights if property is transferred (also called due on sale clause). A **defeasance clause** is used to defeat or cancel a certain right upon the happening of a specific event. A **subordination clause** allows a later recorded mortgage to take priority over an earlier one. A **partial release clause** provides for a lien to be released from part of land if some part of the balance is paid.

5.  The word "mortgage" can be prefaced by different words describing its type or function. A **first mortgage** has first lien position. A **senior mortgage** has a higher lien position. A **second mortgage** has second lien position. A **junior mortgage** has a lower lien position. A **purchase money mortgage** is when the seller takes mortgage for part of purchase price. A **soft money mortgage** is when the borrower gets credit instead of cash. A **hard money mortgage** is when the borrower gets actual cash (e.g., cash-out mortgage). A **bridge mortgage** is a temporary mortgage between two others, repaid with a later mortgage. A **budget mortgage** includes PITI (principal, interest, taxes, insurance)—borrower pays extra 1/12 of taxes and insurance each month (escrowed, then paid when due). A **package mortgage** includes personal property. A **blanket mortgage** is for more than one land parcel. A **construction mortgage** is a temporary loan to finance buildings.

6.  A **land contract** is a real estate installment agreement. Buyer makes payments to seller for right to occupy land, but no title is transferred until all or part of payments are made. (Buyer does get equitable title.) The Ohio Division of Real Estate **reminds licensees not to give legal advice on land contracts.** The deed holder must sign the listing agreement (not just land contract holder).

# Quiz

1. *A promissory note calling for payment of interest only during its term and that results in a balloon payment is known as a(n)*

   a. amortized note.

   b. installment note.

   c. negotiated note.

   d. straight note.

2. *The mortgage clause that permits the lender to declare the entire unpaid loan balance immediately due and payable on default of the borrower is a(n)*

   a. acceleration clause.

   b. defeasance clause.

   c. escalation clause.

   d. forfeiture clause.

3. *A mortgage clause that permits the lender to call the outstanding balance due and payable should the property be sold by the borrower is a(n)*

   a. acceleration clause.

   b. alienation clause.

   c. balloon payment clause.

   d. exculpatory clause.

4. *Which document accompanies the mortgage for a home loan?*

   a. abstract of title

   b. contract of sale

   c. deed

   d. promissory note

5. *In a judicial foreclosure, the debtor can get the property back through an act of*

   a. confirmation.

   b. disintermediation.

   c. non-judicial foreclosure.

   d. redemption.

6. *For which type of mortgage must the borrower be a senior citizen?*

   a. hypothecated

   b. open-ended

   c. package

   d. reverse

7. *A budget mortgage is best defined as one that includes*

   a. payments covering principal, interest, taxes, and insurance.

   b. people with lower incomes.

   c. personal as well as real property.

   d. principal and interest payments.

8. *A buyer finances the construction of a new house through a local bank. If money is released to the builder through the buyer at various stages of construction, this mortgage is probably a(n)*

   a. budget mortgage.

   b. construction mortgage.

   c. option ARM.

   d. package mortgage.

9. *In a mortgage document, the borrower is known as the*

   a. builder.

   b. mortgagee.

   c. mortgagor.

   d. trustor.

10. *Money obtained from a foreclosure sale in excess of the property debt and court costs belongs to the*

    a. court.

    b. debtor.

    c. lender.

    d. sheriff.

# Primary and Secondary Markets

This chapter discusses some of the major and minor participants in the real estate lending market. The major participants in the **primary market** include commercial banks, savings and loans, and mortgage companies. Other sources for various types of real estate lending are also discussed, including commercial lenders and private lending. A discussion on subprime lending explores predatory lending practices. Finally, the **secondary markets**, their purpose and function, and major participants are reviewed.

## Key Terms

**Commercial Banks** Financial institutions that provide a variety of financial services.

**Credit Unions** Financial institutions that are a type of cooperative organization where members share something in common (e.g., an employer), pool their deposits together, pay members better interest rates, and loan money to fellow members.

**Disintermediation** The loss of deposits to competing investments that offer higher returns.

**Fannie Mae (Federal National Mortgage Association)** The nation's largest, privately owned investor in residential mortgages.

**Freddie Mac (Federal Home Loan Mortgage Corporation)** Nonprofit, federally chartered institution (now privately owned) that functions as buyer and seller of residential mortgages.

**Ginnie Mae (Government National Mortgage Association)** Government-owned corporation that guarantees payment of principal and interest to investors who buy its mortgage backed securities on the secondary market.

**Mortgage Banker** One who originates, sells, and services mortgage loans and usually acts as the originator and servicer of loans on behalf of large investors, such as insurance companies, pension plans, or Fannie Mae.

**Mortgage Broker** One who, for a fee, places loans with investors, but typically does not service such loans.

**Portfolio Lenders** Financial institutions that make real estate loans they retain and service in-house instead of selling on the secondary markets.

**Real Estate Owned (REO)** Property acquired by a lending institution through foreclosure and held in inventory.

**Savings and Loan Associations (S & Ls)** Institutions that specialize in taking savings deposits and making mortgage loans.

# Primary Mortgage Market Lenders

**Primary mortgage markets** (or simply **primary markets**) *are lenders who make mortgage loans directly to borrowers*. The primary market is comprised of the various local lending institutions (**commercial banks**, **savings and loans**, **mortgage companies**, **credit unions**). The source of funds for the primary market is largely made up of the savings deposits of individuals and businesses in the local area. Lenders use those savings to make real estate loans.

## Commercial Banks

**Commercial banks** are *financial institutions that provide a variety of financial services, including loans.* These are normally the large lenders in most cities and towns, and are usually very visible due to their presence and sponsorship of everything from sporting to community events.

Although banks remain the largest source of investment funds in the country today, their activities had been focused on relatively short-term commercial and consumer loans. Residential mortgages were not always a major part of their business, primarily due to government limitations on the amount of long-term investments they could make. These limitations were imposed on commercial banks because the vast majority of the deposits they hold are **demand deposits**—*money a customer may elect to withdraw from the bank at any time*. Checks and checking accounts fall into this category. Demand deposits (which are immediately accessible) are considered less reliable for reinvesting in long-term real estate loans than other types of bank deposits, such as savings accounts or CDs (which customers are expected or required to leave in the bank for longer periods of time before withdrawal).

Now, commercial banks have increased participation in home mortgage lending for several reasons:

1. Bankers want to capitalize on existing customer relationships built through checking accounts and other traditional services.

2. Bankers hope that mortgage borrowers will become bank customers for other services.

3. Bankers offer certain customers special services and rate discounts on loans provided they have a minimum amount of money in the bank. Most lenders have lowered the minimum required to qualify to deposits of $100,000.

4. There have been important changes in state and federal banking regulations, requiring banks to hold on reserve different percentages of funds for different types of loans, based on their perceived risk. First lien home mortgages are in the lowest risk category. Thus, banks need to maintain fewer funds on reserve to cover losses for home mortgage loans than for other types of loans, leaving more funds available for other loans or investments.

Commercial banks are also approved and involved in the sale of insurance, securities (like mutual funds), and other investments. Commercial lenders can be national or state chartered, and many are now involved in Internet banking; offering their customers full banking services without having to physically enter the bank.

## Savings and Loan Associations

**Savings and loan associations (S&Ls)** are *financial institutions that specialize in taking savings deposits and making mortgage loans*. Traditionally, the major real estate lending institutions were the S&Ls, investing roughly 75% of their assets in single-family mortgages. They were able to dominate local mortgage markets even though commercial banks had more assets to invest, mainly because deposits placed with S&Ls were savings deposits that were less subject to immediate withdrawal than demand (checking) deposits held by banks.

From the mid 1940s to the late 1970s, S&Ls expanded their mortgage operations aggressively. While other lenders feared the risks inherent in long-term conventional loans, S&Ls believed they could succeed by virtue of their local market knowledge and ability to attract long-term deposits. Since they could offer higher interest rates on savings accounts than commercial banks, they had no trouble attracting depositors during times of prosperity. This strategy worked very well until the surge in interest rates in the late '70s and early '80s turned the tables. Since S&Ls were limited by law as to how much interest they could pay on savings deposits, they were unable to offer attractive returns to depositors. The result was widespread **disintermediation**—*loss of deposits to competing investments* (e.g., money market funds, government bonds), which offered much higher returns. To make matters worse, S&Ls were saddled with long-term, non-liquid mortgages at low interest rates (by 1980's standards), which they were unable to sell to the secondary market, since at that time S&Ls were not using the uniform qualifying standards set by the major secondary market investors, such as Fannie Mae.

As interest rates rose sharply and S&Ls were stuck with long-term loans at low rates, they had to do something. In an effort to average out these low-rate loans and get higher returns to attract depositors demanding higher rates, S&Ls began to make riskier investments. Deregulation allowed S&Ls to offer higher rates of return to savings depositors, but made matters worse as S&Ls now had to compete against additional investment vehicles to attract investment dollars.

Management mistakes, economic slumps, and sometimes even fraud led many S&Ls toward insolvency. Many tried new, riskier investments that regulators didn't always have the ability to evaluate. And when insolvency loomed, some S&L officers decided to gamble even more, feeling there was little to lose since their deposits were insured by the federal government. These risky investments resulted in a dramatic increase in the failure rate of S&Ls, which cost the federal government and taxpayers billions of dollars and caused a massive restructuring of the industry.

Despite the crisis, S&Ls remain leading home mortgage lenders (and follow Fannie Mae qualifying standards). S&Ls are required to keep 70% of their assets in mortgage-related activities or change their federal charter to a bank charter. But with fewer S&Ls and more mortgage companies, it's likely the mortgage industry will replace S&Ls as the leading provider of residential mortgages.

## Mortgage Companies

**Mortgage companies** are *institutions that function as intermediaries between borrowers and lenders.* Two types are **mortgage bankers** and **mortgage brokers**.

### Mortgage Bankers

A **mortgage banker** is *one who originates mortgage loans,* usually funding them with a company's own funds. They specialize in mortgages, and this specialization makes them very competitive in pricing. Mortgage bankers may sell the loans or do the servicing. Mortgage bankers often act as originators and servicers of loans on behalf of large investors such as insurance companies, pension plans, or Fannie Mae. Since these large investors operate on a national scale, they have neither the time nor resources to understand the particular risks of local markets, or to deal with the day-to-day management of the loans. Even if loans are sold on the secondary market, mortgage bankers may continue to act as agents and service loans for a fee.

## Mortgage Brokers

A **mortgage broker** is *one who, for a fee, places loans with investors, but typically does not service such loans.* Mortgage brokers do *not* fund their loans, but act as a conduit in residential mortgages. Often they have knowledge of, and access to, lenders able to supply a particular type of loan needed to buy a property. This could be a loan from an investor for a buyer turned down by a traditional lender, for example. Many mortgage brokers have numerous potential investors they can work with, making them a good source of loans for borrowers with special situations.

Mortgage companies are resources of service and expertise more than actual sources of lending capital. Because they invest little of their own money, their activities are largely controlled by the availability of investment capital in the secondary market. Of course, their loan qualification criteria must reflect the standards of the secondary market if they need or want the option to sell the loans.

### Ohio and Federal Mortgage Broker Laws

Since the state of Ohio has always considered itself a consumer-friendly state, in 2001, it started a series of licensing and education requirements for an individual to become, and remain, a mortgage broker. As part of the **Ohio Mortgage Broker Act**, *Ohio Senate Bill 185*, which went into effect January 1, 2007, mortgage brokers experienced additional sweeping changes and impact on their businesses. Among other highlights, the bill required licensing for loan officers. To obtain a license, individuals were required to take 24 hours of classroom education to get into the business, 6 hours of annual continuing education, and to pass an administered exam and background checks.

The state felt it needed legislation that would give the Ohio Attorney General direct enforcement over lending practices and the ability to put a halt to predatory lending. There are 16 unconscionable acts when dealing with mortgage consumers in the Ohio Revised Code 1345.031.

Under **Title V** of the **Safe and Fair Enforcement Licensing Act (SAFE Act)**, which is a major component of the **Housing and Economic Recovery Act of 2008 (HERA)**, our federal government has taken the education, licensing, testing, and supervision of mortgage providers to a higher level than those of the state of Ohio. Just *one* of the many objectives of the SAFE Act is to enhance consumer protection and support anti-fraud measures.

# Other Primary Mortgage Market Lenders for Residential Real Estate

Other types of financial institutions that make *loans directly to borrowers* for residential first or second mortgages include **credit unions**, **portfolio lenders**, and **Internet lenders**.

## Credit Unions

**Credit unions** are *financial institutions that are a type of cooperative organization with members who share something in common* (e.g., an employer), *pool their deposits, pay members better interest rates, and loan money to fellow members.* Traditionally, credit unions made only home improvement loans, and other types of consumer loans. More recently, many credit unions have become involved in mortgage loans. These mortgage loans are often second mortgages in the form of home equity loans, or can even be first mortgages since credit unions can sell qualifying, standardized loans to the secondary market. Credit unions have grown considerably as they have expanded their membership base through relaxed qualifications to join, and many have combined with other credit unions to provide members with extended services.

## Portfolio Lenders

**Portfolio lenders** are *financial institutions that make real estate loans they retain and service instead of selling on the secondary markets*. Portfolio lenders can be major financial institutions, such as banks or other types of non-traditional lenders or investors. Portfolio lenders make these types of loans as a service to customers who may need a loan amount larger than can be sold to the secondary market or as an investment when the lender likes the project, rate of return, or possible future profit sharing in a particular real estate venture. A lender can offer only portfolio lending, or both portfolio and traditional lending at the same time.

If a lender is holding a loan that needs to be foreclosed upon, then the lender takes possession of the property, and it becomes *real estate owned (REO)*. **REO** is *property acquired by a lending institution through foreclosure*. REO property is held in inventory, and sold to recoup all or part of the lender's investment.

## Internet Lenders

The growth of the Internet and the ability to shop for home loans from the privacy of your home 24 hours a day has stimulated the creation of Internet lenders. **Internet lenders** *can either be a mortgage broker or a mortgage banker*. Some of the largest operate as brokers, taking your loan data and selling the loans to other lenders. Others are subsidiaries of brick-and-mortar lenders. A commercial bank can use the Internet to extend its lending into areas where it doesn't have offices. And with low overhead, Internet lending can be very profitable.

# Commercial Real Estate Lenders

Commercial **real estate lenders can be any of the primary market participants we've discussed thus far—commercial banks, savings and loans**, and **mortgage companies**. Even credit unions have begun to offer commercial lending on a limited basis. Others that make direct commercial loans are **insurance companies, pension funds**, and **real estate investment trusts**. All of these lenders like commercial real estate projects because of the potential for high returns. Also, with commercial projects, there is often the possibility a lender can share in profits generated by the commercial venture. This is almost never an option with residential mortgages.

## Insurance Companies

**Insurance companies** are *institutions with large sums of stable, long-term investment capital looking for high-return investments*. The majority of projects they become involved in as primary lenders are large-scale commercial real estate projects with high potential returns. Insurance companies were a major source of lending for residential real estate companies after World War II, peaking at 23.5% of all residential loans in 1951. Since that time, residential lending by insurance companies has declined to less than 3% today.

Life insurance companies are the primary investor in real estate among insurance companies. That's because life insurance policy premiums are held for relatively long terms and are not generally subject to sudden early withdrawal. Of course, insurance companies must keep some reserves to pay claims, but they seek high-return investments with the rest of their money to help pay out future liabilities while still making a profit for shareholders. Real estate provides the potential for long-term growth and higher-than-average returns.

## Pension Funds

**Pension funds** are *sources of large sums of capital for high return investments*. Pension fund managers are conservative investors and play a growing role in real estate finance. Pension fund managers sometimes get involved in commercial real estate projects as primary lenders where there is a potential for high returns. They seek projects through mortgage brokers, but rarely get involved in making direct residential real estate loans. Pension funds are large investors in commercial property ownership, and rent the space as another source of income. State-controlled pension funds are sometimes a large backer of statewide development programs.

## Real Estate Investment Trusts

A **real estate mortgage trust (REMT)** is simply *a group of people who pool funds to make mortgages*. In order to take advantage of tax benefits established under the Federal Real Estate Investment Trust Act of 1960, though, a true *real estate investment trust* (REIT) must be set up (with the help of a lawyer). A **real estate investment trust** is a *real estate investment business with at least 100 investors organized as a trust*.

A **trust** is *an unincorporated association of investors managed by a trustee(s)*. With a trust, investors get flow-through tax advantages of a partnership but keep some benefits of a corporation. Investors receive tax benefits similar to mutual funds and other regulated investment companies. But unlike corporations, whose earnings are subject to double taxation (first at the corporate level and again as personal income when distributed to stockholders), real estate trust earnings are taxed only once—after they are distributed to investors. Another advantage to a REIT is, like corporate shareholders, investors are shielded from liability for the REIT's debts.

Some requirements for a REIT include:

* At least 100 beneficial owners
* Five or fewer persons cannot hold more than 50% of the beneficial interest
* Must issue shares or certificates of interest
* Each share must have a proportionate vote in trust policy decisions
* Cannot hold property primarily for sale to customers
* 90% of its income must be distributed to investors to receive single taxation
* 90% of its gross income must be from investments
* 75% of its gross income must come from real estate investments

REITs are generally most active in commercial real estate since the large number of investors involved means each person would get a very small piece of a residential mortgage transaction. Most REITs specialize in ownership of:

* Retail properties.
* Industrial properties.
* Apartment communities.
* Golf courses.
* Parking garages.

## Private Lending

Private lending has been a steady force in the world of real estate finance. Investors include those who:

- Choose real estate as their primary means of investing.

- Offer mortgages to high-risk borrowers at above-market rates.

- Choose to hold mortgage paper because of the income stream.

- Invest in many different ways, carving out safe or risky niches.

- Put money in both the primary and secondary markets.

For many potential homebuyers, the largest source of private lending is called "The Bank of Mom and Dad."

### Sellers

The majority of private lending in the primary market comes from sellers who extend credit to buyers to help them buy a home. This is often referred to as "taking back" or "carrying back" part of the sale price. This can occur because money from more traditional lenders is too scarce or too expensive. It can also occur when a buyer can't qualify for a conventional loan, or may need help with a down payment for a number of reasons. **Seller financing** can be in the form of a first mortgage, second mortgage, or may even be offered as a lease/option or land contract. These different financing vehicles are discussed later in this textbook.

## Subprime Lending

**Subprime loans** *had more risks than were allowed in the conforming loan market.* (These were also called **B-C Loans** or **B-C Credit.**) From 2004 to 2006, subprime mortgages were the fastest-growing segment in the mortgage industry. Prime loans were made to customers with good credit. For these loans, borrowers typically could find interest rates posted in the newspaper. Yet, for customers with less-than-perfect credit, interest rates were quoted based on the risk the lender associated with the loan. Subprime loans filled a need by helping these customers reach their goal of home ownership. Some lenders and investors were willing to make these riskier loans because they could get much higher interest rates and fees than with other real estate loans.

To underwrite a subprime loan, the lender was not examining whether the borrower was worthy of credit as much as where he belonged on the risk scale. Credit scoring was a helpful factor in making this determination. Appraisals were also very important, as the property may have been the lender's only recourse in case of default. It took an experienced underwriter to wade through the risk factors.

By early 2007, the subprime mortgage meltdown was upon us. After the meltdown, there was virtually no interest in these loans.

### Predatory Lending Practices

Along with the advantages of subprime lending, which extended credit to people who might not have otherwise been able to qualify for a home mortgage, come some of the inevitable negative by-products—lenders taking advantage of borrowers. This happens with ill-informed and often desperate borrowers who have little knowledge of, or defense against, predatory lending practices. *Loans may be considered **predatory** if the loan costs and fees are unusually or excessively high, or if the loan terms are misrepresented* *by a lender*. New regulations are aimed at ensuring that complete and clear disclosures are made to borrowers.

However, the difference between a **prime loan**, a **subprime loan**, and a **predatory loan** is hard to define. Many predatory loans have terms that make it hard for the borrower to ever get out of a bad situation as there may be prepayment fees, negative amortization, and interest-only loans that never pay down any principal. The law specifically prohibits certain practices, including:

- "Packing" a loan with credit insurance and other extra fees the borrower is pushed into paying for

- Extending credit to people with no income and, thus, little chance of repaying the loan (the lender forecloses on the property and keeps the excess equity to cover "costs")

- Refinancing the lender's own high-cost loan with another fee-rich loan in less than a year's time (unless a lender can show the new loan benefits the borrower)

# Secondary Mortgage Markets

Now that all these loans are made by this huge variety of primary lenders, what happens to them? Are they held in the bank as portfolio loans? Some may be, but most loans are sold. The question is: To whom—and why? In this section, we discuss what happens to a loan once a lender makes it, and why and how a home loan may end up with a lender in another state or maybe even another country you've never heard of.

**Secondary mortgage markets** (or simply **secondary markets**) are *private investors and government agencies that buy and sell real estate mortgages.* Secondary mortgage markets were originally established by the federal government to steady local real estate cycles. (Some of these agencies have since been privatized.) The difference between primary and secondary markets is that secondary markets buy real estate loans as investments from all over the country, whereas primary markets are usually local in nature (with local lenders making local loans to potential homeowners).

## Function of Secondary Markets

The function of secondary markets is to buy and sell the mortgages of primary market lenders. Loans are bought and sold for several reasons. The primary and secondary markets are both trying to maximize the returns on their investment dollars. As interest rates increase, it is more profitable to sell off older loans that have lower interest rates so the lender has new money to lend again at higher interest rates. Buying and selling mortgages can also make more funds available to be loaned again, thus stabilizing local real estate markets. Let's look at how this works:

1. When secondary market participants buy mortgages from local banks, those local banks then have more money they can lend again to other potential homeowners in their area.

2. When local banks invest surplus funds in real estate investments from other regions of the country that may be going through different phases of a real estate cycle, the effects of local real estate cycles can be moderated.

3. An important by-product of secondary mortgage markets is the standardization of loan criteria. Any changes implemented by secondary mortgage markets become requirements around the country for those wanting to sell mortgages on the secondary market.

All these points help make local real estate markets more stable.

## For Example

**Example A:** Tenth Bank is in an area of town that's booming. Businesses are coming to the area and lots of people are moving there. Many of these people are looking to purchase a home, and have come to Tenth Bank to borrow money. Trouble is, most of Tenth Bank's deposits are already tied up in real estate loans. But, by selling its current home mortgage loans in the secondary market, Tenth Bank can get additional funds to make new loans. Tenth Bank and its customers are happy, and the effects of a potential credit crunch in the local real estate market are moderated.

**Example B:** Later, Tenth Bank finds itself in a different situation. The local community is still doing well, so Tenth Bank has lots of people putting deposits in the bank, but there's little activity in the real estate market. With this surplus of deposits, Tenth Bank may have trouble finding enough local investments to buy with a high enough return. In this case, Tenth Bank could buy real estate mortgage loans on the secondary market. Since Tenth Bank would then hold real estate investments from all over the country, Tenth Bank would not need to worry as much about a downturn in the local real estate market because it's holding loans from other areas, as well.

**Example C:** Tenth Bank is considering some new home mortgage requests. The loans seem riskier for several reasons having to do with the borrowers and the properties. Tenth Bank is slow to approve these loans because, if they don't meet the criteria of the secondary markets, Tenth Bank must hold the loans and can't sell them to the secondary market. This situation helps to stabilize the local real estate market because it discourages banks from making too many risky loans. Furthermore, the standardized criteria helps Tenth Bank feel fairly secure in the mortgage investments it buys on the secondary market from other areas of the country, even though it may never see the actual borrowers and properties it is helping to finance.

## The Flow of Mortgage Funds

The availability of funds in the primary market depends a great deal on the existence of secondary markets. Let's briefly look at the flow of mortgage funds. First, mortgage funds are loaned to a homebuyer by a lending institution in the primary market. The mortgage is then sold to a secondary market agency, which may sell it to other investors in the form of mortgage-backed securities. A **mortgage-backed security**, or **MBS**, is *a group of similar mortgages bound together into a bundle, or pool, for the purpose of generating interest payments for an investor who buys into that particular pool.* Because the primary lender sold the mortgage on the secondary market, the lender can take the money it receives from the sale and make another mortgage loan, then sell that new loan to the secondary market and continue the cycle.

The secondary market agency can pool the mortgages it buys to create mortgage-backed securities, which the secondary market participants sell to investors. As the secondary market agency sells the mortgage-backed securities to investors, it has more funds to buy more mortgages. It can then create more MBS pools to sell to investors and the cycle continues.

### How Secondary Markets Work

The secondary market is able to function as it does because standardized underwriting criteria are used to qualify borrowers and property. A mortgage will be purchased by the secondary mortgage market only if the primary market lender conformed to the secondary markets' underwriting standards.

Although we define secondary markets as private investors and government agencies that buy and sell real estate mortgages, private investors actually are a very small percentage of the secondary markets. These private investors can be brokers, high-risk investors, insurance companies, or pension plans. Our discussion focuses on three agencies responsible for most of the secondary mortgage market activity:

1. **Fannie Mae**—The Federal National Mortgage Association (FNMA)
2. **Ginnie Mae**—The Government National Mortgage Association (GNMA)
3. **Freddie Mac**—The Federal Home Loan Mortgage Corporation (FHLMC)

## Fannie Mae—Federal National Mortgage Association

**Fannie Mae** is *the nation's largest investor in residential mortgages*. Fannie Mae was created in 1938 as part of President Roosevelt's New Deal and as the first government-sponsored secondary market institution. It was originally formed as a government-owned corporation but, in 1968, it became a stockholder-owned corporation. However, on September 6, 2008, developments in the housing market required the Director of the **Federal Housing Finance Agency (FHFA)** to "shore up" the operations of Fannie Mae by appointing the FHFA as its conservator. Fannie Mae, although still a private corporation, is currently obligated to send profits directly to the U.S. treasury under the terms of the bailout, and the U.S. government has warrants that allow them to come in and purchase 80% of stock at any time of their choosing. As such, while the government is not the owner legally, they effectively control the company and absorb all profits currently. Fannie Mae can purchase conventional mortgages as well as FHA and VA mortgages and has consistently been ranked as one of the top 10 largest businesses in the world.

Fannie Mae funds its operation by **securitization**—the *act of pooling mortgages, then selling them as mortgage-backed securities*. Conventional loans may be guaranteed by Fannie Mae with full and timely payments of both principal and interest. Fannie Mae buys mortgages or interests in a pool of mortgages from lenders. Lenders who wish to sell loans to Fannie Mae must own a certain amount of stock in Fannie Mae. The lender assembles a pool (collection) of loans and a participation interest in that pool (usually 50%–95%) is then sold to Fannie Mae. In this way, both the lender and Fannie Mae own interest in the loans. Loans sold to Fannie Mae are usually serviced by the originating lender or another mortgage servicing company. Fannie Mae pays a service fee to lenders who continue to service the loans.

## Ginnie Mae—Government National Mortgage Association

**Ginnie Mae** was created in 1968 as a government-owned corporation operating under the Department of Housing and Urban Development (HUD).

The primary functions of Ginnie Mae are to promote investment by guaranteeing the payment of principal and interest on FHA and VA mortgages through its mortgage-backed securities program, and to serve low- and moderate-income homebuyers. It also provides assistance to the Department of Agriculture's Rural Housing Loans. This program, supported by the federal government's borrowing power, guarantees interest and principal mortgage payments to mortgage holders. Ginnie Mae is the only mortgage-backed security that carries the full faith and credit of the United States Government.

Mortgage-backed securities fall into two general types:

1. **Bond-type securities** are *long-term, pay interest semiannually, and provide for repayment at a specified date*.

2. **Pass-through securities**, which are more common, *pay interest and principal payments on a monthly basis*. Some types pay even if payments aren't collected from the mortgagor.

Ginnie Mae also provides "special assistance" financing for urban renewal and housing projects, with below-market rates to low-income families. Ginnie Mae's activity here has decreased as its mortgage-backed securities program has grown.

## Freddie Mac—Federal Home Loan Mortgage Corporation

**Freddie Mac** was created in 1970 as a nonprofit, federally chartered institution controlled by the Federal Home Loan Bank System. Freddie Mac, like Fannie Mae, is currently under the conservatorship of the Federal Housing Finance Agency (FHFA). Freddie Mac *does not guarantee* payment of its mortgages. The primary function of Freddie Mac is to help savings and loans acquire additional funds for lending in the mortgage market by purchasing the mortgages they already held. Freddie Mac may deal in FHA, VA, and conventional mortgages. While Fannie Mae emphasizes the purchase of mortgage loans, Freddie Mac also actively sells the mortgage loans from its portfolio, thus acting as a conduit for mortgage investments. The funds generated by the sale of the mortgages are then used to purchase more mortgages.

Freddie Mac issues its own mortgage-backed securities, which are backed by the conventional mortgages it purchases. Freddie Mac purchases mortgages through the following programs:

- **Immediate delivery program**—*The lender must deliver the mortgages that Freddie Mac has agreed to purchase within 60 days*. Failure to deliver can mean a seller will be banned from further Freddie Mac sales for two years. The immediate loan delivery program can involve either whole loan purchases or participation purchases.

- **Forward commitment purchase program**—*Commitments are made for six- and eight-month periods, but sale and delivery of mortgages is at the option of the lender*. There's a non-refundable commitment fee payable to Freddie Mac.

## Secondary Market Quality Control

Both Fannie Mae and Freddie Mac, along with other secondary market agencies, have been actively involved in developing underwriting standards for mortgage loans. The standards include such items as loan-to-value (LTV) ratios and income-expense ratios. We'll explain the mechanics of these later, but for now it's only important to understand that these underwriting standards assure a *uniform quality control*. This inspires confidence in purchasers of the mortgage-backed securities. The purchasers know the mortgages backing the securities must be of a minimum quality, thus lessening their risk in investing in properties they can't view or assess themselves. Without the assurance of these underwriting standards, someone in Utah would be unlikely to invest in site-unseen property in Ohio.

Furthermore, since lenders want to sell their loans to secondary agencies, they must follow the underwriting guidelines of those agencies. In their efforts to increase the quality of loans they purchase, the agencies force the lenders to upgrade the quality of loans they make. Not only can the agencies refuse to purchase loans that don't follow their guidelines, they can also request lenders repurchase already sold loans if it's later discovered that the lender violated underwriting guidelines. Thus, the secondary market encourages lenders to implement their own quality control programs, and review buyer and property qualifications more carefully.

Finally, because the secondary market performs such an important function in providing liquidity of mortgage funds, the standards set by the secondary market have a large influence on lending activities in the primary market.

### For Example

Once secondary agencies began accepting adjustable rate mortgages (ARMs), 15-year fixed-rate mortgages, and convertible ARMs, these types of financing became more readily available in the primary market. Lenders were more willing to make these types of loans when they knew the loans could be sold to the secondary market. In contrast, option ARMs and no documentation/no qualification loans are not being purchased by the secondary market; therefore, due to the tightening of mortgage qualifications, these types of financing are virtually nonexistent today.

## Other Secondary Mortgage Players

In addition to the agencies just described, there are several additional secondary market participants of note. Insurance companies buy residential mortgages on the secondary market to help provide a cushion of stability against commercial real estate projects that can be high-risk, high-reward ventures. Pension fund managers are also becoming increasingly active in the secondary mortgage markets as they buy up blocks of stable residential real estate mortgage investments, in addition to being large investors in mortgage-backed securities issued by Fannie Mae and Freddie Mac.

In contrast, private investors do not directly buy mortgages on the secondary market since this would require large amounts of capital, and buying only a few mortgages would entail a greater risk of default. Instead, they purchase mortgage-backed securities. With mortgage-backed securities, the investor buys an interest in a pool of mortgages, with the principal and interest payments, made by the homeowners, passed through directly to the investor. Mortgage-backed securities offered by Ginnie Mae are backed by the government (the government will pay if the homeowner defaults on the loan). Because of this security, the rates of return on investment offered by Ginnie Mae are relatively low, but very safe. Some private companies also offer mortgage-backed securities to investors. They are not guaranteed by the government, but the rates of return offered to investors are higher.

## Present Day Mortgage Lending (As of this writing)

The creation of Fannie Mae in 1938 was really the birth of the modern day mortgage industry. Although initially S&Ls enjoyed a prominent place in the mortgage industry, their role diminished as they lost deposits to competing investments that offered higher rates of return. Furthermore, S&Ls were holding mortgage paper at much lower rates than the prevailing interest rates. This crisis was exacerbated by bad loans and tax law changes, as described earlier.

These circumstances, along with the rising interest rates and a desire to shift credit risk, caused lenders to place even greater emphasis on the ability to sell their loans. As more and more options became available, the secondary mortgage market, led by Fannie Mae, grew in importance as a source of funds for lenders and a means of readily available capital for potential homeowners at attractive interest rates.

# Summary

1. The **primary market** consists of *lenders making mortgage loans directly to borrowers.* Primary lenders are commercial banks, savings and loans, and mortgage companies. *Banks* are a large source of funds and provide mortgage loans to existing customers. *Savings and loans* were the largest provider of home mortgage loans, but were significantly hurt by deregulation. Risky S&L investments aimed for high returns, but left many insolvent. Disintermediation forced S&Ls to use the secondary markets. A *mortgage company* is a mortgage banker or broker. *Mortgage bankers* originate loans, usually fund loans with a company's own funds, and may sell or service those loans. *Mortgage brokers* place loans with investors, usually don't service loans, and don't fund their loans, but have access to different lenders and loan programs.

2. Other **primary mortgage market lenders** are credit unions, finance companies, portfolio lenders, and mutual savings banks. *REO (real estate owned)* is property acquired via foreclosure and held in inventory. Most primary lenders rely heavily on secondary markets, and, thus, have adopted uniform loan underwriting standards— making the national primary market more uniform.

3. **Commercial real estate lenders** are primary market lenders, plus insurance companies and pension plans. Commercial real estate projects are sought out for their potential high returns, and for the possibility of participating in profits. *REITs (real estate investment trusts)* are also commercial real estate investors, where 100+ investors organize as a trust to have income and profits pass through like a partnership, but with limited liability like a corporation. (IRS rules for REITs must be followed.)

4. **Private lending** is popular when interest rates are high, or when buyers can't qualify for conventional loans or need help with a down payment. Most private lending comes from sellers; it can be a first mortgage, second mortgage, lease/option, or land contract. Befor the tightening of mortgage qualifications, buyers with trouble qualifying could also use subprime lenders. **Subprime loans** (B-C Loans, B-C Credit) had more risk than was allowed in the conforming market. Borrower risk factors determined interest rate and terms. Rates and fees were higher. **Predatory lending** is when fees are excessive, a loan is made to borrower with no income to repay, or the loan is refinanced often.

5. The **secondary market** consists of private investors and government agencies that buy and sell home mortgages. This was established to moderate local real estate cycles. It gives lenders money to lend again when they sell their mortgages. Local lenders can obtain loans from other areas. Standardized loan criteria means better-quality loans. Insurance companies and pension funds use secondary markets as the sole means of investing in residential mortgages.

6. **Fannie Mae** is the largest investor in residential mortgages. Fannie Mae buys loans then sells securities backed by its pool of mortgages. **Ginnie Mae** was formed from part of Fannie Mae. It is government-owned and managed by HUD. Ginnie Mae guarantees payment of principal and interest on FHA and VA loans for its mortgage-backed securities. **Freddie Mac** issues mortgage-backed securities. Freddie Mac is privately owned but, like Fannie Mae, is currently under the conservatorship of the Federal Housing Finance Agency (FHFA).

# Quiz

1. **The largest providers of residential market loans today are**
   a. mortgage companies.
   b. mutual savings banks.
   c. pension funds.
   d. savings and loan associations.

2. **Commercial banks**
   a. focus on long-term investments.
   b. invest primarily in single-family residential housing.
   c. rely on savings deposits for most of their funds.
   d. specialize in short-term commercial lending activities.

3. **The real estate investment that enjoys special tax treatment is the**
   a. insurance company.
   b. mortgage company.
   c. REIT.
   d. savings and loan association.

4. **Life insurance companies prefer making loans for**
   a. large-scale commercial real estate projects.
   b. resale to the secondary market.
   c. short-term business purposes.
   d. single-family homes.

5. **Mortgage brokers do NOT**
   a. act as intermediaries between borrowers and lenders.
   b. have a variety of lenders from which they can obtain loans for borrowers.
   c. invest little of their own money in the loans they arrange.
   d. service the loan (collect the payments) after the loan closes.

6. **Lenders making loans directly to real estate purchasers are part of the**
   a. pension market.
   b. primary market.
   b. secondary market.
   c. tertiary market.

7. **Which is NOT a primary lender for residential properties?**
   a. commercial bank
   b. insurance company
   c. mortgage company
   d. savings and loan association

8. **Which agency is the conservator of Fannie Mae and Freddie Mac?**
   a. Federal Housing Administration
   b. Federal Housing Finance Agency
   c. Housing and Urban Development
   d. Office of Federal Housing Enterprise Oversight

9. **Which agency helps to even out the money supply for mortgage loans?**
   a. Fannie Mae
   b. FHA
   c. FHFA
   d. HUD

10. **Private investors and government agencies that buy and sell real estate mortgages are known as the**
    a. intermediate market.
    b. primary market.
    c. secondary market.
    d. tertiary market.

11. **To sell loans to the secondary market, the primary market lender must**
    a. allow the secondary agencies to audit its books.
    b. be a federal government-affiliated lender.
    c. be willing to suffer significant discounting losses.
    d. follow the underwriting guidelines of the secondary market agencies.

12. **The purpose of subprime loans was to**
    a. allow lenders to justify charging excessive fees.
    b. give borrowers, with no income or means of repaying, a mortgage loan.
    c. let lenders add additional unnecessary fee items (like credit insurance) beyond the mortgage amount.
    d. offer borrowers with less-than-perfect credit or other qualifying difficulties an opportunity to obtain a mortgage loan.

# Conventional Financing

I f seller financing is not available, a home buyer most likely will have to go to a primary market lender for a loan. There are two types of financing for residential home loans in Ohio: *Conventional financing* and *government financing*. In this chapter, we look at the different types of conventional loans (conforming and nonconforming), and also how private mortgage insurance and secondary financing have made conventional loans easier to obtain.

**Amortized Loan** Loan with payments applied to principal and interest.

**Balloon Payment** A final payment at the end of a loan term to pay off the entire remaining balance of principal and interest not covered by payments during the loan term.

**Call Provision** Clause that lets lenders demand full payment of a loan immediately. Also referred to as **call a note**.

**Conforming Loan** Loan that meets Fannie Mae/Freddie Mac standards and can be sold on the secondary market.

**Conventional Loan** Loan not insured or guaranteed by a government entity.

**Fixed Rate Loan** Loan with a constant interest rate remaining for the duration of the loan.

**Fully Amortized Loan** Loan where the total payments over the life of the loan pay off the entire balance of principal and interest due at the end of the loan term.

**Loan-to-Value Ratio (LTV)** The amount of money borrowed compared to the value or price of the property.

**Negative Amortization** When a loan balance grows because of deferred interest.

**Partially Amortized Loan** Loan where payments are applied to principal and interest, but the payments do not retire the debt when the agreed upon loan term expires, thus requiring a balloon payment at the end of the loan term.

**Private Mortgage Insurance (PMI)** Insurance offered by private companies to insure a lender against default on a loan by a borrower.

**Secondary Financing** When a buyer borrowers money from another source in addition to the primary lender to pay for part of the purchase price or closing costs.

**Key Terms**

# Conventional Financing

**Conventional financing** is when real estate is *paid for or financed with a conventional loan.* A **conventional loan** is *any loan **not** insured or guaranteed by a government agency.* We'll begin by looking at traditional conventional loans, then at variations seen today in conventional financing.

## Traditional Conventional Loans

Traditional conventional loans are typically **long-term**, **fully amortized**, **fixed-rate** real estate loans. These are the type of loan borrowers are most familiar with.

**Long-term real estate loans** *generally have total payments spread out over 25–30 years,* and today even 40-year home loans are available. While the long-term nature of conventional loans seems natural, before the Federal Housing Administration (FHA) was formed in 1934, home loans were typically for three- to five-year terms, and had to be paid off at the end of the specified period. Loans were limited to 50% of the home's value and the payments were interest only (straight notes), meaning that the mortgagor never paid any of the original principal. Less than four of every ten families actually owned a home.

The FHA first proposed loans of 15 years with 20% down. Of course, homes were less expensive then, but few people could afford to buy their own home. Payments were often high with short loan terms, and **balloon payments** *to pay off the balance were required at the end of the loan term.* This meant people had to refinance their loans frequently, posing problems for those who could not come up with the required balloon payment or whose qualifying situation may have changed at an inopportune time. Today, long-term loans of 25–40 years provide homebuyers with a reasonable payment and the security to choose if and when to refinance.

**Amortized loans** have *payments applied to principal **and** interest* (as opposed to interest-only loans). A **fully amortized loan** is one where *the total payments over the life of a loan will pay off the entire balance of principal and interest due at the end of the term.* Again, this is very different from how things were before the FHA, when loans had only partial amortization or none at all. This created **negative amortization**—*the loan balance grows because of deferred interest,* resulting in even larger balloon payments for the borrower.

Today, the main advantage to traditional conventional loans is that they are **self-liquidating**—*making all payments on time means the loan will be paid off with the last scheduled payment.* Payments are manageable when spread over 25–40 years, and stay constant for the entire loan term. Although the payment stays the same for the life of the loan, the amounts applied to principal and interest are adjusted each month.

### $150,000 Loan @ 6.25%, 30-year Term (Figures Approximate)

| Payment Number | Principal Balance | Total Payment | Interest Portion | Principal Portion | Ending Balance |
|---|---|---|---|---|---|
| 1 | $150,000.00 | $923.58 | $781.25 | $142.33 | $149,857.67 |
| 2 | $149,857.67 | $923.58 | $780.51 | $143.07 | $149,714.61 |
| 3 | $149,714.61 | $923.58 | $779.76 | $143.81 | $149,570.79 |
| 4 | $149,570.79 | $923.58 | $779.01 | $144.56 | $149,426.23 |
| 5 | $149,426.23 | $923.58 | $778.26 | $145.31 | $149,280.92 |

**Fixed rate loans** are *loans with an interest rate that remains constant for the duration of the loan.* This is good and bad for the borrower and the lender. Of course, the biggest advantage to a borrower is he doesn't need to worry about increasing rates; if rates decrease enough, he can refinance. From the lender's perspective, there's a guaranteed rate of return but the rate is locked in for 30 years, even if interest rates rise during that time.

√ **Note:** In contrast, the concept of adjustable rate mortgages (ARMs) has been around for over 50 years, but it was not until the advent of rate adjustment periods and lifetime caps on interest rates that the public became less fearful of taking out an ARM. A percentage of homebuyers have always been attracted to adjustable rate mortgages because they start out with a lower interest rate (thus a lower payment). We will cover ARMs in detail in Chapter 6.

## 15-Year Mortgage Loans

What makes 15-year mortgages appealing is that they save homebuyers money. Over the life of the mortgage, the total payments on a 15-year mortgage are about one-third less than a 30-year mortgage at the same interest rate. Often times, a lender will give a homebuyer a better interest rate on a 15-year mortgage because the shorter term means less risk for them. An added benefit is the homebuyer can attain full ownership in half the time it takes to pay off a 30-year mortgage.

Of course, there are *disadvantages* to a 15-year mortgage:

- Higher payments consume financial resources that could have been invested other ways and could have earned a higher return than the interest rate paid on the mortgage

- The borrower loses their federal tax deduction sooner as their loan is paid off more quickly

- Payments are higher (but not double when compared to a 30-year loan)

- Larger down payments may be required to keep payments manageable and help the buyers qualify

One way to achieve some of the benefits of 15-year mortgages (saving interest and paying less over the life of the mortgage) without the legal obligation is for the homebuyer to get a 30-year mortgage and then *make additional principal payments each month.* Of course, this takes discipline, but most mortgages will allow it (***always check with the lender***). Thus, a homebuyer can retire the debt earlier and save interest without having to worry about the contractual burden of higher payments.

| 15-Year Mortgage vs. 30-Year Mortgage Comparison of Interest Paid, 6% Interest Rate | | | |
|---|---|---|---|
| Loan Amount | Term | Monthly Payment | Total Interest Paid |
| $50,000 | 15 Years | $421.93 | $25,947.00 |
| | 30 Years | $299.78 | $57,919.09 |
| $100,000 | 15 Years | $843.86 | $51,894.23 |
| | 30 Years | $599.55 | $115,838.19 |
| $150,000 | 15 Years | $1265.79 | $77,841.34 |
| | 30 Years | $899.33 | $173,757.28 |

## 40-Year Mortgage Loans

Due to the increasing price of homes, especially on the East and West Coasts, some people cannot afford the high cost of the homes without a longer loan period to keep the payments lower. Since the term is ten years longer, the downside is that the home purchaser will pay significantly more interest over the life of the loan.

## Conforming Versus Nonconforming Loans

**Conforming loans** *meet Fannie Mae/Freddie Mac underwriting standards and can be sold on the secondary market.* Lenders try to make many of their loans conforming loans, because they like the option of being able to liquidate (sell for cash) their real estate loans on the secondary market if they need more funds.

**Nonconforming loans** *do not meet Fannie Mae/Freddie Mac underwriting standards and cannot be sold to Fannie Mae or Freddie Mac.* (There are other secondary markets where nonconforming loans can be sold, however.) Lenders with the option of keeping loans in their portfolio (mostly banks and S&Ls) can, within the limits of the law, deviate from the standards set by secondary markets.

The two main reasons loans get classified as nonconforming are:

- Size of the loan.
- Credit quality of the borrower.

### For Example

**Jumbo loans** *exceed the maximum loan amount established by Fannie Mae and Freddie Mac* for conforming mortgage loans. The current loan limit is $417,000 on a single-family home (higher on two-, three-, and four-family homes) and changes occasionally, so these jumbo loans are considered nonconforming loans.

Loans for which the borrower does not meet the minimum standards established by Fannie Mae/Freddie Mac are also nonconforming loans. Subprime lenders, portfolio lenders, or neighborhood banks offer these loans to fulfill their obligation under the Community Reinvestment Act; however, these nonconforming loans cannot be sold to Fannie Mae or Freddie Mac.

While there are always lenders willing to deviate from Fannie Mae/Freddie Mac standards, the majority of loans made conform to the secondary market criteria because of the importance of being able to liquidate them. Be aware that the distinctions between conforming and nonconforming loans continue to become more blurred. Fannie Mae and Freddie Mac constantly implement new loan program standards to meet the needs of consumers, and the conforming market eagerly follows into territory once the sole domain of the nonconforming market.

### For Example

Fannie Mae/Freddie Mac offer 97% LTV loans and even 105% LTV loans for those with "golden credit."

# Conventional Loan Products

Conventional loan products fall into *categories based on the percentage of down payment the borrower pays to get the loan.* Remember, 15-year and 30-year mortgages can both be conventional loans. Conventional loans are defined as loans *not* insured or guaranteed by a government entity. Generally, when we discuss conventional loans in this chapter, we are referring to 30-year, fixed-rate mortgages, which are still the most common loan for residential property. We also present these loans with the conditions and standards you will likely encounter on the test.

In the real world, there are many variations on these loan products. Lenders constantly offer innovative loan products to meet the needs of customers and to attract business in a competitive environment. As we discuss these "typical" loan products and "typical" down payments with PMI, remember some lenders offer high LTV loans where PMI is not necessary (but fees may be higher, or conditions and standards imposed).

## 80% Conventional Loan

For years, the 80% conventional loan has been the standard conventional loan. An 80% conventional loan means that the **loan-to-value ratio (LTV)** is 80% of the appraised value or sale price of a property, whichever is less. **LTV** is the *amount of money borrowed divided by the value (or price) of the property.* With this type of loan, the buyer makes a 20% down payment and obtains a 30-year, fixed rate conventional loan for the balance of the purchase price.

### For Example

A buyer wants to purchase a house that costs $100,000—he needs a 20% down payment, or $20,000. An 80% conventional loan means he can borrow 80%, or $80,000, of the sale price of the home, assuming the home appraises for $100,000 or more. If the house appraises for less than $100,000—for example, $95,000—he could borrow only 80% of the appraised value. In this case, if he moved forward at the asking price of $100,000, he'd need to come up with the difference as part of his down payment:

**$95,000 x 20% = $19,000 + $5,000 = $24,000**

## 90% Conventional Loan

If a buyer does not have enough money for a 20% down payment but still wants a conventional loan, he can try to get a 90% conventional loan with a 10% down payment. The 90% conventional loan became possible with the advent of private mortgage insurance (which we'll discuss shortly). The qualifying standards for 90% conventional loans tend to be more stringent, and lenders adhere to those standards more strictly even though the loan is insured.

### Down Payment

For a 90% loan, the buyer must make a **10% down payment**, with at least half of the down payment **(5%) from his own cash reserves**. The rest of the down payment may be a gift from a family member, equity in other property traded to the seller, or credit for rent already paid under a lease/purchase.

### Interest Rate and Fees

A 90% loan usually has the same interest rate as an 80% loan (although it may be higher, based on the borrower's credit situation). A 90% loan *also has a private mortgage insurance (PMI) premium*, making it more expensive than an 80% loan, both in closing costs and monthly payments.

## 95% Conventional Loan

When a buyer does not have enough money for a 10% down payment but still wants a conventional loan, he may qualify for a 95% conventional loan with a 5% down payment. This higher loan-to-value ratio of 95% *requires owner-occupancy*.

### Down Payment

For a 95% loan, a buyer must make the **5% down payment from his own cash reserves**, without using secondary (owner) financing or gifts.

### Interest Rate and Fees

A 95% loan usually has the same interest rate as an 80% or 90% loan (although it may be higher, based on the borrower's credit situation). Typically, the PMI premium is higher, making a 95% loan more costly than a 90% loan.

## Other Conventional Loan Products

Both Fannie Mae and Freddie Mac have loan products to fit an individual borrower's needs depending on down payment, income, and credit score situation. What follows is a brief overview of some of the products and their features.

### Freddie Mac

**Home Possible®97 Mortgage**—Requires a 3% down payment (which can come from a variety of sources), a 640-700 credit score, loan term to 40 years, and low private mortgage insurance of 18% (see PMI chart on page 76). There are income limits depending on the location of the home and homebuyer education is required for first-time home buyers.

**ALT 97® Mortgage**—Requires a 5% down payment (which can come from a variety of sources), a 620-700 credit score, no income limits, and debt to income ratios to 45%. However, private mortgage insurance can be 35% coverage (see PMI chart on page 76).

**A- (MINUS) Mortgage**—Requires a 5% down payment and higher mortgage insurance, and is intended for a borrower who has some credit "blemishes."

### Fannie Mae

**My Community Mortgage®**—Requires a 3% down payment (which can come from a variety of sources), a credit score of 660, loan term to 40 years, debt to income ratios to a maximum of 45%, low private mortgage insurance (18% coverage—see PMI chart on page 76), and non-traditional credit can be accepted. There are income limits depending on the location of the property and homebuyer education is required for first-time home buyers.

**Flexible 97® Mortgage**—Requires a 3% down payment (which can come from a variety of sources), loan term to 40 years, and no income limits. Mortgage insurance (PMI) can be as high as 35% coverage (see PMI chart on page 76).

Once a customer decides upon a conventional loan program, a lender may offer him a fixed rate mortgage, adjustable rate mortgage (ARM), or a balloon mortgage. The following illustrates some of the options a lender may present to a customer:

- **Fixed rate mortgages**
  10, 15, 20, 25, 30, 40 year
- **ARMs**
  10/1, 7/1, 5/1, 3/1, 1/1
- **Balloon mortgages**
  7/23, 5/25

The type of mortgage the customer is offered and the option he accepts will depend upon his finances, time frame, and other considerations.

### For Example

For a customer who plans to purchase an expensive home in which he hopes to retire, a 30- or 40-year fixed rate mortgage may be the best option. For a customer whose job requires him to relocate every five years, a long-term loan may not be logical. In this case, the lender may be able to offer the customer a better rate on a 5/1 ARM.

### Best Practices

Due to the Patriot Act and other anti-terrorism legislation, there is more scrutiny on buyers with large home down payments. It is important to note if a real estate agent assists someone in purchasing a home with the use of illegally obtained funds, there could be liability to the agent, broker, and even the seller. When a buyer has a larger-than-normal down payment, it is wise for the real estate agent to consult with her broker for guidance.

# Conventional Loans with Less than a 20% Down Payment

In the discussion of conventional loans, you learned that it's possible to make less than the standard 20% down payment. There are actually two ways to accomplish this: **Private mortgage insurance** and/or **secondary financing**.

## Private Mortgage Insurance (PMI)

**Private mortgage insurance (PMI)** is *offered by private companies to insure a lender against default on a loan by a borrower.* PMI is what makes 90% and 95% loans possible. Prior to PMI, lenders would loan only 80% of the property value because it was thought that a 20% down payment was the incentive needed for the borrower to keep mortgage payments current. The lender felt comfortable that, in the event of default, a foreclosure sale would yield 80% of the original sale price (or appraised value), recovering the original loan amount.

PMI evolved to compensate the lender for reduced borrower equity, making loans easier for borrowers and safer for lenders. Both Fannie Mae and Freddie Mac also require third-party insurance on home loans with less than 20% down payments.

## How Mortgage Insurance Works

When insuring a loan, the mortgage insurance company shares the lender's risk—but only part of the risk. The insurer does *not* insure the entire loan amount but, rather, the upper portion of the loan—the loan amount that exceeds the standard 80% LTV. The amount of coverage can vary but is typically 20%–25% of the loan amount.

| MONTHLY PMI PREMIUM | | FIXED | | TEMPORARY BUYDOWNS | | ARMs | |
|---|---|---|---|---|---|---|---|
| | | 30-yr | 15-yr | 30-yr | 15-yr | 30-yr | 15-yr |
| Base LTV | PMI Coverage | 1st month and renewal to Yr 10 | | 1st month and renewal to Yr 10 | | 1st month and renewal to Yr 10 | |
| **95%** to 90.01% | 35% | 1.06% | 0.83% | 1.21% | 1.10% | 1.25% | 1.13% |
| | 30% | 0.94 | 0.81 | 1.04 | 0.92 | 1.08 | 0.95 |
| | 25% | 0.84 | 0.70 | 0.90 | 0.77 | 0.94 | 0.81 |
| **90%** to 85.01% | 30% | 0.69 | 0.54 | 0.84 | 0.71 | 0.89 | 0.77 |
| | 25% | 0.62 | 0.48 | 0.73 | 0.60 | 0.78 | 0.65 |
| | 17% | 0.49 | 0.33 | 0.56 | 0.36 | 0.61 | 0.44 |
| **85%** & under | 17% | 0.43 | 0.30 | 0.44 | 0.30 | 0.49 | 0.36 |
| | 12% | 0.38 | 0.26 | 0.39 | 0.27 | 0.44 | 0.31 |
| | 6% | 0.34 | 0.24 | 0.36 | 0.25 | 0.40 | 0.28 |

*Sample PMI Rate Card*

In the event of default and foreclosure, the insurer will take over the property or allow the lender to sell the property. Either way, the lender can make a claim for reimbursement of actual losses (if any) up to the face amount of the policy. Losses incurred by the lender take the form of unpaid principal and interest, property taxes and hazard insurance, attorney's fees, costs of preserving the property during the period of foreclosure and resale, and the expense of selling the property.

## PMI Premiums

There are actually three ways a buyer can pay for private mortgage insurance:

1. **Monthly mortgage insurance** is easy to calculate and, in time, can be cancelled; thus reducing the monthly mortgage payment.

### For Example

If the sale price of a home is $100,000, on a 90% LTV 30-year fixed mortgage, the PMI can be calculated using the rate card. Let's use the Fannie Mae/Freddie Mac required 25% coverage, at a rate of 0.62%:

| | |
|---|---|
| $100,000 | Sale Price |
| $ 90,000 | LoanAmount (90% LTV) |
| $ 90,000 | Loan Amount |
| x   0.0062 | Rate Card Factor |
| **$558** | **Annual PMI cost** |

Then, divide $558 by 12 ($558 ÷ 12 = $46.50). So, $46.50 is added to the borrower's *monthly* mortgage payment.

Although our example shows only a fixed rate mortgage, you can see from the rate card that private mortgage insurance companies also insure ARMs. (The chart is only intended as a guide.)

2. **One-time PMI premium** is offered by some private mortgage insurance companies, with no renewal fee. Combining the initial premium and renewal premiums into one single payment allows the buyer to finance the PMI premium, thus no extra cash is required at closing and monthly payments are often lower than if the premium is added to the regular mortgage payment.

3. **No PMI premium, but a higher interest rate** is another approach to paying PMI. Basically the borrower pays the lender a higher interest rate on the higher risk loan. This allows the money to be deducted as interest on a borrower's federal income tax. Most lenders call this a "Lender-Paid PMI (LPMI)" loan. The lender then buys PMI coverage for itself and when the home is in better equity position, it cancels the PMI coverage. The borrower continues to pay the slightly higher interest rate, usually 0.25% to 0.5% higher. The advantage is this usually results in a lower monthly payment for the borrower than a traditional PMI-type loan.

---

## FINANCE EXERCISE 4-1

Let's review our formula for calculating a monthly loan payment on a 30-year fixed rate loan that is fully amortized:

**(Loan Amount) ÷ (1,000) x (Factor) = Monthly Payment**

Now, let's compare the cost of a traditional PMI-type payment with a No PMI loan. The PMI monthly premium is 0.62% annually. Remember, PMI applies to the loan amount and must be divided by 12 to arrive at a monthly dollar figure. Let's compare the monthly payments for 30-year loan of a $200,000 home with a 10% down payment and 6.5% PMI loan and 7% No PMI loan.

1. What is the monthly payment on the 6.5% PMI loan?

2. What is the monthly payment on the 7% No PMI loan?

3. What are the advantages and disadvantages of each?

*See the Appendix for answers to check your work. How did you do?*

## PMI Cancellation

Lenders require mortgage insurance on high-LTV, low-down-payment loans as protection against borrower default. Once the increased risk of borrower default is gone (when the loan-to-value ratio is reduced to 80% or less), mortgage insurance has fulfilled its purpose. In the past, many lenders did not cancel PMI, even when the risk was reduced. But the federal Homeowners Protection Act of 1998 says that for all loans made after July 29, 1999, lenders must automatically cancel PMI when a home has been paid down to **78% of its original value**, provided the borrower is not delinquent. The law also requires lenders to give borrowers an initial disclosure regarding PMI cancellation rules, and annual disclosures reminding borrowers of their PMI cancellation rights.

The law has some exceptions, such as multi-family units, non-owner-occupant homes, mortgages on second homes, and second mortgages. As is often the case, the law sets a minimum but the market moves the bar higher.

### For Example

Fannie Mae and Freddie Mac have adopted rules that apply the 78% cancellation rule to all of their mortgages—even those closed *before* July 1999—and have also expanded the rules to cover investment properties and second homes. Plus, Fannie Mae and Freddie Mac will consider the present value of the home—not just the original value as required by the law. This effectively cancels PMI *more quickly* for most borrowers since they can count the appreciation of their homes. Most lenders now follow these guidelines.

The law also says that for loans closed after July 29, 1999, lenders must drop PMI coverage at a borrower's request if a new borrower-paid, lender-approved appraisal shows the loan has been paid down to 80% or less of the home's original value and mortgage payments are current. Again, Fannie Mae and Freddie Mac have gone a step further, allowing borrowers to use 80% of the home's current value if no payments have been more than 30 days late in the prior 12 months for fixed-rate loans (or 24 months for ARMs). Fannie Mae and Freddie Mac also apply these rules to all loans, but can require up to five years of seasoning (outstanding age) on the loan before the rules apply. If loan payments are not made on time, the borrower can be considered high risk, and the lender could require PMI coverage for a longer time.

Whether through automatic or borrower-requested cancellation, when PMI is terminated, the lender cancels the policy and reduces the monthly mortgage payment by the PMI amount.

√ **Note:** The law and Fannie Mae/Freddie Mac rules do not apply to any up-front or one-time PMI premium paid.

### Disclosures for Existing Residential Mortgages

For residential mortgages consummated before the Act took effect (July 29, 1999), if PMI was required, the servicer must provide to the borrower an annual written statement that:

- States that PMI may be canceled with the consent of the lender or in accordance with state law.

- Provides the servicer's address and telephone number so that the borrower can contact the servicer to determine whether the borrower may cancel PMI.

## Secondary Financing

**Secondary financing** is *when a buyer borrows money from another source (sometimes the primary lender) to pay part of the purchase price or closing costs.* This is another way a buyer can get a conventional loan *without* a 20% down payment.

With secondary financing, it's often the seller that "carries" the extra financing. In effect, the borrower has been extended credit by the seller, just as if the money had been borrowed from a finance company. For conventional loans, the primary lender often insists on certain conditions with secondary financing from any source:

1. **Borrower must make a 5% down payment.** For owner-occupied property, the total of the first and second mortgages must not exceed 95% of the appraised value or sale price, whichever is less. The borrower must pay the remaining 5% of the purchase price out of her own funds. The first mortgage cannot exceed 80% LTV.

2. **Term of second loan cannot exceed 30 years, or be less than 5 years.** The *term* of the loan is the *repayment period*. The rationale here is that a second mortgage should not take longer to pay off than the first mortgage.

3. **No prepayment penalty is permitted.** The second mortgage must be payable in full or in part at any time, without penalizing the borrower for paying the debt early.

4. **Scheduled payments must be due on a regular basis.** Although payments must be on a regular basis, they do not have to be monthly. Secondary finance payments can be monthly, quarterly, semi-annually, or any other regular schedule. Payments can fully amortize the debt, partially amortize the debt, or pay interest only.

5. **No negative amortization.** The payments on the second mortgage must at least equal the interest on the loan. A loan balance cannot grow because of deferred interest.

6. **Buyer must be able to afford payments on first *and* second mortgages.** This means the primary lender on the first mortgage will count both mortgages when qualifying the buyer for the mortgage debt.

7. **Secondary financing mortgage needs a subordination clause.** Most primary lenders require secondary financing to have a *subordination clause* to ensure the primary lender's lien will take priority, even if the second mortgage is recorded first.

### For Example

Here's how secondary financing might work on a $120,000 home:

| | |
|---|---|
| $ 96,000 | 80% First Mortgage (primary lender) |
| $ 12,000 | 10% Second Mortgage (from seller or lender) |
| $ 12,000 | 10% Down Payment (from borrower) |
| **$120,000** | **100% Total Sale Price** |

Asking the seller to carry a second mortgage has been a popular way to finance conventional loans since the first long-term, fully amortized mortgages. The popularity of secondary financing increases when interest rates rise. Let's take a brief look at some ways a second mortgage can be repaid. Keep in mind it's not always the seller who carries a second mortgage. A second mortgage can be carried by any lender, investor, or financial institution. In fact, sometimes the same lender may finance the first and second mortgage. This allows the lender to charge a higher interest rate on the second mortgage. (We'll discuss this shortly.)

## Fully Amortized Second Mortgage

A **fully amortized** loan is one where the *total payments over the life of a loan will pay off the entire balance of principal and interest due at the end of the term*. This makes the term agreed upon between borrower and seller/lender important because if the term is too short, the payments will be higher. Don't forget that when underwriting the loan, the primary lender will include this amount as part of the borrower's monthly housing expense.

### For Example

A house costs $100,000. The buyer makes $10,000 (10%) down payment, gets an $80,000 (80%) first mortgage for 30 years at 6.5%, and a $10,000 (10%) second mortgage for 5 years at 7.875%. The buyer's housing expense will be:

|  |  |
|---|---|
| $505.65 | Payment on First Mortgage ($80,000, 6.5%, 30 years) |
| + $202.17 | Payment on Second Mortgage ($10,000, 7.875%, 5 years, fully amortized) |
| **$707.82** | **Total Housing Expense (Principal and Interest Only)** |

## Partially Amortized Second Mortgage with Balloon Payment

A **partially amortized** loan is one where *payments are applied to principal and interest, but the payments do not retire the debt when the agreed upon loan term expires*. Thus, a **balloon payment** is required as a final payment at the end of the loan term to pay off the entire remaining balance of principal and interest not covered by payments during the loan term.

The lender and borrower figure the monthly payment as if the borrower is going to pay off the entire debt over a long period of time. This keeps the payments low. But, at an agreed upon earlier date, the borrower agrees to repay the remaining balance of the loan. For example, it may be agreed that the payments are figured as if the second mortgage is going to be repaid over 30 years (keeping the payments low), but the borrower agrees to repay the remaining balance of the loan after only five years (with a balloon payment).

There's a good reason for doing this. If a second mortgage is scheduled to fully amortize within its term (five years), the monthly payments will be larger than if it is scheduled to partially amortize with a balloon payment (schedule payments as if the second mortgage is for 30 years, but then pay the balance after five years). The rationale behind the partially amortized mortgage is that the smaller monthly payments make the total housing expense less burdensome for the borrower, making it easier to qualify for a loan. Of course, the danger is that the borrower can't come up with the second mortgage loan balance (or can't refinance) after five years. But overall, this can be a useful tool for getting a buyer qualified for the house.

### For Example

A house costs $100,000. The buyer makes a $10,000 (10%) down payment, gets an $80,000 (80%) first mortgage for 30 years at 6.5%, and a $10,000 (10%) second mortgage amortized over 30 years at 7.875%, but with a balloon payment due in 5 years. The buyer's housing expense will be:

|  |  |
|---|---|
| $505.65 | Payment on First Mortgage ($80,000, 6.5%, 30 years) |
| + $72.51 | Payment on Second Mortgage ($10,000, 7.875%, partially amortized) |
| **$578.16** | **Total Housing Expense (Principal and Interest Only)** |

When you compare the two previous examples, it's clear the partially amortized second mortgage eases the buyer's qualifying burden, and may be the preferred financing arrangement when the buyer's income is borderline.

## Setting Up a Partial Amortization Schedule

The previous example states that the payments for the partially amortized mortgage are based on a 30-year repayment (amortization) plan. This means the payments are scheduled as though the debt will be paid in full over a 30-year period, even though the entire balance will be due and payable after only five years. When the repayment term is 30 years, as opposed to five years, the payments are lower but the debt is retired very gradually. In fact, after five years, payments based on a 30-year amortization will have only reduced the original loan balance by a relatively small amount. If the second mortgage is to be paid at that time, there will be a substantial balloon payment due (or the loan will have to be refinanced). The following chart illustrates how a $10,000 second mortgage steadily declines over 30 years, if allowed to do so. It also shows the balloon payment due after just five years.

If all monthly payments are made on time, a 30-year $10,000 loan at 7 7/8% will have a balance of about $9,496 after five years. This is the balloon payment amount.

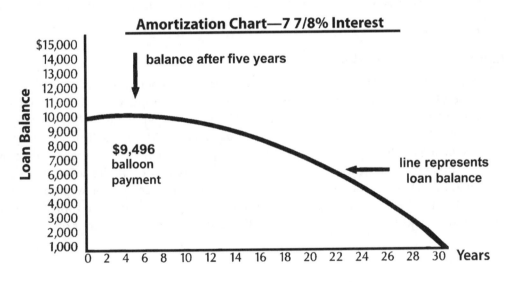

**Amortization Chart—7 7/8% Interest**

## Interest-Only Second Mortgage

An interest-only loan is one for which scheduled payments pay only the accrued interest, and do not pay any portion of the principal. Of course, if no principal is paid during the loan term, the balloon payment will be the original amount borrowed. This reduces monthly payments even more. With interest-only loans, no amortization is used. Simply multiply the loan amount by the interest rate and divide by 12 (months).

### For Example

A house costs $100,000. The buyer makes a $10,000 (10%) down payment, gets an $80,000 (80%) first mortgage for 30 years at 6.5%, and a $10,000 (10%) interest-only second mortgage at 7.875%, with a balloon payment due in 5 years. The buyer's housing expense will be:

| | |
|---|---|
| $505.65 | Payment on First Mortgage ($80,000, 6.5%, 30 yrs) |
| + $65.63 | Payment on Second Mortgage ($10,000 x 0.07875 ÷ 12) |
| $571.28 | **Total Housing Expense (Principal and Interest Only)** |

Of the previous three examples, the final example gives a borrower the lowest housing expense.

## Lender First and Lender Second

As we discussed previously, sellers don't always carry the second mortgage. A lender may make two different loans at different interest rates (e.g., first mortgage for 80% of a home's price at 6.5% interest, and second mortgage for 10% of a home's price at 7.875% interest) to reflect the riskier nature of the upper end of the loan amount. This gives the lender a better yield for taking on the increased risk. When the upper portion of the loan represented by the second mortgage is paid off, the risk is gone and the borrower still has a first mortgage at a good interest rate. The repayment plan is a matter of agreement between borrower and lender. The loan can be paid off as fully amortized, partially amortized with balloon, or interest-only with balloon. (The lender will usually charge a loan fee for both loans.)

---

### FINANCE EXERCISE 4-2

Let's see how a house payment works in this situation, and use the payment skills we learned earlier. Recall the formula for a fully amortized loan:

**(Loan Amount) ÷ (1,000) x (Factor) = Monthly Payment**

And the formula for a straight note is:

**(Loan Amount) x (Interest Rate) ÷ (Months in a Year) = Monthly Payment**

A couple purchases a $200,000 home. They take out an 80% LTV, fully amortized 30-year fixed rate loan, first mortgage at 6.5% and a 10% LTV second mortgage at 8.5% for 10 years on a straight note. They make a 10% down payment. Lenders call this an 80-10-10.

1. What is the monthly payment on the 30-year amortized loan?

2. What is the monthly payment on the straight note?

3. How much will the balloon payment be at the end of ten years?

*See the Appendix for answers to check your work. How did you do?*

---

## Prepayment Penalties

**Prepayment penalties** are *fees a lender charges the borrower for paying off a loan early.* While the time periods and amount of the penalty may vary considerably, the basic effect of these penalties is to charge the debtor extra money to make up for interest income a lender loses when the debtor pays off the loan early.

In the past, conventional lenders charged penalties for early loan repayment to discourage it, but most lenders today would rather have the money to reinvest. Standard Fannie Mae and Freddie Mac notes and mortgages don't have prepayment penalties, and they are prohibited in FHA and VA loans. It is always wise to check as many subprime loans and even some first-time homebuyer programs have prepayment penalties, and it is better to know prior to selling a home or refinancing a mortgage.

---

### FINANCE EXERCISE 4-3

A borrower is purchasing a home and wants a fixed rate, conventional loan. The sale price is $189,500 and the property was appraised at $200,000. The buyer will make a 5% down payment at an interest rate of 6.50% interest for 30 years fully amortized. The lender will charge a 1.5% loan fee on the mortgage.

1. What will the loan amount be?

2. How much will the buyer pay at closing for down payment plus the loan fee?

3. What is the monthly payment on the mortgage, including principal and interest?

*See the Appendix for answers to check your work.*

---

# Fannie Mae and Freddie Mac Underwriting Standards

When qualifying a buyer for a conventional loan, Fannie Mae and Freddie Mac underwriting criteria should be used. Some of the most important criteria evaluated in qualifying a borrower for a particular mortgage loan are income, credit history, and net worth.

## Income Qualifying Standards

When considering a borrower's income, there are two important income ratios to consider:

- Housing expense ratio
- Total debt service ratio

## Housing Expense Ratio

A borrower's **housing expense ratio** is the *relationship of the borrower's total monthly housing expense to gross monthly income, expressed as a percentage*:

**Total Housing Expense ÷ Gross Monthly Income = Ratio %**

Conventional lenders consider a borrower's income adequate for a loan if the proposed total mortgage payment of principal, interest, taxes, and insurance (**PITI**) does not exceed *28% of stable monthly income*.

## For Example

$2,900 = Stable Monthly Income

$700 = Proposed Mortgage Payment (PITI)

**$700 ÷ $2,900 = 0.24 = 24%**

The borrower's housing expense ratio would be 24%, which is less than 28%, so the borrower would qualify for the loan.

## Total Debt Service Ratio

A borrower's **total debt service ratio** is the *relationship of the borrower's total monthly debt obligations (including housing and long-term debts with more than ten payments left) to gross income, expressed as a percentage*:

**Total Debt Service ÷ Income = Ratio %**

Conventional lenders want to be sure the borrower's housing expenses (as explained previously), plus any installment debts with more than ten payments left, do not exceed *36% of his stable monthly gross income*. Alimony, child support, or any other court-ordered obligations must count as debt against this ratio. Note also that debts with less than 10 payments may still be counted against the borrower if the payments are high (e.g., $600 car payment). Car leases are always counted.

## For Example

| | |
|---|---|
| $2,900 | Stable Monthly GrossIncome |
| $700 | Proposed Mortgage Payment (PITI) |
| $225 | Car Payment (18 payments left) |
| $100 | Child Support Payment |
| **$1,025** | **Total Debt Service** |

**$1,025 ÷ $2,900 = 0.35 = 35%**

The borrower's total debt service ratio would be 35%, which is less than 36%, so the borrower would qualify for the loan.

The total debt service ratio is a more realistic measure of the borrower's ability to support the loan payments. Since the total debt service ratio takes all debt into consideration, the mortgage payment determined by calculating the total debt service ratio is also likely to be smaller than the housing expense ratio. Since the borrower must qualify under **both** ratios, the smaller of the two is the maximum allowable mortgage payment.

## For Example

Mary Smith has a stable monthly gross income of $3,200. She has three long-term monthly debt obligations:

- $220 car payment
- $75 personal loan payment
- $50 revolving charge card payment

What's the maximum monthly mortgage payment for which she can qualify?

Housing expense ratio = 28%

**$3,200 (Monthly Income) x 0.28 (Income Ratio) = $896 (Maximum Mortgage Payment)**

Total debt service ratio = 36%

**$3,200 (Monthly Income) x 0.36 (Income Ratio) = $1,152 (Maximum Total Debt Service)**

| | |
|---|---|
| $1,152 | Maximum Total Debt Service |
| – $220 | Car Payment |
| – $75 | Personal Loan Payment |
| – $50 | Revolving Charge Card Payment |
| **$807** | **Maximum Mortgage Payment, Total Debt Service Ratio** |

Thus, the maximum monthly mortgage payment Mary qualifies for is $807.

Remember, Mary must qualify under both ratios, so the lower figure is the most she can get. Of course, if she could pay off some of her debt and reduce her total long-term monthly obligations, she would qualify for a larger mortgage payment.

In Chapter 7, we will take maximum mortgage payments and show you how that equates into a loan amount.

# Summary

1. **Conventional loans** are *not* insured or guaranteed by a government entity. Traditional conventional loans are long-term, fully amortized, fixed rate. An **amortized loan** has payments applied to principal and interest; a fully amortized loan has total payments that over the life of the loan pay all principal and interest due. *Conventional loans* can have a 15- to 40-year term, and can be either conforming or nonconforming. A 15-year loan pays off sooner and saves interest, but requires higher payments and a potentially higher down payment. *Conforming loans* meet Fannie Mae/Freddie Mac standards and can be sold on the secondary market. *Nonconforming loans* don't meet these standards and cannot be sold to Fannie Mae/Freddie Mac, but can be sold on the secondary market to other buyers. Nonconforming loans can be due to credit quality or loan size ("jumbo loan" exceeds Fannie Mae/Freddie Mac maximum loan amount: $417,000).

2. Conventional loan programs include **80%, 90%, 95%, and 97% LTVs.** For example, an *80% conventional loan* means the loan-to-value ratio (LTV) is 80% of appraised value or sale price of the property, whichever is less. For an 80% loan, buyers must make a 20% down payment; for a 90% loan, buyers must make a 10% down payment with 5% from personal cash reserves (no gifts, loans, etc.); for a 95% loan, buyers must make a 5% down payment, all from personal cash. For these loans, interest rate and fees may be higher on higher LTVs, and PMI is always higher.

3. **Private mortgage insurance** (PMI) protects the lender against borrower default. PMI compensates lenders for lower borrower down payments and shares partial risk (upper part) with lender. PMI can take the form of a fee at closing and renewal premium, a one-time PMI premium, or no PMI premium but a higher interest rate. *Federal law* dictates that loans made after July 1999 must drop PMI when LTV is 78% of original value, or if the borrower asks and the appraisal is 80% of original value. Fannie Mae/Freddie Mac rules that PMI is to be dropped if LTV is 78% (or borrower-paid appraisal is 80%) of current value.

4. **Secondary financing** is when a buyer borrows money for part of the purchase price or closing costs. Conditions for secondary financing: 1. Borrower must make 5% down payment, 2. Term of second loan must be 5–30 years, 3. No prepayment penalty, 4. Scheduled payments due on regular basis, 5. No negative amortization, 6. Buyer must be able to afford payments on first *and* second mortgages, and 7. Secondary financing mortgage needs a subordination clause.

5. A **second mortgage** can be fully amortized, partially amortized with a balloon payment to pay off balance, or interest-only with a balloon payment to pay off principal at the end of the loan. *Partial amortization* is when payments are scheduled as if the loan term is longer (e.g., 30 years), but the balance is due sooner (e.g., 5 years). *Partially amortized and interest-only* loans have smaller payments than fully amortized loans, and may help buyer qualify. The same lender can give both loans at different interest rates.

6. **Assumption** means one party (buyer) takes over primary liability for the loan of another party (seller). When trying to assume a loan: 1. Lender can accept assumption and leave terms in tact, 2. Lender can accept assumption and charge fee or increase interest rate, or 3. Lender will *not* allow assumption and call the note. Prepayment penalties can be charged for paying a loan early. The FHA/VA prohibits this. Always consult with a lender or lawyer on loan assumptions.

# Quiz

1. **A conventional loan**
   a. follows the secondary market's underwriting guidelines.
   b. has an adjustable interest rate.
   c. has normal seller financing terms.
   d. is not insured or guaranteed by any government entity.

2. **A loan repaid with periodic payments of both principal and interest so the entire loan amount is paid in full at the end of the loan term is a(n)**
   a. annualized loan.
   b. conventional loan.
   c. fully amortized loan.
   d. partially amortized loan.

3. **All are representative of 15-year mortgages, EXCEPT**
   a. the borrower loses his Federal tax deduction faster because his loan is paid off earlier.
   b. higher interest rates.
   c. higher monthly payments.
   d. lower interest rates.

4. **Private mortgage insurance is required when the loan-to-value ratio (LTV) is**
   a. 75% or higher.
   b. over 80%.
   c. 90% or higher only.
   d. over 95% only.

5. **Private mortgage insurance typically covers _____ of the loan amount.**
   a. 20–25%
   b. 50%
   c. 75–80%
   d. 100%

6. **An advantage to a No PMI loan for the homebuyer is**
   a. higher interest rates.
   b. the loan is paid sooner.
   c. lower monthly payments as compared to a loan with PMI.
   d. None of the above—these loans are risker.

7. **Which would likely have the highest PMI cost?**
   a. 80% loan
   b. 90% loan
   c. 95% loan
   d. house purchased with cash

8. **PMI must be canceled**
   a. at the discretion of the borrower.
   b. only if the lender is satisfied the buyer is no longer a credit risk.
   c. when a home has been paid down to 78% of its original value for loans made after July 1999.
   d. whenever a new appraisal is ordered, regardless of the value.

9. **The provision that penalizes borrowers who pay off loans sooner than agreed is a(n)**
   a. alienation clause.
   b. assumption clause.
   c. incorporation clause.
   d. prepayment penalty clause.

10. **Lenders are often willing to charge lower interest rates for 15-year mortgages because the**
    a. borrower is always a better risk.
    b. interest rate is fixed for a longer period of time.
    c. loan funds will be repaid more quickly.
    d. loan qualifications are much more stringent.

# Government Financing

This chapter discusses government-sponsored programs that assist buyers with a home purchase. **Government financing** means real estate loans are insured, guaranteed, or sponsored by government programs. All support for government financing occurs on the federal level. (Don't confuse this with government involvement in the secondary mortgage markets.) The two main federal programs in real estate finance are **FHA-insured** and **VA-guaranteed** loans. We will also discuss the USDA Rural Development Housing Program.

# FHA-Insured Loans

The National Housing Act of 1934 established the Federal Housing Administration (FHA). Prior to the FHA, most home loans were for three to five years and required a 50% or greater down payment, resulting in a home ownership rate of 40% or less. The FHA was the first to issue long-term loans, up to 30 years, with lower down payments, sometimes as low as $0 down.

**FHA-insured loans** are *insured by the federal government* through the Department of Housing and Urban Development (HUD). The **Federal Housing Administration** is a *government agency under HUD that actually insures the loans*. The FHA's main purpose is to assist in providing housing opportunities for low- and moderate-income families. However, the FHA does *not* have income limits to determine who is eligible for assistance. Any U.S. citizen, permanent resident, or non-permanent resident with a work visa may apply. Instead, the FHA sets a **maximum mortgage amount** it will insure.

The FHA does not provide mortgage funds to borrowers, and does not build houses. Rather, the FHA is a *federal mortgage insurance agency*. The FHA's **Mutual Mortgage Insurance Plan (MMIP)** provides a function similar to private mortgage insurance companies, insuring private lenders against losses caused by borrower defaults on FHA-insured loans.

Under the plan, lenders approved by the FHA to make insured loans either submit applications from prospective borrowers to the local FHA office for approval or may act as *direct endorsers*. **Direct endorsers** are *lenders authorized to underwrite their own FHA loan applications*. These lenders are responsible for the entire mortgage process through closing, and perform underwriting functions themselves (credit examination, appraisal review). When a direct endorser has approved and closed a loan, the application for mortgage insurance is submitted to the FHA. Most FHA loans are currently processed through the direct endorsement program.

### Best Practices

It is important to note that lenders who make FHA loans must be approved by HUD. Real estate professionals need to know what loan programs different lenders do or do not provide. You can find approved lenders by asking your broker or consulting the HUD website (www.hud.gov).

# FHA Loan Guidelines

Since the government insures FHA loans, it's only natural the FHA establishes underwriting guidelines for approving borrowers and property, and sets other loan regulations. FHA regulations have the force and effect of law. As we discuss these items, keep in mind that all generally apply to *standard FHA 203(b) loans*, considered by most to be "regular" FHA loans on one- to four-family homes. Other FHA loan types may have different guidelines or additional criteria.

## FHA Loan Borrower Guidelines

The main criteria for FHA loan approval are the borrower's:

- Credit history
- Amount of income

The FHA is more lenient in both areas than traditional conventional lenders.

## Credit History

More flexibility is allowed in trying to "understand" a borrower's past situation and difficulties. Even with this philosophy, a borrower may have open collections, but outstanding court ordered judgments must be paid before closing. There is an *exception* to this if the judgments are medical related or a payment arrangement is in effect with a creditor.

## Amount of Income

There is *no minimum or maximum income* a borrower must have to get an FHA loan. However, the borrower *must have sufficient income to service the debt on the home mortgage and all other credit obligations.* Lenders multiply the potential borrower's income by debt service ratios to determine how much debt the borrower should be able to afford. Later, when we discuss qualifying the buyer, we'll discuss this more thoroughly.

The FHA allows lenders to approve borrowers with a higher debt service ratio than traditional conventional lenders allow. Borrowers can qualify for an FHA loan with:

- A mortgage payment up to **31%** of their gross monthly income.

- Total payments for all debts (including the proposed mortgage payment) up to **43%** of their gross income.

Sometimes, these guidelines are stretched even farther if a borrower is buying a new construction or energy-efficient home. The FHA requires a borrower's property taxes, insurance, and homeowners association dues (e.g., condo fees) to be included as part of the proposed mortgage payment when qualifying, but the higher ratios make it easier to qualify for an FHA loan than a traditional conventional loan.

### Other FHA Regulations

- A borrower may *not* use secondary financing for the minimum FHA down payment (which can be as low as 3.5%).

- The minimum down payment can be a *non-repayable gift or loan* from a relative, or even a grant from a non-profit home buying type of organization.

- At least one borrower must occupy the home.

Other items affecting borrowers will be discussed shortly with FHA loan regulations.

# Property Guidelines for FHA Loans

The main criteria for FHA loan approval are **condition of the property** and the **maximum mortgage amount** permitted in the county where the property is located.

### Condition of the Property

The FHA is more strict than other lenders about condition of the property. There are two reasons for this:

1. Since many FHA buyers have lower incomes and not much surplus cash, often borrowers cannot afford the repairs necessary to make the home habitable.

2. With lower down payments, there's theoretically a higher risk of default, so the FHA does not want to be left with houses in need of repair that can't easily be resold. (The FHA now requires appraisers to identify potential problems and deficiencies as part of the appraisal for FHA loans.)

## Maximum Mortgage Amount

This is a key requirement as it determines FHA loan eligibility. Remember, borrowers can have any income level to qualify, but they may *not* borrow more than the FHA maximum mortgage amount. *The maximum loan amount depends on the median range of housing costs in a particular community.* This results in varying mortgage amounts from one community to another (e.g., loan limits are higher in areas of higher-cost housing).

As of January 1, 2010, the maximum loan amount for standard 203(b) loans for single-family homes in Ohio ranges from $271,050-$432,500 and up to $831,750 for a four-family building, as long as the homeowner occupies the building. The maximum loan amounts vary by county.

> √ **Note:** Loan amounts are evaluated once a year. For a current schedule of FHA mortgage limits, visit the HUD website: https://entp.hud.gov/idapp/html/hicostlook.cfm.

In higher-cost areas where the median price of homes significantly exceeds listed amounts, HUD has increased the maximum allowable loan amount. Areas determined to be "high cost" have loan limits ranging from $729,750 for a single-family home to $1,403,400 for a four-family home. In Alaska, Hawaii, Guam, and the U.S. Virgin Islands, the maximum is 150% of the high cost limit: $1,094,625 for a single-family home to $2,105,100 for a four-family home. Although HUD loan limits are reviewed annually, a petition to review a high-cost area can be made anytime.

# FHA Loan Regulations

In addition to those criteria for borrowers and properties already mentioned, there are other important rules for FHA loans: **Secondary financing**, **down payment**, **LTV calculations**, **mortgage insurance**, **buydown limits**, **assumability of loans**, **prepayment penalties**, and **items paid by the seller**.

## Secondary Financing

The FHA does *not* permit secondary financing, such as credit cards or second mortgages, to meet its minimum down payment requirement (which can be as low as 3.5%), nor can secondary financing be used to pay for closing costs. The minimum down payment must be *paid by the buyer in cash, or it may be a gift* from a relative, *or grant* from a non-profit group.

Secondary financing (other than for part of the down payment) *is permitted for FHA loans if the following conditions are met:*

1. Borrower's income must be sufficient to qualify for the combined total of both payments on the FHA and non-FHA mortgages.
2. Payments on the second mortgage, if any, must be *monthly*, with all payments being substantially the same amount.
3. Second mortgage may *not* have a balloon due sooner than ten years (unless approved by the FHA Commissioner).
4. Second mortgage *must permit prepayment* without penalty after giving the lender 30 days' notice.

Second mortgages with FHA loans are most beneficial to the buyer if the second mortgage is at an interest rate lower than the prevailing rate. This option becomes more popular as interest rates rise.

> √ **Note:** These second mortgage restrictions do not apply if the mortgage is held by the federal, state, or local government.

## Down Payment

Minimum down payments are calculated differently for FHA loans. The FHA requires that:

1.  Closing costs are *not* added when figuring the maximum mortgage amount.

2.  The borrower must make a minimum 3.5% cash investment (down payment).

Both of these FHA policies can have an impact on the buyer's out-of-pocket expenses, and may also affect contract negotiations between buyer and seller. Let's explain and then look at some examples to clarify.

### Closing Costs Are Not Added

Estimated closing costs may *not* be added in when figuring the maximum amount the buyer can finance as part of the loan. What often happens, though, is the seller agrees to pay all or some of the buyer's closing costs (up to the FHA's limits), and then simply raises the contract price. Of course, the buyer can still pay closing costs separately in cash (to avoid paying interest for 30 years on the higher sale price) or finance the initial MIP (mortgage insurance premium).

### Minimum 3.5% Cash Investment (Down Payment)

The 3.5% investment figure is based on the property's sale price. This "cash investment" is usually the buyer's down payment, but the buyer's 3.5% cash may be applied toward any part of the acquisition cost. The **acquisition cost** is the *purchase price of a property, plus (allowable) buyer-paid closing costs.* Closing costs paid by the seller are *not* included (unless they end up increasing the contract price of a home).

Since FHA borrower investment calculations use the sale price but allow the money to be applied toward down payment or closing costs, it can be tricky to figure out how much the borrower needs to bring to the closing. Check with an FHA-approved lender for the exact calculation of the down payment.

## Mortgage Insurance

A mortgage insurance premium (MIP—not to be confused with PMI for conventional loans) is required for all FHA loans, regardless of down payment size. For most FHA programs, the MIP has an initial premium and an annual premium. The initial MIP is 1.75% of the loan amount for 30-year loans, with an annual premium of 1.35% of the outstanding loan balance (divided into 12 monthly payments).

The 15-year mortgage has the added benefit of a lower annual MIP. The initial MIP premium is 1.75% of the loan amount, but the annual premium is only 0.70% of the outstanding loan balance (divided into 12 equal monthly payments). See the chart below for more detailed information.

√ **Note:** Initial and annual MIP rates change often, responding to varied economic conditions. The chart below is used to illustrate the effects of MIP rates on an FHA insured loan. Consult with an FHA lender for current MIP rates.

| FHA MIP Factors | 30-Year Loans | |
| --- | --- | --- |
| LTV | Initial MIP | Renewal |
| Greater Than 95% | 1.75% | 1.35% |
| Less Than or Equal to 95% | 1.75% | 1.30% |

| FHA MIP Factors | 15-Year Loans | |
| --- | --- | --- |
| LTV | Initial MIP | Renewal |
| Greater Than 90% | 1.75% | 0.70% |
| Less Than or Equal to 90% | 1.75% | 0.45% |

## Cancellation

For loans made after January 1, 2001, the MIP is automatically canceled when the LTV reaches 78% of the original value (for 30-year mortgages, the annual MIP must be current for at least five years).

For loans made after June 3, 2013, the FHA will collect the annual MIP for the maximum duration permitted under statute. See 12 U.S.C. § 1709(c)(2)(B).

- For **all** mortgages regardless of their amortization terms, any mortgage involving an original principal obligation (excluding financed Up-Front MIP (UFMIP)) less than or equal to 90 percent LTV, the annual MIP will be assessed until the end of the mortgage term or for the first 11 years of the mortgage term, whichever occurs first.

- For any mortgage involving an original principal obligation (excluding financed UFMIP) with an LTV greater than 90 percent, FHA will assess the annual MIP until the end of the mortgage term or for the first 30 years of the term, whichever occurs first.

## Financing

If the initial MIP premium for 15-year or 30-year loans is paid in cash at closing, it may be paid by the buyer, seller, or any third party (e.g., relative). If the MIP is financed, the initial premium is added to the loan so the total loan amount may then exceed the FHA maximum, but only by the MIP amount. Monthly payments are calculated with the annual MIP, according to the chosen loan program.

### For Example

A 30-year loan on a house will be $80,000, after down payment. This is also the maximum LTV amount. Determine the initial MIP premium **(A)**, and the maximum FHA mortgage if the MIP is financed **(B)**.

**A.**

| $80,000 | 30-Year Loan Amount |
|---|---|
| x 0.0175 | MIP Factor |
| $ 1,400 | Initial MIP Premium |

**B.**

| $80,000 | Loan Amount Without MIP |
|---|---|
| + $ 1,400 | Initial MIP Premium |
| $81,400 | Maximum FHA Mortgage |

So, even though the maximum FHA loan is $80,000 based on the LTV, the total amount financed may exceed the $80,000 maximum by the $1,400 MIP, resulting in a total maximum FHA mortgage amount of $81,400 for the FHA loan.

## Seller Contribution Limits

FHA regulations limit the amount of seller contributions that may be paid in connection with FHA-insured loans. As of April 2010, the maximum amount of points the seller can pay for the buyer is six. If a seller pays more than 6%, the excess is applied, dollar for dollar, to reduce the sale price in calculating the maximum loan amount. For this rule, a seller-paid contribution includes discount points, prepaid interest, and closing costs normally paid by the buyer (such as initial MIP, escrows, loan origination fee).

√ **Note:** As of this writing, the FHA is considering lowering the seller contribution from 6% to 3%. It is important for real estate professionals to stay up-to-date on laws, regulations, and guidelines relating to their industry.

For FHA fixed rate loans with temporary buydowns, a buyer must qualify at the note interest rate.

## For Example

If a 6% FHA loan had a temporary buydown of two percentage points (making the loan 4%), a buyer must still qualify for the loan as if it were a 6% loan. (Temporary buydowns may still be used to make a house payment more affordable, but there is no ability to qualify for the loan based on the lower initial loan rate.)

## Assumability of Loans

For loans that are FHA insured or endorsed after December 15, 1989, the FHA has the right to perform a credit check of the borrower. FHA requires the buyer to sign a statement saying that if the property is transferred to another person whose credit has not been approved by the FHA, the entire mortgage balance is immediately *due in full*. Thus, any offers involving mortgage assumptions must be investigated thoroughly with the lender (and perhaps even with legal counsel—ask about your broker's policy).

## Prepayment Penalties

FHA regulations do not allow provisions for prepayment penalties to be included in FHA loans. FHA loans may be paid off at any time without additional charges or penalties of any kind. However, if a house is sold or refinanced after the first day of the installment period, then a lender may require an entire month's interest be paid.

Current FHA rules do *not* allow lenders to require 30 days' written notice in advance of a payoff—even if the mortgage or note gives the lender that right. *This FHA rule supersedes any agreement in the private loan documents.* However, there is a scenario in which borrowers can end up paying an extra month of interest on FHA loans. The lender may require that the prepayment be made on the normal installment due date (usually the first of the month). If prepayment is made *after* the normal installment due date, the lender can require the borrower to pay the interest that would be due from the prepayment date up until the next installment due date.

Thus, since the entire month's interest may become due as noted above, people with FHA mortgages try to sell, pay off, or refinance the mortgage close to the end of the month to be sure it's closed before the first of the month (or first day of the installment period). The borrower may prepay without giving the lender advance notice, but if prepayment is offered on any day other than the normal payment due date, the lender may refuse to accept payment until the next due date or charge interest until that date. Each lender is required to give borrowers a written disclosure of its prepayment policy.

## HUD Regulations on Payment of Costs

FHA and HUD regulations govern some items *the seller may or may not pay* for the buyer. For example, the seller cannot pay for the buyer's minimum down payment.

HUD regulations dictate that some lender fees *may not be paid by the buyer* and must be paid by the seller (or the lender must absorb these fees). For example, the FHA will not allow a buyer to pay for a tax service fee. This type of non-allowable fee is often collectively referred to as a "*junk fee.*"

**Junk fees** are *lender charges that do not show up as points on the loan, but are set dollar amounts rather than a percentage of the loan amount.* Some lenders charge these fees to improve their profit or yield on a loan. From HUD's perspective, though, these fees do not directly benefit the buyer, so buyers are not permitted to pay them. In this instance, it may fall on the seller to pay these fees if the seller wants the loan to close. This can lead to stress at the closing table if the seller has not thoroughly examined the closing statement beforehand, and is not prepared to have these fees taken out of the proceeds the seller receives from the closing.

The seller can also pay for:

- The buyer's initial MIP premium.

- Escrows for taxes and insurance, since these are now open to negotiation between the buyer and seller.

Keep in mind that as of April 2010, the maximum number of points or other forms of seller contributions the seller can pay is limited to six (6%).

### Best Practices

Never assume closing costs are, or aren't, automatically included in the purchase contract. Always negotiate closing costs upfront, or when the original offer is presented.

For example, a seller agrees to pay $1,000 in closing costs. What does this include? If the buyer assumes that particular fees are covered by the $1,000, you may experience some trouble at closing. The buyer may not come to the closing with the necessary funds and/or the seller may end up with less than anticipated.

### Other FHA Regulations

As you review the regulations we've discussed or as you encounter others in your real estate practice, be aware that FHA rules and regulations change all the time. For example, at one time, the FHA:

- Made investor loans (it no longer does).
- Set maximum interest rates (now rates are market driven, although FHA loans can still be lower due to the perceived lower risk of government-insured mortgages).
- Allowed the use of temporary buydowns to qualify for a larger mortgage.
- Didn't allow sellers to pay escrows or points for buyers (now these are a matter of negotiation between the parties).

As the needs of borrowers changed, the FHA began allowing ARM loans and secondary financing with FHA loans. Current rules can be obtained from a lender, or by visiting http://www.hud.gov.

## FHA Loan Programs

There are several FHA loan programs authorized under the federal statute that created the Federal Housing Administration. Most of these loan programs are referred to by the section number of the federal statute that describes them. For example, the most common type of loan for which a buyer will be eligible is called a Section 203(b) loan (after the statute section and paragraph that explains the requirements). All of the rules and regulations we've discussed apply to the standard Section 203(b) loan. Many of these rules also apply to the other FHA loans we will mention here, with exceptions noted where applicable.

√ **Note:** For specific FHA loan questions, call 1-800-440-8647 or visit http://www.hud.gov.

There are many types of FHA home loans, some of which most agents will never hear about or use in their career. We will cover the most common loan types along with several others you may encounter in your real estate career.

### Section 203(b)—The Standard FHA Program

Ordinary, owner-occupant buyers are most suited for 203(b) loans. All the points discussed regarding FHA loans apply to the Standard FHA Program.

### Section 203(k)—Rehabilitation Loans

Section 203(k) insures mortgages covering the purchase or refinancing and rehabilitation of a home of at least one year old. A portion of the loan proceeds is used to pay the seller or, in a refinance, to pay off the existing mortgage. The remaining funds are placed in an escrow account and released as rehabilitation is completed. The cost of the rehabilitation must be at least $5,000, but the total value of the property must still fall within the FHA mortgage limit for the area. The value of the property is determined by the lesser of:

- The value of the property before rehabilitation plus the cost of rehabilitation.
- 110% of the appraised value of the property after rehabilitation.

Many of the rules and restrictions that make the FHA's basic single-family mortgage insurance product (Section 203(b)) relatively convenient for borrowers also apply here. But lenders may charge additional fees, such as a supplemental origination fee, fees to cover the preparation of architectural documents and review of the rehabilitation plan, and a higher appraisal fee.

### Streamlined 203(k) Loan

HUD developed the Streamlined 203(k), or "Streamlined (K)" Limited Repair Program, that permits homebuyers to finance, into their mortgage, up to an *additional* $35,000 (with no dollar minimum) for repairs. The money can be used to purchase and improve or upgrade the home before move in or to refinance an existing mortgage and add up to $35,000 in repairs or improvements. With this product, homebuyers can quickly and easily tap into cash to pay for property repairs or improvements, such as those identified by a home inspector or FHA appraiser. Unlike the standard 203(k) program, *any FHA-approved lender* may originate a Streamlined (K) mortgage.

The following repairs can be financed with a Streamlined 203(K) loan:

- Repair/replacement of roofs, gutters, and downspouts
- Repair/replacement/upgrade of existing HVAC systems
- Repair/replacement/upgrade of plumbing and electrical systems
- Repair/replacement of existing flooring
- Minor remodeling (e.g., kitchen with no structural repairs)
- Exterior and interior painting
- Weatherization, including storm windows and doors, insulation, weather-stripping, etc.
- Purchase and installation of appliances, including freestanding ranges, refrigerators, washers/dryers, dishwashers, and microwaves
- Improvements for disability accessibility
- Lead-based paint stabilization or abatement of lead-based paint hazards
- Repair, replacement, or addition of exterior decks, patios, or porches
- Basement remodeling with no structural repairs

- Basement waterproofing
- Window and door replacement and exterior siding replacement
- Well or septic system repair or replacement

### Section 234(c)—Condominiums

The 234(c) program insures lenders against foreclosure losses for purchases of a condominium unit with mortgage terms of up to 30 years. The condominium project must be approved for participation under general approval guidelines or under Federal Housing Administration (FHA) procedures. Generally, projects eligible for approval must contain at least four dwelling units; they can be detached or semi-detached, a row house, a walk-up, or an elevator structure. The loan is made by an approved FHA lender, such as a mortgage company, bank, or savings and loan association, and is insured by the FHA.

Starting in November 2009, the FHA allowed lenders to determine project eligibility under several "approval processing options." Two of the many conditions for condominium FHA financing approval are:

- How much *investor concentration* is there as a percentage of total units?
- What is the condition of the condominium homeowners association related to a percentage of delinquent homeowners on their association dues?

Any creditworthy potential owner-occupant who meets FHA underwriting criteria and makes the condominium unit her principal residence is eligible for a mortgage insured under this program. Most of the features of Section 234(c) mortgage insurance are the same as those governing HUD's basic FHA mortgage insurance program, Section 203(b); however, there are additional owner-occupancy restrictions.

√ **Note:** To find out if a particular condominium project is FHA approved, visit the following HUD website: https://entp.hud.gov/idapp/html/condlook.cfm.

## Home Equity Conversion Mortgage

To be eligible for a federally insured **Home Equity Conversion Mortgage** (**HECM**), or **reverse mortgage**, all borrowers:

- Must be at least 62 years or older.
- Own and occupy the property.
- Should have either no mortgage or one small enough to be paid off with the proceeds of the HECM loan. Life estates and living trusts may also qualify.
- Must have attended counseling from a HUD-approved counseling agency.

The property may be an existing single-family home, condominium unit, manufactured home, or a two- to four-family residential unit, as long as the borrower occupies one of the units. Newly constructed residences are also eligible provided:

- A certificate of occupancy (or equivalent) has been issued for the new home by the local authority.
- The residence is 100% complete, and the owner is occupying it.

Both existing and new units must meet HUD eligibility standards.

### Section 251—FHA ARM Loans

This FHA loan program offering insured adjustable rate mortgages (ARMs) was started by HUD in the early 1980s as a response to the increasing popularity of ARMs among borrowers and lenders. The FHA ARM plan is limited to one- to four-family dwellings and condominium units. The FHA offers a standard one-year ARM and four "hybrid" ARM products. **Hybrid ARMs** *offer an initial interest rate that is constant for the first three, five, seven, or ten years.* After the initial period, the interest rate *adjusts annually.* Following are the interest rate cap structures for various ARM products:

| ARM Loan | Annual Cap | Life-of-the Loan Cap |
|---|---|---|
| One-year and three-year hybrid | One percentage point | Five percentage points (e.g., if a borrower's initial interest rate is 5%, the highest possible interest rate is 10%). |
| Five-, seven-, and ten-year hybrid | Two percentage points | Six percentage points |

## Special Loan Conditions

All loan requirements, conditions, and criteria for standard 203(b) loans also apply to Section 251 ARM loans. Maximum loan amounts are the same as for 203(b) loans. No buydowns are permitted to help the buyer qualify, who also must qualify for the loan at the second year's interest rate.

### For Example

If the initial interest rate for the loan is 6%, the buyer must qualify at 7%. This is because the maximum interest rate for the loan in the second year is the initial interest rate (6%), plus a maximum 1% increase (FHA cap).

The FHA may insure only 10% of all Title II single-family mortgages insured during the previous fiscal year (e.g., 203(b) loans). FHA ARMs are more popular when interest rates are high.

## Other Special FHA Loan Programs

### Good Neighbor Next Door (GNND)

The GNND is an FHA program specifically designed for EMTs, firefighters, K-12 teachers, and law enforcement officers for HUD properties. Some benefits and details of the program are:

- Buyers pay 50% of the list price of the property.
- Homes are in revitalization areas and available properties change weekly (usually a limited supply).
- Owners must occupy the home for 36 months and a 203(k) or a Streamlined 203(k)K rehab can be incorporated into the loan.
- FHA takes a "silent second" mortgage on the home, but as long as the occupancy requirement is met, no interest or payments are required.

### Non-Occupying Borrowers ("Kiddie Condo")

The FHA allows a non-occupying borrower to buy a home under certain conditions. When borrowers are related by blood, marriage, or law (e.g., spouses, parents, children, siblings, step-children, aunts/uncles, nieces/nephews), maximum financing is available.

If a parent buys a home for a child but will not occupy the property with them, many lenders refer to this as a "Kiddie Condo." Although the name may suggest otherwise, the dwelling does not have to be a condominium; this program can be used for the purchase of a single-family residence or a town home.

### For Example

Julie's son is a recent graduate but he does not have the financial ability to buy a home. Julie can purchase the home with her son but the financing will based on Julie's income and debt structure.

The "Kiddie Condo" program allows parents to purchase the property with a minimum down payment (3.5%) as opposed to buying the property as an investment that might require 20% or more as a down payment. At closing, all parties must sign the security instrument and the mortgage note.

## Manufactured Housing

A **manufactured home** is defined as *a structure that is transportable in one or more sections*. In traveling mode, the home is 8 feet or more in width and 40 or more feet in length. It is built on a permanent chassis and is designed to be used as a dwelling when connected to the required utilities (including plumbing, heating, air-conditioning, and electricity).

√ **Note:** A **modular home** is also factory built (to local and state codes) and is *not* considered manufactured housing. The home is delivered in sections to the site and then installed.

Other names for manufactured homes include:

- Mobile homes
- Sectionals
- Multi-sectionals
- Singlewides
- Doublewides
- Triplewides

A manufactured home may not be eligible for FHA financing if it does not meet the following criteria. In order to be eligible for FHA financing, the manufactured home, when erected on site, must:

- Be build on or after June 15, 1976.
- Be at least 400 sq. ft. in gross living area.
- Be built and remain upon a permanent chassis.
- Be designed to be used as a dwelling with a permanent foundation, which is designed and constructed to HUD/FHA criteria.
- Show a HUD Certification Label/Seal affixed to the home's exterior.
- Carry a one-year manufacturer's warranty if it is a new manufactured home.
- Be installed on a site that meets local suitability and has an adequate water supply and sewage facilities.

# VA-Guaranteed Home Loans

The **Veterans Administration (VA)** Home Loan Program is for veterans, active duty military personnel (referred to here as veterans), and certain members of the reserves and National Guard. The VA's program provides an excellent product and benefits for individuals who have served, or are serving, to protect our families and our nation; it also provides real estate professionals with an additional form of financing that allows them to sell more homes.

For those unfamiliar with the program, there are several advantages to using the VA's Home Loan Program. The VA allows a veteran who qualifies to purchase a primary residence *without putting money down toward the sale price,* as long as the sale price does not exceed the appraised value. Veterans do, however, need money toward closing costs and the earnest money deposit, which the seller generally requires when a sales contract is signed. Closing costs may be paid by the seller, which is an item to consider when the sale price is being negotiated.

Other benefits of using the VA's program (other than 100% financing of sale price) include:

- Loans are assumable, provided the assumer is qualified

- Veterans' closing costs are limited by the VA

- Additional assistance is offered by the VA if veterans have problems making home loan payments in the future

- The loan can be prepaid without a penalty

Here are some quick facts you may find useful concerning purchase transactions:

- The VA does *not* have a maximum loan amount. However, lenders do sell loans on the secondary mortgage market, so they will generally limit loans to $417,000 (the limit is $1,094,625 in parts of Colorado) with no down payment. With a down payment, loans may exceed **these amounts**.

- The veteran must qualify income- and credit-wise.

- The veteran must occupy the home as the primary residence.

- The veteran does *not* have to be a first-time homebuyer and may reuse his benefit.

- *The lender*, not the VA, sets the interest rate and discount points; these may vary from lender to lender.

- Private mortgage insurance is not required, but the VA does charge an upfront VA funding fee, which may be financed. Veterans in receipt of VA service-connected monthly disability payments are exempt from this fee.

- The seller can pay for closing costs up to 4%, but only certain items are considered as part of the concession (e.g., payment of pre-paids, VA funding fee, payoff of credit balances or judgments on behalf of the veteran, funds for temporary buydowns). Discount points are excluded from seller concessions.

- The veteran is *not* allowed to pay for the wood-destroying insect (termite) report; it is generally paid by the seller.

- The VA does not approve the majority of loans. Most transactions are handled directly by the lender with little VA intervention.

# VA Loan Guidelines

Since the government guarantees VA loans, it's only natural that there are government guidelines for approving borrowers and property, and other VA loan rules. As we discuss these items, keep in mind there are a limited number of VA loan programs.

## Borrower Guidelines for VA Loans

For a veteran to obtain a VA loan, the lender needs two documents:

1. DD-214
2. Certificate of Eligibility

The **DD-214** (commonly called **Discharge Papers** or **Report of Separation**) is issued by the Department of Defense to all military personnel who saw active duty service or received active duty training for more than 90 days. The DD-214 identifies the veteran's condition of discharge (honorable, general, other than honorable, dishonorable, or bad conduct), thus establishing eligibility for benefits. The DD-214 *cannot* be downloaded, viewed, or requested online. Federal law requires all requests for a veteran's records and information be submitted in writing. Standard Form 180 is used to request a duplicate DD-214.

A **Certificate of Eligibility (COE)** is *issued by the VA to those who qualify for VA loans*. This is required by a lender to establish the amount and status of the veteran's eligibility under the VA loan guarantee program. A borrower can check with the VA to determine his eligibility status. VA Form 26-1880 is used to request the Certificate of Eligibility. The borrower's eligibility will depend on his military service.

Although the lender will examine the borrower's credit history, amount of income, and other factors before approving the loan, the main criterion for a borrower being considered for a VA loan is the borrower's **military eligibility**.

## Military Eligibility

Eligibility for a VA loan is based on a *person's length of continuous active service in the U.S. Armed Forces*. Military service requirements will vary based on when and how the veteran served. A veteran who is unsure what he will qualify for should be referred to the VA Regional Service Center.

### Best Practices

Helping a veteran determine eligibility for a VA loan is tricky and should not be attempted by an agent. If a veteran feels he may be eligible for benefits, refer him to a VA-approved lender for assistance with the forms, or direct the individual to the VA Regional Service Center. Some non-veterans may also qualify, such as spouses of veterans who died on active duty or who are MIA. These restrictions are complicated, so seek guidance from the VA.

## Other Regulations Concerning Borrowers

A veteran must occupy the property as his primary residence, may not have more than one VA loan at a time, and may not own more than two homes at the same time acquired with VA loans.

### For Example

If the veteran bought a home with a VA loan, paid off the loan but kept the home, then bought a second home with a VA loan, paid off the loan and kept the home, one of those homes would have to be sold before a third home could be purchased with a VA loan.

## Sample Standard Form 180 - Request for Duplicate DD-214 Discharge Papers    Page 2 of 2*

Standard Form 180 (Rev. 09/08)  (Page 1)
Prescribed by NARA (36 CFR 1228.168(b))

Authorized for local reproduction
Previous edition unusable

OMB No. 3095-0029  Expires 10/31/2011

# REQUEST PERTAINING TO MILITARY RECORDS

\* Requests from veterans or deceased veteran's next-of-kin may be submitted online by using eVetRecs at http://www.archives.gov/veterans/evetrecs/ \*

*(To ensure the best possible service, please thoroughly review the accompanying instructions before filling out this form.  Please print clearly or type.)*

### SECTION I - INFORMATION NEEDED TO LOCATE RECORDS (Furnish as much as possible.)

| 1. NAME USED DURING SERVICE (last, first, and middle) | 2. SOCIAL SECURITY NO. | 3. DATE OF BIRTH | 4. PLACE OF BIRTH |
|---|---|---|---|

**5. SERVICE, PAST AND PRESENT**  (For an effective records search, it is important that all service be shown below.)

| | BRANCH OF SERVICE | DATE ENTERED | DATE RELEASED | OFFICER | ENLISTED | SERVICE NUMBER (If unknown, write "unknown") |
|---|---|---|---|---|---|---|
| a. ACTIVE COMPONENT | | | | | | |
| b. RESERVE COMPONENT | | | | | | |
| c. NATIONAL GUARD | | | | | | |

6. IS THIS PERSON DECEASED?  If "YES" enter the date of death.
☐ NO  ☐ YES _____

7. IS (WAS) THIS PERSON RETIRED FROM MILITARY SERVICE?
☐ NO  ☐ YES

### SECTION II – INFORMATION AND/OR DOCUMENTS REQUESTED

**1. CHECK THE ITEM(S) YOU WOULD LIKE TO REQUEST A COPY OF:**

☐ **DD Form 214 or equivalent.** This form contains information normally needed to verify military service. A copy may be sent to the veteran, the deceased veteran's next of kin, or other persons or organizations if authorized in Section III, below. NOTE: If more than one period of service was performed, even in the same branch, there may be more than one DD214.  **Check the appropriate box below to specify a deleted or undeleted copy.**  When was the DD Form(s) 214 issued?  YEAR(S):

  ☐ **UNDELETED:** Ordinarily required to determine eligibility for benefits.  Sensitive items, such as, the character of separation, authority for separation, reason for separation, reenlistment eligibility code, separation (SPD/SPN) code, and dates of time lost are usually shown.

  ☐ **DELETED:** The following items are deleted: authority for separation, reason for separation, reenlistment eligibility code, separation (SPD/SPN) code, and for separations after June 30, 1979, character of separation and dates of time lost.

☐ **All Documents in Official Military Personnel File (OMPF)**

☐ **Medical Records** (Includes Service Treatment Records (outpatient), inpatient and dental records.)  If hospitalized, provide facility name and date for each admission:

☐ **Other** (Specify):

**2. PURPOSE:** (An explanation of the purpose of the request is **strictly voluntary**; however, such information may help to provide the best possible response and may result in a faster reply.  Information provided will in no way be used to make a decision to deny the request.)  Check appropriate box:

☐ Benefits  ☐ Employment  ☐ VA Loan Programs  ☐ Medical  ☐ Medals/Awards  ☐ Genealogy  ☐ Correction  ☐ Personal
☐ Other, explain:

### SECTION III - RETURN ADDRESS AND SIGNATURE

**1. REQUESTER IS:**  *(Signature Required in # 3 below of veteran, next of kin, legal guardian, authorized government agent or "other" authorized representative.  If "other" authorized representative, provide copy of authorization letter.)*

☐ Military service member or veteran identified in Section I, above

☐ Next of kin of deceased veteran  (Must provide proof of death).
  *Show relationship:* _____
  (See item 2a on accompanying instructions.)

☐ Legal guardian (Must submit copy of court appointment.)

☐ Other (specify) _____

**3. AUTHORIZATION SIGNATURE REQUIRED** *(See items 2a or 3a on accompanying instructions.)*  I declare (or certify, verify, or state) under penalty of perjury under the laws of the United States of America that the information in this Section III is true and correct.

**2. SEND INFORMATION/DOCUMENTS TO:**
*(Please print or type.  See item 4 on accompanying instructions.)*

Name _____

Street _____  Apt. _____

City _____  State _____  Zip Code _____

**Signature Required** - Do not print

(     )
Date of this request _____  Daytime phone _____

Email address _____

*This form is available at http://www.archives.gov/research/order/standard-form-180.pdf on the National Archives and Records Administration (NARA) web site.*

[ RESET ]

*Side 1 [not shown] contains information about this Form.*

OMB Control No. 2900-0086
Respondent Burden: 15 minutes

| VA Department of Veterans Affairs | FOR VA USE ONLY COE REF. NO. | MAIL COMPLETED APPLICATION TO: |
|---|---|---|
| **REQUEST FOR A CERTIFICATE OF ELIGIBILITY** | | Atlanta Regional Loan Center<br>Attn: COE (262)<br>P. O. Box 100034<br>Decatur, GA 30031 |

**NOTE: Please read information on reverse before completing this form. If additional space is required, attach a separate sheet.**

| 1. NAME OF VETERAN *(First, Middle, Last)* | 2. DATE OF BIRTH | 3. SOCIAL SECURITY NUMBER |
|---|---|---|

4A. DID YOU SERVE UNDER ANOTHER NAME?  ☐ YES  ☐ NO *(If "Yes," complete Item 4B)*    4B. NAME(S) USED DURING MILITARY SERVICE *(If different from name in Item 1)*

| 5. DAYTIME TELEPHONE NUMBER | 6. E-MAIL ADDRESS *(If applicable)* |
|---|---|

| 7A. ADDRESS *(Number and street or rural route, city or P.O., State and ZIP Code)* | 7B. MAIL CERTIFICATE OF ELIGIBILITY TO: *(Complete ONLY if the Certificate is to be mailed to an address different from the one listed in Item 7A.)* |
|---|---|

8A. WERE YOU DISCHARGED, RETIRED, OR SEPARATED FROM SERVICE BECAUSE OF DISABILITY?  ☐ YES  ☐ NO          8B. VA CLAIM NUMBER *(If known)*

**MILITARY SERVICE (SEE INSTRUCTIONS FOR PROOF OF SERVICE ON THE NEXT PAGE)**

9A. ARE YOU CURRENTLY ON ACTIVE DUTY? *(If you currently serving on active duty, leave the "Date Separated" field blank.)*  ☐ YES  ☐ NO

| | BRANCH OF SERVICE | DATE ENTERED | DATE SEPARATED | OFFICER OR ENLISTED | SERVICE NUMBER *(if different from Social Security Number)* |
|---|---|---|---|---|---|
| **IMPORTANT:** Please provide your dates of service. In many cases eligibility can be established based on data in VA systems. However, it is recommended that proof of service be provided, if readily available. Proof of service is required for persons who entered service after September 7, 1980 and were discharged after serving less than 2 years. | | | | | |
| 9B. ACTIVE SERVICE - *Do not* include any periods of Active Duty for Training or Active Guard Reserve service. *Do* include any activation for duty under Title 10 U.S.C. (e.g. Reserve or Guard unit mobilized.) | | | | | |
| 9C. RESERVE OR NATIONAL GUARD SERVICE *Include any periods of Active Duty for Training (ADT) or Active Guard Reserve service.* **Do not** *include any activation for duty under Title 10 U.S.C. (e.g. Reserve or Guard unit mobilized.)* | | | | | |

**PREVIOUS VA LOANS (SEE INSTRUCTIONS ON THE NEXT PAGE - Attach a separate sheet if information for all homes will not fit in Item 10)**

| 10A. DO YOU NOW OWN ANY HOME(S) PURCHASED OR REFINANCED WITH A VA-GUARANTEED LOAN?<br>☐ YES *(If "Yes," complete Items 10B through 10D)*<br>☐ NO *(If "No," skip to Item 14)*<br>☐ NOT APPLICABLE (NA) - I HAVE NEVER OBTAINED A VA-GUARANTEED HOME LOAN *(If "NA," skip to Item 14)* | 10B. DATE OF LOAN *(Month and Year)* | 10C. STREET ADDRESS | 10D. CITY AND STATE |
|---|---|---|---|
| 11A. ARE YOU APPLYING FOR THE **ONE-TIME ONLY RESTORATION** OF ENTITLEMENT TO PURCHASE ANOTHER HOME?<br>☐ YES  ☐ NO *(If "Yes," complete Items 11B through 11D)* | 11B. DATE OF LOAN *(Month and Year)* | 11C. STREET ADDRESS | 11D. CITY AND STATE |
| 12A. ARE YOU APPLYING FOR A RESTORATION OF ENTITLEMENT TO OBTAIN A **REGULAR (CASH-OUT) REFINANCE** ON YOUR CURRENT HOME?<br>☐ YES  ☐ NO *(If "Yes," complete Items 12B through 12D)* | 12B. DATE OF LOAN *(Month and Year)* | 12C. STREET ADDRESS | 12D. CITY AND STATE |
| 13A. ARE YOU REFINANCING AN EXISTING VA LOAN TO OBTAIN A LOWER INTEREST RATE **WITHOUT RECEIVING** ANY CASH PROCEEDS (IRRRL)?<br>☐ YES  ☐ NO *(If "Yes," complete Items 13B through 13D)* | 13B. DATE OF LOAN *(Month and Year)* | 13C. STREET ADDRESS | 13D. CITY AND STATE |

I CERTIFY THAT the statements in this document are true and complete to the best of my knowledge.

| 14A. SIGNATURE OF VETERAN *(Do NOT print)* | 14B. DATE SIGNED |
|---|---|

FEDERAL STATUTES PROVIDE SEVERE PENALTIES FOR FRAUD, INTENTIONAL MISREPRESENTATION, CRIMINAL CONNIVANCE OR CONSPIRACY PURPOSED TO INFLUENCE THE ISSUANCE OF ANY GUARANTY OR INSURANCE BY THE SECRETARY OF VETERANS AFFAIRS

| **FOR VA USE ONLY** *(Please do not write below this line)* | DATE RETURNED |
|---|---|
| REASON(S) FOR RETURN | |

VA FORM
SEP 2011    **26-1880**        SUPERSEDES VA FORM 26-1880, MAR 2011,
WHICH WILL NOT BE USED.

*Side 2 [not shown] contains information about this Form.*

Sample Form 26-8320 - Certificate of Eligibility

---

## Department of Veterans Affairs

## CERTIFICATE OF ELIGIBILITY
FOR LOAN GUARANTY BENEFITS

| NAME OF VETERAN *(First, Middle, Last)* | SERVICE SERIAL NUMBER/SOCIAL SECURITY NUMBER |
|---|---|
| ENTITLEMENT CODE          BRANCH OF SERVICE | DATE OF BIRTH |

Is eligible for the benefits of Chapter 37, Title 38, U.S. Code, and has the amount of entitlement shown as available, subject to the statements *(If checked)* and prior usage shown below.

☐ Valid unless discharged or released subsequent to date of this certificate. A certification of continuous active duty as of date of note is required.

☐ Excluded entitlement previously used for LH _____ as shown herein is available only for use in connection with the property which secured that loan.

☐ Entitlement has been used for manufactured home purposes. Remaining entitlement for additional manufactured home use is: $ _____.

☐ Not eligible for any loan to purchase a manufactured home unit until veteran disposes of unit purchased with manufactured home loan number LHM _____.

*SAMPLE*

| LOAN NUMBER *(Include amount if direct loan)* | ENTITLEMENT | | | DATE AND INITIALS OF VA AGENT |
|---|---|---|---|---|
| | USED | | AVAILABLE* | |
| | 1810 | OTHER | | |
| | | | $36,000 | |
| | | | | |
| | | | | |
| | | | | |

*The amount shown is increased by up to $10,000 for home purchase and construction and condominium loans which are for an amount in excess of $144,000. The guaranty will not exceed 25 percent.
NOTE: The figure shown as available entitlement represents the portion of a loan which may be guaranteed or insured by VA to a lender. For information about maximum loan amounts, see VA Pamphlets 26-4 and 26-71-1, or contact the nearest VA office for further information.

| Available entitlement is subject to reduction if VA incurs actual liability or loss on the loan(s), if any, listed below, obtained by the veteran with the assistance of loan benefits derived from military service in WWII or the Korean conflict. | | | REDUCED | | |
|---|---|---|---|---|---|
| | | | ITEM | DATE | INITIALS OF VA AGENT |
| OUTSTANDING LOAN NUMBER(S) | DATE | INITIALS OF VA AGENT | | | |
| | | | | | |
| | | | | | |
| | | | | | |
| | | | | | |

SECRETARY OF VETERANS AFFAIRS

*(Issuing Office)*

*(Date issued)*                    *(Signature of Authorized Agent)*

VA FORM FEB 1990    **26-8320**    SUPERSEDES VA FORM 26-8320, JUL 1988 WHICH WILL NOT BE USED.    ☆U.S. GOVERNMENT PRINTING OFFICE 1993-721-330

Also, a veteran borrower is responsible for repaying any guarantee amount the VA may have paid to the lender because of the borrower's default on the loan. In the past, this meant the veteran's liability continued even if there was an assumption and default by a subsequent borrower. Now, it is the VA's policy *not to pursue secondary liability against a veteran* unless the seller participated in fraud against the VA. Nevertheless, this underscores the importance of getting a release from liability when a loan is assumed.

√ **Note:** VA rules and regulations are continuously updated and amended. For current information, VA form requests, or questions: Call the VA at 1-800-827-1000 or visit http://www.va.gov.

## Property Guidelines for VA Loans

The main criterion for a property getting approved for a VA loan is the **Certificate of Reasonable Value (CRV)**. You also need to be aware of the **maximum guarantee amount (entitlement)** the VA will authorize.

### Certificate of Reasonable Value (CRV)

The **Certificate of Reasonable Value (CRV)** is a document issued by the VA that states the value of the subject property based on an approved appraisal. The **CRV** (or the sale price, whichever is less) *establishes the maximum mortgage amount a veteran may have on a VA-guaranteed loan for that property.* Although the VA does not limit a home's purchase price, if the price of the property exceeds the CRV, the veteran must make up the difference in cash to buy that property. *The loan amount cannot exceed the CRV.*

### Maximum Guarantee Amount (Entitlement)

The VA places a limit on the guarantee amount a veteran is entitled to receive. The **maximum guarantee amount (entitlement)** *determines how much guarantee assistance a veteran can get on a VA loan.*

The VA guarantee amount has increased over the years. The current maximum loan guarantee amount is $104,250. With the VA providing this loan guarantee amount up to 25% of the purchase price, a veteran can buy a home costing up to $417,000 with no down payment. (A veteran wishing to buy a more expensive home must make a down payment for the portion above $417,000.)

### Restoring Eligibility

When the original home is sold and a new buyer is assuming the loan, the selling veteran may be released from liability and may have his VA loan guarantee entitlement restored, as long as the following conditions are met:

- Loan must be current
- VA must approve buyer's credit
- Buyer must sign a written agreement assuming obligations and liabilities of the veteran (including indemnity obligation)
- Buyer must be a veteran with enough unused entitlement, which he agrees to substitute for seller's entitlement
- VA must issue a release

### Reinstating Eligibility

When the original VA loan is paid in full, the house is sold, and a need for new housing can be demonstrated, the veteran's full VA loan guarantee entitlement is reinstated.

The veteran should contact the local VA office to determine any available guarantee eligibility.

## VA Loan Regulations

In addition to the criteria for borrowers and properties, there are important rules that apply to VA loans. These include rules on **secondary financing**, **down payment**, **LTV calculations**, **variable funding fee** (instead of mortgage insurance), **no buydown limits**, **assumability of loans**, **prepayment penalties**, and **items paid by seller**.

### Secondary Financing

VA permits secondary financing to pay for all or part of a down payment, or if the secondary financing is at a lower interest rate than the VA loan; giving the borrower a lower total mortgage payment.

Secondary financing is allowed for VA loans if the following conditions are met:

1.  First and second mortgages *together may not exceed the reasonable value of the property*, as determined by the CRV

2.  Borrower's income must be sufficient to *qualify for the combined total* of both payments on the VA and non-VA mortgages

3.  Second mortgage interest rate may *not* exceed the interest rate of the first mortgage

4.  Conditions on the second mortgage may not be more stringent than the first mortgage (e.g., late payment penalty), *but* the second mortgage can include a due-on-sale clause

Veterans taking out a VA loan may need a second mortgage if they do not have enough entitlement to qualify for a large enough loan or for a no-down-payment loan, or they do not have enough cash available to make up the difference.

√ **Remember:** The veteran *cannot* use secondary financing *to pay for any amount of the home's cost above the CRV.* Amounts above the CRV must be paid by the veteran in cash.

### Down Payment

Unlike most loans, a typical VA loan may be obtained by an eligible veteran with no down payment. For zero-down loans, most lenders require the VA loan guarantee to equal at least 25% of the loan amount. A veteran with complete entitlement of $104,250 available can buy a home for up to $417,000 with no down payment. (Veterans with less than the full entitlement amount can buy a home for up to four times the amount of their entitlement.)

If the veteran's remaining entitlement is insufficient, or if the purchase price exceeds $417,000, the veteran can provide a down payment so the combination of the entitlement and the down payment equal 25%. If the veteran is buying a home with a sale price greater than the CRV, the amount over the CRV must be paid by the veteran in cash as a down payment. If the CRV is too much below the sale price of the home and the seller is not willing to accept less, or the veteran cannot come up with enough money as a down payment, the transaction is effectively dead.

Also note that *closing costs may not be financed as part of a VA loan.* If the CRV is high enough, it may be possible to raise the purchase price and have the seller pay the closing costs. More often than not, however, the CRV comes in at or below the sale price. When that happens, either the seller can pay the closing costs and accept less money for the home, or the veteran must come up with more cash. (This is when secondary financing may be an option.)

## Variable Funding Fee

A *variable funding fee is charged on all VA loans.* This is a one-time fee, due at closing, based on the status of the veteran, how many times he has used the program, and the amount (if any) of down payment. Remember, there is no mortgage insurance with VA loans, but this variable funding fee is due at closing—or may be financed if the loan total does not exceed the CRV. Note that the variable funding fee is *waived for disabled veterans.*

| VA Variable Funding Fees* | | | |
|---|---|---|---|
| | **Down Payment** | **1st Time User**<br>**% of Loan Amount** | **Subsequent User**<br>**% of Loan Amount** |
| Veterans | No Down Payment<br>5% - 9.99%<br>10% or More | 2.15%<br>1.50%<br>1.25% | 3.30%<br>1.50%<br>1.25% |
| National Guard &<br>Reservists | No Down Payment<br>5% - 9.99%<br>10% or More | 2.40%<br>1.75%<br>1.50% | 3.30%<br>1.75%<br>1.50% |

*\* To refinance for a lower interest rate, the fee for all users is 0.50% (1.00% on manufactured home loans).*

## Assumability of Loans

When a VA-guaranteed home loan is assumed, the VA has the right to require a credit check to make sure the new borrower meets the minimum credit qualifications. (For the original veteran to restore or reinstate eligibility, the loan must be assumed by another qualifying veteran.)

When the VA loan will not be paid off (e.g., an assumption), other considerations are important to consider. When a veteran obtains a guaranteed loan from the VA, he becomes legally obligated to **indemnify** the United States Government for any claim paid by the VA under the guarantee.

√ *In Other Words:* If the VA has to pay any money to the lender because the veteran defaults on the loan, the veteran must repay that amount to the government.

In the past, this meant the veteran's liability continued even if there was an assumption and default by a subsequent borrower. Now, it is the VA's policy not to pursue secondary liability against a veteran unless the seller participated in fraud against the VA. Nevertheless, it is still useful to know the steps a veteran can take to be released from this liability.

## Release from Liability

A veteran can be released from liability on a VA loan *only if* the following conditions are met:

1. The loan must be current.

2. The buyer must be an acceptable credit risk.

3. The buyer must agree, in writing, to assume the liabilities and obligations of the veteran, including the indemnity obligation.

4. The VA must issue a release.

To facilitate a veteran's release from liability for a buyer assuming his loan, it's best to include a provision in the contract. The sales agreement should state the buyer will assume all of the seller's loan obligations (including the potential liability for indemnity on the VA loan), and the sale will not be closed *unless and until* the VA approves the income and credit of the buyer and issues a release. Ask your broker or an attorney for help with these contract clauses.

## Restoring Entitlement

The person assuming a VA loan does not have to be a veteran, but the seller's veteran entitlement for future VA loans can be restored only if the buyer is a veteran who agrees to substitute his entitlement for that of the selling veteran and all other conditions for release of liability are met. If the buyer is a veteran and the seller wants a substitution of VA entitlement, a stipulation to that effect should also be included in the contract. Again, ask your broker or an attorney for help with these contract clauses.

## Prepayment Penalties

The VA doesn't allow clauses for prepayment penalties to be included in VA loans. *VA loans may be paid off early without additional charges or penalties of any kind.* (But the VA does allow these clauses for secondary financing.)

## Items Paid by the Seller

Who pays for VA loan fees, points, etc., is open to negotiation. VA rules allow any item to be paid by the seller. The only rule in this area is that veterans, as buyers, cannot be charged commissions, brokerage fees, or "buyer broker" fees. These items must be paid by the seller.

## Co-signing for a VA Loan

An important VA rule is that **only the veteran's spouse can co-sign for a VA loan**.

√ ***Note:*** As you review the rules we've discussed, or encounter others in your real estate practice, be aware that VA rules change all the time. Current rules can always be obtained from a lender, or by visiting http://www.va.gov.

# VA Loan Programs

A limited number of VA loan programs are offered by the government. The most popular is a fixed-rate, fully amortized loan with a term of 15 or 30 years. Several ARM loans are also available.

Sample Form 26-0592  -  Counseling Checklist for Military Homebuyers

 **Department of
Veterans Affairs**

## COUNSELING CHECKLIST FOR MILITARY HOMEBUYERS

1. Failure on the part of a borrower on active duty to disclose that he/she expects to leave the area within 12 months due to transfer orders or completion of his/her enlistment period may constitute "bad faith." If your loan is foreclosed under circumstances which include such bad faith, you may be required to repay VA for any loss suffered by the Government under the guaranty. (In ANY case in which VA suffers a loss under the guaranty, the loss must be repaid before your loan benefits can be restored to use in obtaining another VA loan.)

2. Although real estate values have historically risen in most areas, there is no assurance that the property for which you are seeking financing will increase in value or even retain its present value.

3. It is possible that you may encounter difficulty in selling your house, recovering your investment or making any profit, particularly if there is an active new home market in the area.

4. Receiving military orders for a permanent change of duty station or an unexpected early discharge due to a reduction in force will not relieve you of your obligation to make your mortgage payments on the first of each month.

5. "Letting the house go back" is **NOT** an acceptable option. A decision to do so may be considered "bad faith". A foreclosure will result in a bad credit record, a possible debt you will owe the government and difficulty in getting more credit in the future.

6. If unexpected circumstances lead to difficulty in making your payments, contact your mortgage company promptly. It will be easier to resolve any problems if you act quickly and be open and honest with the mortgage company.

7. **YOUR VA LOAN MAY NOT BE ASSUMED WITHOUT THE PRIOR APPROVAL OF VA OR YOUR LENDER**.

8. **DO NOT BE MISLED!** VA does not guarantee the **CONDITION** of the house which you are buying, whether it is new or previously occupied. VA guarantees only the **LOAN.** You may talk to many people when you are in the process of buying a house. Particularly with a previously occupied house, you may pick up the impression along the way that you need not be overly concerned about any needed repairs or hidden defects since VA will be sure to find them and require them to be repaired. This is **NOT TRUE!** In every case, ultimately, it is your responsibility to be an informed buyer and to assure yourself that what you are buying is satisfactory to you in all respects. Remember, VA guarantees only the loan - **NOT** the condition.

9. If you have any doubts about the condition of the house which you are buying, it is in your best interest to seek expert advice before you legally commit yourself in a purchase agreement. Particularly with a previously occupied house, most sellers and their real estate agents are willing to permit you, at your expense, to arrange for an inspection by a qualified residential inspection service. Also, most sellers and agents are willing to negotiate with you concerning what repairs are to be included in the purchase agreement. Steps of this kind can prevent many later problems, disagreements, and major disappointments.

10. Proper maintenance is the best way to protect your home and improve the chance that its value will increase.

11. If you are buying a previously owned house, you should look into making energy efficient improvements. You can add up to $6,000 to your VA loan to have energy efficient improvements installed. Consult your lender or the local VA office.

**I HEREBY CERTIFY THAT** the lender has counseled me and I fully understand the counseling items set forth above.

_____        _____
(Borrower's Signature)                                                          (Date)

**I HEREBY CERTIFY THAT** the borrower has been counseled regarding the counseling items set forth above.

_____        _____
(Lender's Signature)                                                            (Date)

VA Form
JUN 1995  **26-0592**          EXISTING STOCK OF VA FORM 26-0592, JUL 1990, WILL
BE USED.

# USDA Rural Development Housing Programs

The USDA Rural Development's direct and guaranteed loan programs provide low-interest, no-down-payment loans to help eligible families living in rural communities and rural areas purchase existing or new homes. The direct loan program is geared toward low-income individuals. No down payment is required and closing costs may be included in the loan. Eligible applicants are qualified for a loan amount up to a county-by-county loan limit based on their debt-to-income ratios. In addition, the applicant must have an acceptable credit history (preferable credit score of 620 better) and adequate and dependable income sufficient to meet all obligations.

Loans may be made up to 100% of the appraised value for the purchase of a home and, in some cases, the loan may include closing costs. The end result is less cash upfront from borrowers for loans made under this program.

Buyers (or borrowers) must personally occupy the dwelling following the purchase. Dwellings must be structurally sound, functionally adequate, and in good condition.

Some other homebuyer benefits include:

*   No mortgage insurance (3% guarantee fee (subject to change) which can be financed into the loan)
*   30-year fixed rate
*   No loan limit
*   No reserve requirements
*   Closing costs can be gifted, paid by the seller, or paid by a nonprofit organization

Anyone seeking more information about homeownership financing or any other USDA Rural Development program may visit http://www.rurdev.usda.gov. This program was formerly called Farmer's Home Administration, FmHA.

### Best Practices

If a buyer is eligible, or may be best suited, for a government loan, you may have to shop around for an approved lender. It might help to ask your broker for a source, or you may explore the FHA, VA, or USDA websites to find approved lenders for your area.

## FINANCE EXERCISE 5-1

A borrower wants an FHA loan for a home that costs $103,500 and appraised for $107,000. Estimated closing costs are $1,500. The borrower also wants to finance the initial MIP premium. The borrower has good credit, a six-figure income, and meets all other FHA standards.

1.  How much is the minimum investment the buyer must make to buy this home?

2.  What's the most the seller can pay (in points and dollars)?

*See the Appendix for answers to check your work.*

## FINANCE EXERCISE 5-2

A first-time borrower who served in active duty for more than six years wants a VA loan. The home costs $88,900, estimated closing costs are $1,100, and the borrower wants to finance the variable funding fee. The borrower has good credit, but little cash.

1.  What's the loan amount for this home?

2.  How much will the buyer pay at closing including the down payment and closing costs? What if the funding fee is paid in cash?

*See the Appendix for answers to check your work.*

# Summary

1. **Government financing** means real estate loans are insured or guaranteed by government programs. This occurs at the federal level (and should not be confused with government involvement in secondary markets). Government programs include FHA-insured, VA-guaranteed, and USDA Rural Development loans.

2. FHA Loan Review:

    • **Less stringent qualifying standards for borrowers.** It's generally easier for buyers to qualify for FHA loans because higher debt ratios are allowed.

    • **Higher property standards.** The FHA scrutinizes properties to see if they need any obvious, major repairs so buyers don't need to spend money fixing them.

    • **Low down payments.** An FHA down payment is often lower than conventional loans, and although the minimum down payment can't be borrowed, it can be a gift.

    • **MIP is required.** MIP initial premium can be financed, even over FHA limits.

    • **Long-term loans.** Most FHA loans are 30 years, which keeps payments lower.

    • **Loans are assumable.** FHA loans may be assumed, with FHA completing a credit check and approving the new borrower.

    • **No prepayment penalty.** FHA loans may not contain prepayment penalties, but a borrower may have to pay an extra month's interest if the loan is paid off after the payment due date.

3. **FHA loan programs**: 203(b)—Standard; 203(k)—Rehab loans (can borrow to fix up); Streamlined 203(k) to repair homes; 234(c)—Condos (only approved condos, no multi-family); 251—FHA ARM.

4. **VA-guaranteed loans** help eligible veterans buy a home with no down payment. Veteran must occupy the home, can't have more than one loan at a time, nor more than two VA-purchased homes at once. The VA doesn't limit a home's price, but limits guarantee amount the lender can recover for default ($104,250). VA automatic endorsers underwrite VA loans.

5. VA Loan Review:

    • **Borrower must be an eligible veteran.** Eligibility is based on the dates and length of active military duty. Veterans should check with the VA to determine benefits.

    • **No price limit for homes.** The VA does not limit the price of a home a veteran can buy, but does limit the guarantee amount to $104,250. (Loan can't exceed the CRV.)

    • **No down payment.** Unlike most mortgage loans, a typical VA loan may be obtained with no down payment. (The mortgage limit is $417,000 when there is no down payment.)

    • **Closing costs may *not* be financed.** Although closing costs cannot be financed, they can be paid by the seller, the buying veteran, or through the lender.

    • **Variable funding fee is required.** While there is no mortgage insurance on VA loans, there is a one-time funding fee due at closing (or it can be financed). This fee is waived for disabled veterans.

    • **No seller contribution limits.** Points can be paid by anyone including the buyer or seller. The seller is limited to paying 4% of closing costs, but there is no limit regarding discount points.

    • **Loans are assumable.** VA loans may be assumed, with the VA completing a credit check and approving the new borrower. The new buyer should also be a veteran, and the seller should get released from indemnity.

    • **No prepayment penalty.** VA loans may *not* contain prepayment penalties.

# Quiz

1. **The Federal Housing Administration (FHA)**
   a. allows for prepayment charges if the loan is paid off within five years.
   b. makes residential loans.
   c. requires alienation clauses.
   d. requires MIP.

2. **FHA programs are directed primarily at**
   a. investors looking to generate high-return government subsidized housing.
   b. low- to middle-income homebuyers.
   c. luxury homebuyers.
   d. middle- to high-income homebuyers buying second homes.

3. **A buyer can get an FHA loan for**
   a. certain condominiums.
   b. purchasing a home to live in that needs some repairs.
   c. a reverse mortgage.
   d. all of the above

4. **FHA interest rates are set by**
   a. federal regulations.
   b. the FHA.
   c. the market.
   d. negotiation between buyer and seller.

5. **The FHA requires mortgage insurance (MIP) when the**
   a. buyer cannot pay the required down payment in cash.
   b. LTV exceeds 80%.
   c. LTV exceeds 90%.
   d. All FHA loans must have MIP.

6. **Which is an advantage of FHA financing?**
   a. less stringent qualifying standards
   b. long-term loans
   c. low down payments
   d. all of the above

7. **Maximum loan limits for FHA loans depend on the**
   a. amount of the buyer's down payment.
   b. county in which the home is located in each state.
   c. median home prices in the area.
   d. type of dwelling (e.g., one to four units).

8. **A loan guaranteed by the Veterans Administration (VA) requires a minimum down payment of**
   a. $0.
   b. at least 3% of the loan amount.
   c. 10% of the loan amount.
   d. It depends on the property type.

9. **VA loans are available for**
   a. apartment buildings.
   b. commercial buildings.
   c. multiple-family residences of five or more units.
   d. one- to four-unit owner-occupied residences.

10. **The VA sets the maximum loan amount by looking at the**
    a. county the home is located in.
    b. CRV.
    c. current interest rates.
    d. type of dwelling (e.g., one to four units).

11. **The amount a qualified veteran can borrow is determined by the**
    a. financial qualifications of the veteran.
    b. veteran's cash flow analysis for residual income.
    c. veteran's previous use of the program and remaining eligibility.
    d. all of the above

12. **Which is NOT a characteristic of a VA loan?**
    a. no credit check of an assuming veteran
    b. no due on sale clause
    c. no prepayment penalty
    d. Veterans can buy investment property with zero down.

13. **With a loan assumption, a veteran seller is still liable for the loan amount after the property is transferred, unless the**

   a. buyer gives written assumption of liability and the VA issues a release.

   b. buyer is an acceptable credit risk approved by the lender.

   c. loan is current.

   d. all of the above

14. **Full VA entitlement can be restored to a veteran**

   a. at no time—the program can be used only once.

   b. if a dishonorably discharged veteran assumes the loan.

   c. when half of the loan amount has been repaid.

   d. when a veteran sells his home and pays off the loan.

# *Nontraditional Financing Tools*

Alternative financing tools are useful when interest rates are high or when buyers have trouble qualifying for a loan. Financing tools can also help buyers achieve other goals, such as getting a lower interest rate, buying a bigger house, or paying off a loan sooner. We'll start by looking at the most popular financing tools: Buydowns (or discounts) and adjustable rate mortgages (ARMs). Then we'll discuss sub-prime loans, no document loans, structured mortgages, and buyer assistance programs. Finally, we'll explore some of the newest types of loans available and talk about seller financing.

## Key Terms

**Adjustable Rate Mortgage (ARM)** A mortgage that permits the lender to periodically adjust the interest rate to reflect fluctuations in the cost of money.

**Buydown** Additional funds in the form of points paid to a lender at the beginning of a loan to lower the interest rate and monthly payments.

**Caps** Limits, usually used with ARMs, to protect a borrower from large payment increases. There can be caps on interest rates, payments, or negative amortization.

**Discount Points** An amount paid to a lender when a loan is made to make up the difference between the current market interest rate and the rate a lender gives a borrower on a note. Discount points increase a lender's yield, allowing the lender to give a borrower a lower interest rate. Also referred to as **Discounts** or **Points.**

**Index** A statistical report that is generally a reliable indicator of the approximate change in the cost of money, and is often used to adjust the interest rate in ARMs.

**Margin** The difference between the index value and the interest rate charged to the borrower with an ARM loan (e.g., the lender's profit).

**Permanent Buydown** When points are paid to a lender to reduce the interest rate and loan payments for the entire life of the loan.

**Prime Rate** The lowest interest rate that banks charge their best commercial customers.

**Rate Adjustment Period** The interval at which a borrower's actual interest rate changes with an ARM.

**Temporary Buydown** When points are paid to a lender to reduce the interest rate and payments early in a loan, with interest rate and payments rising later.

## Purpose of Nontraditional Financing Tools

The **Housing and Economic Recovery Act of 2008 (HERA)** was passed for several reasons, including the modernization of the **Federal Housing Administration,** foreclosure prevention, and the enhancement of consumer protection. Part of this Act (HB 3221, Page 159, Part 6) defines a *nontraditional mortgage* as "anything other than a 30-year fixed rate mortgage." When interest rates are high or buyers can't qualify for traditional financing, nontraditional financing tools are often used to lower a buyer's monthly payment and/or down payment, or help them qualify in some other way. Financing tools are important elements of real estate finance that can help buyers achieve their goals.

One of the biggest reasons buyers use special financing tools is to buy a particular home; usually one that's more expensive than they would qualify for traditionally. Financing tools can often help a buyer get a lower interest rate, a lower payment, or both. By starting out with a lower payment, a buyer can get a more expensive home now and grow into larger payments over time.

### For Example

Sometimes, a buyer wants a variable interest rate to get a lower rate, but wants to make sure that the payment will not increase. This is accomplished by structuring the mortgage in a particular way. Other times, the size of the payment is not as important so a mortgage is structured to help a buyer achieve some other financial goal, such as paying off a home more quickly and saving interest.

Nontraditional financing tools may be needed to help a buyer who has less-than-perfect credit or some other high-risk factor that disqualifies her from getting a traditional loan. With the wide variety of nontraditional financing available in today's market, it's important for you to understand how these tools work so you can help your clients reach their real estate goals.

## Types of Financing Tools

Buyers have many different goals, and there are just as many financing tools available to help them finance the perfect property. If the goal is a lower interest rate or a lower monthly payment, additional payments to the lender at the beginning of the loan may be initiated. Other times a loan is structured to defer higher interest rates or higher payments until later in the loan. Both financing tools fall under the general category of **buydowns**, which involve **discounts** and the payment of **points** to the lender.

Another way to decrease the initial interest rate on a loan (thus decreasing monthly payments) is for the borrower to assume part of the lender's interest rate risk by taking an adjustable rate mortgage (ARM). An ARM allows the lender to raise or lower the interest rate as the cost of money changes.

Before the mortgage crisis in 2007, other nontraditional financing tools were available. However, mortgage lending qualifications have tightened and these financing tools are now virtually unavailable.

## For Example

As a real estate professional, you may run into some customers who, in the past, obtained **subprime loans**. These loans were given to borrowers with less than perfect credit, or some other risk factor that did not allow them to qualify for a conventional loan. These loans allowed the lender to charge an interest rate above what is typical for conventional mortgages.

A variation of the subprime loan was the **no document (no doc) loan** or **low document loan.** *These loans required no verification of income* and were used when a borrower was too busy, or found it difficult, to provide income verification. The decision to fund the loan was based upon other merits (e.g., credit score, occupation).

Finally, lenders may offer other nontraditional financing programs to help borrowers qualify more easily, obtain a larger loan, or pay a reduced down payment. These types of loans are often referred to as **homebuyer assistance programs**.

# Buydowns

**Buydowns** are *additional funds in the form of points paid to a lender at the beginning of a loan term to lower the interest rate and monthly payments.* In order to understand buydowns, you must also understand the concept of **discount points**.

## Discount Points

**Discount points** are *paid to a lender to make up the difference between the current market interest rate and the rate given to a borrower on a note.* Discount points increase a lender's return on loans with lower-than-market interest rates, allowing the lender to give the borrower a loan with a lower interest rate.

√ **In Other Words:** By paying a one-time fee to a lender, a borrower gets a discount on the interest rate of the loan.

Discount points are also called **discounts** or **points**. The term *point* is short for percentage point. A **point** is *one percent of the loan amount.*

## For Example

On a $100,000 loan, the borrower would pay an additional $1,000 for every point the lender charged.

The lender can charge points as a way of lowering the borrower's interest rate. Thus, the borrower can get a rate that's below the current market interest rate. Essentially, the lender is discounting the normal interest rate (called the **nominal rate**, **note rate**, or **coupon rate**).

## Best Practices

Lenders may charge other fees to make a loan, but they may not lower the buyers' interest rate. These fees are called **closing costs** by most lenders and, depending on the type of loan program, can be quite expensive. Make sure your buyers know how these costs affect how much money they need to close their loan and their monthly payment.

√ **Note:** There are two important things to remember about points thus far:
- Points are computed only on the loan amount, not the sale price.
- Points can be combined with closing costs as fees charged to the buyer.

## Purpose of Discount Points

Simply put, discount points can *help lenders and buyers get what they want.* Discount points have traditionally been associated with FHA and VA loans, but points for conventional loans are becoming more common.

Although paying discount points to get a lower interest rate seems to benefit the buyer, they can also benefit the seller. Who pays the points is open to negotiation, and often a seller will pay them to make the subject property more marketable and affordable for a buyer. It's far easier to sell when the buyer's interest rate is lower. However, in effect, having the seller pay the points as part of the negotiated purchase price lowers the seller's net proceeds. *When points are paid to reduce the buyer's interest rate*, it's called a **buydown**.

### For Example

The Clark family entered into a contract to buy a home for $180,000 with a loan amount of $162,000. Their lender told them that to qualify for their payment, they needed a lower interest rate. If the seller paid two points to reduce the Clark family's interest rate, the cost to the seller would be $3,240 ($162,000 x 2% = $3,240).

Many times, if the seller knows he is getting full price for his home (or close to it), this incentive could influence whether or not the contract closes.

## Buydown Plans

One of the easiest ways to make a loan less expensive is with a buydown. A **buydown** is when *additional funds, in the form of points, are paid to the lender at the beginning of a loan to lower the interest rate and monthly payments.* Since the result is that the buyer's mortgage payments are lowered, this could help in qualifying the buyer for the loan. Sellers, builders, or any party—including buyers—can make a lump sum payment to the lender at the time the loan is made to buydown the interest rate. The money paid to the lender is used to reduce the borrower's payments *early in the loan* (**temporary buydown**) or *throughout the life of the loan* (**permanent buydown**).

### Paying for a Buydown

As we've discussed, a buydown can be paid in cash at closing by any party (e.g., seller, buyer, builder). This is typically how a buyer would pay for a buydown; by simply increasing the cash needed at closing.

If the seller pays for the buydown, the lender calculates the buydown, and subtracts it from the loan proceeds paid to the seller for the property. However, the buyer still signs a note for the full amount. The seller just agrees to receive less at closing.

### How a Buydown Lowers Payments

A buydown lowers a buyer's payments because of the lower interest rate that results from paying the discount points. There are *two main advantages* to a buydown plan:

1. The buyer's monthly payment is lower than normal.
2. The lender qualifies the buyer for the loan on the basis of a reduced payment.

## Permanent Buydown

A **permanent buydown** is when *points are paid to a lender to reduce the interest rate and loan payments for the entire life of the loan.* When a buyer's interest rate is **permanently** lowered by a buydown, the lender will write that interest rate into the promissory note. Thus, the nominal rate (or coupon rate) stated in the note is the actual reduced interest rate.

Permanent buydowns were very popular in the early 1980s as the mortgage interest rates reached as high as 18.5%. Sellers and builders offered a lower permanent buydown to entice buyers in the market to purchase their homes.

Permanent buydowns reappeared with builders during the recession that started in the second half of 2006. When the interest rates were 6.5%, some builders offered a 5.5% fixed 30-year permanent buydown to influence buyers to purchase their homes verses other homes on the market.

### Calculating Permanent Buydowns

To accurately determine buydown rates, you should get a quote from the lender.

---

### FINANCE EXERCISE 6-1

Rob Morris finds a $120,000 home he wants to purchase; he will make a $20,000 down payment. Today's interest rate with no points is 6.5% on a 30-year fixed rate, fully amortized loan. To qualify, Rob needs a rate of 6%.

1. What if the lender charges 3½ points for the rate reduction? What would the cost of the points be?

   *100,000 × .035 = 3500*

2. Calculate the payment at a 6.5% fully amortized, 30-year fixed loan. Compare the 6.5% payment to the 6% payment. How much would Rob save?

   *32*

3. How many months would Rob have to stay in the home to save enough to get his points money back?

   *3500 ÷ 32 = 109 months*

4. Can you think of another way for Rob to spend the money paid for discount points that might make more financial sense?

   *put more down*

*See the Appendix for answers to check your work.*

As you can see, buydowns can help buyers qualify for loans and make mortgage payments more attractive. That's why, at times, sellers are willing to pay discount points for buyers. It means less money in the seller's pocket, but may be necessary to close the transaction.

## Temporary Buydown

A **temporary buydown** is *when points are paid to a lender to reduce the interest rate and payments early in a loan, with both rising later.* When interest rates are high, temporary buydowns are a popular way to reduce payments early in the loan. Many buyers feel they can grow into a larger payment, but need time to get established.

### Graduated Payment

A **graduated payment** buydown is a plan where *payment subsidies in the early years keep payments low.* Payments increase each year until they're high enough to fully amortize the loan. In the past, the FHA allowed builders, or other sellers, to help buyers qualify for a loan at the *bought down* interest rate. This is no longer the case. In recent years, the FHA changed the guideline; if a buydown is used, the buyer must now qualify at the *note rate*. The loan is usually structured so the subsidy lasts only two or three years.

The most common type of graduated payment buydown plan is often referred to as a **2-1 buydown**. 2-1 buydowns and 3-2-1 buydowns are often incorporated with homes priced for first-time buyers. These buydowns allow purchasers to lower their payments early on, which allows them to purchase much more house than they could afford otherwise.

A **2-1 buydown** is a *graduated payment buydown where the payments are lower for only two years.*

### For Example

The lender makes a 30-year loan for $170,000 at 6.75% interest rate. The builder agrees to a 2-1 buydown.

| | | | | | | | |
|---|---|---|---|---|---|---|---|
| | | | GRADUATED PAYMENT EXAMPLE | | | | |
| Year | Note Interest Rate | Buydown | Effective Interest Rate | Monthly Payment at 6.75% | Actual Monthly Payment | Monthly Subsidy | Annual Subsidy |
| 1 | 6.75% | 2% | 4.75% | $1,103 | $887 | $216 | $2,592 |
| 2 | 6.75% | 1% | 5.75% | $1,103 | $993 | $110 | $1,320 |
| 3 | 6.75% | -0- | 6.75% | $1,103 | $1,103 | -0- | -0- |
| | | | | | | TOTAL BUYDOWN: | $3912 |

### Calculating Temporary Buydowns

To accurately determine temporary buydown rates, **always** have clients get a quote from the lender. As a rough estimate, 2-1 buydowns cost about 2.5 points.

## Limits on Seller-Paid Points

In Chapter 5, we discussed Fannie Mae, Freddie Mac, VA, and FHA limits on points and other contributions paid by the seller (or other interested parties). Let's review these briefly.

## Fannie Mae and Freddie Mac

Fannie Mae and Freddie Mac guidelines limit discounts, buydowns, and other forms of seller contributions including finance costs such as prepaid interest, escrows for property taxes, hazard insurance, and mortgage insurance. Limits are placed on these items to prevent buyers from acquiring property they will not be able to afford in the future.

Contributions by sellers or other interested parties are limited to a percentage of the property's sale price or appraised value, *whichever is less*. If contributions exceed Fannie Mae and Freddie Mac guidelines, the contribution amount must be deducted from the property's value or sale price before determining the maximum loan amount. Maximum contributions are based on the type of property and the LTV. Please consult the lender for complete rules as these vary by loan program.

| Maximum Contribution | Property Type | LTV |
|---|---|---|
| 2% | Investment Property | |
| 3% | Principal Residence | 90% or higher LTV |
| 6% | Principal Residence | Between 90% and 75% LTV |
| 9% | Principal Residence | 75% or lower LTV |

## FHA

FHA guidelines also impose limits on discounts, buydowns, and other forms of seller contributions. Effective April 2010, the FHA allows a maximum seller contribution of 6%. If the contribution is more than 6%, the FHA, like Fannie Mae and Freddie Mac, deducts the excess from the maximum loan amount.

 **Note:** As was mentioned in Chapter 5, as of this writing, the FHA is considering lowering the seller contribution from 6% to 3%. It is important for real estate professionals to stay up-to-date on laws, regulations, and guidelines related to their industry.

For this rule, remember that seller-paid contributions include any items normally paid by the buyer. Family contributions are also excluded.

### Best Practices

Even though smaller payments are due at the beginning of the loan term, they will continue to increase. Buyers must consider whether this may pose a problem down the road. Failure to consider this increase is one of the reasons for the rise in foreclosure rates, especially for new builds. Remember, an increase in tax payments may occur as well, adding to the monthly financial obligation.

# Adjustable Rate Mortgages (ARMs)

**Adjustable rate mortgages (ARMs)** permit the lender to periodically adjust the interest rate so it reflects fluctuations in the cost of money. ARMs are popular alternative financing tools because they can help borrowers qualify more easily for a home loan, or qualify for a larger home loan. Many lenders like ARMs because they pass the risk of fluctuating interest rates on to borrowers. With an ARM, the borrower is affected by interest rate movements: If rates climb, payments go up; if they decline, payments go down.

Because ARMs shift the risk of interest rate fluctuations to the borrower, lenders normally charge a lower rate for an ARM than for a fixed rate loan. Although the majority of borrowers prefer the security of a fixed rate (provided the rate is not too high), ARMs have maintained a place in the market despite comparatively low mortgage rates. Of course, as interest rates rise, so does ARM popularity.

## How ARMs Work

The borrower's interest rate is determined initially by the cost of money when the loan is made. The three main elements of an ARM are:

- Rate
- Index
- Margin

Once the initial interest rate for the loan is set, it is tied to a widely recognized and published index. An **index** is a *statistical report that is generally a reliable indicator of the approximate cost of money.* Thus, future interest rate adjustments for ARM loans are based on the up and down movement of the index.

A simple example is a home equity line of credit where lenders often quote the interest rate as *prime rate* plus or minus a certain percentage. **Prime rate** is the lowest rate banks charge their best commercial customers. Here, the prime rate serves as the index and the additional percentage serves as the lender's margin. A **margin** is the *difference between the index value and the interest rate charged on an ARM.* The lender adds a margin to the index to ensure sufficient income for administrative expenses and profit.

The prime rate is rarely used for long-term home mortgages because, for these types of loans, lenders like to choose an index that is more responsive to actual economic fluctuations and takes into consideration other risk factors.

Let's look at a hypothetical illustration where a lender chose Treasury securities:

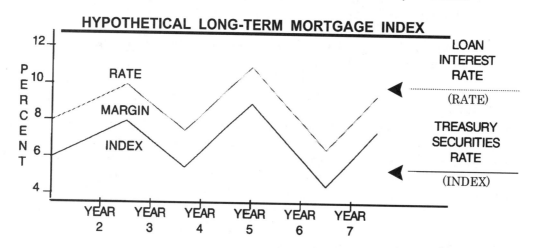

In the previous illustration, you can see the interest *rate* runs roughly parallel to the Treasury securities *index*, but is always a few percentage points above it. This is the *margin* the lender added to the index. In fact, between lenders who use the same index, it's the size of the margin that makes the difference in interest charges a borrower pays (margins for ARMs usually vary from 2% to 3%):

**Index + Margin = Adjustable Interest Rate Borrower Pays on the Loan**

*For Example*

If the current index value is 4.25% and the lender's margin is 2%, the current ARM interest rate will be 6.25%.

Several acceptable indexes are published periodically that are easily available to lenders and borrowers. Three of the most commonly used indexes for ARM loans are:

1. **Average One-year Treasury Constant Maturity Index (TCM)**
   The 12-Month Treasury Average is also known as the Monthly Treasury Average. It is an average of the monthly yields of U.S. Treasury securities adjusted to a constant maturity of one year. This index typically fluctuates slightly more than the COFI index.

2. **Cost of Funds Index of the 11th District Federal Home Loan Bank (COFI)**
   This index is the monthly weighted-average interest rate paid by the 11th Federal Home Loan Bank (FHLB); district savings institutions for savings, checking, advances from the FHLB; and other sources of funds. Historically, the COFI index has not fluctuated as rapidly as market interest rates (prime rate, the discount rate, or Treasury Bill rates).

3. **London InterBank Offering Rate (LIBOR)**
   The LIBOR index is the rate of interest that London banks charge one another. Several different LIBOR rates can be used for ARM indexes including the one-, three-, and six-month, and the one-year. The six-month is the most popular for an ARM index.

Let's compare where these indexes have been from 2005-2010.

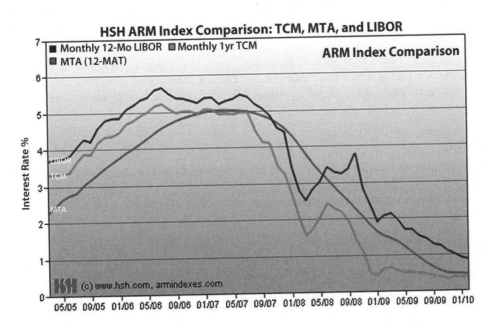

*One-year Treasury (TCN) vs Fannie Mae LIBOR vs MTA (monthly values). Printed with permission of HSH Associates Financial Publishers*

At the time a loan is made, the lender selects an index. Thereafter, the loan interest rate will rise and fall with the rates reported by that index. The index fluctuates (because of market forces) during the term of the loan and causes the borrower's interest rate to increase and decrease, but the lender's margin remains constant.

√ **Note:** The lender has the option of increasing the borrower's interest rate (or leaving it unchanged) when the selected index rises, but if the index falls, a reduction in the borrower's rate is mandatory. Any applicable guidelines or requirements of Fannie Mae, Freddie Mac, and the FHA and/or private mortgage insurers must be followed as well.

## Elements of ARM Loans

There are several elements of an adjustable rate mortgage, including:

- Index
- Margin
- Rate adjustment period
- Interest rate cap (if any)
- Negative amortization (if any)
- Conversion option (if any)

### Index

As future interest rate adjustments for ARM loans are based on the movements of the index, most lenders try to use an index that is responsive to economic fluctuations (TCM, LIBOR, or COFI).

COFI is less volatile than the one-year Treasury index (TCM). In other words, COFI doesn't rise as much over the long term, but it also doesn't fall as much. LIBOR is also becoming more popular. These indexes move in step with other short-term interest rate debt instruments.

From the borrower's perspective, knowing which index is chosen is not as important as knowing whether it is one the lender can or cannot manipulate. The index should be one that is determined and affected by market conditions, and is regularly listed in a major publication.

### Margin

A lender adds a margin (also referred to as a **spread**) to the index to ensure sufficient income for administrative expenses and profit. The lender's margin generally remains fixed for the duration of the loan, and the movement of interest rates or other factors in the financial markets do not affect it.

This is where it benefits customers to shop around for a loan. Margins can vary greatly from one lender to the next, and may vary among loan programs offered by the same lender.

## Rate Adjustment Period

The **rate adjustment period** is the *interval at which a borrower's interest rate changes with ARMs*. This interval can range from monthly to ten years; however, the most common rate adjustment period is every year. After checking movement in the selected index, the lender will notify the borrower, in writing, of any increase or decrease in the rate.

## Interest Rate Cap

**Caps** are *limits*. Interest rate caps are used with ARMs to protect a borrower from large interest rate increases. This is one way lenders limit the magnitude of payment changes that occur with interest rate adjustments. Placing a limit on the number of percentage points an interest rate can be increased during the term of a loan helps eliminate *payment shock*: The result of large and frequent payment increases that may put mortgage payments above the borrower's means.

In addition to protecting borrowers from payment shock, industry leaders (especially secondary market investors) demanded caps on ARMs to protect themselves from portfolio shock (*carrying loans that borrowers no longer have the ability to pay*). Today, most ARMs have some type of cap; this is a result of uniform ARM lending practices combined with a period of self-regulation.

### Fannie Mae and Freddie Mac Caps

Both Fannie Mae and Freddie Mac use guidelines to determine ARM interest rate caps.

|  | Per Year | Over the Life of the Loan |
|---|---|---|
| Fannie Mae | 2% | 6% |
| Freddie Mac | 2% | 5% |

While these guidelines are not necessarily regulations, most lenders include these, or stricter, caps in their loans (especially if they want to sell them on the secondary market).

### FHA/VA Caps

| FHA Loan Type | Per Year | Over the Life of the Loan |
|---|---|---|
| One-year, 3/1 ARMs | 1% | 5% |
| 5/1, 7/1, 10/1 ARMs | 2% | 6% |

## Teaser Rates

**Teaser rates** are *initial interest rates that are much lower than typical adjustable interest rates*. Teaser interest rates usually return to normal after the first adjustment period. They are designed to entice borrowers to accept ARMs because lenders see them as an opportunity to increase earnings and insulate themselves from fluctuations in interest rates.

Initially, teaser rates were offered without caps, which eventually led to payment and portfolio shock. Teaser rates are one of the reasons the movement toward payment caps was so strong. They also led the government to impose regulations on the disclosure of interest rates and the true costs of ARMs.

## Negative Amortization

**Negative amortization** is when a *loan balance increases, rather than decreases, because payments don't cover interest on the loan.* This can be a problem for both borrowers and lenders.

Many lenders view, within acceptable limits, interest rate and payment increases as a way to avoid interest shortfalls and negative amortization. Keep in mind, negative amortization would occur only if interest rates increased several percent a year, for many years, without relief. Negative amortization is most likely to occur when there are frequent rate changes (e.g., every six months) and infrequent payment adjustments (e.g., every three years). If interest rates reach very high levels and/or rise quickly, lenders may rely on negative amortization instead of large payment increases. If the loan balance reaches a certain limit because of negative amortization, the loan is rewritten at the new balance and further negative amortization is prohibited.

## Conversion Option

A **conversion option** in an ARM means the borrower has the right to convert from an adjustable rate to a fixed rate mortgage. ARMs with a conversion option typically include a:

- Higher interest rate (often both the initial and converted rate are higher)
- Limited time to convert (e.g., between the first and fifth year)
- Conversion cost fee

### For Example

A Fannie Mae convertible ARM program may be converted between the 13th and 60th month for a processing fee paid to the lender. The initial rate on the ARM loan is the same as for other Fannie Mae ARMs but, if converted, the fixed rate is 0.125% higher than the standard fixed rate at the time of conversion.

# ARM Loan-to-Value Ratios

ARM loans with loan-to-value ratios (LTVs) of 80%, 90%, and 95% are available. Loans with higher LTVs are often subject to restrictions.

### For Example

Many lenders refuse to make 90% or 95% ARM loans if there's a possibility of negative amortization.

Furthermore, in most cases where borrowers are seeking 90% or 95% ARMs, they'll be required to occupy the property because owner-occupants are considered better credit risks than non-occupant borrowers.

## Fannie Mae and Freddie Mac LTVs for ARMs

Fannie Mae and Freddie Mac have stricter LTV guidelines for ARMs than for fixed-rate loans. LTV *ratios may not exceed 95%* for standard ARMs purchased by Fannie Mae and Freddie Mac. The LTV requirements are based on the potential risk of increasing payments when the interest rate is adjusted.

# ARM Disclosures

Lenders offering residential financing, including ARMs, must comply with federal guidelines under **Regulation Z** of the **Truth in Lending Act**. Regulation Z requires a *general brochure* be given to borrowers, *certain specific disclosures* be made if relevant to the ARM program, and disclosure of the **annual percentage rate (APR)**.

## General Brochure

A lender complies with this requirement by giving loan applicants a booklet called *The Consumer Handbook on Adjustable Rate Mortgages*, prepared by the Federal Reserve and the Federal Home Loan Bank Board. Lenders sometimes refer to this booklet as the **CHARM**.

## Disclosures

Disclosures must be provided to the borrower when the loan application is made or before payment of any non-refundable fees, whichever occurs first. These disclosures must explain how the mortgage works, the terms, and how it will be adjusted. The lender must give the borrower advance notice of any change in payment, interest rate, index, or loan balance. Such disclosures must be given at least 25 days in advance, but not more than 120, before a new payment level takes effect. The lender must also give the borrower an example, based on a $10,000 loan, showing how the payments and loan balance are affected by changes.

## Annual Percentage Rate (APR)

The **annual percentage rate (APR)** is *the relationship between the cost of borrowing money and the total amount financed, represented as a percentage.* **Regulation Z** disclosures regarding the APR cannot be made based solely on an ARMs initial rate. The disclosure of the APR must be based on the initial rate plus the lender's margin, and should reflect a composite annual percentage rate based on the lower rate for a certain number of years and the higher rate for the remaining years on the loan term.

## Best Practices

As an agent, you must always be prepared to answer your customers' questions regarding financing their new home. You are expected to be a knowledgeable real estate professional. When it comes to ARM loans, it is reasonable to expect the following questions.

### 1. What will my interest rate be?

Be sure you know the initial ARM interest rates. Monitor local rates because they change regularly. (The rates are usually published in the Business or Home section of the daily or Sunday newspaper.) At first, a buyer will be more concerned with the total rate, but as the home purchase gets closer, a buyer may be interested in more specific information. Refer the buyer to the lender for specifics.

### 2. How often will my interest rate change?

Rate adjustments will be explained in detail in the loan papers and in the disclosures available from the lender.

### 3. Is there any limit to how much my interest rate can increase?

Most ARMs have interest rate caps. The most common annual interest rate caps are usually 1%–2%; the most common life-of-the-loan caps are 5% and 6% and are set by Fannie Mae and Freddie Mac; FHA caps are 1% and 5% for some programs and 2% and 6% for other programs. Refer the buyer to the lender for specifics.

(continued on next page)

## Best Practices (continued)

**4. Is there a limit to how much my payment can increase at any one time?**

Some ARMs have payment caps while others keep increases under control with interest rate caps. If there are payment caps, they're usually 7.5%–15% of the payment amount, which is equal to about a 1%–2% interest rate change.

**5. What is the probability of runaway negative amortization?**

This is not very likely. Interest rate caps, negative amortization caps, and re-amortization requirements protect both the borrower and lender. Of course, if interest rates rise sharply and rapidly, there's always a possibility for negative amortization. But with the changing nature of money markets, interest rates have not increased dramatically. They rise and fall, so the borrower's rate will increase at one interval and be reduced at another. If there's negative amortization at one point, when interest due exceeds interest paid, there's a good chance that soon afterwards, index declines will result in accelerated amortization. This up and down pattern, though unpredictable, should continue through the life of the loan.

**6. Can my ARM be converted to a fixed-rate loan?**

Many ARMs now have conversion options that allow borrowers to convert to fixed rate loans, for a fee, at certain periods or points in the loan term. ARMs with conversion options often have higher interest rates than those without. Check the loan documents and disclosures, and ask about the lender's policies.

# Other Structured Mortgages

This section is a catch-all for other types of mortgages and alternative financing tools that can help borrowers achieve their goals. If a borrower has a definite financing goal, there's probably a way to structure a mortgage to reach it. Let's look at a few common types of structured mortgages.

## Bi-weekly Mortgage

A **bi-weekly mortgage** is a *fixed-rate mortgage set up like a standard 30-year conventional loan.* The main difference is that the *borrower makes a payment every two weeks instead of once a month.* This alternative financing tool can help a borrower pay off a mortgage earlier, thus saving thousands in interest. Bi-weekly mortgages save interest because 26 payments are made each year, which is equal to one extra monthly payment. Bi-weekly loans are usually paid off in about 24.8 years, instead of 30 years. Let's look at an example:

### $70,000/5.75%/30-year Amortization

| Payment Schedule | Payment Amount | Number of Payments | Total Amount Paid |
| --- | --- | --- | --- |
| Monthly | $408.50 | 360 | $147,060 |
| Bi-weekly | $204.25 | 643 (approximately) | $131,332 |

Bi-weekly mortgages do require more servicing for lenders, and they can be an extra burden for borrowers. Because Fannie Mae does purchase bi-weekly mortgages, it can alleviate some of the lender's burden. Many regular monthly loans allow borrowers to make extra payments, but it requires discipline on the part of the borrower to make them voluntarily.

Some third-party companies claim to offer a means for borrowers to deposit bi-weekly payments with them, but borrowers need to research these carefully because some of them do not pay the lender early (so much of the interest savings is lost). Instead, they simply collect 52 weekly payments, which amounts to a 13th monthly payment to the lender to help reduce the balance and interest faster (but much less quickly than true bi-weekly payments).

## Reverse Mortgage

A **reverse mortgage** is *when a homeowner mortgages her home and, in return, receives a monthly check from the lender*. Reverse equity mortgages help elderly homeowners maintain financial security or achieve other financial goals by converting their home's equity into cash.

A reverse mortgage borrower must be over age 62 and own a home with little or no outstanding mortgage. *The monthly payment depends on the appraised value of the home, the age of the homeowner, the length of the loan, when the loan must be repaid, and the amount of interest charged.* The most popular reverse mortgage programs are lump sum, monthly payment, line of credit, or a combination of the three.

## Shared Appreciation Mortgage (SAM)

A **shared appreciation mortgage (SAM)** is a loan where *the lender charges below-market interest in exchange for a share of the borrower's equity*. This can help a lender or borrower achieve various goals, including shared risk and/or shared reward, on commercial projects.

## Graduated Payment Mortgage (GPM)

A **graduated payment mortgage,** often referred to as **GPM**, is a mortgage with *low initial monthly payments, which gradually increase over time*. With a graduated payment mortgage, the borrower starts by making the lowest monthly payment allowed. Over time, typically 5 to 15 years, monthly payments increase every year by a predetermined percentage.

### For Example

A borrower has a 30-year graduated payment mortgage with monthly payments that increase by 7% every year for five years. At the end of five years, the increases stop. The borrower then pays this new increased amount monthly for the rest of the 25-year loan term.

## Interest Only Mortgage

An **interest-only mortgage loan** is a *non-amortized home loan where, for a set period (usually early in the loan), the majority of the monthly payment goes toward interest; payments are due at regular, pre-determined intervals*. In the U.S., that period often ranges from 5, 10, or 15 years (exact terms vary from lender to lender). At maturity, or the remainder of the loan period, the balance of the loan amount due is paid at regular monthly intervals.

## Hybrid ARMs

Often advertised as 3/1, 5/1, or 7/1 ARMs, these loans are a mix, or a hybrid, of a fixed-rate period and an adjustable-rate period. The interest rate is fixed for the first few years of the loans (e.g., five years in a 5/1 ARM). After that, the rate may adjust annually until the loan is paid off. In the case of 3/1, 5/1, or 7/1 ARMs, the first number tells you the fixed interest rate period and the second number tells you how often the rate will adjust after the initial period.

Lenders often quote hybrid ARMs for potential buyers due to the popularity of this type of loan product.

You may have also seen ads in the past for 2/28 or 3/27 ARMs. The first number indicated how long the fixed interest rate period was, and the second number indicated the number of years the rates on the loan would be adjustable. Some 2/28 and 3/27 mortgages adjusted every six months, not annually.

# Structured Mortgages That are No Longer Available

Some loan types that were popular in the past (e.g., **subprime loans, low doc** or **no doc loans**) are no longer available due to the tightening of mortgage qualifications after the mortgage crisis of 2007. However, real estate professionals may encounter clients who are still paying off these types of loans, or who obtained them in the past and are curious as to why they are longer an option.

## Growth Equity Mortgage

A **growth equity mortgage (GEM)** was a *fixed rate mortgage set up like a 30-year conventional loan, but payments increased regularly, like an ARM*. This was an alternative financing tool that helped a borrower reach the goals of paying off a mortgage faster and of saving interest. The fixed interest rate of a GEM allowed 100% of the annual payment increases to reduce the principal balance.

## Low Doc or No Doc Loans

As their name implies, **low doc loans** and **no doc loans** were mortgage loans that *required less than full documentation of income, employment, and assets*. The name is a bit of a misnomer because the borrowers still had to complete a loan application (although they actually had to fill out less of the application) and have a credit report pulled. An appraisal of the subject property was still required. The loans ranged from stated income to stated assets to no ratio loans, and were mostly dependent on the amount of the buyer's down payment combined with how good their credit score was.

## Option or Payment Option ARMs.

Payment option ARMs were one of the fastest growing types of mortgages before the mortgage crisis in 2007. A **payment option ARM** was an *adjustable rate mortgage that allowed the borrower to choose among several payment options each month*. The options typically included:

- **Traditional payment of principal and interest,** which reduced the amount owed on the mortgage. Payments were based on a set loan term, such as a 15-, 30-, or 40-year payment schedule.

- **Interest-only payment,** which paid the interest but did not reduce the amount owed on the loan principal.

- **Minimum (or limited) payment** that may have been less than the amount of interest due that month and may not have reduced the amount owed on the mortgage. The amount of interest not paid was added to the principal of the loan, which **increased the amount owed and future monthly payments**, and increased the amount of interest paid over the life of the loan.

The interest rate on a payment option ARM was typically very low for the first few months, six months, or one year. (e.g., 2% for the first one to three months). After that, the interest rate typically rose to a rate closer to that of other mortgage loans. Payments during the first year were based on the initial low rate, meaning that if only the minimum payment was made each month, it did not reduce the principal and may not have covered the interest due. The unpaid interest was added to the amount owed and the loan balance increased, resulting in negative amortization.

Payment option ARMs had a built-in recalculation period, usually every five years. At this point, the monthly payment was recalculated (lenders used the term *"recast"*) based on the remaining term of the loan.

At the end of year 5 of a 30-year loan, the payment for the remaining 25 years was recalculated. If the loan balance increased because only minimum payments were made, or if interest rates rose, payments increased each time the loan was recast. At each recast, the new minimum payment was fully amortized and payment caps did not apply. This meant the monthly payment could increase greatly at each recast.

Lenders may have recalculated loan payments before the recast period if the amount of principal owed grew beyond a pre-set limit, usually 110%, or 125% of the original mortgage amount.

## For Example

Only minimum payments were made on a $200,000 mortgage and any unpaid interest was added to the balance. If the balance grew to $250,000 (125% of $200,000), the lender would recalculate the payments so the loan could still be paid off by the end of the term. It was likely payments would go up substantially.

## Subprime Loans (B/C Loans)

Generally, **subprime mortgages** were for *borrowers with credit scores that did not meet traditional, conforming, or FHA/VA guidelines.* In general, credit scores range from around 300 to 850, with most consumers landing in the 600s and 700s. Those who are habitually late in paying bills, and especially those who fall behind on debts by 30, 60, 90 days, or more, suffer plummeting credit scores. Those consumers who fell below traditional guidelines were in subprime territory.

Few lenders used the term "subprime" to describe these consumers or loans because it was considered bad salesmanship. The word "non-prime" was used or, more likely, an adjective wasn't used to describe the mortgage at all.

Mortgages for those with excellent credit are somewhat a commodity, with rates that don't vary much from lender to lender for equivalent loans. That's wasn't the case with subprime mortgages. Clients may have received widely differing offers from different subprime lenders because of different ways of weighing the risk of granting credit. For that reason, it was important to comparison shop when a credit score was low.

Subprime loans usually had higher rates than equivalent prime loans. Lenders considered many factors when they came up with mortgage rates and terms, using a process called risk-based pricing. This made it impossible to generalize subprime rates. They were higher, but how much higher depended on factors such as credit score, down payment, and what types of delinquencies the borrower had in the recent past (from a mortgage lender's standpoint, late mortgage or rent payments were worse than late credit card payments). A subprime loan also was more likely to have a prepayment penalty, a balloon payment, or both.

## Predatory Lending

Predatory tactics were sometimes used to get a customer to take a subprime loan. Some lenders charged naive borrowers outrageous fees and sky-high interest rates. These lenders were likely to tell the borrower that his credit score was lower than it really was. Another predatory tactic was to pressure a homeowner to refinance the mortgage frequently, charging high closing fees each time, and rolling the closing costs into the mortgage amount. That goes hand-in-hand with another predatory tactic: Issuing a loan regardless of the borrower's ability to repay it. When the borrower inevitably defaulted, the predatory lender foreclosed and sold the property.

An ethical mortgage lender doesn't want to foreclose on a property because it is a costly process. An ethical lender makes money by charging interest and loses money by foreclosing. A predatory lender, on the other hand, profits by repeatedly collecting closing fees, then seizing the house.

### Best Practices

Most real estate agents do not hold dual licenses as mortgage brokers or financial consultants. The alternative financing arena, unfortunately, is full of hazards for real estate professionals. Be careful to not overstep your bounds by making lender and program recommendations you do not understand and are not qualified to explain. Always recommend more than one lending source and encourage buyers to shop around to get professional advice.

# Homebuyer Assistance Programs

**Homebuyer assistance programs** can include down payment assistance (sometimes referred to collectively as **DAP programs**), subsidized mortgage interest rates, help with closing costs, or a combination of these. These programs may be offered by government or non-profit organizations to promote home ownership or by lenders as part of their obligation under the Community Reinvestment Act.

Some programs allow people to buy homes with lower down payments than conventional loans, often 3% or less. This type of assistance may be offered by cities, counties, or the state and the money may be targeted to specific neighborhoods. Often a portion or all of the required down payment is paid on behalf of the buyer. Money for these programs is limited and administered on a first-come, first-served basis. Various bond issues or levies may replenish the funding for the program, but it is hard to predict when money will become available. Some non-profit organizations also provide grants, gifts, or otherwise arrange money for down payment.

Interest rate subsidies may also be obtained from a variety of sources. Ohio bond money is available from time-to-time, whereby the state issues bonds and uses the funds to subsidize the interest rate paid on mortgages by low-income families. Underwriting requirements are the same as they are for conventional, FHA, VA, and rural housing loans, but the interest rate is lower.

## Ohio Housing Finance Agency

One program that offers both down payment assistance and interest rate subsidies is available through the **Ohio Housing Finance Agency (OHFA)**. This is a state agency that assists first-time homebuyers or people who haven't owned a home in the past three years. Agents should check with a lender to make sure that the OHFA has funding for loans.

> √ **Note:** The three-year requirement is waived for borrowers who are qualifying veterans or buying in a *targeted* area (economically distressed areas as designated by HUD).

Help is available through a 2.5% down payment assistance grant to qualified borrowers based on the purchase price of the home or a 3% grant from a second mortgage. These are low-interest loans to reduce monthly mortgage payments, or money that can be applied toward the buyer's closing costs. Participants in OHFA's program must meet federal income guidelines and home sale price restrictions; minimum credit scores may apply. Maximum allowable sale prices vary for new and existing homes, and for targeted and non-targeted areas.

Other programs are available for military personnel, firefighters, emergency medical technicians, health care providers, police, and K-12 teachers. OHFA even has a program designed for recent college graduates.

> √ **Note:** For information and availability go to http://www.ohiohome.org.

## Community Reinvestment Act (CRA)

The **Community Reinvestment Act (CRA)** is a federal law passed in 1977 and updated in 1995 to emphasize that regulated *financial institutions have a continuing obligation to help meet the credit needs of the local communities in which they operate (especially low-income neighborhoods)*. CRA requires each lender's record in this area be evaluated periodically, and considered in conjunction with any application for deposit facilities or merger and acquisition requests.

**First Time Home Buyer Loans** or **Community Home Buyer Programs** are some of the generic names for the various programs lenders have created in response to the Community Reinvestment Act. The Act requires lenders to offer financing more flexible than conforming loans in regard to credit, income, and down payment as a means of supporting the community. The law does not require lenders to make high-risk loans, but loans in the community should be made whenever possible while maintaining the safety of the institution. Buyers may have to complete a course on financial responsibility to qualify for a loan.

All of these government and private sector programs have numerous rules buyers must follow to qualify for the assistance program. Nevertheless, the programs offer hope to some who otherwise might not be able to buy a home on their own. Supporters of these programs applaud the fact that they help more people buy homes; detractors worry about high potential default rates for people with little money to put down on a home or money to spend on upkeep.

# Seller Financing

Another possibility when discussing alternative financing tools is seller-assisted financing. **Seller financing** is *when a seller extends credit to a buyer to finance the purchase of the property;* this can be instead of, or in addition to, the buyer obtaining a loan from a third party, such as an institutional lender. Seller financing includes seller first mortgages, seller second or piggyback mortgages, land contracts, loan assumptions, or even lease-option or lease purchase transactions. The goal is to get buyers into homes they may not usually be able to purchase and provide sellers with options that enable them to sell their home.

A seller may help with financing for several reasons:

- The buyer may be unable to come up with all the cash necessary for a conventional mortgage down payment.

- The buyer may be unable to qualify for a loan from a lender for various reasons.

- In buyer's markets, sometimes the only way sellers can make a deal is to finance part of the purchase price themselves.

- Mortgage money from traditional lenders may be too costly, in terms of interest rates, or may be simply unavailable.

In any case, sellers can often enhance the salability of their properties by offering complete or partial financing. Two of the most common seller financing vehicles are **purchase money mortgages** and **land contracts**.

## Purchase Money Mortgage

A **purchase money mortgage** is *a mortgage given by a buyer to a seller to secure part or all of the money borrowed to purchase property*. An individual seller can be a mortgagee just as easily as an institutional lender can. The central advantage of this arrangement is that sellers are not bound by institutional policies regarding loan ratios, interest rates, or qualifying standards. To make the sale, a seller may finance all or part of the purchase price for the buyer, relying on the mortgage as security. If the seller finances the entire purchase, he is in a first lien position. The seller may charge a below market interest rate, and may offer financing to a buyer considered a credit risk by institutional lenders. Whether the seller finances all or part of the purchase, they are taking a risk; but the risk may be justified if it allows the sale to proceed or enables the seller to get a higher price for the home. Of course, with any form of seller financing, the seller must not need an immediate cash-out from the sale.

If the seller does not need immediate cash, purchase money financing can be advantageous for several reasons:

- It can mean the difference between selling and not selling a home.

- A seller can often get a higher price for a home.

- It may be a tax benefit.

In regard to taxation, since the seller receives the profit from the sale of the home over several years, the seller may benefit from a lower rate of income taxation. Taking the full profit at the time of sale could push the seller into a higher tax bracket; but when the profit is paid on an installment basis over time, only the amount actually received is considered taxable income for the year. At the very least, the seller gets the benefit of deferred taxation until the money is actually received, and the seller may get a desired income stream.

## Best Practices

The seller's property must be free and clear of all mortgages or the seller will have a problem with the alienation or due on sale clause that requires the loan to be paid off if the ownership of the property is transferred. It is important for a buyer to determine if a property has financial encumbrances and to consult with a real estate attorney for drawing up the documents needed for seller financing.

# Purchase Money Second Mortgage

A **purchase money second mortgage** is in a *second lien position*. If the seller finances only part of the purchase price, he would be in a junior lien position with the institutional lender taking the first lien position. Even in cases where there's an assumable loan, or where the buyer can obtain financing from an institutional lender, it may be beneficial for the seller to provide additional financing in the form of a second mortgage. If the buyer doesn't have sufficient cash to cover the difference between the sale price and the institutional financing, a purchase money second mortgage can become the key to closing the sale.

## For Example

Chris owns property with an existing $90,000 mortgage. The mortgage is assumable, and has 120 payments of $750 remaining. Pat is interested in buying the property, but doesn't have the $45,000 cash needed to meet the sale price of $135,000. Pat offers to buy the house with a $20,000 down payment if Chris will take a second mortgage for the remaining $25,000. Chris agrees and the sale is finalized.

## Loan Assumption

**Assumption** of a loan means that *one party agrees to take over payments of another party's debt, with the terms of the note remaining the same.* The FHA and VA permit assumptions (with a credit check of the buyer).

√ **Note:** Always consult the lender or a lawyer before discussing loan assumptions with your buyers.

Buyers can simply agree to take over the payment of the seller's debt and the terms of the note remain the same. The property is still security for the loan, but the buyer becomes primarily liable for repayment. A seller needs to get permission from the lender for a loan assumption and the new buyer needs to be approved by the lender. This ensures that the seller is not liable if the buyer defaults on the loan. This is usually referred to as getting a *"full release of liability."*

## Land Contract

A **land contract** is *a real estate installment agreement where the buyer makes payments to the seller in exchange for the right to occupy and use the property, but no deed or title is transferred until all, or a specified portion, of the payments have been made.*

√ ***Remember:*** The seller retains legal title to the subject property; the buyer becomes only an owner in fact, having possession and *equitable title*, but no actual title and no deed.

**Equitable title** is *an interest in real property created upon the execution of a valid sales contract.* Even though actual title won't be transferred until a future date, the person holding equitable title still enjoys certain rights and privileges (e.g., the benefit of minerals found on the land after a valid sales contract was signed and entered into, but before the passage of actual title to the new owner).

In its simplest form, the land contract is made by a seller who owns the property free and clear. Such a seller need only negotiate the term and interest rate of the contract, along with the amount of down payment, if any.

Land contracts are a popular form of purchase money financing in some parts of Ohio, especially in rural areas or for buying homes that may not be suitable for regular financing (e.g., mobile homes, vacant land).

### Advantages and Disadvantages

Land contracts have many of the same advantages and disadvantages as purchase money mortgages:

| Advantages | Disadvantages |
|---|---|
| • Freedom from institutional loan qualifying standards<br>• Deferral of income taxation<br>• Flexibility of terms | • Can't be resold to Fannie Mae (although a few private secondary market investors may be willing to buy them) |

### Best Practices

Land contracts, if not properly prepared, can be a source of trouble for buyers, sellers, and agents. Contracts and contract clauses are complex and have unforeseen legal ramifications. You should never attempt to write land contract terms, clauses, or any other legal clause or document yourself. This may be considered unauthorized practice of law, and can be grounds for license suspension, revocation, or other disciplinary action. It is also a disservice to your clients and might even result in a lawsuit against you and/or your broker. Always recommend that all parties involved in a transaction seek competent, professional legal advice.

## Lease/Options

A **lease/option** is *when a seller leases property to someone for a specific term, with an option to buy the property at a predetermined price during the lease term.* The lease/option plan is comprised of two elements:

• **Lease**—A contract where one party pays rent to the other in exchange for possession of real estate

- **Option**—A contract giving one party the right to do something within a designated time, without obligating him to do it

Obviously, the lease/option is not the equivalent of a sale, but there's at least a good possibility that a sale will eventually take place.

The option agreement retains rights, for a predetermined period of time, to make an offer to purchase or to sell the property at a predetermined price. The *prospective purchaser* is the **optionee**; the *property owner* is the **optionor**. For the most part, the option contract assures the optionee the right to purchase the property. Usually, the optionee is interested in the property, but won't exercise his right to complete the purchase unless certain terms are met or questions are answered beforehand.

Some of the instances in which an option might be used include:

- **Profit**—A prospective buyer plans on selling the option to someone else for a profit
- **Speculation**—A prospective buyer thinks the property will increase in value (e.g., based on a change in zoning)
- **Investment**—A prospective buyer thinks the property is a good investment, but wants to find other investors willing to share the risk
- **Comparison**—A prospective buyer thinks the property is a good deal, but wants to investigate other properties before coming to a final decision
- **Time to acquire cash**—A prospective buyer needs time to get the cash needed to close
- **Qualifying**—A prospective buyer can't qualify for a loan now, but believes circumstances will change shortly (e.g., raise at work)
- **Rent credit**—The property owner agrees to credit part of the lease payments to the down payment, loan amount, or sale price, thus reducing the cost and making it easier for the prospective buyer to obtain the property

## Consideration for an Option

An **option** is simply another *type of contract*. So, like all contracts, an option must be supported by *consideration* to be enforceable. **Consideration** is *anything of value given to induce another person to enter into a contract*. Here, consideration is given by the optionee to the optionor in return for a commitment to sell the property to the optionee at some time in the future. The consideration is usually a sum of money (sometimes called **option money**), but it can be anything of value.

Once paid, the option money is not refundable, regardless of whether the optionee proceeds with the purchase. If the buyer chooses not to exercise the option to buy, the seller keeps the money as compensation for keeping the property off the market and not selling it to anyone else during the option period. In many instances, buyers and sellers agree that if the purchase actually goes through, the option money will be credited to the purchase price, much like a good faith deposit in an ordinary purchase and sale agreement. This is not always the case, however, so such an arrangement should be clearly spelled out in the option contract. In fact, if the buyer and the seller have not clearly agreed in the written option contract to credit the option money against the purchase price, it's presumed that the balance due is the full price stated in the option (not including the option money).

### How Does a Lease/Option Work?

The seller/lessor leases the property to the buyer/tenant for a specific term (e.g., six months, one year) with the provision that part of the rental payments may be applied to the purchase price if the tenant decides to buy before the lease expires.

### Advantages and Disadvantages

| Advantages | Disadvantages |
|---|---|
| • Keeps a sale alive until the parties are in a position to close | • Seller cannot sell the property to anyone other than the tenant during the term of the option |
| • Allows buyer to reduce the selling price over time, making it easier to come up with a down payment or to qualify for a loan when the option is exercised. Some sellers will allow a small part of the lease payment to go towards the eventual closing. This is done as an incentive to the buyer to close and reduces what he has to come up with at the closing. | • Used only when it seems unlikely that additional/better offers will be forthcoming in the near future |
| • Buyer gets advantage of occupying and using the property during the option period | • Sellers cannot occupy the property during the term of the lease (this plan normally involves sellers who have already purchased a new property or who have been holding the subject property as an investment rather than for personal use) |
| • Seller receives income from the property, which can be used to make payments on a new property, or to cover payments on existing financing | |

## Lease/Purchase

A **lease/purchase** is *when a seller leases property to someone for a specific term, with the tenant agreeing to buy the property at a set price during or following the lease term*. The lease/purchase plan is comprised of two elements:

- **Lease**
- **Purchase contract**

The lease/purchase is the equivalent of a sale, but there are additional considerations to take into account because the sale is delayed until a later date.

The purchase agreement locks in a predetermined price for the property and sets a date for the sale transaction to be completed. Here, the buyer is interested in the property and committed to its purchase, but can't buy it right away until certain issues are resolved or other events take place.

Some instances when a lease/purchase might be used include:

- **Time to acquire cash**—A buyer needs time to get the cash needed to close. Here, the buyer must have a definite plan (e.g., house for sale, large commission check coming) in order to commit to a lease/purchase.

- **Qualifying**—A buyer knows circumstances will change shortly, so he can qualify for the loan. Here again, the buyer must have a definite plan (e.g., raise scheduled in a work contract, large debt that will be paid off shortly) in order to commit to a lease/purchase.

- **Rent credit**—The seller agrees to credit part of the lease payments to the down payment, loan amount, or sale price, thus reducing the cost and making it easier for the buyer to obtain the property.

## How Does a Lease/Purchase Work?

The seller/lessor leases the property to the buyer/tenant for a specific term (e.g., six months, one year) with the provision that part of the rental payments may be applied to the purchase price. In addition to a lease agreement, a purchase agreement is also prepared which spells out the terms and conditions of the purchase, as well as the date it is to take place. Both contracts must conform to all laws governing real estate contracts.

## Advantages and Disadvantages

| Advantages | Disadvantages |
|---|---|
| • Guarantees a sale by locking the parties into an agreement (makes the transaction a certainty, as opposed to a lease/option)<br><br>• Allows the buyer (by making monthly payments) to reduce the final sale price over time, making it easier to come up with a down payment or to qualify for a loan when the purchase date comes<br><br>• Buyer can occupy and use the property during the lease<br><br>• Seller receives income from the property and is assured a sale by a certain date | • Buyer and seller are locked in the transaction (buyer can't change his mind; seller can't sell to anyone other than the tenant, even if a better deal comes along)<br><br>• Seller can't occupy property during the term of the lease (this plan normally involves sellers who have already bought another property or who don't need immediate cash from the property to use for the purchase of another one) |

# Equity Exchange

An **equity exchange** is *when value in one property is traded for value in another*. This is also called a **tax-deferred exchange**, **tax-free exchange,** or **Section 1031** (referencing the section number of IRS law). General rules for a tax-deferred equity exchange of real estate are:

• The properties must be exchanged, or qualify as **delayed exchange** (promise to provide a replacement within 45 days and closed within 180 days)

• The properties must be **like-kind property** (real estate for real estate)

• The properties must be held for **use in a trade or business,** or held by the party **as an investment**

When property is exchanged as part of an equity exchange, the parties defer paying taxes until a **capital gain** (*profit*) is actually realized from the transaction (usually means when the property is sold in the future). If the transaction does qualify as a tax-free exchange, any gain that is purely a result of the exchange is deferred. The succeeding property may be sold again as a 1031 exchange as long as the rules are followed. However, any property or money that does not qualify (is not like-kind property held for income, business, or investment) is taxable.

Equity exchanges are often used when a buyer can't come up with sufficient cash for a purchase. The difference between what the buyer has in cash and the purchase price of the property can be made up with other assets the seller would be willing to accept as part of the down payment. (e.g., land, another house, cars, boats, any other property in which the buyer has an equity interest). If the equity exchange involves real estate that meets the IRS criteria mentioned previously, there are no immediate tax consequences for the seller.

A tax-free exchange is not available for owner-occupied properties or for property held for sale by a **dealer** (person who holds property for the sole purpose of reselling it). Always seek professional tax advice and legal counsel for any transaction involving equity exchanges or tax deferrals.

## Participation Plan

Primarily used in the financing of commercial real estate, a **participation plan** is *when a buyer and another investor (or seller, lender, etc.) enter into a partnership, with the buyer paying an equity share in lieu of interest.* This is also called a **shared equity plan**. In a participation plan, the buyer enters into a form of partnership with an investor who provides cash for the sale. The investor may be the seller, a bank, or any private investor.

Instead of charging interest, the investor in a participation plan receives a percentage of the equity (the difference between the property's value and the indebtedness secured by the property). The buyer must still make principal payments, although these may be deferred. Different investors have varying requirements as to the percentage of equity shared and the method of repaying the investment. These issues are a matter of institutional policy or negotiation between the buyer and the investor.

### Best Practices

We've discussed a few creative financing arrangements in this chapter, but this is by no means a comprehensive list. Some things we discussed earlier, like a builder-paid buydown, can also be classified as seller financing. The old saying, "Where there's a will, there's a way" is the focal point of creative financing. The advantages of open-minded negotiation among buyers, sellers, lenders, and agents can't be overemphasized.

## Selecting and Executing Seller Financing

Once you know what each party desires from the transaction, a solution can be found and seller financing may help everyone reach their goals. It all comes down to a matter of negotiating *price versus terms*, and finding out which is most important to the parties. A seller can get a better price if he is willing to be more generous on the loan terms.

Conversely, buyers who want or need especially good terms are usually not in a position to dictate price. There's always give and take because the issue of price versus terms (payments or interest rate) is a trade-off. Your broker's experience and guidance can help you see the numerous possibilities that can help your clients get what they want to close the transaction.

The variety of creative financing plans is almost without limit, which makes it very important that the rights and obligations of all parties—buyer, seller, lender (if any), and real estate agent—be taken into account. This requires real estate professionals involved in negotiating creative transactions to be well informed, take particular care to represent their clients properly, and make necessary disclosures. Until you have much more experience, you should *not* be negotiating these transactions on your own. Ask your broker about his policies, procedures, and for advice. And always get your broker involved throughout the process. Finally, it's always advisable to seek the counsel of real estate attorneys, tax consultants, and/or certified public accountants to ensure the transaction closes without problems (now or down the road).

## FINANCE EXERCISE 6-2

A borrower wants to buy a $150,000 home, and plans to make a $15,000 down payment. The borrower is seeking a conventional loan but doesn't want to pay more than 6.5% interest. The lender agrees to make a 6.5% interest loan if it is discounted three points.

1. What's the total number of points (in dollars and percentage) the lender will receive for making this loan?

2. If the seller agrees to pay the discount points, how much will the seller net from the transaction? (Assume seller pays no other costs.)

*See Appendix for answers to check your work.*

## FINANCE EXERCISE 6-3

A borrower secures a 5/1ARM for $152,000. The initial interest rate is 4.5%, but after five years, the rate will go to the LIBOR index (currently at <1% plus 3% margin). The interest rate will be adjusted annually. Rate caps are 2% per year and 5% over the life of the loan.

1. What is the index and margin on this loan?

2. What's the highest the rate can be at the beginning of the sixth year?

3. What is the highest rate the borrower would ever have?

4. What is the lowest rate the borrower would ever have?

5. Is negative amortization likely to occur on this loan?

*See Appendix for answers to check your work.*

# Summary

1.  **Alternative financing** means real estate is financed with terms or concessions other than those typical for conventional loans. Alternative financing tools can help buyers qualify for larger loans, or help them reach other financial goals. The most popular alternative financing tools are buydowns and adjustable rate mortgages (ARMs). Other types include hybrid ARMs and homebuyer assistance programs.

2.  **Buydowns** are points (or additional money) paid to the lender at the beginning of a loan term to lower interest rate and payments. Discount points are paid to lenders to make up the difference between the market interest rate and the rate the buyer gets in the note. One point equals 1% of the loan amount. Buydowns are often paid by the seller: The home sells with less difficulty since the buyer qualifies more easily (lower rate equals lower payment). A permanent buydown (for the life of the loan) has a reduced rate stated in note. A temporary buydown (early in loan) can be a graduated payment (e.g., 2-1). The Fannie Mae/Freddie Mac limit on seller paid payments is three points when LTV is greater than 90% and six points when LTV is less than 90%. Effective April 2010, the FHA limit on seller paid payments is six points.

3.  **ARMs** let lenders adjust interest rates. The lender picks an *index* (statistical report reflecting cost of money) and adds a *margin* (profit margin), which results in the *rate* paid on the loan. Loan documents state the rate, index, margin, and payment adjustment period; caps (if any) on rate, payments or negative amortization; and conversion option (if any). The rate and payment don't have to adjust at the same time. If the rate changes more often than payments are received, *negative amortization* (loan balance grows from deferred interest) occurs. Caps keep loans from growing out of control. Conversion option: Buyer can convert to fixed rate (limited).

4.  Other limits on ARMs: Fannie Mae/Freddie Mac LTV limited to 95%. ARM rules under Regulation Z of Truth in Lending Act: Brochure is given to buyer, specific disclosures are made, and annual percentage rate (APR) is disclosed. The APR is the composite rate: It reflects a lower rate for a certain number of years and a higher rate for later years. Lenders can't disclose only the initial low rate (teaser rate).

5.  Other alternative financing can help borrowers reach other financial goals. *Bi-weekly*: Payments every two weeks so balance is paid faster because money is saved in interest. *Growth equity*: Fixed rate, but payments increase to pay off balance faster. *Reduction option*: Buyer can reduce rate once, with less of a cost to refinance. *Reverse*: People over the age of 62 get a monthly check from the lender. *Shared appreciation*: Lender shares equity in a commercial project.

6.  **Subprime loans** had more risk than generally allowed by the conventional market and after the mortgage crisis of 2007 are virtually unavailable. Homebuyer assistance programs can consist of down payment assistance programs (called DAP programs), subsidized mortgage interest rates, help with closing costs, or a combination of these. Programs can be offered by government, non-profit groups, or by lenders as an obligation under the Community Reinvestment Act.

7.  **Seller financing** is when the seller extends credit (all or partial) to the buyer to finance the purchase of property. This can help a buyer who doesn't have enough cash to buy a property, can't qualify for a conventional loan, or wants/needs a lower-than-market interest rate. The seller gets the benefit of selling the home with less difficulty, can often get a better price by offering terms, and gets tax deferment on the gain from the home sale.

8. A **purchase money mortgage** is given by the buyer to the lender or seller to secure part or all of the money borrowed to purchase property. It can be done only if the seller doesn't need all the cash from the deal. The seller can finance all (first mortgage) or part (second mortgage) of the purchase price. Unencumbered property with no liens is easiest since the transaction is between the buyer and seller. Encumbered property with liens requires a loan assumption. *Assumption* is when the buyer takes responsibility for the mortgage, but the seller must get a release. (An alienation clause can stop this.) A land contract is an installment contract where the buyer pays the seller for possession of property, but the seller keeps the title until all (or some) payments have been made.

9. **Lease/option** is when the seller leases the subject property and the tenant has the right (but no obligation) to buy it at a set price within a certain time. An option can be used for profit, speculation, investment, comparison, or to give buyer time to acquire cash, time to qualify, or extend rent credit toward the purchase price. An option needs consideration (option money). The contract should say how much option money and what portion of the lease payments go toward the purchase price. A lease/option can keep the sale alive, but the buyer may change his mind. A lease/purchase is better for the seller because it locks in a sale date.

10. **Equity exchange** (tax-deferred exchange, Section 1031) is when property is traded for value in other property. Properties must be exchanged (or delayed exchange) for like-kind property and held for trade, business, or investment. Capital gains tax is deferred. Tax-free exchange isn't available for residential property. Participation plans have investors share equity instead of getting interest.

# Quiz

1. *The Jones family is buying a home for $105,000 and it appraised for $102,000. On an $80,000 loan, six points is equal to*
   a. $4,800.
   b. $4,896.
   c. $6,120.
   d. $6,300.

2. *If the sale price of a home is $120,000, it appraises for $122,000, and the buyer takes out a loan for $96,000, the discount points charged by the lender are computed on*
   a. $96,000.
   b. $114,000.
   c. $120,000.
   d. $122,000.

3. *Typical "nontraditional financing programs" include*
   a. adjustable rate mortgages.
   b. permanent buydowns.
   c. temporary buydowns.
   d. all of the above

4. *A permanent buydown plan can reduce the borrower's payments*
   a. early in the loan only, but will require a balloon payment at the end of the term.
   b. for the entire life of the loan.
   c. for the entire life of the loan, but with an automatic prepayment penalty.
   d. through gradual payment decreases throughout the life of the loan.

5. *The advantages of a permanent buydown for borrowers include*
   a. easier qualifying standards.
   b. lower monthly payments.
   c. the possibility of qualifying for a larger loan.
   d. all of the above

6. *Adjustable rate mortgages*
   a. allow the lender to adjust the interest rate in accordance with a chosen index at specified intervals.
   b. may cause mortgage payments to increase or decrease over time.
   c. pass part of the risk of interest rate fluctuations from the lender to the buyer.
   d. all of the above

7. *There may be a difference in interest rates among lenders who use the same index primarily because of the*
   a. commissions paid to real estate agents.
   b. lender's stock value.
   c. loan balance.
   d. profit and/or the administrative expenses of the lender.

8. *The margin is the difference between the*
   a. APR and the cost-of-funds index (COFI).
   b. index value and the interest rate charged to the borrower.
   c. value of the home and the amount borrowed.
   d. none of the above

9. *Which is NOT an element of an ARM?*
   a. index
   b. margin
   c. positive amortization cap
   d. rate

10. *Negative amortization occurs when*
    a. interest rate adjustments occur more frequently than mortgage payment adjustments.
    b. the interest rate rises but payments are locked at a low amount due to payment caps.
    c. the loan balance grows from deferred interest.
    d. all of the above

11. *A typical hybrid arm loan might also be called a(n)*
    a. 7/1 ARM.
    b. option ARM.
    c. piggyback loan.
    d. VA loan.

12. *In Ohio, to learn more about first-time homebuyer loans, you should check with the*
    a. Federal Reserve Bank.
    b. Home Loan Bank Board.
    c. Ohio Housing Finance Agency.
    d. Veterans Administration.

13. *A reverse mortgage is available to persons who*
    a. are over age 62.
    b. are under age 55.
    c. own a home with a large outstanding mortgage.
    d. all of the above

14. *Bob, the buyer, takes over Sally's, the seller, mortgage. Bob is now personally liable for the debt and agrees to pay the balance of the purchase price to Sally under a contract. Bob and Sally now have a(n)*
    a. assumption and release.
    b. encumbered property cash-out.
    c. land contract subject to an existing mortgage.
    d. land contract with assumption of an existing mortgage.

15. *One disadvantage to a lease/option agreement is that it*
    a. allows prospective buyers to occupy the property for an extended period of time before a commitment to buy is made.
    b. can result in no sale (and no commission).
    c. requires only a minimal cash investment from the tenant/prospective buyer.
    d. all of the above

# Qualifying the Buyer

As a real estate professional, you must have a thorough understanding of the mortgage loan process. Pre-qualification and pre-approval are concepts you need to become familiar with and understand the differences between the two. We will discuss the process of qualifying buyers for conventional, FHA, and VA loans, as well as standards relating to income, credit history, and net worth. We'll also review the housing expense ratios and total debt service ratios allowed by Fannie Mae, the FHA, and the VA.

## Key Terms

**Assets** Items of value; usually items owned by a borrower.

**Credit History** A person's record of debt repayment detailing how a person paid credit accounts in the past. Credit history is used as a guide to how likely the borrower is to pay accounts on time and as agreed in the future.

**Credit Scoring** A means by which the lender makes certain determinations regarding the creditworthiness of potential borrowers. This involves a lender assigning specified numerical values to different aspects of a borrower.

**Debt** Recurring monetary obligation that cannot be canceled (e.g., monthly bills).

**Housing Expense Ratio** The relationship of a borrower's total monthly housing expense to income, expressed as a percentage.

**Liabilities** Financial obligations or debt. Any money that is owed.

**Pre-Approval** Process by which a lender determines if potential borrowers can be financed through the lender, and for what amount of money.

**Pre-Qualification** Process of pre-determining how large a loan a potential homebuyer might be eligible to borrow. Pre-qualification is typically done by an agent or lender, but it doesn't guarantee approval.

**Reserves** Cash on deposit or other highly liquid assets a borrower must have in order to cover two months of PITI mortgage payments, after they make the cash down payment and pay all closing costs.

(continued on page 155)

# Getting a Buyer Approved

In the past, mortgage loan applications were completed only when buyers were ready to purchase a particular home. For that reason, loan applications ask for detailed information about prospective buyers so lenders can make informed decisions about whether to grant credit. However, there's a growing trend toward pre-approving buyers for loans because, among other things, pre-approval can be a useful negotiating tool. This is not the same as pre-qualifying buyers; the two terms are not interchangeable.

## Pre-Qualification

**Pre-qualification** is the process of pre-determining the loan amount a potential homebuyer may be eligible to borrow. An agent or a lender can pre-qualify a buyer; however, it does *not* guarantee approval. Pre-qualification of a buyer is *not binding on the lender*, which is why the distinction is very important. The lender is only saying it looks favorable that the buyer will be approved. Often, there's more background research and information the lender has not thoroughly investigated, and won't do so until a loan application is submitted.

Pre-qualification is usually a simple process of asking the prospective borrower questions about income and debts. An *in-file credit report* (a quick and summarized credit report) may be pulled by a lender, or the buyer may be asked questions about his financial situation. A real estate agent's pre-qualification of a prospective buyer may be as simple as making sure that the borrower has a steady job and no glaring credit problems (e.g., a recent bankruptcy). Often, a real estate agent will compute the buyer's income and debt ratios, which we will discuss how this is done later, to get an idea of how much house the prospective buyer may be able to afford.

## Pre-Approval

**Pre-approval** is the process by which a lender determines if potential borrowers can be financed, and for what amount of money. Real estate agents can't give a buyer a pre-approval. For pre-approval, a buyer goes through many steps in the loan process. Furthermore, with pre-approval, a lender states that the prospective buyer's situation has been evaluated and, providing all circumstances stay the same, the lender is willing to loan money (up to a specific amount) to the potential buyer. This is helpful when working with buyers and a powerful tool in getting an offer accepted by a seller.

Of course, a buyer's circumstances can and do change and pre-approval from some lenders means more than others. This is where familiarity with the loan process is important and where you should take advantage of the wisdom and experience your broker and other senior real estate professionals in your office can share. Above all else, get pre-approvals from lenders in writing and always follow the policies and procedures established by your broker.

### Best Practices

Many lenders today will offer a pre-approval when what they are issuing is a pre-qualification. Be very careful to discern between the two or you may spend a lot of time and effort working with a buyer who may have hidden credit or loan problems. Read the pre-approval document from the lender carefully and if it is subject to things like "successful credit review," "verification of income and debts," or "underwriting review," your buyers may actually be only pre-qualified. Ask questions to ensure the lender has done all the research necessary to successfully pre-approve the buyers and not just pre-qualify them.

# The Loan Approval Process

The **real estate loan approval process consists of four steps:**

1. Consult with the lender

2. Complete the loan application

3. Process the loan application

4. Analyze the borrower and the subject property

Traditionally, borrowers went to a lender's office for face-to-face meetings. Today, with busy schedules and a competitive environment, many lenders offer the option to meet with the borrower in their home or workplace. And, of course, the Internet provides even more options. Many steps can be accomplished quickly and conveniently online or through other electronic means; from asking initial questions, filling out the loan application, getting final approval, and closing the loan.

Most of this chapter will be presented from the traditional "walk-in and meet the lender" perspective, but we'll also discuss commonly used Internet-based lender processes. Keep in mind that even with variations in the mechanics of the loan process, the steps taken, information needed, and results are the same.

# Consulting with the Lender

Potential borrowers can consult with lenders in a variety of ways, including in-person or online. Before any steps are taken, it's important for the borrower to select the right lender. If a buyer already has a relationship with a lender, this is a good place to start. On the other hand, if a buyer has credit problems, it may be helpful to go through a mortgage company that deals with many different lenders. As buyers decide how to proceed with applying for a loan, they may ask you for advice. To avoid confusion or problems, remember these points:

- Do not interject your own opinion into the situation—let a credit professional, such as a lender, decide the buyers' credit situation.

- Always let clients or customers have the final say as to how they apply for a loan and with whom.

- Disclose the type of compensation you or your broker will receive for a referral.

- Always consult with your broker regarding his policies in all areas before giving any type of advice or recommendation.

Remember, it is the agent's job to educate the buyer about options—not to make the final decisions.

**Stable Income** Income expected to continue in the future.

**Total Debt Service Ratio** The relationship of a borrower's total monthly debt to income, expressed as a percentage. Debt obligations include housing and long-term debts with more than ten payments remaining.

**Underwriter** Individual who evaluates a loan application to determine its risk level for a lender or investor; final decision maker on a loan application.

**Key Terms**

After the buyer selects a lender, initial discussions usually involve the various types of mortgages offered by the lender (e.g., 30-year, 15-year, fixed rate, ARM). This allows the buyer to decide which loan best suits his needs. A buyer will need to give the lender both personal and financial data in order to make the lending decision. Providing this information early will help speed up the approval process.

When going for an actual *loan approval* (not a pre-approval), the purchase and sale agreements may be examined. The lender wants to see if compliance with the terms of the agreement is feasible. Of particular concern is the closing date. Often, a contract will call for a closing date that's too early to be realistic. If it's impossible for the lender to meet the closing date, a more feasible date can be agreed upon by all parties to the contract to avoid frustration. Loan fees must also be discussed.

### Best Practices

It is a good idea for an agent to consult the buyer's lender prior to writing the purchase agreement. The lender will be able to give helpful information regarding costs the buyer will incur and underwriting restrictions that may be encountered. Writing these into the offer in advance will eliminate surprises and addendums as the transaction progresses.

## Common Fees Associated with Real Estate Loans

Buyer's can expect to incur expenses for processing of the real estate loan application, including fees for:

- Pulling a credit bureau report.
- A property appraisal report.
- A preliminary title report.
- Required inspections.

When a loan closes, additional expenses will apply, including title insurance and recording fees. Fees that occur only when a loan closes are likely to be paid out of the closing funds, but early expenses incurred by lenders must be paid, even if the loan doesn't close. This is when having a relationship with a lender can help because they may agree to absorb some of the smaller costs, such as pulling a credit report. When no relationship exists, a deposit ensures the lender that fees will be paid, even if the loan does not close.

Other more costly items, such as a property appraisal, may have to be paid upfront by the borrower. For loans that close, lenders may also charge a **loan origination fee** (also called a **loan service fee**) to cover the administrative costs of making and servicing the loan. This fee is usually based on a percentage of the loan amount (1% equals 1 point) and paid out of the closing funds.

RESPA requires lenders to provide a **Loan Estimate** that includes a "good faith" estimate of settlement costs no later than **three business days** following the date of a completed mortgage loan application. The Loan Estimate includes estimated closing costs, projected monthly payments, and the true cost of credit as an annual percentage rate.

# Completing the Loan Application

The **loan application** is a required form that potential borrowers must complete, *listing all pertinent information about the borrower and the subject property.* Loan applications were designed for those who would follow through with the loan and actually borrow funds (upon loan approval), so a great deal of information is required. The same application is often used for pre-approvals, since the lender anticipates a pre-approval will eventually lead to a loan. If the buyer doesn't provide all of the necessary data during the initial consultation, it will be necessary to provide it later, which may delay the loan process.

The information on the loan application includes:

- New home purchase and sale agreement (not necessary for pre-approvals, once the buyer finds a home, this can be supplied)
- Residence history (past two years)
    - Landlord or rental agent's name, address, and phone number (if applicable)
    - Current type of mortgage loan including the lender's name, phone number, and address (if applicable)
- Employment history (past two to three years)
    - Name, address, and phone number of all employers
    - Description of position held, employment status (full time, part time, temporary, etc.), and income earned
    - Tax returns, including a year-to-date income and expense statement (if self-employed or fully commissioned)
    - Corporate tax returns (if major stockholder owning 25% or more in a corporation's stock)
- Income information
    - Amount and source of income, including regular salary and secondary sources like pensions, Social Security, disability, child support, alimony, etc.
    - Documentation of income or verification of benefits from the income sources outlined above; child support and/or alimony require a copy of the divorce decree only if indicated as a source of income
- List of assets
    - Names, addresses, and account numbers of all bank accounts
    - Value of personal property
    - Make, model, year, and value of vehicles owned
    - Cash and face value of insurance policies or other assets (e.g., stocks)
    - Address, description, and value of real estate owned
- List of liabilities
    - Balance, monthly payment, and account number for each creditor (along with name, address, and phone number)
    - Copy of divorce decree (if paying child support or alimony)
- Copy of gift letter, if source of down payment or closing costs
    - Letter must be signed by donor and state that funds do not need to be repaid
- Certificate of Eligibility and DD-214 (Discharge Papers)—VA loans only
- Existing home sale information (if applicable)
    - Net amount of the sale (after commissions and expenses)
    - Letter from the buyer's company stating what moving costs will be paid, if applicable
- Other relevant documentation or additional documentation requested by lender

# The Loan Application

The buyer(s) typically completes a loan application during the initial consultation with the lender. Lenders expect their loans to be repaid in a timely manner without collection, servicing, or foreclosure. Thus, employment stability, income potential, history of debt management, and net worth are important considerations made by the lender.

The loan application details the borrower's financial and employment history and elicits responses to determine financial trends and attitudes in order to predict loan repayment. This explains why borrowers must supply so much information.

Let's take an in-depth look at each section of a typical loan application.

I. **Type of Mortgage and Terms of Loan.** Details the mortgage option chosen.

II. **Property Information and Purpose of Loan.** Location and legal description of the subject property, its value, and the manner of taking title. To determine how much security the property provides for the loan, lenders are interested in the current value and trend of the value, as well as any improvements that have or will be made.

Lenders generally consider loans on a primary residence a better risk than those on a secondary residence or investment property. When money is tight, lenders sense that most people will pay for their primary residence before spending money on other real estate loans. The lender also asks about the borrower's source of down payment, settlement charges, and secondary financing as another means of ascertaining a borrower's financial stability.

III. **Borrower Information.** Personal information (e.g., name, address, phone number, Social Security number, age, schooling, marital status), including number of dependents (although children help stabilize a borrower, they add considerably to financial obligations). If less than two years at the present address, previous address information must be provided. A parallel section exists for co-borrowers (e.g., spouse).

IV. **Employment Information.** Current job including how many years in the same line of work; this demonstrates job stability. If less than two years at current job, previous employment information must be included..

If **self-employed** (owns 25% or more of the business used for income qualification), this must be noted on the application. Again, there's a parallel section for the co-borrower's information.

V. **Monthly Income and Combined Housing Expense Information.** Primary employment income, overtime, bonuses, commissions, dividends, interest, net rental income, and income from any other sources. Note that income derived from alimony or child support does not need to be disclosed, unless the borrower wants this considered as part of his income to qualify for a larger loan. Those who are self-employed may need to supply additional supporting documents (e.g., personal tax returns, corporate tax returns, financial statements).

Monthly housing expenses (e.g., rent, mortgage payments, secondary financing, insurance, real estate taxes) are also requested here. The lender wants to know what the borrower is currently paying along with the proposed payment on the new mortgage. This helps gauge the extra burden for the new loan as compared to the current.

VI. **Assets and Liabilities.** All assets and liabilities; this is used to determine the borrower's net worth. **Assets** are *items of value owned by the borrower*, such as cash on hand, checking or savings accounts, stocks, bonds, insurance policies, real estate, retirement funds, automobiles, and personal property. **Liabilities** *are financial obligations or debts owed* by a borrower. **Debts** are *recurring monetary obligations that cannot be* *canceled*. The distinction is that *liabilities are money owed; debts specifically refer to recurring obligations* (e.g., monthly bills).

Note that any pledged assets, where collateral on another loan, are considered liabilities up to the amount of money owed. A borrower must reveal alimony or child support as a liability if owed. Generally, the lender will not consider debts with less than ten remaining payments (except leases, which always count regardless of how few payments remain). Still, borrowers must list all debts, including collections, slow pays, judgments, etc. Lenders will pull a credit report revealing these accounts anyway, so it's best to be honest from the start. Lenders may also use some debtors as credit references.

**Net worth** is *determined by subtracting liabilities from total assets*. Most lenders feel a borrower's net worth is a good indicator of creditworthiness. A high net worth shows an ability to manage money and may help offset other marginal items on an application. Furthermore, liquid assets that can be sold in an emergency to make payments give lenders additional security in making the loan.

VII. **Details of the Transaction.** Information on the real estate transaction itself—purchase price, prepaid items (e.g., escrows for taxes, insurance), estimated closing costs, mortgage insurance, etc. The borrower must also indicate secondary financing, seller-paid closing costs, and any other credits, such as equity from selling the current home and deposits being held by a broker or title company. By adding and subtracting these amounts, along with the amount the borrower is financing, the lender can estimate the cash the borrower must bring to closing.

VIII. **Declarations.** This section is basically a catchall. Here, the lender asks the borrower and co-borrower to declare, by signing the Acknowledgement and Agreement section, that they have had no outstanding judgments, bankruptcies, foreclosures, etc., which may not have shown up during the lender's research. The borrower and co-borrower must also declare whether they are obligated to pay alimony or child support, have borrowed any part of the down payment, are co-signers on any other debts, are U.S. citizens or permanent residents, and whether they intend to occupy the property as a primary residence.

IX. **Acknowledgement and Agreement.** The borrower and co-borrower date and sign the application, acknowledging they have answered everything truthfully and understand and agree to be bound by the terms of the loan, if granted.

X. **Information for Government Monitoring Purposes.** This section is mandatory and is used by the government to monitor lender compliance with equal credit and equal housing laws. Remember, the **Equal Credit Opportunity Act (ECOA)** prohibits discrimination in granting credit based on age, sex, race, marital status, color, religion, national origin, or receipt of public assistance.

## Processing and Analyzing the Borrower and Property

Once the application is completed, the lender can begin gathering other pertinent information on the buyer. Many times, this is done by a person called a **loan processor**, or just processor. The processor is a good source of information as to the status of the loan. Some lenders will accept a borrower's check stubs or W-2 forms, copies of bank statements, and other original documents; others still use verification forms sent to the buyer's employer, banks, other creditors, and previous mortgage lenders. A credit report will be ordered and a preliminary title report prepared. An approved appraiser will also be contacted to appraise the subject property.

# Uniform Residential Loan Application

This application is designed to be completed by the applicant(s) with the Lender's assistance. Applicants should complete this form as "Borrower" or "Co-Borrower," as applicable. Co-Borrower information must also be provided (and the appropriate box checked) when ☐ the income or assets of a person other than the Borrower (including the Borrower's spouse) will be used as a basis for loan qualification or ☐ the income or assets of the Borrower's spouse or other person who has community property rights pursuant to state law will not be used as a basis for loan qualification, but his or her liabilities must be considered because the spouse or other person has community property rights pursuant to applicable law and Borrower resides in a community property state, the security property is located in a community property state, or the Borrower is relying on other property located in a community property state as a basis for repayment of the loan.

If this is an application for joint credit, Borrower and Co-Borrower each agree that we intend to apply for joint credit (sign below):

_____          _____
Borrower                                                                          Co-Borrower

## I. TYPE OF MORTGAGE AND TERMS OF LOAN

| Mortgage Applied for: | ☐ VA<br>☐ FHA | ☐ Conventional<br>☐ USDA/Rural Housing Service | ☐ Other (explain): | Agency Case Number | Lender Case Number |
|---|---|---|---|---|---|

| Amount<br>$ | Interest Rate<br>% | No. of Months | Amortization Type: | ☐ Fixed Rate<br>☐ GPM | ☐ Other (explain):<br>☐ ARM (type): |
|---|---|---|---|---|---|

## II. PROPERTY INFORMATION AND PURPOSE OF LOAN

| Subject Property Address (street, city, state & ZIP) | No. of Units |
|---|---|

| Legal Description of Subject Property (attach description if necessary) | Year Built |
|---|---|

| Purpose of Loan | ☐ Purchase     ☐ Construction     ☐ Other (explain):<br>☐ Refinance     ☐ Construction-Permanent | Property will be:<br>☐ Primary Residence          ☐ Secondary Residence          ☐ Investment |
|---|---|---|

*Complete this line if construction or construction-permanent loan.*

| Year Lot Acquired | Original Cost<br>$ | Amount Existing Liens<br>$ | (a) Present Value of Lot<br>$ | (b) Cost of Improvements<br>$ | Total (a + b)<br>$ |
|---|---|---|---|---|---|

*Complete this line if this is a refinance loan.*

| Year Acquired | Original Cost<br>$ | Amount Existing Liens<br>$ | Purpose of Refinance | Describe Improvements          ☐ made          ☐ to be made<br>Cost: $ |
|---|---|---|---|---|

| Title will be held in what Name(s) | Manner in which Title will be held | Estate will be held in:<br>☐ Fee Simple<br>☐ Leasehold (show expiration date) |
|---|---|---|

| Source of Down Payment, Settlement Charges, and/or Subordinate Financing (explain) |
|---|

## III. BORROWER INFORMATION

| Borrower | Co-Borrower |
|---|---|
| Borrower's Name (include Jr. or Sr. if applicable) | Co-Borrower's Name (include Jr. or Sr. if applicable) |

| Social Security Number | Home Phone (incl. area code) | DOB (mm/dd/yyyy) | Yrs. School | Social Security Number | Home Phone (incl. area code) | DOB (mm/dd/yyyy) | Yrs. School |
|---|---|---|---|---|---|---|---|

| ☐ Married     ☐ Unmarried (include<br>☐ Separated     single, divorced, widowed) | Dependents (not listed by Co-Borrower)<br>no.          ages | ☐ Married     ☐ Unmarried (include<br>☐ Separated     single, divorced, widowed) | Dependents (not listed by Borrower)<br>no.          ages |
|---|---|---|---|

| Present Address (street, city, state, ZIP)     ☐ Own     ☐ Rent ___ No. Yrs. | Present Address (street, city, state, ZIP)     ☐ Own     ☐ Rent ___ No. Yrs. |
|---|---|

| Mailing Address, if different from Present Address | Mailing Address, if different from Present Address |
|---|---|

*If residing at present address for less than two years, complete the following:*

| Former Address (street, city, state, ZIP)     ☐ Own     ☐ Rent ___ No. Yrs. | Former Address (street, city, state, ZIP)     ☐ Own     ☐ Rent ___ No. Yrs. |
|---|---|

## IV. EMPLOYMENT INFORMATION

| Borrower | Co-Borrower |
|---|---|
| Name & Address of Employer     ☐ Self Employed | Yrs. on this job | Name & Address of Employer     ☐ Self Employed | Yrs. on this job |
| | Yrs. employed in this line of work/profession | | Yrs. employed in this line of work/profession |

| Position/Title/Type of Business | Business Phone (incl. area code) | Position/Title/Type of Business | Business Phone (incl. area code) |
|---|---|---|---|

*If employed in current position for less than two years or if currently employed in more than one position, complete the following:*

| Borrower | | IV. EMPLOYMENT INFORMATION (cont'd) | | Co-Borrower | |
|---|---|---|---|---|---|
| Name & Address of Employer | ☐ Self Employed | Dates (from – to) | Name & Address of Employer | ☐ Self Employed | Dates (from – to) |
| | | Monthly Income $ | | | Monthly Income $ |
| Position/Title/Type of Business | Business Phone (incl. area code) | | Position/Title/Type of Business | Business Phone (incl. area code) | |
| Name & Address of Employer | ☐ Self Employed | Dates (from – to) | Name & Address of Employer | ☐ Self Employed | Dates (from – to) |
| | | Monthly Income $ | | | Monthly Income $ |
| Position/Title/Type of Business | Business Phone (incl. area code) | | Position/Title/Type of Business | Business Phone (incl. area code) | |

### V. MONTHLY INCOME AND COMBINED HOUSING EXPENSE INFORMATION

| Gross Monthly Income | Borrower | Co-Borrower | Total | Combined Monthly Housing Expense | Present | Proposed |
|---|---|---|---|---|---|---|
| Base Empl. Income* | $ | $ | $ | Rent | $ | |
| Overtime | | | | First Mortgage (P&I) | | $ |
| Bonuses | | | | Other Financing (P&I) | | |
| Commissions | | | | Hazard Insurance | | |
| Dividends/Interest | | | | Real Estate Taxes | | |
| Net Rental Income | | | | Mortgage Insurance | | |
| Other (before completing, see the notice in "describe other income," below) | | | | Homeowner Assn. Dues | | |
| | | | | Other: | | |
| Total | $ | $ | $ | Total | $ | $ |

\*    Self Employed Borrower(s) may be required to provide additional documentation such as tax returns and financial statements.

**Describe Other Income**    *Notice:*  **Alimony, child support, or separate maintenance income need not be revealed if the Borrower (B) or Co-Borrower (C) does not choose to have it considered for repaying this loan.**

| B/C | | Monthly Amount |
|---|---|---|
| | | $ |
| | | |
| | | |

### VI. ASSETS AND LIABILITIES

This Statement and any applicable supporting schedules may be completed jointly by both married and unmarried Co-Borrowers if their assets and liabilities are sufficiently joined so that the Statement can be meaningfully and fairly presented on a combined basis; otherwise, separate Statements and Schedules are required. If the Co-Borrower section was completed about a non-applicant spouse or other person, this Statement and supporting schedules must be completed about that spouse or other person also.

Completed ☐ Jointly ☐ Not Jointly

| ASSETS | Cash or Market Value | Liabilities and Pledged Assets. List the creditor's name, address, and account number for all outstanding debts, including automobile loans, revolving charge accounts, real estate loans, alimony, child support, stock pledges, etc. Use continuation sheet, if necessary. Indicate by (*) those liabilities, which will be satisfied upon sale of real estate owned or upon refinancing of the subject property. | | |
|---|---|---|---|---|
| Description | | | | |
| Cash deposit toward purchase held by: | $ | | | |
| *List checking and savings accounts below* | | **LIABILITIES** | **Monthly Payment & Months Left to Pay** | **Unpaid Balance** |
| Name and address of Bank, S&L, or Credit Union | | Name and address of Company | $ Payment/Months | $ |
| | | | | |
| Acct. no. | $ | Acct. no. | | |
| Name and address of Bank, S&L, or Credit Union | | Name and address of Company | $ Payment/Months | $ |
| | | | | |
| Acct. no. | $ | Acct. no. | | |
| Name and address of Bank, S&L, or Credit Union | | Name and address of Company | $ Payment/Months | $ |
| | | | | |
| Acct. no. | $ | Acct. no. | | |

## VI. ASSETS AND LIABILITIES (cont'd)

| Name and address of Bank, S&L, or Credit Union | | Name and address of Company | $ Payment/Months | $ |
|---|---|---|---|---|
| Acct. no. | $ | Acct. no. | | |
| Stocks & Bonds (Company name/ number & description) | $ | Name and address of Company | $ Payment/Months | $ |
| | | Acct. no. | | |
| Life insurance net cash value | $ | Name and address of Company | $ Payment/Months | $ |
| Face amount: $ | | | | |
| **Subtotal Liquid Assets** | $ | | | |
| Real estate owned (enter market value from schedule of real estate owned) | $ | | | |
| Vested interest in retirement fund | $ | | | |
| Net worth of business(es) owned (attach financial statement) | $ | Acct. no. | | |
| Automobiles owned (make and year) | $ | Alimony/Child Support/Separate Maintenance Payments Owed to: | $ | |
| Other Assets (itemize) | $ | Job-Related Expense (child care, union dues, etc.) | $ | |
| | | **Total Monthly Payments** | $ | |
| **Total Assets a.** | $ | **Net Worth** (a minus b) ▶ $ | **Total Liabilities b.** | $ |

**Schedule of Real Estate Owned** (If additional properties are owned, use continuation sheet.)

| Property Address (enter S if sold, PS if pending sale or R if rental being held for income) ▼ | Type of Property | Present Market Value | Amount of Mortgages & Liens | Gross Rental Income | Mortgage Payments | Insurance, Maintenance, Taxes & Misc. | Net Rental Income |
|---|---|---|---|---|---|---|---|
| | | $ | $ | $ | $ | $ | $ |
| | | | | | | | |
| | | | | | | | |
| Totals | | $ | $ | $ | $ | $ | $ |

List any additional names under which credit has previously been received and indicate appropriate creditor name(s) and account number(s):

| Alternate Name | Creditor Name | Account Number |
|---|---|---|
| | | |
| | | |

## VII. DETAILS OF TRANSACTION

| | | |
|---|---|---|
| a. | Purchase price | $ |
| b. | Alterations, improvements, repairs | |
| c. | Land (if acquired separately) | |
| d. | Refinance (incl. debts to be paid off) | |
| e. | Estimated prepaid items | |
| f. | Estimated closing costs | |
| g. | PMI, MIP, Funding Fee | |
| h. | Discount (if Borrower will pay) | |
| i. | Total costs (add items a through h) | |

## VIII. DECLARATIONS

If you answer "Yes" to any questions a through i, please use continuation sheet for explanation.

| | Borrower | | Co-Borrower | |
|---|---|---|---|---|
| | Yes | No | Yes | No |
| a. Are there any outstanding judgments against you? | ☐ | ☐ | ☐ | ☐ |
| b. Have you been declared bankrupt within the past 7 years? | ☐ | ☐ | ☐ | ☐ |
| c. Have you had property foreclosed upon or given title or deed in lieu thereof in the last 7 years? | ☐ | ☐ | ☐ | ☐ |
| d. Are you a party to a lawsuit? | ☐ | ☐ | ☐ | ☐ |
| e. Have you directly or indirectly been obligated on any loan which resulted in foreclosure, transfer of title in lieu of foreclosure, or judgment? | ☐ | ☐ | ☐ | ☐ |

(This would include such loans as home mortgage loans, SBA loans, home improvement loans, educational loans, manufactured (mobile) home loans, any mortgage, financial obligation, bond, or loan guarantee. If "Yes," provide details, including date, name, and address of Lender, FHA or VA case number, if any, and reasons for the action.)

| VII. DETAILS OF TRANSACTION | | VIII. DECLARATIONS | | | | |
|---|---|---|---|---|---|---|

| VII. DETAILS OF TRANSACTION | | | VIII. DECLARATIONS | Borrower | | Co-Borrower | |
|---|---|---|---|---|---|---|---|
| | | | If you answer "Yes" to any question a through I, please use continuation sheet for explanation. | Yes | No | Yes | No |
| j. | Subordinate financing | | f. Are you presently delinquent or in default on any Federal debt or any other loan, mortgage, financial obligation, bond, or loan guarantee? | ☐ | ☐ | ☐ | ☐ |
| k. | Borrower's closing costs paid by Seller | | g. Are you obligated to pay alimony, child support, or separate maintenance? | ☐ | ☐ | ☐ | ☐ |
| l. | Other Credits (explain) | | h. Is any part of the down payment borrowed? | ☐ | ☐ | ☐ | ☐ |
| | | | i. Are you a co-maker or endorser on a note? | ☐ | ☐ | ☐ | ☐ |
| m. | Loan amount (exclude PMI, MIP, Funding Fee financed) | | ----------------------------------------------------- | | | | |
| | | | j. Are you a U.S. citizen? | ☐ | ☐ | ☐ | ☐ |
| n. | PMI, MIP, Funding Fee financed | | k. Are you a permanent resident alien? | ☐ | ☐ | ☐ | ☐ |
| o. | Loan amount (add m & n) | | l. Do you intend to occupy the property as your primary residence? | ☐ | ☐ | ☐ | ☐ |
| | | | If "Yes," complete question m below. | | | | |
| p. | Cash from/to Borrower (subtract j, k, l & o from i) | | m. Have you had an ownership interest in a property in the last three years? | ☐ | ☐ | ☐ | ☐ |
| | | | (1) What type of property did you own—principal residence (PR), second home (SH), or investment property (IP)? | | | | |
| | | | (2) How did you hold title to the home— by yourself (S), jointly with your spouse or jointly with another person (O)? | | | | |

### IX. ACKNOWLEDGEMENT AND AGREEMENT

Each of the undersigned specifically represents to Lender and to Lender's actual or potential agents, brokers, processors, attorneys, insurers, servicers, successors and assigns and agrees and acknowledges that: (1) the information provided in this application is true and correct as of the date set forth opposite my signature and that any intentional or negligent misrepresentation of this information contained in this application may result in civil liability, including monetary damages, to any person who may suffer any loss due to reliance upon any misrepresentation that I have made on this application, and/or in criminal penalties including, but not limited to, fine or imprisonment or both under the provisions of Title 18, United States Code, Sec. 1001, et seq.; (2) the loan requested pursuant to this application (the "Loan") will be secured by a mortgage or deed of trust on the property described in this application; (3) the property will not be used for any illegal or prohibited purpose or use; (4) all statements made in this application are made for the purpose of obtaining a residential mortgage loan; (5) the property will be occupied as indicated in this application; (6) the Lender, its servicers, successors or assigns may retain the original and/or an electronic record of this application, whether or not the Loan is approved; (7) the Lender and its agents, brokers, insurers, servicers, successors, and assigns may continuously rely on the information contained in the application, and I am obligated to amend and/or supplement the information provided in this application if any of the material facts that I have represented herein should change prior to closing of the Loan; (8) in the event that my payments on the Loan become delinquent, the Lender, its servicers, successors or assigns may, in addition to any other rights and remedies that it may have relating to such delinquency, report my name and account information to one or more consumer reporting agencies; (9) ownership of the Loan and/or administration of the Loan account may be transferred with such notice as may be required by law; (10) neither Lender nor its agents, brokers, insurers, servicers, successors or assigns has made any representation or warranty, express or implied, to me regarding the property or the condition or value of the property; and (11) my transmission of this application as an "electronic record" containing my "electronic signature," as those terms are defined in applicable federal and/or state laws (excluding audio and video recordings), or my facsimile transmission of this application containing a facsimile of my signature, shall be as effective, enforceable and valid as if a paper version of this application were delivered containing my original written signature.

Acknowledgement. Each of the undersigned hereby acknowledges that any owner of the Loan, its servicers, successors and assigns, may verify or reverify any information contained in this application or obtain any information or data relating to the Loan, for any legitimate business purpose through any source, including a source named in this application or a consumer reporting agency.

| Borrower's Signature | | Date | Co-Borrower's Signature | | Date |
|---|---|---|---|---|---|
| X | | | X | | |

### X. INFORMATION FOR GOVERNMENT MONITORING PURPOSES

The following information is requested by the Federal Government for certain types of loans related to a dwelling in order to monitor the lender's compliance with equal credit opportunity, fair housing and home mortgage disclosure laws. You are not required to furnish this information, but are encouraged to do so. The law provides that a lender may not discriminate either on the basis of this information, or on whether you choose to furnish it. If you furnish the information, please provide both ethnicity and race. For race, you may check more than one designation. If you do not furnish ethnicity, race, or sex, under Federal regulations, this lender is required to note the information on the basis of visual observation and surname if you have made this application in person. If you do not wish to furnish the information, please check the box below. (Lender must review the above material to assure that the disclosures satisfy all requirements to which the lender is subject under applicable state law for the particular type of loan applied for.)

| BORROWER ☐ I do not wish to furnish this information | | | CO-BORROWER ☐ I do not wish to furnish this information | | |
|---|---|---|---|---|---|
| Ethnicity: ☐ Hispanic or Latino  ☐ Not Hispanic or Latino | | | Ethnicity: ☐ Hispanic or Latino  ☐ Not Hispanic or Latino | | |
| Race: ☐ American Indian or Alaska Native  ☐ Native Hawaiian or Other Pacific Islander | ☐ Asian  ☐ White | ☐ Black or African American | Race: ☐ American Indian or Alaska Native  ☐ Native Hawaiian or Other Pacific Islander | ☐ Asian  ☐ White | ☐ Black or African American |
| Sex: ☐ Female  ☐ Male | | | Sex: ☐ Female  ☐ Male | | |

To be Completed by Loan Originator:
This information was provided:
☐ In a face-to-face interview
☐ In a telephone interview
☐ By the applicant and submitted by fax or mail
☐ By the applicant and submitted via e-mail or the Internet

| Loan Originator's Signature X | | Date |
|---|---|---|
| Loan Originator's Name (print or type) | Loan Originator Identifier | Loan Originator's Phone Number (including area code) |
| Loan Origination Company's Name | Loan Origination Company Identifier | Loan Origination Company's Address |

| CONTINUATION SHEET/RESIDENTIAL LOAN APPLICATION | | |
|---|---|---|
| Use this continuation sheet if you need more space to complete the Residential Loan Application. Mark **B** f or Borrower or **C** for Co-Borrower. | Borrower: | Agency Case Number: |
| | Co-Borrower: | Lender Case Number: |

I/We fully understand that it is a Federal crime punishable by fine or imprisonment, or both, to knowingly make any false statements concerning any of the above facts as applicable under the provisions of Title 18, United States Code, Section 1001, et seq.

| Borrower's Signature | Date | Co-Borrower's Signature | Date |
|---|---|---|---|
| X | | X | |

After examining the application, the lender may also ask the buyer to submit further information, such as:

- Investment account records, or other documentation.

- Tax returns (if the buyer is self-employed or living on investment income).

- Other documents relevant to a buyer's income or credit status.

As the lender reviews the loan application and decides whether to make the loan, the borrower is evaluated on five criteria, referred to as the five "Cs":

1. **Capacity**—Does the borrower have the financial ability to pay the mortgage along with the other debts and obligations?

2. **Collateral**—Is the borrower's down payment and property value sufficient for the lender to recoup its money if foreclosure occurs?

3. **Credit**—Does the borrower's past payment history show a willingness and ability to repay obligations?

4. **Character**—Does the borrower have stability in a job and in responsibilities such that, even with setbacks, financial obligations will be honored?

5. **Conditions**—Do other factors, such as economic health of borrower's job field, general economic conditions, etc., look favorable?

The lender also wants to know the source of the buyer's down payment. Savings, sale of a prior home, and gifts are all acceptable sources of down payment.

# Underwriting and Approving the Loan Application

Processing the loan application involves reviewing the information submitted and verifying items as necessary. When the lender receives the credit report, verification forms, preliminary title report, and appraisal, a loan package is put together and given to an underwriter. An **underwriter** is *the individual who evaluates a loan application to determine its risk level for a lender or investor* and is usually the final decision maker on whether a loan is approved.

The underwriting process can be automated (where all information is entered into a computer) or done by an individual who works for the lender. Both processes apply various qualifying standards. With automated underwriting, computer software makes a recommendation to accept a loan, or refers it to a human underwriter for review. Loan underwriters carefully examine a loan package and decide to approve, reject, or approve the loan with conditions (e.g., the buyer must bring proof that the previous home was sold and the mortgage is no longer outstanding).

# Automated Underwriting

**Automated underwriting** is *a process whereby information from a loan applicant is entered into a computer and an evaluation comes back within minutes advising the lender to accept the loan applicant, or refer the loan application for further review and analysis by a loan underwriter.* The purpose of automated underwriting is to reduce the cost of examining a loan application and speed up mortgage approvals.

A loan may be referred for review because automated underwriting systems are generally able to evaluate only the first three "Cs" (capacity, collateral, credit), but the last two (character, conditions) are too subjective for a computer.

The computer can evaluate the job and income data as being sufficient or insufficient to support the proposed mortgage payment and other debts. Next, the borrower's total equity position in the house is calculated based on the purchase price and proposed down payment. Finally, the computer determines the loan applicant's credit situation and likelihood of default based on the borrower's credit score and other risk factors. If any of these are marginal, the computer refers the loan applicant to a human underwriter to consider other factors.

Automation is used in all facets of the lending process. Computers have helped the mortgage business become more efficient. And with large databases of statistics and information available, the secondary market has increased efforts to manage credit risk by improving loan criteria. Automation will also determine and make recommendations as to the documentation required for a particular loan.

The two biggest automated underwriting tools used today are Freddie Mac's **Loan Prospector**® and Fannie Mae's **Desktop Underwriter**®. It's important to understand that automated underwriting tools and systems do not actually approve or reject loans. Instead, the system is set up so the computer makes recommendations to the loan underwriter based on programmed risk factors. The Desktop Underwriter® looks at 14 separate factors about the borrower and the property when evaluating the mortgage loan application. The three most important factors are:

1.   Equity in the property.

2.   Credit history of the borrower (including credit score).

3.   Liquid reserves the borrower has in the bank.

Most systems only recommend *approval* or *further evaluation of the loan application* after examining additional documentation. In all cases, the underwriter has the final say, on behalf of the lender, as to whether a loan is approved, and the underwriter has ultimate responsibility for qualifying the buyer.

## The Art of Qualifying a Buyer

**Qualifying a buyer** simply means evaluating a borrower's creditworthiness. According to Fannie Mae, "Underwriting mortgage loans is an art, not a science." Of course, as automated underwriting becomes more widespread in the finance industry, it may seem as if the opposite of that statement is true. Still, when the computer cannot approve a loan application, it is referred back to a human underwriter who goes through the traditional art of qualifying a buyer. And, as a real estate agent, it is helpful for you to understand this process.

Two general steps all lenders take before agreeing to make a real estate loan are to evaluate the:

1.   Borrower (to make sure he meets minimum qualifying standards).

2.   Property.

This evaluation process, **loan underwriting**, is where an underwriter evaluates various risk factors associated with a loan.

The primary concern throughout the loan underwriting process is *determining the degree of risk a loan represents*. The underwriter attempts to answer two fundamental questions:

1.   Does the borrower's overall financial situation, which is comprised of income, credit history, and net worth, indicate he can reasonably be expected to make the proposed monthly loan payments in a timely manner?

2. Is there sufficient value in the property pledged as collateral to assure recovery of the loan amount in the event of default?

Qualifying standards may vary from lender to lender, but with increased lender dependence on the national secondary market, a high degree of standardization in loan underwriting has developed. The majority of lenders throughout the country have incorporated the standards set by the major secondary market investors into their own conventional loan underwriting procedures, specifically Fannie Mae and Freddie Mac.

Since most lenders use Fannie Mae and Freddie Mac conventional underwriting standards, it's important for real estate professionals to know those standards so they can expertly pre-qualify buyers and properties. Portfolio lenders make up their own rules since they hold the loan. Of course, if the loan being contemplated is in conjunction with the FHA or VA, FHA or VA underwriting standards must be used. We'll discuss the FHA and VA later, but first let's look at Fannie Mae and Freddie Mac underwriting standards.

# Fannie Mae and Freddie Mac Underwriting Standards

When qualifying a buyer for a conventional loan, Fannie Mae and Freddie Mac underwriting criteria should be used. Some of the most important criteria evaluated in qualifying a borrower for a particular mortgage loan are **income**, **credit history**, and **net worth**.

## Income Qualifying Standards

When considering a borrower's income, there are two important income factors to consider—**housing expense ratio** and **total debt service ratio**.

### Housing Expense Ratio

A borrower's **housing expense ratio** is the *relationship of the borrower's total monthly housing expense to income, expressed as a percentage*:

**Total Housing Expense ÷ Gross Monthly Income = Ratio %**

Conventional lenders consider a borrower's income adequate for a loan if the proposed total mortgage payment of principal, interest, taxes, and insurance (**PITI**) does not exceed *28% of stable monthly income*. **Stable monthly income** is a *borrower's monthly gross income that can reasonably be expected to continue in the future*. This is usually a borrower's gross monthly income from primary employment and any other income considered reliable and likely to endure.

### For Example

Joe has $2,900 in stable gross monthly income. His proposed mortgage payment (PITI, plus PMI if needed) is $700.

**$700 ÷ $2,900 = 0.24 = 24%**

Joe's housing expense ratio is 24%, which is less than 28%, so he qualifies for the loan.

### Total Debt Service Ratio

A borrower's **total debt service ratio** is the *relationship of the borrower's total monthly debt obligations (including housing and long-term debts with more than ten payments left) to income, expressed as a percentage*:

**Total Monthly Debt Service ÷ Gross Monthly Income = Ratio %**

Conventional lenders want to be sure the borrower's housing expenses (as explained previously) plus any installment debts with more than ten payments left do not exceed *36% of his stable monthly income*. Alimony, child support, or other court-ordered obligations must count as debt against this ratio. Note also that debts with less than ten payments may still be counted against the borrower if payments are high (e.g., *$600 car payment*).

## For Example

Kathy has $2,900 in stable gross monthly income and the following monthly debt payments:

| | |
|---|---|
| $700 | Proposed Mortgage Payment (PITI, plus PMI if needed) |
| $225 | Car Payment (18 payments left) |
| + $100 | Child Support Payment |
| **$1,025** | **Total Monthly Debt Payments** |

$1,025 ÷ $2,900 = 0.35 = 35%

Kathy's total debt service ratio is 35%, which is less than 36%, so she qualifies for the loan.

Using the housing expense ratio and total debt service ratio, it's easy to determine the maximum mortgage payment for which a borrower will qualify:

- First, take the borrower's stable monthly income and multiply it by the maximum **housing expense ratio (28% or 0.28)**. This gives you the maximum mortgage payment allowable under the first ratio.

- Next, take the borrower's stable monthly income and multiply it by the maximum **total debt service ratio (36% or 0.36)**. This gives you the amount of total monthly long-term debts the borrower is permitted to have.

- Take the second amount and subtract the monthly long-term obligations the borrower already has (not including mortgage payments). This will give you a figure that represents the largest mortgage payment allowed under the second ratio.

The total debt service ratio is a more realistic measure of the borrower's ability to support the loan payments because it takes into account all recurring financial obligations. And since the total debt service ratio takes all debt into consideration, the mortgage payment determined by calculating the total debt service ratio is also likely to be smaller than the housing expense ratio. Since the borrower must qualify under both ratios, the smaller of the two is the maximum allowable mortgage payment.

## For Example

Mary has a stable monthly income of $3,200. She has three long-term monthly debt obligations: A $220 car payment, a $75 personal loan payment, and a $50 revolving charge card payment. What is the maximum monthly mortgage payment for which she can qualify?

Housing Expense Ratio = 28%

$3,200 Gross Monthly Income x 0.28 Housing Expense Ratio = **$896 Maximum Mortgage Payment**

Total Debt Service Ratio = 36%

$3,200 Gross Monthly Income x 0.36 Debt Service Ratio = **$1,152 Maximum Total Debt Service**

| | |
|---|---|
| $1,152 | Maximum Total Debt Service |
| – $220 | Car Payment |
| – $75 | Personal Loan Payment |
| – $50 | Revolving Charge Card Payment |
| **$807** | **Maximum Mortgage Payment** |

Remember, Mary must qualify under both ratios, so the lower figure is the most she can get. Of course, if she could pay off some of her debt and reduce her total long-term monthly obligations, she would qualify for a larger mortgage payment.

## Stable Monthly Income

As mentioned earlier, **stable monthly income** is the *monthly income amount that can reasonably be expected to continue in the future.* This is generally meant to include the borrowers' **gross base income** from primary jobs, plus earnings from acceptable secondary sources.

Although the lender may include all these sources, a thorough analysis will be conducted. Before deciding if there's sufficient income, the underwriter must decide what portion of the borrower's total verified earnings are acceptable as a part of his stable monthly income. This is accomplished by studying the **quality** (dependability) and the **durability** (probability of continuance) of the income source(s).

A **quality** source of income is one that is *reasonably reliable*, such as income from an established employer, government agency, interest-yielding investment account, etc. A **durable** source of income is one that is *expected to continue for a sustained period.* Permanent disability, retirement earnings, and interest on established investments clearly are enduring types of income. Temporary unemployment benefits or newly established rental income are not likely to be counted. Let's look at various income sources:

- **Bonuses, commissions, and part-time earnings** are considered durable if a borrower can show they've been a consistent part of earnings for at least one year, but preferably two or more. Proof of consistency can be made with copies of W-2 forms, pay stubs, or federal income tax returns or the lender may send the employer a verification of employment earnings.

- **Overtime** technically may count as part of a borrower's stable monthly income, but many underwriters are reluctant to rely on it because durability is uncertain. When qualifying buyers, don't count overtime earnings unless they are consistent.

- **Disability payments** count as income if they are a permanent source, but the lender will use caution if they are for a limited time.

- **Social Security** will count if it is permanent income for a buyer who has reached retirement age. If these payments are the result of a disability or some other condition, the lender will treat them like other disability payments.

- **Pensions and retirement benefits** generally are considered by lenders to be stable income, although they may investigate the source to determine solvency.

- **Interest-yielding investments** are considered durable if the investments are sound and interest payments have been consistent.

- **Rental income** can be counted if a stable pattern of positive cash flow can be verified. **Cash flow** is *money available to an individual on a regular basis, after subtracting all expenses.* Rents must cover all expenses and mortgage payments, while still leaving excess cash for owner. Authenticated copies of the owner's books showing gross earnings and operating expenses for the prior two years should be submitted along with a borrower's loan application.

- **Alimony, child support, and maintenance** can be considered part of the borrower's stable monthly income if it's determined they are likely to be made on a consistent basis. Such a determination is dependent on whether the payments are required by written agreement or court decree, the length of time the payments have been received, the age of the child (child support payments generally stop at age 18), the overall financial and credit status of the payer, and the ability of the borrower to compel payment if necessary (e.g., through a court order).

  A copy of the divorce decree is generally sufficient to establish the amount and enforceability of the required payments. In some instances, the borrower may be asked to submit proof of receipt. Also, the closer a child gets to age 18, the less durable child support income appears to a lender. There's no official cutoff date used by underwriters, but most underwriters will see support payments as terminal and not include them in the stable monthly income figure, unless at least three years remain before the payments cease.

√ **Note:** Alimony, child support, and/or maintenance do *not* need to be listed as sources of income if a borrower does not want them considered as income for the loan.

- **Unemployment and Welfare** are almost never treated as stable monthly income because they're viewed as temporary. However, if a borrower can show an extended pattern of unemployment compensation received during a certain time (e.g., due to seasonal layoffs), the underwriter may consider it.

### For Example

1. Al has worked as a greens keeper at a golf course for five years. Every winter, he is laid off, receives unemployment, and receives a W-2 from the employment office. His unemployment income should be considered.

2. Brandon has a six-year-old son and receives Aid for Dependent Children. This, too, should be considered.

- **Self-employment income** is documented by personal and corporate tax returns for the past two to three years that the borrower provides. (Remember, self-employed means a person owns 25% or more of the business used for income qualifying.) The lender may also ask to see personal and corporate *financial statements* that show assets and liabilities for an individual (or an entity, such as a company) for a specific time period. Profit and loss statements and/or balance sheets may also be required.

If a borrower has been self-employed for less than two years, it will be difficult to qualify for a loan; and, if the borrower has been in business for less than one year, it will be even more difficult. Underwriters are wary of new businesses and are generally unwavering in their insistence that a self-employed borrower must have operated the business profitably for at least two years.

- **Co-borrowers** are used to help a primary borrower qualify for a real estate loan. The most common co-borrowers are spouses, especially in two-income households. Parents are also becoming a growing source of co-borrowers, as they lend an established earnings pattern and financial status to their children who otherwise would be unable to purchase a home.

√ ***Note:*** Parents cannot co-sign a VA loan.

A **co-borrower** is simply a *person who signs a mortgage and note along with another party* (primary borrower/mortgagor) *and accepts a joint obligation to repay the loan.* Like the primary borrower, the co-borrower must have income, credit history, and assets acceptable to the underwriter. Also keep in mind that the co-borrower must be able to support both his own housing expense plus a proportionate share, if not all, of the proposed housing expense. Marginal co-borrowers should not be relied on heavily, and may do more harm than good.

## Evaluating Income

Keeping in mind what we discussed previously about a lender's general attitude toward certain kinds of income, it's still important to remember that each type of income will be evaluated separately by the lender. Generalizations can help, but all decisions come down to the individual lender evaluating each aspect of a loan application on a case-by-case basis.

When deciding what income will count toward a home purchase, the lender takes each income source and looks at **employment history**, **advancement**, and **education/training** in deciding the strength of each position—particularly for the borrower's primary job.

### Employment History

When evaluating the elements of a borrower's income (quantity, quality, and durability), the underwriter will analyze the individual's employment stability. A borrower with a history of steady, full-time employment will be given more favorable consideration than one who has changed employers frequently, unless the changes are properly explained.

As a general rule, a borrower should have continuous employment for at least two years in the same field. However, every borrower is unique and if there is not an established two-year work history, there may be explainable circumstances that would warrant loan approval, such as having recently finished college or having recently been discharged from the service.

### Advancement

If the borrower has changed employers for the sake of advancement within the same line of work, the underwriter will likely view the change favorably. On the other hand, persistent job hopping without advancement usually signifies a problem of some kind; the underwriter will tend to regard this individual's earnings as unstable.

### Education and Training

Special education or training that prepares a person for a specific kind of work can strengthen a loan application. Such education or training can offset minor weaknesses with respect to earnings or job tenure, especially if the underwriter is convinced there's a continuing demand for people in this line of work, job stability in that particular field, or opportunity for advancement.

## Computing Monthly Income

After deciding which income will count, all gross monthly income from those sources are added together to arrive at a total gross monthly income figure. If a borrower earns an hourly wage, it must be converted to a monthly figure.

To convert hourly wages to monthly earnings:

**Hourly Wage x 40 (Hours in a Work Week) x 52 (Weeks in a Year) ÷ 12 (Months in a Year) = Monthly Earnings**

√ **Note:** It is important to confirm with the borrower that their work week consists of 40 hours—it may be more or less.

### For Example

Our borrower makes $9.50 per hour. Compute the monthly income:

Hourly Wage: $9.50

Weekly Income: $9.50 x 40 (Hours) = $380

Annual Income: $380 x 52 (Weeks in a Year) = $19,760

Monthly Income: $19,760 ÷ 12 (Months in a Year) = $1,647

An easier way to calculate this is to multiply the hourly wage by 2,080 (40 x 52 = 2,080), then divide by 12 to get a monthly figure.

## Verifying Income

Fannie Mae and Freddie Mac have changed income verification procedures. Previously, lenders had to send verification forms to employers. Now, income may be verified by the borrower. The borrower can substantiate employment and income by providing W-2 forms for the previous two years and original payroll stubs or vouchers for the previous 30-day period. The pay stubs must identify the borrower, employer, and the borrower's gross earnings for both the current pay period and year-to-date. Lenders then confirm the employment and earnings with a phone call to the employer. (Self-employed people need to provide two full years worth of tax returns, and possibly year-to-date profit and loss statements to verify income.)

# Credit History

**Credit history** is a *record of debt repayment*, detailing how a person paid credit accounts in the past as an indicator of whether she is likely to pay them on time and as agreed in the future. **Debts** are any *recurring monetary obligation that cannot be canceled*.

## For Example

A car lease is a debt; student loans or court-ordered child supports are also considered debts. Utilities and insurance premiums are not considered debts because they can be canceled. Lenders assume you would turn off your phone before losing your house. Gray areas involve such things as doctor bills. These are not considered a debt unless the borrower has a payment schedule (e.g., for braces).

Borrowers must inform a lender of all debts—even things that may not show up on a credit report.

As a part of the loan evaluation, the underwriter analyzes the borrower's (and any co-borrower's) credit history by obtaining a credit report from a local and/or national credit rating bureau. If the credit history shows a slow payment record or other derogatory credit information (suit, judgment, repossession, collection, foreclosure, or bankruptcy), a loan application could be declined or the borrower put into a high-risk category.

In some cases, derogatory ratings don't prevent a borrower from obtaining a loan if credit problems can be explained. The underwriter must be satisfied that these problems don't represent the borrower's overall attitude toward credit obligations, and the circumstances leading to the problems were temporary and no longer exist.

## Evaluating Credit History

When evaluating a borrower's credit history, lenders use a number of methods. Some methods are more subjective than others, but lenders are moving toward more objective evaluation methods to ensure compliance with the Equal Credit Opportunity Act (ECOA).

Remember, the Act prohibits discrimination in lending based on age (except minors under 18), sex, race, marital status, color, religion, national origin, or receipt of public assistance. As lenders search for uniform ways to evaluate credit to avoid violating any laws, methods of *credit scoring* are becoming increasingly popular.

**Credit scoring** is an *objective means of determining the creditworthiness of potential borrowers based on a number system*. A credit score is a numeric representation of the borrower's credit profile. Credit scoring involves assigning specified numerical values to different aspects of the borrower. These numbers are adjusted up and down based on the strength or weakness of a particular borrower qualification.

## For Example

A person with significant available credit that is rarely used would likely score higher than a person with lower credit limits but whose credit cards are all at the limit. A person with a lengthy employment history with the same company would score higher than a person who just joined a new firm. The numbers are added from all the different categories scored, and the person is given a credit score based on these various criteria and respective scores. The higher the credit score, the better the credit risk.

Credit scores are based on years of computer modeling aimed at predicting who might be a credit risk. The purpose of credit scoring is to reduce the cost of examining a loan applicant's credit report and provide a means to speed up the loan approval process.

While credit scoring is often not the only means of analysis, it provides a benchmark to compare the relative value of the borrower's qualifications. There are several types of credit scores. Credit scoring can be as simple as the lender assigning numerical values to different aspects of a borrower, or as complex as the mathematical formulas used to derive credit bureau reported scores, such as **FICO** or **BEACON**.

## FICO/BEACON Scores

**FICO** is a credit score developed by Fair, Isaac, & Co. and used by Experian (formerly TRW); **BEACON** is a credit score used by Equifax; TransUnion's credit score is called **EMPIRICA**. BEACON score is a common term you will hear lenders talk about. Each of these three main credit bureau scores is calculated a little differently, but they all produce similar credit scores. FICO scores range from about 300 to 850—*the lower the score, the higher the risk of default.*

As a point of reference, Freddie Mac guidelines consider those with credit scores above 720 to be an acceptable credit risk. Those with scores of 620-660 are considered marginal and should be held to a more comprehensive review. Those with scores below 620 are considered high risk, and caution is urged. (Lenders are also encouraged to check the accuracy of credit information.)

FICO weights credit history in five categories and each category comprises a percent of the overall score, as noted below:

- Recent payment history (35%)
- Amount owed on accounts (30%)
- How long individual has been a credit user (15%)
- New credit inquiries or recently opened accounts (10%)
- Types of credit used—mortgage, installment loans, etc. (10%)

These FICO/BEACON scores are the result of very complex calculations carried out by a computer that takes into account every aspect of the borrower's credit file. Items considered in a person's credit file include:

- Number of open accounts
- Total credit limit
- Total amount of debt outstanding
- Number of late payments in the past 30-60-90 days
- Liens
- Judgments
- Bankruptcies
- Number of recent credit inquiries

Lenders can't tell you exactly how each credit score is computed, but they can tell you what cutoff scores they use in qualifying borrowers for various mortgage loan programs. These credit scores also play an important role in automated underwriting since Freddie Mac identified a strong correlation between mortgage performance and credit scores.

## Best Practices

Credit scoring is very important to a buyer in understanding what the interest rate might be, or whether he gets the loan at all. As a result, it is important buyers review their credit from time to time. There are three credit-reporting agencies lenders use. They will normally pull a credit report from all three and use the score that falls in the middle. Once a year, consumers are entitled to a free credit report from each agency, and should periodically check these for errors. Consumers are also entitled to one free credit report if information on their report has resulted in some adverse action (e.g., turned down for any kind of financing), the consumer is the victim of identity theft, or their credit file contains inaccurate information due to fraud. A buyer can get a free report at www.annualcreditreport.com.

## Explaining Derogatory Credit

Most people try to meet credit obligations on time; when they don't, there's usually a reason. Job loss, hospitalization, prolonged illness, death in the family, or divorce can create financial pressures that affect debt-paying habits. If a few derogatory items appear on a credit report, it may be possible to show that the problems occurred during a specific period of time for understandable reasons (e.g., hospitalization, job loss), and that prior and subsequent credit ratings have been good.

When explaining credit difficulties, it's a mistake to blame problems on creditors. If borrowers refuse to accept responsibility for their actions, underwriters will reject such explanations. Underwriters anticipate that a borrower's reluctance to take responsibility for prior credit problems is an indication of what can be expected in the future.

If a borrower's credit report is laced with derogatory ratings over a period of years, there's probably little hope for loan approval through a traditional lender. Perpetual credit problems more likely reflect an attitude rather than a circumstance, and it's reasonable for lenders to presume that pattern will continue.

Most credit problems can be resolved with time, so never assume a buyer can't qualify for a loan. If a buyer indicates credit problems in the past, refer him to a competent lender to get an expert's opinion. Unless you have professional expertise as a mortgage broker or other finance professional, you have the potential to get into trouble if you start telling people they can't get approved for a loan based on personal opinion.

### Bankruptcy

Bankruptcy, as established by federal law, is a court process that cancels debt and provides some relief for creditors. There are two basic proceedings:

| | Chapter 7 Bankruptcy (aka Straight Bankruptcy) | Chapter 13 Bankruptcy |
|---|---|---|
| Description | A liquidation proceeding Debtor turns over all non-exempt property to the bankruptcy trustee, who then converts it to cash for distribution to the creditors Debtor receives a discharge of all dischargeable debts, usually within four months | Filed by those who want to pay off their debts over a period of three to five years Preferable to those who have non-exempt property they want to retain |
| Individuals Must… | Meet certain tests related to income and debt | Have predictable and sufficient income to pay their reasonable expenses with some amount leftover to pay off their debts |
| Will Remain on a Credit Report for… | 10 years | 7 years |

### Bill Consolidation and Refinancing

Even without derogatory ratings, lenders may find other concerns in a credit report that might indicate the borrower is a marginal credit risk. If an individual's credit pattern is one of continually increasing liabilities and periodically "bailing out" through **refinancing** and **bill consolidation** (*borrowing a larger sum of money to pay off many smaller debts*), he may be classified as a marginal risk. This pattern suggests a tendency to live beyond a prudent level. This is a subjective consideration likely to influence the lender's decision if a borrower is weak in other areas, such as income or net worth.

### Verifying Credit History

Lenders will accept only credit reports they obtain directly from credit reporting agencies. Borrowers must give their consent to have a credit bureau report pulled, and there's a statement to that effect on the loan application, or the lender will have borrowers sign a separate statement giving the lender permission to pull the report.

# Net Worth

**Net worth** is determined by *subtracting liabilities from total assets*. In other words, it's the value of all the property (real and personal) accumulated, after subtracting all debts or obligations owed. Fannie Mae says, "Accumulation of net worth is a strong indication of creditworthiness." A borrower who has built up a significant net worth from earnings, savings, and other investment activities clearly has the ability to manage financial affairs and accumulate wealth.

If a borrower has a marginal total debt service ratio, an above-average net worth can offset this deficiency. Underwriters know that net worth (especially in liquid form, such as savings or stocks and bonds) can be used to pay unexpected bills or support a borrower when there's a temporary interruption in income.

### Evaluating Net Worth

Lenders and underwriters are interested in three aspects of a borrower's net worth:

1. Confirming the borrower has sufficient assets and personal money to make the **down payment and pay closing costs** on the property, without borrowing them

2. Determining that the borrower has adequate **reserves** to cover two months' of PITI mortgage payments, after making a down payment and paying closing costs

3. Identifying **other assets** the borrower has (demonstrating an ability to manage money) and that could be sold to handle emergencies and make mortgage payments

### Down Payment

The borrower must have sufficient liquid assets to make the cash down payment and pay the closing costs and other expenses incidental to the purchase of the property. **Liquid assets** are *cash and any other assets (such as stocks or bonds) that can be quickly converted to cash*.

> √ **Note:** A borrower must explain the source of any large and unusual deposits. These *need* to be verified and documented.

### Reserves

**Reserves** are *cash on deposit or other highly liquid assets* a borrower has available. Lenders like to see enough to cover two months' of PITI mortgage payments, after the borrower makes the down payment and pays all closing costs. Lenders may require this as a safeguard against unexpected bills or temporary loss of income, and as an indicator of financial stability. The reserve requirement for investment properties is six months' of PITI.

## Other Assets

Other assets should also be included on the loan application. Real estate *equity* is an important asset to consider. **Equity** is the *difference between the market value of the property and the sum of the mortgages and other liens against it*. It is what the buyer should receive from the sale of the property (minus all selling expenses). If the equity from the sale of a home is the source of money for the purchase of the subject property, the underwriter might require evidence that the sale closed and the borrower received the sale proceeds before making the new loan. If the loan is a construction loan and the borrower owns the home building lot, the underwriter will treat the borrower's equity in that lot as cash or its equivalent when figuring the down payment needed.

Other real estate also counts as an asset, but only the equity of the property (not its total value) contributes to net worth, since only the equity can be converted to cash by selling an interest in, or mortgaging, the property. Real estate with little or no equity, or with income that's equal to or below expenses, hurts a loan application more than it helps because the property may require cash from the borrower. Of course, a lender must be told of any financial obligations or expense shortfalls not covered by property rents.

Other assets (besides cash and real estate) which are typically listed in a loan application, include equity in:

- Automobiles
- Furniture
- Jewelry
- Stocks
- Bonds

Cash value in a life insurance policy may also be considered. The assets that most favorably influence the underwriter's decision are liquid assets—those that can be quickly converted to cash.

## Verifying Deposits for Down Payment/Reserves

In verifying the borrower has sufficient cash to cover the down payment and required reserves, the underwriter will typically send a Request for Verification of Deposit directly to the borrower's bank, and have it returned directly to the underwriter without passing through the borrower's hands. As an alternative, Fannie Mae rules allow the borrower to bring in original bank statements from the previous two or more months to verify the needed funds are on deposit.

When the underwriter receives the completed Verification of Deposit forms or gets original bank statements from borrowers, there are four things for which the underwriter is looking:

1. Does the verified information conform to statements made in the loan application?
2. Is there enough money in the bank to pay the costs of buying the property?
3. Has the bank account been opened within the last few months?
4. Is the present balance notably higher than the average balance?

Recently opened accounts and higher-than-normal balances must be explained, since these are strong indications that the buyer may have borrowed the funds needed to buy the home.

### Gift Letter

If an applicant lacks the necessary funds to close a transaction, a gift of the required amount from relatives is usually acceptable to the underwriter. The gift should be confirmed by means of a **gift letter,** signed by the donor that *clearly states the money represents a gift and does not have to be repaid.* Usually, the gift must be from an immediate family member (although rules can vary).

In addition to the gift letter, a lender must verify that the donor has the funds available to provide the gift with a copy of the gift check and deposit receipt showing funds were deposited and are available for closing. This has proven to be an area of mortgage fraud in the past so it's important to verify the donor listed on the gift letter is indeed who supplied the funds.

Even if the gift letter requirements are satisfied, borrowers typically have to make some cash payment from personal cash resources. Fannie Mae requires that the borrower make at least a *5% down payment* in addition to the gift, unless the gift is 20% or more of the purchase price. If the gift equals 20% or more, the borrower is *not* required to make a 5% down payment in addition to the gift.

## Verifying Assets

Included in every loan application is a section devoted to assets. The underwriter takes all appropriate steps to verify the nature and value of assets held by a borrower. The purpose of the asset verification process is to ensure the borrower has sufficient assets or reserves to handle typical household emergencies.

### Financial Statement

A **financial statement** is *a summary of facts showing the individual's financial condition.* It is a document that shows assets and liabilities for an individual, covering a specific period of time. If a borrower's assets are substantial and diverse, an audited financial statement may be the best way to explain the borrower's creditworthiness to the underwriter because it contains an itemized list of assets and liabilities that serves to disclose net worth.

# Summary of Qualifying the Buyer

A buyer's ability to qualify for a real estate loan depends on many factors, all of which relate to income, credit history, and net worth. There are guidelines for determining adequate income for a given housing expense, but it would be wrong to apply these figures too rigidly.

All aspects of the buyer's financial situation must be considered before a loan decision can be made. Quality, quantity, and durability of a buyer's income are important, but a buyer with a marginal income situation may still qualify for a loan if there's substantial net worth, indicating the ability to manage financial affairs.

Conversely, strong earnings and substantial assets may not be enough to offset the damage caused by poor credit paying habits. A borrower must be both able (income/assets) and willing (credit) to pay the housing expense.

Finally, keep in mind that a good property with a large down payment can offset marginal credit or income, because borrowers who make large investments in their property are far less likely to default than those with little or no equity.

# GIFT LETTER

I _____ of _____
         (Donor)                                       (Address)

_____ am the _____
     (Phone Number)                                   (Relationship)

of _____
         (Recipient)

I will give _____ (or) have given _____ the recipient a free and voluntary gift
                  (Check One)

of $ _____ to be used for the purchase of a home at _____

_____
                  (Address)

This is a bona fide gift and no repayment of this money is expected by me/us.

The above stated gift funds are currently being held at _____
                                           (Bank or Depository)

_____ , in account # _____ ; and I
      (Address)

authorize said Bank or Depository to verify that an amount equal to the said gift funds are readily available to me from that account.

WARNING:    Section 1010 of Title 18 U.S.C. "Department of Housing and Urban Development Transactions", provides, "Whoever, for the purpose of... influencing in any way the action of such Department ... makes, passes, utters or publishes any statement, knowing the same to be false... shall be fined not more than $5,000.00 or imprisoned not more than two years, or both".

_____     _____
(Donor)               (Date)           (Donor)              (Date)

*Sample Gift Letter Used by Lenders and Underwriters.*

# FHA Underwriting Standards

When applying for FHA loans, underwriters or lenders look at the borrower's income, credit history, and net worth just as they do for conventional loans. With FHA loans, though, underwriters can be more lenient when evaluating the borrower. Of course, an underwriter would like to see a stellar credit history, but credit problems are "understood" as long as there are no open collections or outstanding judgments on the credit report.

The underwriter would also feel more secure if the borrower had sufficient cash to pay the down payment and closing costs but, with FHA loans, even the entire down payment may be a non-repayable gift from a relative. The main difference between FHA and conventional loans is that *FHA loans have more liberal income qualifying standards.*

## Income Qualifying Standards

Underwriters making FHA loans look at income sources and verify income in a similar way as for conventional loans following Fannie Mae and Freddie Mac standards. The main difference is *FHA loans can have higher income ratios than conventional loans.*

### Housing Expense Ratio

As we learned when we discussed conventional loans, a borrower's **housing expense ratio** is the borrower's *total monthly housing expense compared to the gross monthly income, expressed as a percentage:*

**Total Housing Expense ÷ Gross Monthly Income = Ratio %**

The FHA considers a borrower's income adequate if the proposed total mortgage payment does not exceed **31%** of stable monthly income. The FHA's maximum mortgage payment must include **p**rincipal, **i**nterest, **t**axes, and **i**nsurance (**PITI**), plus monthly homeowner's association dues, if applicable (e.g., monthly condominium assessments).

As you will see, the FHA's total mortgage payment includes other monthly housing expenses to better assess the true total housing cost. For conventional loans, we divided the borrower's total housing expense by the borrower's income to determine the housing expense ratio. Then we multiplied the borrower's monthly income by the maximum ratio allowed to find the total mortgage payment for which the borrower would qualify, including debts. Both methods work here as well, in addition to one more:

**Total Housing Expense ÷ Maximum Ratio Allowed = Income Needed to Qualify**

### For Example

| | |
|---|---|
| $538.42 | Principal and Interest |
| $53.00 | Property Taxes |
| $25.00 | Homeowner's Insurance |
| + $90.00 | Association Dues |
| $706.42 | **Total Housing Expense** |

FHA allows a maximum housing expense ratio of 31%, so:

**$706.42 ÷ 0.31 = $2,278.77** (the minimum monthly income needed to buy the house)

## Total Debt Service Ratio

As with conventional loans, a borrower's **total debt service ratio** is the *relationship between the borrower's total monthly debt obligations (including housing and long-term debts with more than ten payments left) and income, expressed as a percentage*:

### Total Debt Service ÷ Gross Monthly Income = Ratio %

FHA lenders are interested in this ratio because they want to be sure a borrower's housing expenses (explained previously), plus any installment debts with more than ten payments left, do not exceed **43%** of stable monthly income. Let's calculate:

### *For Example*

| | |
|---|---|
| $706.42 | Housing Expense (from previous example) |
| $292.65 | Auto Payment |
| + $200.00 | Revolving Account |
| **$1,199.07** | **Total Debt Payments** |

FHA allows a maximum total debt service ratio of 43%, so:

**$1,199.07 ÷ 0.43 = $2,788.53** (the minimum monthly income needed to buy the house)

Remember that a borrower must qualify under both ratios, so $2,788.53 is the monthly income needed to buy this home (barring other offsetting factors).

### *Best Practices*

Higher debt ratios are typically allowed if the buyer is purchasing a new build from a builder, or a home that qualifies for higher-than-normal energy efficiencies. Check with the lender for exact rules and guidance.

# VA Underwriting Standards

When applying for a VA loan, the underwriter or lender will also look at the borrower's income, credit history, and net worth. Here again, like FHA loans, credit problems may be "understood." Net worth is also less of an issue since a borrower can get a VA loan with no down payment.

## Income Qualifying Standards

Underwriters making VA loans look at income sources and verify income in a similar way as for other mortgage loans. The main difference is that VA loans use a *residual income* (cash flow) analysis instead of a housing expense ratio.

### Residual Income

**Residual income** is *the amount of income a borrower has left after subtracting taxes, housing expenses, and all recurring debts and obligations*. (This is also referred to as the **cash flow analysis method**.) The residual income method determines the maximum mortgage amount for which a veteran can qualify. A veteran's residual income must meet the VA's minimum requirements. These figures are determined regionally, based on sale price.

Minimum Residual Income Standards are Guidelines

The balance of residual income (or cash flow) available for family support is an important factor in evaluating a VA loan application, but it's not the only consideration. VA standards are intended to be *guidelines* in judging the borrower's relative strength or weakness in regard to residual income, but none of the VA guidelines should be automatic reasons for approving or rejecting a loan. In fact, residual income is only one of many factors considered in evaluating VA loan applications.

## Table of Residual Incomes by Region

| For loan amounts of $79,999 and below | | | | |
|---|---|---|---|---|
| Family Size | Northeast | Midwest | South | West |
| 1 | $390 | $382 | $382 | $425 |
| 2 | $654 | $641 | $641 | $713 |
| 3 | $788 | $772 | $772 | $859 |
| 4 | $888 | $868 | $868 | $967 |
| 5 | $921 | $902 | $902 | $1,004 |
| Over 5 | Add $75 for each additional member up to a family of seven | | | |

| For loan amounts of $80,000 and above | | | | |
|---|---|---|---|---|
| Family Size | Northeast | Midwest | South | West |
| 1 | $450 | $441 | $441 | $491 |
| 2 | $755 | $738 | $738 | $823 |
| 3 | $909 | $889 | $889 | $990 |
| 4 | $1,025 | $1,003 | $1,003 | $1,117 |
| 5 | $1,062 | $1,039 | $1,039 | $1,158 |
| Over 5 | Add $80 for each additional member up to a family of seven | | | |

## Total Debt Service Ratio

The VA also uses a total debt service ratio when evaluating a potential borrower. Again, VA underwriters have more latitude. The VA looks for a total debt service ratio that normally does not exceed **41%**, although you should check with a VA-approved lender for exact details. If underwriters find this percentage to be above 41%, then other factors like sufficient residual income, significant liquid assets, or a substantial down payment must be considered before approving the loan.

# Review of Qualifying Standards

As we've seen, FHA and VA total debt service ratios are more liberal than Fannie Mae and Freddie Mac qualifying ratios for conventional loans. A borrower considered marginal by Fannie Mae and Freddie Mac can qualify more easily for an FHA or VA loan with these more liberal standards. The following chart compares FHA and VA loans.

**Qualifying Income Expense Ratios for Conventional, FHA, and VA Loans**

| | Housing Expense Ratio (PITI) Not to Exceed… | Total Debt Service Ratio (Housing + Debts with 10 or More Payments) Not to Exceed… | Residual Income |
|---|---|---|---|
| Fannie Mae/Freddie Mac Conventional LTV 90% or Less | 28% of Income | 36% of Income | N/A |
| FHA | 31% of Income | 43% of Income | N/A |
| VA | N/A | 41% of Income (includes all recurring debt) | Should equal or exceed regional figures for family size and loan amount |

## Other Factors Considered

In addition to residual income and total debt service ratio, other factors considered by the underwriter when evaluating a VA loan application include the:

- Borrower's demonstrated ability to accumulate cash or other liquid assets (such as stocks or bonds)
- Borrower's demonstrated ability to use credit wisely and avoid incurring excessive debt
- Relationship between the housing expense for the property being acquired and the housing expense the borrower is accustomed to paying
- Number and ages of the borrower's dependents
- Locality and general economic level of the neighborhood where the subject property is located
- Likelihood that the borrower's income may increase or decrease
- Borrower's employment history and work experience
- Borrower's demonstrated ability and willingness to make payments on time
- Amount of any down payment made
- Borrower's available cash after paying all closing costs and any other prepaid items relating to purchase of the property

## Closing the Loan

Loan underwriters carefully examine a loan package and decide to approve, reject, or approve the loan with conditions. Conditional approval usually requires additional items, such as the:

- Closing statement from the sale of the buyer's previous home
- Final inspection report
- Commitment for private mortgage insurance, which is often a condition for approving conventional loans with less than 20% down

After the loan is approved and all conditions are met, the necessary documents are prepared for **closing, settlement,** or **escrow,** which all mean the same thing—*closing the loan.* **Closing** is the *transfer of ownership* of real property from seller to buyer, according to the terms and conditions in the sales contract or escrow agreement. This is the final stage in a real estate transaction; the seller receives value for property (cash, mortgage, etc.) and the buyer gets title.

This consummates the long process of gathering documents, ensuring they're properly signed and recorded, and collecting and disbursing funds per the sales contract with each party getting a settlement statement showing costs. We'll review the highlights here.

## Closing Procedure

There are two types of closings:

- **Escrow closings**—Conducted by a disinterested third party
- **Roundtable closings**—Conducted with all parties present

In both cases, the mechanics of closing are normally the responsibility of an *escrow agent*. This escrow agent may be from the lender's in-house escrow department, an independent escrow company, or a title insurance company. The escrow agent simultaneously follows the instructions of the buyer and seller, as per the sales contract agreement or a separate set of escrow instructions. A copy of the sales contract or escrow instructions must be provided to the escrow agent, title company, and the lender.

The escrow agent gathers all the necessary documents (e.g., promissory note, mortgage, deed) and ensures they're properly signed. If there are no unforeseen problems during the closing (e.g., the seller did not really have title to the property), the loan papers are signed and there's one final check to be sure that everything is in order. The escrow agent calculates the various prorations, adjustments, and fees charged to each party. Loan funds are then disbursed to the proper parties according to the sales contract or escrow instructions. Finally, each party is given a **Closing Disclosure** that complies with **RESPA**.

√ ***Note:*** RESPA is an important potential topic on the real estate licensing exam.

**BORROWER(S) PRE-QUALIFICATION WORKSHEET**

BUYERS NAME(S): _____

PHONE NUMBER: (H) _____ (W) _____

*STEP A*
**BORROWER'S INCOME**
Hourly Rate      $_____
Guaranteed Weekly Hours    ☒_____
Total Gross Income (or Annual Salary) $_____

**CO-BORROWER'S INCOME**
Hourly Rate      $_____
Guaranteed Weekly Hours    ☒_____
Total Gross Income (or Annual Salary) $_____

**TOTAL INCOME** (FROM ABOVE)    $_____

**DIVIDE INCOME BY 12**    $_____

*STEP B*
**MONTHLY DEBT SERVICE**
Car Payment(s)      $_____
Visa      $_____
Master Card      $_____
Student Loan(s)      $_____
Other Charge Cards      $_____
Other      $_____
Other      $_____
**TOTAL OF DEBT SERVICE** $_____

*STEP C*
**ESTIMATE OF MONTHLY ESCROWS** (IF KNOWN)
Mortgage Insurance      $_____
Property Taxes      $_____
Homeowners Insurance      $_____
**TOTAL OF MONTHLY ESCROWS** $_____

*STEP D*
**HOUSING EXPENSE RATIO** (CONVENTIONAL = 28%; FHA = 31%; VA = 41%)
(FROM STEP A) GROSS MONTHLY INCOME    $_____
     (PICK RATIO FROM ABOVE) ☒_____
**EQUAL MAXIMUM PITI**    $_____
(MAX PITI MUST INCLUDE ANY CONDO / ASSOCIATION FEES)

*STEP E*
**TOTAL DEBT SERVICE RATIO** (CONVENTIONAL = 36%; FHA =43%; VA = 41%)
(FROM STEP A) GROSS MONTHLY INCOME    $_____
     (PICK RATIO FROM ABOVE) ☒_____
**EQUALS MAXIMUM PITI AND DEBT**    $_____
**SUBTRACT DEBTS** (FROM STEP B)    $_____
**EQUALS MAXIMUM ALLOWABLE FOR PITI** $_____
(MAX PITI MUST INCLUDE ANY CONDO / ASSOCIATION FEES)

**COMPARE THE AMOUNTS IS STEP D vs. STEP E**

*STEP F*
**ENTER THE LOWER OF STEP D OR STEP E HERE** $_____
IF YOU HAVE AN ANSWER ON THE ESCROW (STEP C), SUBTRACT THAT NUMBER FROM ABOVE. IF YOU DON'T HAVE AN ANSWER FROM STEP C, TAKE (APPROXIMATELY) 80% OF THE NUMBER IN **STEP F** TO FIND THE MAX ALLOWABLE FOR PRINCIPAL AND INTEREST (P & I). ENTER THAT NEW AMOUNT HERE $_____

*STEP G*
**DIVIDE THE MAXIMUM ALLOWABLE P & I, (STEP F), BY THE FACTOR THAT MOST CLOSELY REPRESENTS AN INTEREST RATE YOU WILL BE USING.**

(P & I) (STEP F) DIVIDED BY (FACTOR) (see below) = $_____ MAX MORTGAGE AMOUNT (PLUS YOUR BORROWER'S DOWN PAYMENT).

Principal and Interest Payment Factor Chart

| Mortgage Interest Rate | 5.25% | 5.50% | 5.75% | 6.00% | 6.25% | 6.50% | 6.75% | 7.00% | 7.25% | 7.50% | 7.75% | 8.00% | 8.25% | 8.50% | 8.75% | 9.00% |
|---|---|---|---|---|---|---|---|---|---|---|---|---|---|---|---|---|
| LOAN TERM (30 YEAR) | .00553 | .00568 | .00584 | .00599 | .00616 | .00632 | .00649 | .00665 | .00683 | .00699 | .00716 | .00734 | .00751 | .00769 | .00787 | .00805 |

*Sample Borrower Pre-Qualification Worksheet*

# FINANCE EXERCISE 7-1

Using a Buyer Qualification Worksheet, calculate how much house a buyer qualifies for with the following income and debt parameters:

**Income**

- Annual combined household income: $68,000 per year *

**Debts**

- Car: $350/month
- Visa Credit Card: $165/month
- Major Department Store Credit Card: $100/month
- Student Loan: $ 150/month

**Down Payment**

- Gift FHA: $10,000
- Borrower's own funds Conventional: $25,000

**Estimated Property Taxes**

- $3,000/year

**Estimated Property Insurance**

- $500/year

* Round income to nearest dollar.

1. Calculate an FHA loan at 6.5%, 30-year, fully amortized

2. Calculate a conventional conforming loan at 6.5%, 30-year, fully amortized

3. How much could the borrower qualify for if he took a conventional 3/1 ARM at 5.25% amortized?

*See the Appendix for answers to check your work.*

# Summary

1. Buyers can get *pre-qualified* or *pre-approved*. **Pre-qualification** is when an agent or lender reviews the borrower's financial situation to see if she's likely to get approved for a loan, and for about how much. (Important distinction: Pre-qualification is *not* binding on lender). **Pre-approval** is when a lender determines that potential borrowers can be financed for a certain amount. Real estate agents *cannot* give a buyer a pre-approval.

2. The loan process consists of four steps: 1. Consulting with the lender, 2. Filling out the loan application, 3. Processing the application, and 4. Analyzing the borrower and subject property. Common fees include a credit report, appraisal, title work, inspections, etc. The lender may have an application fee, require a deposit, or get costs from closing. The loan application includes many personal and financial questions. Address and employment information must date back two to three years. Income doesn't have to include alimony/child support. Those who are self-employed may need to provide personal and company tax returns and financial statements. Assets and liabilities must all be disclosed, including alimony/child support if it's an obligation. **Net worth** equals assets minus liabilities. Borrowers must answer the declarations truthfully.

3. The borrower and property are analyzed, and all information is verified. The underwriting process looks at the *five "Cs"*: **Capacity** (ability to pay), **Collateral** (down payment, home value), **Credit** (good payment history), **Character** (job stability, reserves), and **Conditions** (health of job market, economy). *Automated underwriting* has a computer look at the first three Cs; the computer then recommends accepting the loan or referring it to a human for further consideration.

4. **Fannie Mae, Freddie Mac, the FHA, and VA** all evaluate monthly income stability, quality, and durability. Bonuses, commission, part-time earnings, and overtime all count if shown to be a consistent part of a borrower's income for the past few years. Borrowers typically *cannot* count unemployment, welfare, and temporary income. **Credit history** is a record of debt repayment. **Debt** is a recurring obligation that can't be canceled. **Credit scoring** is an objective means of evaluating credit. Lenders will verify assets and may require financial statements. A gift letter can show part of a down payment/closing costs as a non-repayable gift from relative.

5. Fannie Mae/Freddie Mac **income ratios**: 28% for housing expense, 36% for debt service. The **housing expense ratio** is the relationship between a borrower's total monthly housing expense (PITI) and gross monthly income (stable monthly income), expressed as a percentage. The **total debt service ratio** is the relationship between a borrower's total monthly debt obligations (including housing and long-term debts with more than ten payments left) and income (stable monthly income), expressed as a percentage. The FHA's qualifying standards are more lenient than Fannie Mae's (e.g., entire down payment may be a relative's gift). **FHA income ratios**: 31% for housing expense, 43% for debt service. The VA is also more lenient than Fannie Mae (e.g., no down payment). **VA income ratios**: 41% for debt service, but for housing expense VA uses the residual income method (the money a veteran has left after subtracting all debts).

6. **Closing** is the transfer of ownership of real estate from seller to buyer, per terms and conditions in sales contract or escrow agreement. The seller receives value for property (cash, mortgage, etc.) and the buyer gets title. Closings can be *escrow* (done by disinterested third party) or *roundtable* (conducted with all parties present), and **must comply with RESPA** (full disclosure, prevents kickbacks).

# Quiz

1. **Which prevents senior citizens from being discriminated against in the loan process?**
   a. Equal Credit Opportunity Act
   b. Federal Fair Housing Act
   c. Real Estate Settlement Procedures Act
   d. Regulation Z

2. **A borrower must provide how many years' worth of employment information?**
   a. 2–3
   b. 3–4
   c. 4–5
   d. 5–6

3. **If the borrower is self-employed, he should provide**
   a. the average monthly income earned over the previous two years.
   b. employment verification from the last employer.
   c. profit and loss statements for the previous six years.
   d. tax returns for the previous two to three years.

4. **A gift letter**
   a. is never necessary.
   b. may come only from a friend or family member of the borrower.
   c. must be signed by the donor.
   d. must state when the gift is to be repaid.

5. **An escrow agent may be from a(n)**
   a. independent escrow company.
   b. in-house escrow department.
   c. title insurance company.
   d. all of the above

6. **A borrower applying for a VA loan must provide a**
   a. Certificate of Eligibility and DD-214.
   b. Certificate of Value.
   c. military ID card.
   d. referral from a superior officer.

7. **Conforming loans follow the guidelines of**
   a. Fannie Mae/Freddie Mac.
   b. the FHA.
   c. RESPA.
   d. the VA.

8. **There has been _____ dependence on the secondary mortgage market, which has brought a high degree of _____ to loan underwriting.**
   a. decreasing; creativity
   b. decreasing; standardization
   c. increasing; creativity
   d. increasing; standardization

9. **To qualify for a conventional loan, stable monthly income may include**
   a. alimony received (which a borrower chooses to reveal).
   b. a Christmas bonus received last year for the first time.
   c. erratic unemployment earnings.
   d. income from other family members.

10. **_____ can be used to offset a marginal or high total debt service ratio.**
    a. Above-normal net worth
    b. A co-borrower
    c. High credit scores
    d. all of the above

11. **When do strong earnings and substantial assets offset damage caused by poor credit paying habits?**
    a. all of the time
    b. only if the applicant is a veteran
    c. some of the time
    d. when the applicant declares bankruptcy

12. **Age**
    a. can be a legitimate reason for turning down any borrower.
    b. can be a legitimate reason for turning down a borrower over 65.
    c. can't be considered in the loan underwriting process under any circumstances as long as the applicant is over the age of 18.
    d. should always be considered in the loan underwriting process.

13. *The FHA allows a maximum housing expense-to-income ratio of _____ and a total debt service-to-income ratio of _____.*
    a. 28%; 33%
    b. 28%; 36%
    c. 29%; 36%
    d. 31%; 43%

14. *The VA underwrites loans using the*
    a. residual down payment method.
    b. residual income/cash flow analysis method.
    c. total debt expense-to-income ratio.
    d. total housing expense-to-down-payment ratio.

15. *FHA and VA debt-to-income ratio formulas are _____ than conventional ratios.*
    a. harder to calculate
    b. less generous
    c. more generous
    d. the same

16. *Which has its own underwriting standards?*
    a. Fannie Mae
    b. the FHA
    c. the VA
    d. all of the above

# Final Exams

## Final Exam 1

1. **Which Act prohibits discrimination in granting credit?**
   - a. ECOA
   - b. Home Mortgage Disclosure Act
   - c. RESPA
   - d. There is no law prohibiting discrimination.

2. **In real estate finance, disintermediation means**
   - a. a borrower has possession of property.
   - b. a lender has possession of property.
   - c. money flows out of savings institutions into higher return investments.
   - d. an owner has a property free of debt.

3. **Interest rates are a measure of the**
   - a. cost of money.
   - b. demand for money.
   - c. supply of money.
   - d. value of money.

4. **The secondary market for mortgage loans can best be described as the**
   - a. actions of private investors.
   - b. market for trading future contracts.
   - c. operations of the FHA and the VA.
   - d. purchase and/or sale of mortgage loans after origination.

5. **A lender that makes a secured loan for the purchase of real estate is known as the**
   - a. mortgagee.
   - b. mortgagor.
   - c. trustee.
   - d. vendor.

6. **The purpose of an acceleration clause in a mortgage instrument is to**
   - a. allow the interest rate to be increased.
   - b. define that, in the event of default, all future payments become due immediately.
   - c. define that one late payment is an act in default.
   - d. increase payments at periodic intervals.

7. **When assuming a loan, the buyer would**
   - a. be required to be a veteran.
   - b. make sure the lender accelerates the loan.
   - c. not be responsible to make payments on time.
   - d. pay the seller the equity in their property.

8. **Which is NOT a way for a buyer to avoid PMI on a conventional loan?**
   - a. obtain an 80-10-10 loan
   - b. obtain a "No PMI" loan
   - c. make a 10% down payment on a house
   - d. make a 20% or more down payment on a house

9. **Which is NOT a method used by the Federal Reserve to control monetary policy?**
   - a. open market operations
   - b. raise or lower the discount rate
   - c. raise or lower the prime rate
   - d. raise or lower reserve requirements

10. **The interest rate charged by the Federal Reserve for loans to member banks is called the**
    - a. bank rate.
    - b. base rate.
    - c. discount rate.
    - d. prime rate.

11. **Funds for making FHA loans are provided by**
    a. any government agency.
    b. the Federal Reserve.
    c. the FHA.
    d. qualified lending institutions.

12. **The property value acceptable to the FHA as loan collateral is determined**
    a. as the lesser of the appraised value or the purchase price.
    b. by the amount of the MIP commitment.
    c. by the opinion of the loan underwriter.
    d. by the real estate agent.

13. **Which information can be found in a note?**
    a. appraised value of property
    b. details of the purchase
    c. legal description of property
    d. terms and repayment provisions

14. **Which charge is used to increase a lender's yield on real estate loans?**
    a. appraisal
    b. credit report
    c. origination fee
    d. title insurance

15. **A loan that includes periodic payments of principal and interest followed by a balloon payment is known as a**
    a. fully amortized loan.
    b. hybrid mortgage.
    c. partially amortized loan.
    d. straight note.

16. **The Equal Credit Opportunity Act, which is designed to limit discrimination in credit transactions, includes which restriction?**
    a. Credit reports cannot be required if an applicant objects.
    b. No questions may be asked about a borrower's credit history.
    c. No reasons have to be given if credit is denied.
    d. No restrictions can be placed on the source of income received.

17. **Which is NOT included in a borrower's income analysis?**
    a. pensions, interest, and dividends
    b. regular earnings and overtime
    c. revealed alimony and child support
    d. sporadic overtime and commissions

18. **Qualifying guidelines on most FHA loans are ____ housing ratio and ____ total debt ratio.**
    a. 28%; 33%
    b. 28%; 36%
    c. 31%; 43%
    d. 36%; 41%

19. **The minimum cash payment investment needed for a home with an FHA appraised value of $90,000 is**
    a. $900.
    b. $3,150.
    c. $4,500.
    d. $9,000.

20. **Which statement regarding VA loans is FALSE?**
    a. Property is appraised and a CRV is issued.
    b. VA loans are available for investors who are veterans.
    c. Veteran may pay points on a purchase.
    d. Veteran needs a Certificate of Eligibility.

21. **Ann makes a 20% down payment on her $85,000 purchase. Her loan amount is**
    a. $17,000.
    b. $20,000.
    c. $68,000.
    d. $85,000.

22. **Private mortgage insurance covers the risk of the possibility of**
    a. death of the borrower.
    b. default in loan repayment.
    c. failure of lender who makes the loan.
    d. loss in value of the collateral property.

23. **The interest or value remaining in a property after all liens and other debts are taken into account is known as**
    a. assessment.
    b. equity.
    c. surety.
    d. valuation.

24. **A mortgage that covers a number of parcels of real property, and that may provide for the separate sale of each parcel, is known as a(n)**
    a. adjustable rate mortgage.
    b. blanket mortgage.
    c. open-end mortgage.
    d. package mortgage.

**25. With a fixed-rate loan,**

a. assumptions must be allowed.
b. interest rate may increase if the index goes up.
c. a lender may increase the interest rate if the borrower misses two payments in a year.
d. principal and interest payments must remain constant.

**26. On an adjustable rate loan,**

a. the rate is tied to the lender's profitability.
b. the rate is tied to a specific index.
c. the rate is tied to what the borrower can afford.
d. there is always negative amortization.

**27. The Closing Disclosure is NOT required in the settlement of a transaction of a(n)**

a. condominium.
b. owner-occupied four-family housing unit.
c. retail store building.
d. single-family home.

**28. The Real Estate Settlement Procedures Act does NOT require**

a. a good faith estimate of closing costs at the time of the loan application.
b. prohibiting agents from owning shares in lending companies.
c. prohibiting agents from receiving kickbacks.
d. a settlement statement be given to the buyer and the seller.

**29. RESPA does NOT prohibit and/or place limits on**

a. the amount paid for origination fees.
b. the "cushion" of the borrower's prepaid items that a lender may hold in escrow.
c. kickbacks.
d. the length of time for delivery of required information to the applicant/borrower.

**30. An FHA buyer may currently**

a. be eligible only if he is low income.
b. buy a rental property as an investment.
c. use a gift for his entire down payment.
d. use the program for vacation homes.

**31. The VA guarantee program provides eligible veterans with**

a. cash for home down payments.
b. low interest education loans.
c. low interest home loans.
d. the opportunity to buy a home with little or no down payment.

**32. In a purchase transaction, a major source of second mortgages could be**

a. FHA and VA lending agencies.
b. insurance companies and pension funds.
c. real estate investment trusts.
d. sellers.

**33. The annual percentage rate (APR), as required to be disclosed on a Loan Estimate, is**

a. the actual interest rate on the face of the note.
b. always the same as the interest rate.
c. the relationship between total cost of borrowing and the actual amount borrowed.
d. the sum of all costs required to obtain credit.

**34. What statement regarding the Federal Reserve is FALSE?**

a. All federally chartered banks must be members.
b. It sets the discount rate.
c. It sets the prime rate.
d. There are 12 Federal Reserve districts.

**35. Which mortgage requires principal and interest payments at regular intervals until the debt is satisfied?**

a. balloon mortgage
b. first mortgage
c. fully amortized mortgage
d. partially amortized mortgage

**36. In which market can lenders sell mortgages?**

a. acceleration market
b. mortgagee market
c. primary market
d. secondary market

**37. Which clause in a mortgage allows a lender to declare the entire unpaid balance due upon the borrower's default?**

a. acceleration clause
b. escalator clause
c. foreclosure clause
d. forfeiture clause

**38. The act of depositing something of value with a disinterested third party creates a(n)**

a. bond.
b. covenant.
c. deed of trust.
d. escrow.

39. **The Goldbergs, who own their house free of any encumbrances, are selling it to the Irwins for $115,000. The Goldbergs are taking back a straight note for $75,000 at 10% interest for 20 years. The first monthly payment will be**
    a. $625.
    b. $750.
    c. $1,000.
    d. $7,500.

40. **The federal Truth in Lending law**
    a. dictates that all loan applications must be made in person.
    b. regulates advertising with references to a mortgage interest rate.
    c. requires a lender to estimate the seller's closing costs on all residential loans.
    d. would prevent a broker from advertising "FHA financing available" on a property.

41. **An agent should NOT refer a prospective buyer to a lawyer for advice about**
    a. a lien waiver.
    b. market interest rates.
    c. a mechanic's lien.
    d. an opinion of title.

42. **A seller agrees to pay two points on a buyer's loan. The price is $120,000 and the buyer is making a 20% down payment. Two points equal**
    a. $1,200.
    b. $1,920.
    c. $2,000.
    d. $2,400.

43. **A mortgage clause that prevents someone else from assuming a loan is a(n)**
    a. acceleration clause.
    b. alienation clause.
    c. estoppel clause.
    d. power of sale clause.

44. **In a real estate ad for mortgage financing, which statement is permissible if no other information is given?**
    a. "$2,000 down"
    b. "Interest rate only 9%"
    c. "Liberal terms available to qualified buyer"
    d. "Monthly payment only $400"

45. **An adjustable rate mortgage where the loan balance increases is experiencing**
    a. defeasance.
    b. disintermediation.
    c. negative amortization.
    d. reconveyance.

46. **With a VA loan, a veteran has the option of**
    a. defaulting on the loan without incurring any personal liability.
    b. offering the home for rent immediately after purchasing it.
    c. selling the home and transferring his loan to a new home.
    d. selling the home to a non-veteran, who may then assume the balance of the loan.

47. **Gloria qualifies for an FHA loan. She should make her loan application**
    a. at the Cleveland regional FHA office.
    b. on a form that's available from any real estate broker.
    c. through any FHA-approved lender.
    d. with the State of Ohio Division of Real Estate.

48. **In a foreclosure, the debtor can get the house back through**
    a. acceleration.
    b. confirmation.
    c. defeasance.
    d. redemption.

49. **The Federal National Mortgage Association is**
    a. able to purchase only FHA and VA loans.
    b. designed to increase the availability of money to primary lenders.
    c. owned and operated by the federal government.
    d. owned and operated by the Federal Reserve.

50. **The Government National Mortgage Association is**
    a. also known as Ginnie Mae.
    b. the largest buyer of conventional loans in the market.
    c. a private corporation.
    d. under the direction of Fannie Mae.

# Final Exam 2

1. *The law that prohibits discrimination in the lending process is*
   a. the Civil Rights Act of 1866.
   b. the ECOA.
   c. the Ohio Civil Rights Law.
   d. Title VIII.

2. *The best loan for a buyer to obtain for a single-family home in need of repairs is*
   a. the FHA Streamlined 203(k) loan.
   b. Section 234 (c) loan.
   c. the standard FHA Section 203 (b) loan.
   d. a VA guaranteed loan.

3. *A mortgage broker's basic source of income is derived from*
   a. charges for escrow fees for closing a loan.
   b. charges for service fees for collecting loan payments.
   c. loan origination fees charged to the borrower.
   d. loan origination fees charged to the lender.

4. *Which statement regarding a VA loan is TRUE?*
   a. All closing costs can be financed.
   b. All prepaid escrows can be financed.
   c. The funding fee can be financed.
   d. The VA limits the purchase price for a house.

5. *In regard to a mortgage loan, the borrower is referred to as the*
   a. mortgagee.
   b. mortgagor.
   c. trustee.
   d. vendor.

6. *The interest rates charged for FHA and VA loans are established by*
   a. the FHA and/or VA.
   b. Ginnie Mae.
   c. HUD.
   d. the market.

7. *If the borrower obtains a conventional loan and makes a 20% down payment,*
   a. homeowners insurance is not required.
   b. the loan will be insured by a government entity.
   c. private mortgage insurance is not required.
   d. private mortgage insurance is required.

8. *When a mortgage loan is paid off over a shorter term, the major advantage is a reduction in the*
   a. amount of each monthly payment.
   b. number of payments over that which is stated in the note.
   c. total interest costs.
   d. total principal amount.

9. *ECOA refers to*
   a. Economic Concern Overview Act.
   b. Environmental Concern Overview Act.
   c. Equal Community Opportunity Act.
   d. Equal Credit Opportunity Act.

10. *A loan that includes a fixed rate period followed by an adjustable rate period is known as a(n)*
    a. hybrid loan.
    b. interest-only loan.
    c. piggyback loan.
    d. subprime loan.

11. *For an FHA loan, a borrower CANNOT*
    a. buy a rental property.
    b. have the seller pay their closing costs.
    c. pay their own closing costs and prepaids.
    d. receive a gift for the down payment.

12. *The FHA is administered by*
    a. Fannie Mae.
    b. the FDIC.
    c. Freddie Mac.
    d. HUD.

13. *When qualifying for a residential mortgage loan, an applicant's liabilities are most likely to be calculated as*
    a. minimum monthly payment amounts.
    b. a percentage of cash required.
    c. a percentage of the property value.
    d. a ratio against total assets.

14. **The main characteristic of a shorter-term loan is the**
    a. loan is paid off sooner and less equity is built up.
    b. loan is paid off sooner and less principal and interest must be paid.
    c. loan is paid off sooner and less principal is required to be paid.
    d. payments are higher.

15. **What is the minimum down payment for a VA loan on a $75,000 home?**
    a. $750
    b. $1,500
    c. $2,250
    d. There is no minimum requirement for qualified, eligible veterans.

16. **Funding of a construction loan is usually made**
    a. after all construction has been completed and approved by the lender.
    b. after the time for filing liens has expired.
    c. in full at the time when the note and mortgage are signed.
    d. periodically as the house is constructed.

17. **What is the minimum down payment (cash investment) contribution for an FHA loan on a $170,000 home?** 3.5%
    a. $1,700
    b. $5,950
    c. $8,500
    d. There is no minimum requirement.

18. **Which is a voluntary lien?**
    a. assessments
    b. mechanic's lien
    c. mortgage
    d. property taxes

19. **Which is NOT an advantage of an FHA loan?**
    a. borrowers can use secondary financing for the minimum down payment
    b. higher property standards
    c. less borrower out-of-pocket cash up front
    d. less stringent qualifying standards

20. **For a lower-income buyer with higher debt ratios, the best loan choice would most likely be a(n)**
    a. conventional loan.
    b. FHA loan.
    c. REIT.
    d. VA loan.

21. **To be eligible for a VA loan, a veteran must**
    a. be a combat veteran.
    b. be a relative of a veteran.
    c. get a Certificate of Reasonable Value.
    d. meet the VA's eligibility requirements.

22. **To be eligible for an FHA loan, one must**
    a. be a first-time homebuyer.
    b. be a U.S. citizen, permanent resident, or nonpermanent resident with a work visa.
    c. buy a home in a designated target area.
    d. meet the FHA's income requirements.

23. **The income housing expense and total debt service ratios for traditional 10% and 20% down conventional loans normally are**
    a. 28% and 36%.
    b. 28% and 41%.
    c. 29% and 36%.
    d. 29% and 41%.

24. **What loan will NOT have a balloon payment due at the end of the loan term (the termination date, stop date, or due date)?**
    a. $90,000 loan at 8% interest amortized over 20 years
    b. $90,000 loan at 8% interest amortized over 30 years, due in 10 years
    c. $90,000 loan at 8% interest with interest-only payments, due in 10 years
    d. $90,000 loan with variable interest rate of 8% plus CMT index, due in 10 years

25. **The term used when a loan balance grows due to deferred interest is**
    a. disintermediation.
    b. hypothecation.
    c. interest only.
    d. negative amortization.

**26. Broad forces influencing housing cycles are**

a. environment, asbestos, lead paint, and radon gas.
b. Federal Reserve, Treasury, President, and Congress.
c. physical, economic, governmental, and social.
d. reserve requirements, discount rates, open market operations, and moral suasion.

**27. The Federal National Mortgage Association is also known as**

a. Fannie Mae.
b. Freddie Mac.
c. Ginnie Mac.
d. Ginnie Mae.

**28. The federal government influences money supply with**

a. buying and selling stocks.
b. direct and indirect policy.
c. fiscal and monetary policy.
d. physical and monetary policy.

**29. When the interest rate is much lower initially in order to get a buyer to use a particular loan program, then jumps to a higher rate at the end of a specified period, this is said to be a**

a. permanent buydown.
b. prime rate.
c. teaser rate.
d. usury rate.

**30. A person may be turned down for a mortgage loan if**

a. he has poor credit and income too low to qualify.
b. he is a member of a minority group or other protected class.
c. he is too old.
d. his income is too high to qualify.

**31. The one promising to pay the money in a promissory note is known as the**

a. holder.
b. holder in due course.
c. maker.
d. payee.

**32. A debtor may redeem property from the foreclosure process up until the ____ takes place.**

a. appraisal or advertising
b. confirmation of sale
c. foreclosure
d. A debtor cannot redeem property.

**33. If a buyer purchases a $100,000 home and gets an $80,000 mortgage loan at an interest rate of 6%, how much are 4 points?**

a. $320
b. $3,200
c. $4,000
d. $32,000

**34. PMI covers the risk of**

a. the death of the borrower.
b. a default on the loan repayment.
c. a failure of the loan service agent to service the loan properly.
d. a loss in value of the property serving as collateral.

**35. On an ARM, the margin is the difference between the**

a. APR value and the cost-of-funds index.
b. home value and the amount borrowed.
c. index value and the interest rate charged.
d. qualifying ratio and highest ratio allowed.

**36. When determining whether income is durable and stable and can be used in qualifying a person for a mortgage loan, a factor the underwriter will NOT consider is**

a. child support payments that will continue for less than three years.
b. stability in the income or payments.
c. a two-year history of employment at a job (or in the same field).
d. a verification of employment and income.

**37. The Federal Housing Administration (FHA)**

a. insures mortgage lenders against default.
b. makes residential loans.
c. must follow rules of the Federal Reserve.
d. requires a prepayment penalty.

38. **The maximum allowable mortgage for an FHA loan**
    a. depends on the interest rate.
    b. is $108,750.
    c. is set by the lender.
    d. varies by county.

39. **For a conventional mortgage loan, who makes the final decision on approval or denial?**
    a. Fannie Mae
    b. the FHA
    c. loan processor
    d. underwriter

40. **The Veterans Administration (VA)**
    a. guarantees lenders against default.
    b. makes residential loans.
    c. must follow rules of the Federal Reserve.
    d. requires a prepayment penalty.

41. **Which is NOT a benefit of a VA loan?**
    a. Loans are assumable.
    b. Loans are available for homes and business.
    c. Loans are available with no money down.
    d. Most loans are fixed rate amortized loans.

42. **On a VA loan, who makes the final decision on the approval or denial of a loan?**
    a. the FHA and the underwriter
    b. Ginnie Mae and the secondary market
    c. HUD and the loan officer
    d. the VA and the underwriter

43. **Three main secondary market sources are**
    a. Fannie Mae, Freddie Mac, and Ginnie Mae.
    b. Federal Reserve, S&Ls, and Fannie Mae.
    c. the FHA, the VA, and conventional.
    d. REIT, federal government, and insurance companies.

44. **Conventional loans follow the underwriting guidelines of**
    a. Fannie Mae.
    b. the FHA
    c. Freddie Mac.
    d. both a and c

45. **A seller takes back a second mortgage for $12,000 at 10% interest. The note calls for monthly interest-only payments for five years, then a balloon. What is the first payment amount?**
    a. $100
    b. $1,000
    c. $1,200
    d. $12,000

46. **A lender gives Jenny a $15,000 second mortgage at 9.5% interest. Payments are interest-only for 10 years. What balloon payment will be due?**
    a. $150
    b. $1,500
    c. $15,000
    d. There will not be any balloon payment due.

47. **Regulation Z applies to**
    a. any real estate purchase transactions.
    b. business loans with collateral.
    c. commercial real estate loans only.
    d. real estate credit transactions for personal use.

48. **RESPA applies to all**
    a. business loans with collateral.
    b. commercial real estate loans only.
    c. real estate credit transactions for one- to four-dwelling units.
    d. real estate purchase transactions.

49. **Which is NOT a trigger statement in regard to advertising under the Truth In Lending Act?**
    a. "20% down"
    b. "No down payment"
    c. "Only 360 monthly payments"
    d. "Pay only $700 per month"

50. **Which is NOT covered by RESPA laws?**
    a. Buyer will get a good faith estimate of closing costs.
    b. Buyer will get a Closing Disclosure at closing.
    c. Lender may not discriminate based on source of income.
    d. No kickbacks allowed.

# Final Exam 1 Answer Key

1. a ECOA
2. c money flows out of savings institutions into higher return investments.
3. a cost of money.
4. d purchase and/or sale of mortgage loans after origination.
5. a mortgagee.
6. b define that, in the event of default, all future payments become due immediately.
7. d pay the seller the equity in their property.
8. c make a 10% down payment on a house
9. c raise or lower the prime rate
10. c discount rate.
11. d qualified lending institutions.
12. a as the less of the appraised value or the purchase price.
13. d terms and repayment provisions
14. c origination fee
15. c partially amortized loan.
16. d No restrictions can be placed on the source of income received.
17. d sporadic overtime and commissions
18. c 31%; 43%
19. b $3,150.
20. b VA loans are available for investors who are veterans.
21. c $68,000.
22. b default in loan repayment.
23. b equity.
24. b blanket mortgage.
25. d principal and interest payments must remain constant.
26. b the rate is tied to a specific index.
27. c retail store building.
28. b prohibiting agents from owning shares in lending companies.
29. a the amount paid for origination fees.
30. c use a gift for his entire down payment.
31. d the opportunity to buy a home with little or no down payment.
32. d sellers.
33. c the relationship between total cost of borrowing and the actual amount borrowed.
34. c It sets the prime rate.
35. c fully amortized mortgage
36. d secondary market
37. a acceleration clause
38. d escrow.
39. a $625.
40. b regulates advertising with references to a mortgage interest rate.
41. b market interest rates.
42. b $1,920.
43. b alienation clause.
44. c "Liberal terms available to qualified buyer"
45. c negative amortization.
46. d selling the home to a non-veteran, who may then assume the balance of the loan.
47. c through any FHA-approved lender.
48. d redemption.
49. b designed to increase the availability of money to primary lenders.
50. a also known as Ginne Mae.

# Final Exam 2 Answer Key

1. b  the ECOA.
2. a  the FHA Streamlined 203(k) loan.
3. c  loan origination fees charged to the borrower.
4. c  The funding fee can be financed.
5. b  mortgagor.
6. d  the market.
7. c  private mortgage insurance is not required.
8. c  total interest costs.
9. d  Equal Credit Opportunity Act.
10. a  hybrid loan.
11. a  buy a rental property.
12. d  HUD.
13. a  minimum monthly payment amounts.
14. d  payments are higher.
15. d  There is no minimum requirement for qualified, eligible veterans.
16. d  periodically as the house is constructed.
17. b  $5,950
18. c  mortgage
19. a  borrowers can use secondary financing for the minimum down payment
20. b  FHA loan
21. d  meet the VA's eligibility requirements.
22. b  be a U.S. citizen, permanent resident, or nonpermanent resident with a work visa.
23. a  28% and 36%.
24. a  $90,000 loan at 8% interest amortized over 20 years
25. d  negative amortization
26. c  physical, economic, governmental, and social.
27. a  Fannie Mae.
28. c  fiscal and monetary policy.
29. c  teaser rate.
30. a  he has poor credit and income too low to qualify.
31. c  maker.

32. b  confirmation of sale
33. b  $3,200
34. b  a default on the loan repayment.
35. c  index value and the interest rate charged.
36. a  child support payments that will continue for less than three years.
37. a  insures mortgage lenders against default.
38. d  varies by country.
39. d  underwriter
40. a  guarantees lenders against default.
41. b  Loans are available for homes and business.
42. d  the VA and the underwriter
43. a  Fannie Mae, Freddie Mac, and Ginnie Mae.
44. d  both a and c
45. a  $100
46. c  $15,000
47. d  real estate credit transactions for personal use.
48. c  real estate credit transactions for one- to four-dwelling units.
49. b  "No down payment"
50. c  Lender may not discriminate based on source of income

# *Appendix*

## CHAPTER ANSWER KEY

### Chapter 1—Housing Cycles, Money Supply, and Government Regulation

#### Chapter 1 Quiz (pg. 36)

1. d  seller's market
2. c  structure
3. a  fiscal and monetary policy
4. d  all of the above
5. c  3
6. c  12
7. b  discount rates and reserve requirements
8. a  the Equal Credit Opportunity Act
9. a  first home
10. a  0
11. c  Loan Estimate
12. c  mortgage fraud
13. d  social
14. b  fiscal
15. c  RESPA
16. c  reserve requirements
17. a  APR
18. d  Lenders cannot deny a homebuyer's application when income is not ongoing and/or verifiable
19. a  economic
20. d  14 years

### Chapter 2—Types of Finance Instruments

#### Chapter 2 Quiz (pg. 60)

1. d  straight note
2. a  acceleration clause
3. b  alienation clause
4. d  promissory note
5. d  redemption
6. d  reverse
7. a  payments covering principal, interest, taxes, and insurance
8. b  construction mortgage
9. c  mortgagor
10. b  debtor

### Chapter 3—Primary and Secondary Markets

#### Chapter 3 Quiz (pg. 74)

1. a  mortgage companies
2. d  specialize in short-term commercial lending activities
3. c  REIT
4. a  large-scale commercial real estate projects
5. d  service the loan (collect the payments) after the loan closes
6. b  primary market
7. b  insurance company
8. b  Federal Housing Finance Agency
9. a  Fannie Mae
10. c  secondary market

11. d follow the underwriting guidelines of the secondary market agencies

12. d offer borrowers with less-than-perfect credit or other qualifying difficulties an opportunity to obtain a mortgage loan

## Chapter 4—Conventional Financing

### Finance Exercise 4-1 (pg. 83)

1. Monthly Payment for 6.5% PMI loan: $1,230.60
$200,000 purchase price x 10% = $20,000 down payment
$200,000 - $20,000 down payment = $180,000 loan amount
Factor for 6.5% is 6.32 ÷ 1,000
$180,000 ÷ 1,000 = $180 x 6.32 = $1,137.60 monthly P&I payment
$180,000 loan amount x 0.0062 (PMI monthly premium) = $1,116.00
$1,116.00 ÷ 12 = $93.00 per month PMI premium
$1,137.60 P&I payment + $93.00 PMI premium = $1,230.60 total monthly payment

2. Monthly Payment for the 7% No PMI loan: $1,197.00
$200,000 purchase price x 10% = $20,000 down payment
$200,000 - $20,000 down payment = $180,000 loan amount
Factor for 7% is 6.65 ÷ 1,000
$180,000 ÷ 1,000 = $180 x 6.65 = $1,197.00 monthly P&I payment

3. **6.5% PMI loan**
Disadvantages: It has a slightly higher monthly payment (an extra $33.60).
Advantages: The extra $93 PMI premium ends once the LTV reaches 78% of its original value.
**7% No PMI loan**
Disadvantages: The higher interest rate (an extra 0.5%) is permanent—lasts for the life of the loan.
Advantages: It has a lower monthly payment at the beginning of the loan.

### Finance Exercise 4-2 (pg. 89)

1. First Mortgage (Amortized):
$200,000 purchase price x 80% LTV = $160,000 loan amount
Factor for 6.5% is 6.32 ÷ 1,000
$160,000 ÷ 1,000 = $160 x 6.32 = $1,011.20 monthly P&I payment

2. Second Mortgage (Straight)
$200,000 x 10% = $20,000
$20,000 x 8.5% (straight note) = $1,700 annual payment
$1,700 ÷ 12 = $141.67 monthly interest payment

3. Balloon Payment at the end of 10 years: $20,000
The entire second mortgage amount is due since the couple paid interest only.

### Finance Exercise 4-3 (pg. 90)

1. $189,500 x 0.95 = $180,025 (Loan Amount)

2. $189,500 x 0.05 = $9,475 (Down Payment)

$180,025 x 0.015 = $2,700.38 (Loan Origination Fee)

$9,475 + $2,700.38 = $12,175.38 (Total Due at Closing from Buyer)

3. $180,025 x 6.32 ÷ 1,000 = $1,137.76 (Monthly Principal and Interest on Loan)

*(Note: This equation uses the Interest Rate Factors Chart)*

### Chapter 4 Quiz (pg. 94)

1. d is not insured or guaranteed by any government entity
2. c fully amortized loan
3. b higher interest rates
4. b over 80%
5. a 20-25%
6. c lower monthly payments as compared to a loan with PMI
7. c 95% loan
8. c when a home has been paid down to 78% of its original value for loans made after July 1999
9. d prepayment penalty clause
10. c loan funds will be repaid more quickly

## Chapter 5—Government Financing

### Finance Exercise 5-1 (pg. 118)

1. The minimum investment the buyer must make is 3.5% of the sale price or appraised value, whichever is lower, so: $103,500 x 3.5% (0.035) = $3,622.50 minimum investment.

2. The most a seller can pay for a buyer on an FHA loan (as of May 2010) is 6 points (or 6%*), so: $103,500 x 6% = $6,210.00

   *This is subject to any changes the FHA may make to seller paid limits.

### Finance Exercise 5-2 (pg. 118)

1. $88,900 Home Price + $1,911.35 (2.15% Funding Fee) = $90,811.35 Loan Amount

2. The buyer will not have to make any down payment, but he will have to pay $1,100 in closing costs because they can't be financed. If the funding fee is paid in cash, the buyer will have to bring $3,011.35 to closing: $1,911.35 Funding Fee + $1,100 Estimated Closing Costs = $3,011.35.

### Chapter 5 Quiz (pg. 120)

1. d requires MIP
2. b low- to middle-income homebuyers
3. d all of the above
4. c the market
5. d All FHA loans must have MIP
6. d all of the above
7. b county in which the home is located in each state
8. a $0
9. d one- to four-unit owner-occupied residences
10. b CRV
11. d all of the above
12. d Veterans can buy investment property with zero down.
13. d all of the above
14. d when a veteran sells his home and pays off the loan

## Chapter 6—Alternative Financing Tools

### Finance Exercise 6-1 (pg. 127)

1. The lender will receive 3.5 discount points: $100,000 x 0.035 = $3,500. Remember, points are calculated on the loan amount.

2. $100,000 x 6.5% (factor: 6.32 ÷ 1,000) = $632.00.

   $100,000 x 6% (factor: 6.00 ÷ 1,000) = $600.00.

   $632.00 - $600.00 = $32.00 savings per month.

3. $3,500 Paid in Points ÷ $32 Savings Per Month = 109. Rob would have to stay in the home 109 months to get the money he paid in points back in savings.

4. Rob is very close to putting 20% down if he uses the dollars for points plus another $500. If he gets conventional financing and puts 20% down, he will not require mortgage insurance.

### Finance Exercise 6-2 (pg. 149)

1. The lender will receive 3 discount points. Total points are 3, total amount is $4,050 ($135,000 x 0.03 = $4,050). ($150,000 price - $15,000 down payment = $135,000 loan amount).

2. The seller will receive the $150,000 sale price - $4,050 seller-paid points = $145,950.00, the amount the seller will net.

### Finance Exercise 6-3 (pg. 149)

1. The index is currently at <1%; the margin is +3%.

2. 6.5% would be the highest rate the borrower would have going into year six: Start rate of 4.5% + 2% per year increase = 6.5%.

3. 4.5% Start Rate + Lifetime Cap of 5% = 9.5%.

4. The lowest rate this borrower would ever have would be the lender's margin of 3%.

5. No, negative amortization will not occur on this loan since its rate will reset on its anniversary, which is annually.

## Chapter 6 Quiz (pg. 151)

1.  a  $4,800
2.  a  $96,000
3.  d  all of the above
4.  b  for the entire life of the loan
5.  d  all of the above
6.  d  all of the above
7.  d  profit and/or the administrative expenses of the lender
8.  b  index value and the interest rate charged to the borrower
9.  c  positive amortization cap
10. d  all of the above
11. a  7/1 ARM
12. c  Ohio Housing Finance Agency
13. a  are over age 62
14. d  land contract with assumption of an existing mortgage
15. d  all of the above

# Chapter 7—Qualifying the Buyer

## Finance Exercise 7-1 (pg. 186)

Income: $68,000 ÷ 12 = $5,667.00 per month (rounded).

Debt: Add all monthly debt together: $765 per month.

1.  FHA: $5,667.00 x 31% = $1,756.77

    $5,667.00 x 43% = $2,436.81

    $2,436.81 - $765 (monthly debt payments) = $1,671.81. Since the 31% ratio amount is higher than the 43% ratio, we must use the lower dollar amount.

    Now, subtract taxes ($3,000 ÷ 12 = $250) and insurance ($500 ÷ 12 = $42, rounded). $1,617 - $250 - $42 = $1,379.81 P&I.

    $1,379.81 ÷ 6.5% (factor: 6.32 ÷ 1,000) = $218,324.37.

2.  Conventional: $5,667.00 x 28% = $1,586.76

    $5,667.00 x 36% = $2,040.12

    $2,040.12 - $765 (monthly debt payments) = $1,275.12. Since the 36% ratio is the lower dollar amount we will back the taxes and insurance off that number.

    $1,275.12 - $250 (taxes) - $42 (insurance) = $983.12 P&I.

    $983.12 ÷ 6.5% (factor: 6.32 ÷ 1,000) = $155,556.96.

3.  Use the same numbers from above but use the lower interest rate of 5.25% in step G (factor is 5.53 ÷ 1,000).

    $983.12 ÷ 5.53 = $177.7793 x 1000 = $177,779.39.

## BORROWER(S) PRE-QUALIFICATION WORKSHEET

BUYERS NAME(S): _____

PHONE NUMBER: (H) _____ (W) _____

*STEP A*
**BORROWER'S INCOME**
Hourly Rate ............................ $ _____
Guaranteed Weekly Hours ........ ☒ _____
**Total Gross Income (or Annual Salary)** $ _68,000.00_

**CO-BORROWER'S INCOME**
Hourly Rate ............................ $ _____
Guaranteed Weekly Hours ........ ☒ _____
**Total Gross Income (or Annual Salary)** $ ____0____

**TOTAL INCOME** (FROM ABOVE) ...... $ _68,000.00_

**DIVIDE INCOME BY 12** ............... $ _5,667.00_

*STEP B*
**MONTHLY DEBT SERVICE**
Car Payment(s) ...................... $ _350.00_
Visa ...................................... $ _165.00_
Master Card ........................... $ _____
Student Loan(s) ...................... $ _150.00_
Other Charge Cards ................. $ _100.00_
Other .................................... $ _____
Other .................................... $ _____
**TOTAL OF DEBT SERVICE** $ _765.00_

*STEP C*
**ESTIMATE OF MONTHLY ESCROWS** (IF KNOWN)
Mortgage Insurance ................. $ _____
Property Taxes ....................... $ _250.00_
Homeowners Insurance ............. $ _42.00_
**TOTAL OF MONTHLY ESCROWS** $ _292.00_

*STEP D*
**HOUSING EXPENSE RATIO** (CONVENTIONAL = 28%; FHA = 31%; VA = 41%)
(FROM STEP A) GROSS MONTHLY INCOME $ _5,667.00_
(PICK RATIO FROM ABOVE) ☒ _31%_
EQUAL MAXIMUM PITI $ _1,756.77_
(MAX PITI MUST INCLUDE ANY CONDO / ASSOCIATION FEES)

*STEP E*
**TOTAL DEBT SERVICE RATIO** (CONVENTIONAL = 36%; FHA =43%; VA = 41%)
(FROM STEP A) GROSS MONTHLY INCOME $ _5,667.00_
(PICK RATIO FROM ABOVE) ☒ _43%_
EQUALS MAXIMUM PITI AND DEBT $ _2,436.81_
SUBTRACT DEBTS (FROM STEP B) $ _765.00_
**EQUALS MAXIMUM ALLOWABLE FOR PITI** $ _1671.81_
(MAX PITI MUST INCLUDE ANY CONDO / ASSOCIATION FEES)

**COMPARE THE AMOUNTS IS STEP D vs. STEP E**

*STEP F*
**ENTER THE LOWER OF STEP D OR STEP E HERE** $ _1,671.81_
IF YOU HAVE AN ANSWER ON THE ESCROW (STEP C), SUBTRACT THAT NUMBER FROM ABOVE. IF YOU DON'T
HAVE AN ANSWER FROM STEP C, TAKE (APPROXIMATELY) 80% OF THE NUMBER IN **STEP F** TO FIND THE MAX
ALLOWABLE FOR PRINCIPAL AND INTEREST (P & I). ENTER THAT NEW AMOUNT HERE $ _1,379.81_

*STEP G*
**DIVIDE THE MAXIMUM ALLOWABLE P & I, (STEP F),
BY THE FACTOR THAT MOST CLOSELY REPRESENTS
AN INTEREST RATE YOU WILL BE USING.**

(P & I) (STEP F) DIVIDED BY (FACTOR) (see below) = $ _218,324.37_ MAX
MORTGAGE AMOUNT (PLUS YOUR BORROWER'S DOWN PAYMENT).

*D.P + 10,000 +/-*

Principal and Interest Payment Factor Chart

| Mortgage Interest Rate | 5.25% | 5.50% | 5.75% | 6.00% | 6.25% | 6.50% | 6.75% | 7.00% | 7.25% | 7.50% | 7.75% | 8.00% | 8.25% | 8.50% | 8.75% | 9.00% |
|---|---|---|---|---|---|---|---|---|---|---|---|---|---|---|---|---|
| LOAN TERM (30 YEAR) | .00553 | .00568 | .00584 | .00599 | .00616 | .00632 | .00649 | .00665 | .00683 | .00699 | .00716 | .00734 | .00751 | .00769 | .00787 | .00805 |

---

## BORROWER(S) PRE-QUALIFICATION WORKSHEET

BUYERS NAME(S): _____

PHONE NUMBER: (H) _____ (W) _____

*STEP A*
**BORROWER'S INCOME**
Hourly Rate ............................ $ _____
Guaranteed Weekly Hours ........ ☒ _____
**Total Gross Income (or Annual Salary)** $ _68,000.00_

**CO-BORROWER'S INCOME**
Hourly Rate ............................ $ _____
Guaranteed Weekly Hours ........ ☒ _____
**Total Gross Income (or Annual Salary)** $ _____

**TOTAL INCOME** (FROM ABOVE) ...... $ _68,000.00_

**DIVIDE INCOME BY 12** ............... $ _5,667.00_

*STEP B*
**MONTHLY DEBT SERVICE**
Car Payment(s) ...................... $ _350.00_
Visa ...................................... $ _165.00_
Master Card ........................... $ _____
Student Loan(s) ...................... $ _150.00_
Other Charge Cards ................. $ _100.00_
Other .................................... $ _____
Other .................................... $ _____
**TOTAL OF DEBT SERVICE** $ _765.00_

*STEP C*
**ESTIMATE OF MONTHLY ESCROWS** (IF KNOWN)
Mortgage Insurance ................. $ _____
Property Taxes ....................... $ _250.00_
Homeowners Insurance ............. $ _42.00_
**TOTAL OF MONTHLY ESCROWS** $ _292.00_

*STEP D*
**HOUSING EXPENSE RATIO** (CONVENTIONAL = 28%; FHA = 31%; VA = 41%)
(FROM STEP A) GROSS MONTHLY INCOME $ _5,667.00_
(PICK RATIO FROM ABOVE) ☒ _28%_
EQUAL MAXIMUM PITI $ _1,586.76_
(MAX PITI MUST INCLUDE ANY CONDO / ASSOCIATION FEES)

*STEP E*
**TOTAL DEBT SERVICE RATIO** (CONVENTIONAL = 36%; FHA =43%; VA = 41%)
(FROM STEP A) GROSS MONTHLY INCOME $ _5,667.00_
(PICK RATIO FROM ABOVE) ☒ _36%_
EQUALS MAXIMUM PITI AND DEBT $ _2,040.12_
SUBTRACT DEBTS (FROM STEP B) $ _765.00_
**EQUALS MAXIMUM ALLOWABLE FOR PITI** $ _1275.12_
(MAX PITI MUST INCLUDE ANY CONDO / ASSOCIATION FEES)

**COMPARE THE AMOUNTS IS STEP D vs. STEP E**

*STEP F*
**ENTER THE LOWER OF STEP D OR STEP E HERE** $ _1,275.12_
IF YOU HAVE AN ANSWER ON THE ESCROW (STEP C), SUBTRACT THAT NUMBER FROM ABOVE. IF YOU DON'T
HAVE AN ANSWER FROM STEP C, TAKE (APPROXIMATELY) 80% OF THE NUMBER IN **STEP F** TO FIND THE MAX
ALLOWABLE FOR PRINCIPAL AND INTEREST (P & I). ENTER THAT NEW AMOUNT HERE $ _983.12_

*STEP G*
**DIVIDE THE MAXIMUM ALLOWABLE P & I, (STEP F),
BY THE FACTOR THAT MOST CLOSELY REPRESENTS
AN INTEREST RATE YOU WILL BE USING.**

(P & I) (STEP F) DIVIDED BY (FACTOR) (see below) = $ _155,556.96_ MAX
MORTGAGE AMOUNT (PLUS YOUR BORROWER'S DOWN PAYMENT).

*D.P. + $25,000 +/-*

Principal and Interest Payment Factor Chart

| Mortgage Interest Rate | 5.25% | 5.50% | 5.75% | 6.00% | 6.25% | 6.50% | 6.75% | 7.00% | 7.25% | 7.50% | 7.75% | 8.00% | 8.25% | 8.50% | 8.75% | 9.00% |
|---|---|---|---|---|---|---|---|---|---|---|---|---|---|---|---|---|
| LOAN TERM (30 YEAR) | .00553 | .00568 | .00584 | .00599 | .00616 | .00632 | .00649 | .00665 | .00683 | .00699 | .00716 | .00734 | .00751 | .00769 | .00787 | .00805 |

## BORROWER(S) PRE-QUALIFICATION WORKSHEET

BUYERS NAME(S): _____

PHONE NUMBER: (H) _____ (W) _____

### STEP A
**BORROWER'S INCOME**

| | |
|---|---|
| Hourly Rate | $ _____ |
| Guaranteed Weekly Hours | ☒ |
| Total Gross Income (or Annual Salary) | $ _68,000.00_ |

**CO-BORROWER'S INCOME**

| | |
|---|---|
| Hourly Rate | $ _____ |
| Guaranteed Weekly Hours | ☒ |
| Total Gross Income (or Annual Salary) | $ _____ |

**TOTAL INCOME** (FROM ABOVE)  $ _68,000.00_

**DIVIDE INCOME BY 12**  $ _5,667.00_

### STEP B
**MONTHLY DEBT SERVICE**

| | |
|---|---|
| Car Payment(s) | $ _350.00_ |
| Visa | $ _165.00_ |
| Master Card | $ _____ |
| Student Loan(s) | $ _150.00_ |
| Other Charge Cards | $ _100.00_ |
| Other | $ _____ |
| Other | $ _____ |
| **TOTAL OF DEBT SERVICE** | $ _765.00_ |

### STEP C
**ESTIMATE OF MONTHLY ESCROWS** (IF KNOWN)

| | |
|---|---|
| Mortgage Insurance | $ _____ |
| Property Taxes | $ _250.00_ |
| Homeowners Insurance | $ _42.00_ |
| **TOTAL OF MONTHLY ESCROWS** | $ _292.00_ |

### STEP D
**HOUSING EXPENSE RATIO** (CONVENTIONAL = 28%; FHA = 31%; VA = 41%)

| | | |
|---|---|---|
| (FROM STEP A) GROSS MONTHLY INCOME | | $ _5,667.00_ |
| (PICK RATIO FROM ABOVE) | ☒ | _28%_ |
| EQUAL MAXIMUM PITI | | $ _1,586.76_ |

(MAX PITI MUST INCLUDE ANY CONDO / ASSOCIATION FEES)

### STEP E
**TOTAL DEBT SERVICE RATIO** (CONVENTIONAL = 36%; FHA = 43%; VA = 41%)

| | | |
|---|---|---|
| (FROM STEP A) GROSS MONTHLY INCOME | | $ _5,667.00_ |
| (PICK RATIO FROM ABOVE) | ☒ | _36%_ |
| EQUALS MAXIMUM PITI AND DEBT | | $ _2,040.12_ |
| SUBTRACT DEBTS (FROM STEP B) | | $ _765.00_ |
| EQUALS MAXIMUM ALLOWABLE FOR PITI | | $ _1275.12_ |

(MAX PITI MUST INCLUDE ANY CONDO / ASSOCIATION FEES)

**COMPARE THE AMOUNTS IS STEP D vs. STEP E**

### STEP F
**ENTER THE LOWER OF STEP D OR STEP E HERE** $ _1,275.12_

IF YOU HAVE AN ANSWER ON THE ESCROW (STEP C), SUBTRACT THAT NUMBER FROM ABOVE. IF YOU DON'T HAVE AN ANSWER FROM STEP C, TAKE (APPROXIMATELY) 80% OF THE NUMBER IN STEP F TO FIND THE MAX ALLOWABLE FOR PRINCIPAL AND INTEREST (P & I). ENTER THAT NEW AMOUNT HERE $ _983.12_

### STEP G
**DIVIDE THE MAXIMUM ALLOWABLE P & I, (STEP F), BY THE FACTOR THAT MOST CLOSELY REPRESENTS AN INTEREST RATE YOU WILL BE USING.**

(P & I) (STEP F) DIVIDED BY (FACTOR) (see below) = $ _177,779.39_ MAX MORTGAGE AMOUNT (PLUS YOUR BORROWER'S DOWN PAYMENT).

D.P. $25,000 +/-

Principal and Interest Payment Factor Chart

| Mortgage Interest Rate | 5.25% | 5.50% | 5.75% | 6.00% | 6.25% | 6.50% | 6.75% | 7.00% | 7.25% | 7.50% | 7.75% | 8.00% | 8.25% | 8.50% | 8.75% | 9.00% |
|---|---|---|---|---|---|---|---|---|---|---|---|---|---|---|---|---|
| LOAN TERM (30 YEAR) | .00553 | .00568 | .00584 | .00599 | .00616 | .00632 | .00649 | .00665 | .00683 | .00699 | .00716 | .00734 | .00751 | .00769 | .00787 | .00805 |

## Chapter 7 Quiz (pg. 188)

1. a Equal Credit Opportunity Act
2. a 2-3
3. d tax returns for the previous two to three years
4. c must be signed by the donor
5. d all of the above
6. a Certificate of Eligibility and DD-214
7. a Fannie Mae/Freddie Mac
8. d increasing; standardization
9. a alimony received (which a borrower chooses to reveal)
10. d all of the above
11. c some of the time
12. c can't be considered in the loan underwriting process under any circumstances as long as the applicant is over the age of 18
13. d 31%; 43%
14. b residual income/cash flow analysis method
15. c more generous
16. d all of the above

# *ESTIMATED* BUYER'S CLOSING COSTS COMPARISONS

| | Conventional | | FHA | | VA | |
|---|---|---|---|---|---|---|
| **Loan Origination Fee** | 1.00% | BSL | 1.00% | BSL | 1.00% | BSL |
| **Loan Discount Points** | VARIES | BSL | VARIES | BSL | VARIES | BSL |
| **Appraisal Fee** | $450.00 | BSL | $450.00 | BSL | $450.00 | BSL |
| **Credit Report** | $50.00 | BSL | $50.00 | BSL | $50.00 | BSL |
| **Settlement Fee** | $250.00 | BSL | $250.00 | BSL | $250.00 | SL |
| **Title Insurance** | $100.00 | BSL | $100.00 | BSL | $100.00 | BSL |
| **Title Binder** | $50.00 | BSL | $50.00 | BSL | $50.00 | BSL |
| **Underwriting Fee** | $395.00 | BSL | $395.00 | BSL | | |
| **Processing Fee** | $300.00 | BSL | $300.00 | BSL | $300.00 | SL |
| **Tax Service Fee** | $72.00 | BSL | $72.00 | SL | $72.00 | SL |
| **Document Preparation** | $125.00 | BSL | $125.00 | BSL | $125.00 | SL |
| **Recording Fees** | $200.00 | BSL | $200.00 | BSL | $200.00 | BSL |
| **Survey** | $160.00 | BSL | $160.00 | BSL | $160.00 | BSL |
| **Flood Certificate** | $20.00 | BSL | $20.00 | BSL | $20.00 | BSL |
| **ARM Endorsement** | $75.00 | BSL | $75.00 | BSL | $75.00 | BSL |
| **EPA Endorsement** | **$75.00** | **BSL** | **$75.00** | **BSL** | **$75.00** | **BSL** |
| **Survey Endorsement** | **$50.00** | **BSL** | **$50.00** | **BSL** | **$50.00** | **BSL** |
| **Buydowns** | VARIES | BSL | VARIES | BSL | VARIES | BSL |
| *Prepaids* | | | | | | |
| **PMI/MIP/Funding Fee** | * | BSL | 2.25% | BSLF | ** | BSLF |
| **Hazard Insurance** | 1 Yr. | BSL | 1 Yr. | BSL | 1 Yr. | BSL |
| **Hazard Insurance Escrow** | 2 Mo. | BSL | 2 Mo. | BSL | 2 Mo. | BSL |
| **Property Tax Escrow** | 2 Mo. | BSL | 2 Mo. | BSL | 2 Mo. | BSL |
| **Interest (15 days)** | | BSL | | BSL | | BSL |

**B = Borrower   S = Property Seller   L = Lender   F = Financed**

| | | | |
|---|---|---|---|
| Seller's Contribution | LTV >90.01  3%<br>LTV <90.00  6%<br>LTV <75.00  9% | 6%*** | 4% (+ Discount Points) |

**Investment Property any LTV = 2%**

\*    Conventional mortgage insurance varies with loan to value.

\*\*   If veteran has never used the entitlement, figure funding fee @ 2.15% with 0% down,
     1.50% if between 5%–10% down, and 1.25% if down payment is at least 10% or greater.

\*\*\* As of April 2010, the FHA limit of seller contributions is 6 points (6%). This is subject to change.

*Revised 03/05/2010*

**Please Note: This page is for *illustration purposes* only. Other fees can apply based on "local traditions," your local board contract, and can vary by lender. For the most accurate estimate of closing costs, the buyer should consult with the loan officer.**

**Sample Amortization Schedule**

## Amortization Results

| | | |
|---|---|---|
| Loan amount: | | $100,000.00 |
| Interest rate: | | 8.5% |
| Term of loan: | | 30 Years |
| Mortgage payment: | | $768.91 |

| Year | Loan Balance | Principal | Interest | Total Payments | Total Interest |
|---|---|---|---|---|---|
| 1 | $99,939.42 | $60.58 | $708.33 | $768.91 | $708.33 |
| 2 | $99,178.10 | $65.93 | $702.98 | $9,995.88 | $9,173.98 |
| 3 | $98,349.49 | $71.76 | $697.15 | $19,222.84 | $17,572.33 |
| 4 | $97,447.64 | $78.11 | $690.81 | $28,449.80 | $25,897.44 |
| 5 | $96,466.07 | $85.01 | $683.90 | $37,676.76 | $34,142.83 |
| 6 | $95,397.74 | $92.52 | $676.39 | $46,903.72 | $42,301.46 |
| 7 | $94,234.98 | $100.70 | $668.21 | $56,130.68 | $50,365.67 |
| 8 | $92,969.44 | $109.60 | $659.31 | $65,357.65 | $58,327.09 |
| 9 | $91,592.04 | $119.29 | $649.62 | $74,584.61 | $66,176.65 |
| 10 | $90,092.89 | $129.84 | $639.08 | $83,811.57 | $73,904.46 |
| 11 | $88,461.23 | $141.31 | $627.60 | $93,038.53 | $81,499.77 |
| 12 | $86,685.35 | $153.80 | $615.11 | $102,265.49 | $88,950.84 |
| 13 | $84,752.49 | $167.40 | $601.52 | $111,492.46 | $96,244.95 |
| 14 | $82,648.79 | $182.19 | $586.72 | $120,719.42 | $103,368.21 |
| 15 | $80,359.14 | $198.30 | $570.62 | $129,946.38 | $110,305.52 |
| 16 | $77,867.10 | $215.83 | $553.09 | $139,173.34 | $117,040.44 |
| 17 | $75,154.79 | $234.90 | $534.01 | $148,400.30 | $123,555.10 |
| 18 | $72,202.74 | $255.67 | $513.25 | $157,627.26 | $129,830.00 |
| 19 | $68,989.75 | $278.27 | $490.65 | $166,854.23 | $135,843.98 |
| 20 | $65,492.77 | $302.86 | $466.05 | $176,081.19 | $141,573.95 |
| 21 | $61,686.68 | $329.63 | $439.28 | $185,308.15 | $146,994.83 |
| 22 | $57,544.17 | $358.77 | $410.15 | $194,535.11 | $152,079.28 |
| 23 | $53,035.49 | $390.48 | $378.43 | $203,762.07 | $156,797.57 |
| 24 | $48,128.30 | $424.99 | $343.92 | $212,989.03 | $161,117.33 |
| 25 | $42,787.35 | $462.56 | $306.35 | $222,216.00 | $165,003.34 |
| 26 | $36,974.31 | $503.45 | $265.47 | $231,442.96 | $168,417.27 |
| 27 | $30,647.45 | $547.95 | $220.97 | $240,669.92 | $171,317.37 |
| 28 | $23,761.35 | $596.38 | $172.53 | $249,896.88 | $173,658.23 |
| 29 | $16,266.58 | $649.09 | $119.82 | $259,123.84 | $175,390.43 |
| 30 | $8,109.35 | $706.47 | $62.45 | $268,350.81 | $176,460.15 |
| END | $0.00 | $763.51 | $5.41 | $276,039.94 | $176,808.85 |

NOTE: This amortization schedule assumes that all payments were made on time and for the exact payment amounts. Late payments may add additional interest and/or late charges. Early payments or payments larger than the scheduled payments could result in the balance being paid sooner and/or less total interest being paid over the life of the loan.

## Equal Monthly Payment Needed to Amortize a Loan of $1,000

| TERM RATE | 15 YRS. | 20 YRS. | 25 YRS. | 30 YRS. | TERM RATE | 15 YRS. | 20 YRS. | 25 YRS. | 30 YRS. |
|---|---|---|---|---|---|---|---|---|---|
| 5 % | 7.91 | 6.60 | 5.83 | 5.37 | 9 % | 10.15 | 9.00 | 8.40 | 8.05 |
| 5 1/8 | 7.97 | 6.67 | 5.90 | 5.45 | 9 1/8 | 10.22 | 9.08 | 8.48 | 8.14 |
| 5 1/4 | 8.04 | 6.74 | 5.98 | 5.52 | 9 1/4 | 10.30 | 9.16 | 8.57 | 8.23 |
| 5 3/8 | 8.11 | 6.81 | 6.06 | 5.60 | 9 3/8 | 10.37 | 9.24 | 8.66 | 8.32 |
| 5 1/2 | 8.17 | 6.88 | 6.13 | 5.68 | 9 1/2 | 10.45 | 9.33 | 8.74 | 8.41 |
| 5 5/8 | 8.24 | 6.95 | 6.21 | 5.76 | 9 5/8 | 10.52 | 9.41 | 8.83 | 8.50 |
| 5 3/4 | 8.30 | 7.02 | 6.28 | 5.84 | 9 3/4 | 10.60 | 9.49 | 8.92 | 8.60 |
| 5 7/8 | 8.37 | 7.10 | 6.36 | 5.92 | 9 7/8 | 10.67 | 9.57 | 9.00 | 8.69 |
| 6 % | 8.44 | 7.16 | 6.44 | 6.00 | 10 % | 10.75 | 9.66 | 9.09 | 8.78 |
| 6 1/8 | 8.51 | 7.24 | 6.52 | 6.08 | 10 1/8 | 10.83 | 9.74 | 9.18 | 8.87 |
| 6 1/4 | 8.57 | 7.31 | 6.60 | 6.16 | 10 1/4 | 10.90 | 9.82 | 9.27 | 8.97 |
| 6 3/8 | 8.64 | 7.38 | 6.67 | 6.24 | 10 3/8 | 10.98 | 9.90 | 9.36 | 9.06 |
| 6 1/2 | 8.71 | 7.46 | 6.75 | 6.32 | 10 1/2 | 11.06 | 9.99 | 9.45 | 9.15 |
| 6 5/8 | 8.78 | 7.53 | 6.83 | 6.40 | 10 5/8 | 11.14 | 10.07 | 9.54 | 9.25 |
| 6 3/4 | 8.85 | 7.60 | 6.91 | 6.49 | 10 3/4 | 11.21 | 10.16 | 9.63 | 9.34 |
| 6 7/8 | 8.92 | 7.68 | 6.99 | 6.57 | 10 7/8 | 11.29 | 10.24 | 9.72 | 9.43 |
| 7 % | 8.99 | 7.76 | 7.07 | 6.66 | 11 % | 11.37 | 10.33 | 9.81 | 9.53 |
| 7 1/8 | 9.06 | 7.83 | 7.15 | 6.74 | 11 1/8 | 11.45 | 10.41 | 9.90 | 9.62 |
| 7 1/4 | 9.13 | 7.91 | 7.23 | 6.83 | 11 1/4 | 11.53 | 10.50 | 9.99 | 9.72 |
| 7 3/8 | 9.20 | 7.98 | 7.31 | 6.91 | 11 3/8 | 11.61 | 10.58 | 10.08 | 9.81 |
| 7 1/2 | 9.28 | 8.06 | 7.39 | 7.00 | 11 1/2 | 11.69 | 10.67 | 10.17 | 9.91 |
| 7 5/8 | 9.35 | 8.14 | 7.48 | 7.08 | 11 5/8 | 11.77 | 10.76 | 10.26 | 10.00 |
| 7 3/4 | 9.42 | 8.21 | 7.56 | 7.17 | 11 3/4 | 11.85 | 10.84 | 10.35 | 10.10 |
| 7 7/8 | 9.49 | 8.29 | 7.64 | 7.26 | 11 7/8 | 11.93 | 10.93 | 10.44 | 10.20 |
| 8 % | 9.56 | 8.37 | 7.72 | 7.34 | 12 % | 12.01 | 11.02 | 10.54 | 10.29 |
| 8 1/8 | 9.63 | 8.45 | 7.81 | 7.43 | 12 1/8 | 12.09 | 11.10 | 10.63 | 10.39 |
| 8 1/4 | 9.71 | 8.53 | 7.89 | 7.52 | 12 1/4 | 12.17 | 11.19 | 10.72 | 10.48 |
| 8 3/8 | 9.78 | 8.60 | 7.97 | 7.61 | 12 3/8 | 12.25 | 11.28 | 10.82 | 10.58 |
| 8 1/2 | 9.85 | 8.68 | 8.06 | 7.69 | 12 1/2 | 12.33 | 11.37 | 10.91 | 10.68 |
| 8 5/8 | 9.93 | 8.76 | 8.14 | 7.78 | 12 5/8 | 12.41 | 11.45 | 11.00 | 10.77 |
| 8 3/4 | 10.00 | 8.84 | 8.23 | 7.87 | 12 3/4 | 12.49 | 11.54 | 11.10 | 10.87 |
| 8 7/8 | 10.07 | 8.92 | 8.31 | 7.96 | 12 7/8 | 12.58 | 11.63 | 11.19 | 10.97 |

# Online Resources

## Federal Regulations/Loan Programs

| | |
|---|---|
| Federal Housing Administration | www.fha.gov |
| FHA Maximum County Loan Limits | www.fhaloan.com/fha_limits.cfm |
| Housing and Urban Development | www.hud.gov |
| United States Department of Agriculture/ Rural Housing Development | www.rurdev.usda.gov/rhs |
| Veterans Administration | www.va.gov |

## Secondary Markets

| | |
|---|---|
| Federal Home Loan Mortgage Corporation (Freddie Mac) | www.freddiemac.com |
| Federal National Mortgage Association (Fannie Mae) | www.efanniemae.com |
| | www.fanniemae.com |
| Government National Mortgage Association (Ginnie Mae) | www.ginniemae.com |

## Miscellaneous

| | |
|---|---|
| Annual Credit Report | www.annualcreditreport.com |
| County Auditors Association of Ohio | www.caao.org |
| Fair Isaac Corporation—Credit Scores | www.myfico.com |
| National Do Not Call Registry | www.donotcall.gov |
| Ohio Housing Finance Agency | www.ohiohome.org |
| PSI Exam Test Site | www.psiexams.com |

# Glossary

The definitions provided here relate to real estate. Some of the terms have additional meanings outside of real estate. Consult your dictionary for additional meanings.

**2-1 Buydown** A graduated payment buydown where payments are subsidized for only two years, usually 2% the first year and 1% the second year.

**Accelerate** Hasten the repayment of a loan by demanding all payments immediately rather than in installments.

**Acceleration Clause** A contract clause that gives the lender the right to declare the entire loan amount due immediately because of borrower's default, or other reasons as stated in the contract.

**Acceptance** 1. Agreeing to the terms of an offer to enter into a contract, thereby creating a binding contract. 2. Taking delivery of a deed.

**Acknowledgment** When a person who has signed a document formally declares to an authorized official (usually a notary public) that he or she signed voluntarily. The official certifies the signature is voluntary and genuine. *Compare:* **Attestation.**

**Acquisition Cost** The purchase price of a property, plus allowable buyer paid closing costs.

**Act** A law enacted by a legislative body like the U.S. Congress.

**Adjustable Rate Loan** A loan made by savings and loan associations similar to an adjustable rate mortgage. Also called **ALM.**

**Adjustable Rate Mortgage (ARM)** A mortgage that permits the lender to periodically adjust the interest rate to reflect fluctuations in the cost of money.

**Adjustment Period, Mortgage Payment** The interval at which a borrower's actual mortgage payments change with an ARM (adjustable rate mortgage).

**Adjustment Period, Rate** The interval at which a borrower's actual interest rate changes with an ARM.

**Administrative Agency** A government agency (federal, state, or local) that administers a complex area of law. Responsible for adopting and enforcing detailed regulations that have the force of law.

**Advancement (job)** An improvement in one's employment position, given as a reason for changing jobs (as opposed to job-hopping for no reason).

**Advertisements** Any public notification of property being offered for sale that must follow guidelines of **Regulation Z** of the **Truth In Lending Act**.

**Advertising (foreclosure)** Required notification of foreclosure sale, by notifying the public of the date and time of the sale, for three consecutive weeks in a general circulation newspaper in the county.

**Alienation** The transfer of ownership or an interest in property from one person to another, by any means.

**Alienation, Involuntary** The transfer of an interest in property against the will of the owner, or without action by the owner, occurring through operation of law, natural processes, or adverse possession.

**Alienation, Voluntary** When an owner voluntarily transfers interest to someone else.

**Alienation Clause** A contract clause that gives the lender certain stated rights when there's a transfer of ownership in property. (Often called a **due-on-sale clause.**)

**Alimony** Money paid to an ex-spouse as part of a divorce settlement. Alimony does not have to be revealed as a source of income if it's not counted to help repay the loan, but must be revealed as a debt obligation.

**Amortization** When a loan balance decreases because of periodic installments paid on principal and interest. *Compare:* **Negative Amortization**. *See:* **Re-amortization**.

**Amortization Schedule** A table or chart that shows the periodic payments, interest and principal requirements, and unpaid loan balance for each period of the life of a loan.

**Amortize** To calculate payments to pay off a debt by periodic installments, with payments going toward the principal and interest.

**Amortized Loan** Loan with payments applied to principal and interest. *Compare:* **Fully Amortized Loan** and **Partially Amortized Loan**

**Annual Percentage Rate (APR)** Relationship between the cost of borrowing and the total amount financed, represented as a percentage.

**Appraisal** An estimate or opinion of the value of a piece of property as of a certain date. Also called **valuation**.

**Arm's Length Transaction** A transaction occurring under typical market conditions in the marketplace with each party acting in his or her own best interest.

**Assets** Items of value; usually items owned by a borrower. *See:* **Liquid Assets**.

**Assign** 1. To transfer a right or interest to another. 2. When a tenant transfers his or her right of possession, or other interest in leased property, to another person for entire remainder of the lease term.

**Assumable** Any loan for which an **assumption** may be exercised.

**Assumption** When one party takes over responsibility for the loan of another party and the terms of the loan or note remain unchanged. (Usually lender approval is needed. A **release** is needed or original party remains **secondarily liable** for the loan.)

**Attestation** When witnesses sign a legal document to affirm that the parties' signatures are real; the act of witnessing the execution of a legal document (such as a deed or will). *Compare:* **Acknowledgment**.

**Auction** Method of selling property to the highest bidder, required for foreclosure sales to ensure the highest price is obtained.

**Automated Underwriting** Process where loan applicant information is entered into a computer and an evaluation comes back within minutes advising the lender to accept the loan, or refers the loan application for further review.

**Balloon Payment** A final payment at the end of a loan term to pay off the entire remaining balance of principal and interest not covered by payments during the loan term.

**BEACON Score** Credit scoring where a number from 300-900 is assigned to a consumer's credit history. The *lower* the score, the *greater* the risk of default. Another type of credit score is **FICO Score**.

**Beneficiary** One who receives a benefit; refers to the lender in a **trust deed**.

**Bill Consolidation** Borrowing a lump sum of money to pay off many smaller debts.

**Blank Endorsement** When the holder of a note simply signs his or her name on the back of the note. (Done to transfer or cash in the note.)

**Blockbusting** The illegal practice of inducing owners to sell their homes (often at a deflated price) by suggesting that the ethnic or racial composition of the neighborhood is changing, with implication that property values will decline as a result. Also called **panic selling** and **panic peddling**.

**Board of Governors** A seven-member committee that controls the Federal Reserve System. Also called the **Federal Reserve Board**, or **the Fed**.

**Bond-type Securities** Mortgage backed securities issued by Ginnie Mae, which are long-term, pay interest semi-annually, and provide for repayment at a specified date.

**Bonuses** Money paid to someone in addition to his or her regular salary and may be counted as income only if consistent.

**Boot** Unlike property thrown into a deal to balance the value and are taxable as part of an exchange. *See:* **Equity Exchange**.

**Business Cycles** General swings in business activity, resulting in expanding or contracting activity during different phases of the cycle.

**Buydown** Additional funds in the form of points paid to a lender at the beginning of a loan to lower the interest rate and monthly payments.

**Buydown, Permanent** When points are paid to a lender to reduce the interest rate and loan payments for the entire life of the loan.

**Buydown, Temporary** When points are paid to a lender to reduce the interest rate and payments early in a loan, with interest rate and payments rising later.

**Buyer's Market** A situation in the housing market where buyers have a large selection of properties from which to choose.

**Call Provision** Clause that lets lenders demand full payment of a loan immediately. Also referred to as **call a note**.

**Cancellation** Terminating an obligation, such as when a note is canceled after payment, or when PMI is canceled after certain conditions are met.

**Cap** Limits, usually used with ARMs, to protect a borrower from large payment increases. There can be caps on interest rates, payments, or negative amortization.

**Cap, Interest Rate** A limit on the amount of interest rate increase that can occur with an adjustable rate mortgage.

**Cap, Mortgage Payment** A limit on the amount of mortgage payment increase that can occur with an adjustable rate mortgage.

**Cap, Negative Amortization** A limit on the amount of negative amortization that can occur with an adjustable rate mortgage.

**Capacity** Legal ability to perform some act, such as enter into a contract or execute a deed or will. *See:* **Minor**.

**Capital Gain** Profit made from an investment.

**Cash Flow** Money available to an individual after subtracting all expenses. *See:* **Residual Income**.

**Certificate of Eligibility** A certificate issued by the VA to establish status and amount of a veteran's eligibility to qualify for loan guarantee.

**Certificate of Reasonable Value (CRV)** A document issued by the VA that states the value of the subject property based on an approved appraisal. The VA loan amount cannot exceed the CRV.

**Character** Stability in job and responsibilities such that, even with setbacks, financial obligations will be honored by the borrower.

**Child Support** Money paid to the parent or guardian of children as part of a divorce settlement. Child support does not have to be revealed as a source of income if it's not counted to help repay the loan, but it must be revealed as a debt obligation.

**Civil Rights** Fundamental rights guaranteed to all persons by the law. The term is primarily used in reference to constitutional and statutory protections against discrimination based on race, religion, sex, or national origin.

**Civil Rights Act of 1866** Federal law prohibiting public and private racial discrimination in any property transaction in the U.S.

**Civil Rights Act of 1968** Federal law prohibiting discrimination based on race, color, religion, sex, national origin, disability, or familial status. Also called **Title VIII** or **Federal Fair Housing Act**.

**Clause** A paragraph or section of a contract or other document that defines or assigns specific rights and duties.

**Closing** The final stage in a real estate transaction where ownership of real property is transferred from seller to buyer according to the terms and conditions set forth in a sales contract or escrow agreement. *See:* **Roundtable Closing** and **Escrow Closing**.

**Closing Costs** Expenses incurred in the transfer of real estate in addition to the purchase price (e.g., the appraisal fee, title insurance premiums, broker's commission, transfer tax, etc.)

**Closing Disclosure** A settlement statement prepared by the lender or closing agent itemizing all expenses and costs paid by the buyer and seller needed to close the real estate transaction as required for RESPA-related transactions.

**Co-Borrower** A person who signs a note or other debt obligation with another party, thus accepting joint obligation to repay the note.

**Co-Mortgagor** A person who signs a mortgage with another party (primary mortgagor), thus accepting a joint obligation to repay the loan. Also called **Co-Borrower** or **Co-Signer**.

**Commercial Banks** Financial institutions that provide a variety of financial services.

**Commercial Real Estate Lenders** Lenders who lend money for commercial real estate projects.

**Commissions** The compensation paid to someone in lieu of, or in addition to, regular salary. Commissions may be a flat rate or percentage of sale price, but can be counted as income only if they are consistent.

**Community Reinvestment Act (CRA)** Federal law emphasizing that regulated financial institutions have a continuing obligation to help meet the credit needs of the local communities in which they operate, especially low-income neighborhoods.

213

**Compound Interest** Interest calculated as a percentage of both the principal and accumulated unpaid interest. *Compare:* **Simple Interest**.

**Condition** 1. A provision in a contract, deed, law, regulation, guideline, etc., that makes the parties' rights and obligations depend on the occurrence, or non-occurrence, of a particular event. Also called a **Contingency Clause**. 2. A provision of a contract, law, regulation, guideline, etc., that allows, or does not allow, something else to occur based on whether certain other events occur or do not occur. 3. Other factors that reflect the general state of something as good or bad (e.g., economic conditions of an area, property condition, etc.).

**Condominium** A property developed for co-ownership, where each co-owner has a separate interest in an individual unit, combined with an undivided interest in common areas of the property. *Compare:* **Cooperative.**

**Confirmation of Sale** A document filed by the court finalizing the sale of property at foreclosure, and after which time the equitable right of redemption is no longer available to the original defaulting borrower.

**Conforming Loan** Loan that meets Fannie Mae/Freddie Mac standards and can be sold on the secondary market. *Compare:* **Nonconforming Loan.**

**Consideration** Anything of value, such as money, services, goods, or promises, given to induce another to enter into a contract. Sometimes called **valuable consideration**. Consideration for an option is **option money**.

**Constant Maturity (of one-year U.S. Treasury security)** When the due date is adjusted to current dollars; an Index used for ARM loans.

**Contingent Interest** A term used to describe the lender's share of the appreciation paid on a shared appreciation mortgage (SAM) loan or other participation plan loan.

**Contract** An agreement between two or more parties to do, or not do, a certain thing. The requirements for an enforceable contract are: **Capacity**, **mutual consent**, **lawful objective**, and **consideration**. In addition, certain contracts must be in writing to be enforceable.

**Contract, Land** A real estate installment agreement where buyer makes payment to seller in exchange for right to occupy and use property, but no deed or title is transferred until all, or a specified portion of, payments have been made. Also called **installment sales contract**, **land installment contract**, **land sales contract**, **real estate contract**, and other names.

**Contract, Escrow** An approach used to ensure that payments are made on an existing mortgage, whereby an escrow account or servicing agreement is set up. Buyer makes payments into the escrow account; escrow agent then pays the existing mortgage and passes the surplus money to seller. Often used for land contracts with existing mortgages.

**Conventional Financing** When real estate is paid for or financed with a conventional loan.

**Conventional Loan** Loan not insured or guaranteed by a government entity.

**Conversion Option** A right the borrower has to convert from an ARM to a fixed rate mortgage one time during the loan term, provided certain conditions be met.

**Convertible** Able to be changed or converted; such as with an ARM loan where the borrower can change from a variable rate to a fixed rate. Often stated in a **conversion option** clause.

**Conveyance** The transfer of title to real property from one person to another by means of a written document, such as a deed.

**Conveyance, Voluntary** When a debtor returns property to the lender in lieu of foreclosure. Generally, the debtor does not receive any compensation for surrendering title to the property, but does avoid foreclosure. *See:* **Deed in Lieu of Foreclosure**.

**Cooperative** A building owned by a corporation, where residents are shareholders in the corporation; each shareholder receives a proprietary lease on an individual unit and has the right to use common areas. *Compare:* **Condominium**.

**Cost of Funds Index (COFI)** An index that reflects the cost of borrowing money as per the 11th District Federal Home Loan Bank. This index is used by Fannie Mae when purchasing ARM loans.

**Cost Inflation** An increase in the cost of goods or services. *Compare:* **Demand Inflation**.

**Cost of Money** The interest rate that consumers or businesses pay to use another's money for their own purpose.

**Coupon Rate** The interest rate stated in a note. Also called **Nominal Rate** or **Note Rate**.

**Covenant** 1. A contract. 2. A promise. 3. A guarantee (express or implied) in a document such as a deed or lease. 4. A restrictive covenant. Typical covenants compel or prevent certain actions by the property owner or uses for the property.

**Credit** 1. The availability of money; the ability to borrow money. 2. A sum of money to be received. *See:* **Rent Credit**.

**Credit History** A person's record of debt repayment detailing how a person paid credit accounts in the past. Credit history is used as a guide to how likely the borrower is to pay accounts on time and as agreed in the future.

**Credit Report** A listing of a borrower's credit history, including amount of debt, record of repayment, job info, address info, etc.

**Credit Scoring** A means by which the lender makes certain determinations regarding the creditworthiness of potential borrowers. This involves a lender assigning specified numerical values to different aspects of a borrower. *See:* **BEACON Score**.

**Credit Unions** Financial institutions that are a type of cooperative organization where members share something in common (e.g., an employer), pool their deposits together, pay members better interest rates, and loan money to fellow members.

**Creditor** A person or other entity, such as a bank, who is owed a debt.

**Creditor, Secured** A creditor with a lien on specific property, which enables him or her to foreclose and collect the debt from the sale proceeds if it is not otherwise paid.

**Dealer** A person who holds property for the sole purpose of reselling it.

**Debit** A sum of money that is owed.

**Debt** Recurring monetary obligation that cannot be canceled (e.g., monthly bills).

**Debtor** A person or other entity who owes money to another.

**Deed** An instrument that conveys ownership of real property from the grantor to the grantee.

**Deed in Lieu of Foreclosure** Deed given by borrower to lender to satisfy a debt, avoiding foreclosure. Also called **Voluntary Conveyance**.

**Deed of Trust** An instrument held by a third party as security for the payment of a note (rarely used in Ohio). Like a mortgage, it creates a voluntary lien on real property to secure repayment of a debt. Parties to a deed of trust are grantor or trustor (borrower),

beneficiary (lender), and trustee (neutral third party). Unlike a mortgage, a trust deed has a power of sale, allowing trustee to foreclose non-judicially. Also called a **Trust Deed**. *Compare:* **Mortgage**.

**Default** Failure to fulfill an obligation, duty, or promise, as when borrower fails to make payments, tenant fails to pay rent, or party fails to perform a contract. Mortgage, note, or other document will define what constitutes default.

**Default, Notice of** The first step in the foreclosure process; a letter or other communication stating that the borrower has failed to meet the debt obligation and demanding payment is made in full.

**Defeasance Clause** 1. Used to defeat or cancel a certain right upon the happening of a specific event (e.g., upon final payment, words of grant in a mortgage are void and the mortgage is thereby canceled and title is re-vested to mortgagor). 2. Used to give a borrower the right to redeem real estate after default on a note by paying the full amount due plus fees and court costs. 3. Used in title theory states, whereby a mortgagee agrees to deed property back to the mortgagor after all contract terms have been performed as agreed.

**Defenses** Reasons used to justify certain actions, such as non-payment of a note.

**Deferment** Permission to delay fulfillment of an obligation (e.g., paying taxes) until a later date.

**Deferred Interest** Accrued interest that is not paid by regularly scheduled payments; interest that is accumulated during payment periods but is not paid until a later date. This can be a common element of ARMs and may cause **negative amortization** to occur.

**Deficiency Judgment** A court order stating that the debtor owes money to the creditor when the collateral property does not bring enough at foreclosure sale to cover the entire loan amount, accrued interest, and other costs.

**Deficit Spending** When the government spends more money than it takes in from tax revenue.

**Demand Deposits** Money that is immediately accessible and a customer may elect to withdraw from the bank at any time.

**Demand Inflation** Too much money chasing too few goods.

**Deposit** 1. Money offered as an indication of good faith regarding the future performance of a purchase agreement. Also called **earnest money**. 2. A tenant's security deposit.

**Depreciate** To decline in value.

**Depreciation** 1. A loss in property value for any reason. 2. For taxes, the expensing of the cost of business or investment property over a set number of years, determined by IRS to be an asset's useful life.

**Derogatory Credit** Credit history showing previous problems in meeting financial obligations.

**Direct Endorser** Lender authorized to underwrite their FHA loan applications and who is responsible for the entire loan process through closing.

**Disability Payments** Payments made as a result of an injury, illness, or other infirmary. The payments may be permanent if the disability is permanent, and thus may be counted as stable monthly income.

**Disclosure Statement** A document required by law that reveals specific information. For example, federal law requires that lenders give buyers a disclosure statement detailing the actual cost of borrowing money from the lender.

**Disclosures** Points or facts that must be revealed. For example, the law requires certain specific disclosures for ARMs, and disclosures under Truth In Lending Act.

**Discount** The difference between the stated amount of an obligation and the amount paid.

**Discount Points** An amount paid to a lender when a loan is made to make up the difference between the current market interest rate and the rate a lender gives a borrower on a note. Discount points increase a lender's yield, allowing the lender to give a borrower a lower interest rate. Also referred to as **Discounts** or **Points**. *See:* **Points**.

**Discount Rate** The interest rate charged by Federal Reserve Banks on loans to member commercial banks. Also referred to as the **Federal Discount Rate**.

**Discrimination** Violating civil rights law by treating people unequally because of their race, religion, sex, national origin, age, or some other characteristic of a protected class.

**Disintermediation** The loss of deposits to competing investments that offer higher returns.

**Down Payment** The amount of money a buyer pays to obtain a property in addition to the money that the buyer borrows.

**Due on Sale Clause** Mortgage clause which prohibits assignment by making the entire balance due when property is sold.

**Durability (of stable monthly income)** The likelihood or probability a person's source of income will continue into the future.

**Economic Base** The main business or industry that a community uses to support and sustain itself. A good economic base is critical for home values.

**Eminent Domain** The government's constitutional power to take (appropriate or condemn) private property for public use, as long as the owner is paid just compensation.

**Employment History** Past stability of a person's job tenure at various companies, used on loan applications to help gauge income durability and reliability.

**Encroachment** A physical object intruding onto neighboring property, often due to a mistake regarding the boundary.

**Encumbered Property** Property with mortgages, liens, or other restrictions against it that prevent or restrict its transfer.

**Encumbrance** A non-possessory interest in property; a lien, easement, or restrictive covenant burdening the property owner's title.

**Endorsement** Signing one's name to a note, check, or other instrument as a means of approving its deposit, transfer, etc.; the signature itself is also referred to as an **endorsement**. An endorsement may be **blank**, **qualified**, **restrictive,** or **special**.

**Environmental Impact Statement (EIS)** Study required for all federal and federally related projects by the National Environmental Policy Act, which details a development project's impact on energy use, sewage systems, drainage, water facilities, schools, and other environmental, economic, and social areas.

**Equal Credit Opportunity Act (ECOA)** Federal law that prohibits discrimination in granting credit to people based on sex, age, marital status, race, color, religion, national origin, or receipt of public assistance.

**Equitable Right of Redemption** The right of a debtor to redeem property from foreclosure proceedings prior to confirmation of sale.

**Equity** The difference between the market value of the property and the sum of the mortgages and liens against it.

**Equity Exchange** When value in a property is traded for value in another property. Properties must be of **like kind**, held for use in trade or business, or as investment to qualify for tax deferment. An equity exchange can also be a **delayed exchange**, with a promise to provide a replacement property. To qualify for tax deferment, the replacement property must be located within 45 days and closed within 180 days of the first exchange. Also called **Tax-Deferred Exchange**, **Tax-Free Exchange,** or **Section 1031** (from the section number of IRS law).

**Errors and Omissions Insurance** Professional liability insurance that protects real estate licensees from mistakes or negligence.

**Escheat** When property reverts to the state after a person without a valid will and without heirs dies.

**Escrow** The system in which things of value, like money or documents, are held on behalf of the parties to a transaction by a disinterested third party, or escrow agent, until specified conditions have all been met. *Compare:* **Escrows**.

**Escrow Closing** A closing by a disinterested third party, often an escrow agent.

**Escrow Instructions** The contract that authorizes an escrow agent to deliver items deposited in escrow once the parties have complied with specified conditions. This can be the purchase contract for real estate or a separate document.

**Escrows** Prepayable expenses the lender requires a borrower to set aside prior to closing (e.g., property taxes, insurance). Also called **impounds**. *See:* **Escrow**.

**Estimate Closing Costs** An approximation of the amount of money a borrower will need to buy a particular property.

**Estoppel** A legal doctrine that prevents a person from asserting rights or facts inconsistent with his or her earlier actions or statements when he or she failed to object or attempt to stop another person's actions.

**Estoppel Letter** A lender's written consent to a sale acknowledging the transfer and waiving any right to accelerate the loan because of the sale.

**Failure of Consideration** When the maker of a note never gets what the original holder promised (e.g., the maker doesn't end up with good title to land).

**Familial Status** A protected group under the Federal Fair Housing Act and Ohio Civil Rights Law, making it illegal to discriminate against a person because he or she is the parent or guardian of a child younger than 18 years of age.

**Fannie Mae (Federal National Mortgage Association)** The nation's largest, privately owned, investor in residential mortgages.

**Farmer's Home Administration (FmHA)** Former name of the program now called **Rural Economic Community Development (RECD).**

**Fed Funds Rate** The Federal Reserve's target for short-term interest rates.

**Federal Advisory Council** A body of 12 members, elected one each by the 12 Federal Reserve Banks as district representatives. They meet quarterly with the Board of Governors to discuss business conditions and make policy recommendations.

**Federal Budget Deficit** When federal government income is less than its expenditures.

**Federal Deposit Insurance Corporation (FDIC)** A public corporation, established in 1933, which insures up to $100,000 for each depositor for most member commercial banks and S&Ls. The FDIC has its own reserves and can borrow from the U.S. Treasury.

**Federal Discount Rate** The interest rate charged to banks by the Federal Reserve on loans to member commercial banks.

**Federal Fair Housing Act** Common name for Title VIII of the Civil Rights Act of 1968.

**Federal Funds Rate** The Federal Reserve's target for short-term interest rates.

**Federal Housing Administration (FHA)** Government agency that insures mortgage loans.

**Federal Open Market Committee (FOMC)** A body that controls the Fed's sale and purchase of government securities. The FOMC consists of the seven members of the Federal Reserve Board, plus the President of the Federal Reserve Bank of New York, and four other Federal Reserve Bank Presidents.

**Federal Regulations** Laws enacted by the federal government.

**Federal Reserve Banks** Banks that provide services to financial institutions (e.g., check clearing), which have one main office in each Federal Reserve district. All nationally chartered commercial banks must join the Federal Reserve and buy stock in its district reserve bank.

**Federal Reserve Board (the Fed)** The body responsible for U.S. monetary policy, maintaining economic stability, and regulating commercial banks. Also referred to as the **Board of Governors**, but most commonly called **the Fed**.

**Federal Reserve System** Established by the Federal Reserve Act of 1913 with 12 Federal Reserve Banks as a lender of last resort.

**Fee** 1. An estate of inheritance; title to real property that can be willed or descend to heirs. 2. Charge made for services rendered.

**Fee at Closing** Refers to a PMI payment due at closing. *See:* **Private Mortgage Insurance**.

**Fiduciary** Person in a position of trust, held by law to high standards of good faith and loyalty.

**Finance Companies** Financial institutions specializing in higher risk loans at higher interest rates.

**Finance Instrument** A written document used in the borrowing or lending of money. The most common type is a **promissory note**.

**Financial Institutions Reform, Recovery, and Enforcement Act (FIRREA)** A federal law passed in 1990 in response to the crisis in the savings and loan industry. It revised the regulation of thrifts (S&Ls) and created several new agencies, such as **Office of Thrift Supervision (OTS)** and **Resolution Trust Corporation (RTC)**.

**Financial Statement** A document that shows assets and liabilities for an individual, covering a specific period of time or point in time.

**Financing Statement** A brief document that, when recorded, gives constructive notice of a creditor's security interest in an item of personal property.

**Financing Tools** Alternative financing methods that can help a borrower get approved for a loan more easily or with less of a down payment.

**Finder's Fee** A referral fee paid for directing a buyer or seller to a real estate agent.

**First Lien Position** The spot held by the lien with highest priority when there's more than one mortgage or other debt or obligation secured by the property.

**Fiscal Policy** The government's plan for spending, taxation, and debt management.

**Fixed Disbursement Plan** A type of construction mortgage payout schedule where a percentage of funds is paid at a set time.

**Fixed Rate Loan** Loan with a constant interest rate remaining for the duration of the loan.

**Fixed Term** A period of time with a definite ending date.

**Foreclosure** When a lien holder causes property to be sold, so the unpaid debt secured by the lien can be satisfied from the sale proceeds.

**Foreclosure, Judicial** A lawsuit filed by a lender or other creditor to foreclose on a mortgage or other lien; a court ordered sheriff's sale of the property to repay the debt.

**Foreclosure, Non-judicial** Foreclosure by a trustee under the power of sale clause in a deed of trust, without the involvement of a court. (Not used in some states, such as Ohio.)

**Foreclosure, Strict** Foreclosure with a strict deadline, past which a mortgagor can no longer reclaim interest in the real property from the foreclosure proceedings by bringing the mortgage current.

**Foreclosure Action** A lawsuit filed by a creditor to begin foreclosure proceedings.

**Foreign Real Estate** Any real estate situated outside the state of Ohio (or state in which you work).

**Foreign Real Estate Broker/Salesperson** Any real estate broker/salesperson licensed to engage exclusively in real estate sales for land situated outside the state of Ohio (or state in which you work).

**Forfeiture** Loss of a right or something else of value as a result of failure to perform an obligation or condition.

**Forgery** A note or signature that is not genuine.

**Forward Commitment Purchase Program** Program with a commitment made by Freddie Mac to buy mortgages for six to eight months, with delivery of mortgages at the option of the seller.

**Fraud** An intentional or negligent misrepresentation or concealment of a material fact; making statements that a person knows, or should realize, are false or misleading.

**Fraud in the Inducement** When the holder of a note convinces the maker to grant the loan by making false statements.

**Freddie Mac (Federal Home Loan Mortgage Corporation)** Nonprofit, federally chartered institution (now privately owned) that functions as buyer and seller of residential mortgages.

**Freely Transferable** When the lender or creditor can obtain immediate cash by selling the note (e.g., when real estate notes are sold to the secondary market).

**Fully Amortized Loan** Loan where the total payments over the life of the loan pay off the entire balance of principal and interest due at the end of the loan term.

**Fully Amortized Second Mortgage** A second mortgage that is a fully amortized loan. *See:* **Fully Amortized Loans**.

**Funding Fee** A fee charged on VA-guaranteed loans in place of mortgage insurance.

**Garnishment** Legal process by which a creditor gains access to a debtor's personal property or funds in the hands of a third party. If a debtor's wages are garnished, the employer pays part of the paycheck directly to a creditor.

**General Brochure** A booklet required to be given to a borrower under Regulation Z of the Truth In Lending Act. A lender may comply with this by giving loan applicants a copy of the *Consumer Handbook on Adjustable Rate Mortgages* prepared by the Federal Reserve and the Federal Home Loan Bank Board.

**Ginnie Mae (Government National Mortgage Association)** Government-owned corporation that guarantees payment of principal and interest to investors who buy its mortgage backed securities on the secondary market.

**Government Financing** Real estate loans that are insured, guaranteed, or sponsored by government programs on the federal level. Traditionally, this does not refer to involvement of the government in the secondary markets.

**Graduated Payment Buydown** A temporary buydown plan where payment subsidies in the early years of the loan keep payments low, but payments increase each year until they're sufficient to fully amortize loan.

**Graduated Payment Term** The number of years during which payments may be adjusted in a graduated payment mortgage.

**Gross Income** Income before taxes and expenses have been deducted.

**Guardian** A person appointed by a court to administer the affairs of a minor or an incompetent person.

**Highest and Best Use** The most profitable, legally permitted, feasible, and physically possible use of a piece of property.

**Holder in Due Course** One who acquires a negotiable instrument in good faith and for consideration, and thus has certain rights above the original payee.

**Home Equity Line of Credit (HELOC)** Available money that can be borrowed by a homeowner and secured by a second mortgage on the principal residence. Home equity lines of credit can be accessed at any time up to a predetermined borrowing limit and are often used for non-housing expenditures.) *Compare:* **Home Equity Loan**.

**Home Equity Loan** A loan taken by a homeowner, secured by a second mortgage on the principal residence. Home equity loans are usually a one-time loan for a specific amount of money and obtained for a specific, and often non-housing, expenditure). *Compare:* **Home Equity Line of Credit**.

**Home Mortgage Disclosure Act (HMDA)** A law requiring all institutional mortgage lenders with assets of more than $10 million to make annual reports of all mortgage loans made in a given geographic area where they have at least one office. This law is designed to help the government detect patterns of **redlining**.

**Homestead Protection** Limited protection for a debtor against claims of judgment creditors; applies to property of the debtor's residence.

**Housing Expense Ratio** The relationship of a borrower's total monthly housing expense to income, expressed as a percentage.

**HUD** The Department of Housing and Urban Development; government agency that deals with housing issues.

**Hypothecate** To pledge property as security for a loan without giving up possession of it, as with a mortgage.

**Illegality of Instrument** A note based on illegal activities, such as gambling, and therefore not valid.

**Immediate Delivery Program** A Freddie Mac program whereby sellers have up to 60 days to deliver mortgages that Freddie Mac has agreed to buy on the secondary market.

**Immobility** A physical characteristic of real estate referring to the fact that it can't move from one place to another.

**Incapacity** When someone is not able to sign a note or enter into any other kind of contract (e.g., because of age or mental incompetence).

**Income** The money one receives from a job, investment, or other use of skills or capital.

**Income Qualifying Standards** The criteria used to evaluate the quality and durability of a borrower's sources of income, in conjunction with an assessment of the borrower's housing expense ratio and total debt service ratio.

**Incompetent** Not legally competent; not of sound mind; mentally ill, senile, or feebleminded.

**Indemnify** 1. To protect another against loss or damage. 2. To compensate a party for loss.

**Index** A statistical report that is generally a reliable indicator of the approximate change in the cost of money, and is often used to adjust the interest rate in ARMs.

**Inflation** An increase in the cost of goods or services; or too much money chasing too few goods.

**Inflation, Cost** An increase in the cost of goods or services.

**Inflation, Demand** Too much money chasing too few goods.

**Initial Premium** The first insurance premium paid for PMI. *See:* **Private Mortgage Insurance**.

**Installment Note** A note that calls for periodic payments of principal and/or interest during the term of the note. (In reality, a balloon payment is often required to pay the balance, but **on the state sales exam, Installment Note always assumes there's NO balloon**.)

**Instrument** Any document that transfers title (such as a deed), creates a lien (such as a mortgage), or gives a right to payment (such as a note or contract).

**Insurance Companies** Institutions with large sums of stable, long-term investment capital, looking for high return investments, such as long-term commercial real estate projects; investors in secondary mortgage markets.

**Interest** 1. A right or share in something, such as a piece of real estate. 2. A charge a borrower pays to a lender for the use of the lender's money. *Compare:* **Principal**.

**Interest-Only Loan** A loan where scheduled payments only pay accrued interest, and do not pay any portion of principal.

**Interest-Only Second** A second mortgage that is an interest-only loan.

**Interest Rate** The rate which is charged or paid for the use of money, generally expressed as a percentage of the principal.

**Interest Shortfall** Any accumulated interest accrued, but not collected, through regular payments because of the adjustable rate or graduated payment feature of a loan.

**Interest-Yielding Investments** Investments that pay interest or other dividends as a form of income to the holder or bearer. This may be counted as stable monthly income if the payments are consistent and do not deplete the principal amount of the investment.

**Intermediary** A person or institution that originates and/or services loans on behalf of another party (e.g., a mortgage broker).

**Invalid** Not legally binding or legally effective; not valid.

**Investment** A use of capital designed to produce income and/or profit.

**Jumbo Loans** Loans that exceed the maximum loan amount that Fannie Mae and Freddie Mac will buy, making them nonconforming. As of 2010, the limit is $417,000 on a single-family home.

**Just Compensation** Appropriate or fair value for private land taken by the government for public use. *See:* **Eminent Domain**.

**Kickbacks** Fees or other compensation given for services not performed, but as a means of undisclosed commission for business referrals. Kickbacks are prohibited by RESPA.

**Land Contract** A real estate installment agreement where a buyer makes payment to a seller in exchange for the right to occupy and use property, but no deed or title transfers until all, or a specified portion of, payments have been made. Also called **installment sales contract**, **land installment contract**, **land sales contract**, **real estate contract**, and other names.

**Land Use Controls** Public or private restrictions on how land may be used (e.g., zoning).

**Lawful Objective** A legal purpose.

**Lease** A contract where one party pays the other rent in exchange for possession of real estate; a conveyance of a leasehold estate from the fee owner to a tenant.

**Lease/Option** When a seller leases property to someone for a specific term, with an option to buy the property at a predetermined price during the lease term, usually with a portion of the lease payments applied to the purchase price. *See:* **Lease; Option.**

**Lease/Purchase** When a seller leases property to someone for a specific term, with the tenant agreeing to buy the property at a set price during or following the lease term.

**Lender First and Lender Second** When a lender holds two different mortgages on the same property, often at different interest rates.

**Lessee** A person who leases property from another; a tenant.

**Lessor** A person who leases property to another; a landlord.

**Level Payment** A buydown plan where the interest rate reduction, and hence the payment, is constant throughout the buydown period.

**Liabilities** Financial obligations or debt. Any money that is owed. *Compare:* **Debt.**

**Lien** A non-possessory interest in property, giving a lien holder the right to foreclose if the owner does not pay a debt owed to the lien holder; a financial encumbrance on the owner's title.

**Lien, General** A lien that attaches to all of the debtor's property. *Compare:* **Lien, Specific.**

**Lien, Involuntary** A lien that arises by operation of law, without the consent of the property owner. Also called a **statutory lien**.

**Lien, Materialman's** Similar to a mechanic's lien, but based on a debt owed to someone who supplied materials, equipment, or fuel for a project rather than labor.

**Lien, Mechanic's** A specific lien claimed by someone who performed work on the property (construction, repairs, or improvements) and has not been paid. This term is often used in a general sense, referring to materialman's liens as well as actual mechanic's liens.

**Lien, Specific** A lien that attaches only to a particular piece of property. *Compare:* **lien, general.**

**Lien, Tax** A lien on real property to secure the payment of taxes.

**Lien, Voluntary** A lien placed against property with the consent of the owner; a mortgage or, in other states, a deed of trust.

**Lien Priority** The order in which liens are paid off out of the proceeds of a foreclosure sale. For example, tax liens always have the highest priority and a first mortgage would have the next highest priority.

**Lien Theory States** States where a mortgagee holds only a lien against property (not actual title) until the loan is repaid. The mortgagor holds the actual title. *Compare:* **Title Theory States.**

**Lienholder, Junior** Secured creditor with a lower priority lien than another lien on the same land.

**Like Kind Property** The same type of property (such as real estate for real estate), as a necessary condition for a tax-free exchange.

**Limited Real Estate Broker/Salesperson** Person licensed exclusively to sell cemetery interment rights for a fee.

**Line of Credit** Available money that a borrower can access at any time up to a predetermined borrowing limit. If the loan is secured by a second mortgage on the borrower's principal residence, it is referred to as a **home equity line of credit**.

**Liquid Assets** Cash and other assets, such as stocks or bonds, which can quickly be converted to cash.

**Listing** A written agency contract between a seller and a real estate broker, stating the broker will be paid a commission for finding (or attempting to find) a buyer for the seller's real property.

**Loan Application** The form lenders require potential borrowers to complete, listing all pertinent information about the borrower and property.

**Loan Estimate** A lender disclosure containing a "good faith estimate" of closing costs, loan terms, and the costs that the borrower must pay for a real estate loan, including the annual percentage rate (APR). The lender must give this to the borrower within three business days of a completed loan application. Required by RESPA and the Truth in Lending Act for all federally related residential transactions.

**Loan Origination Fee** Fee charged by lender to cover the administrative costs of making a loan, usually based on a percentage of the loan amount (1% = 1 point).

**Loan-to-Value Ratio (LTV)** The amount of money borrowed compared to the value or price of the property.

**Location** Exact position of real estate.

**Location Survey** A survey that determines if a property's buildings encroach on adjoining property, or if any adjoining property's buildings encroach on the subject property.

**London InterBank Offering Rate (LIBOR)** An index used by lenders when making ARM loans; the rate (in Euros) that international banks charge each other for loans.

**Long-Term** Loans in real estate that have payments spread out over 25-30 years.

**Lot** Parcel of land; a parcel in a subdivision.

**Maintenance Payments** Money paid as part of a divorce settlement. Maintenance payments do not have to be revealed as a source of income if not counted to help repay a loan, but must be revealed as a debt obligation.

**Majority, Age of** The age at which a person gains legal capacity; in Ohio, 18 years old. *Compare:* **Minor**.

**Maker** One promising to pay money in a note.

**Margin** The difference between the index value and the interest rate charged to the borrower with an ARM loan (e.g., the lender's profit).

**Market Price** The price for which real estate actually sold.

**Market Value** The most probably price that a property should bring in a competitive and open market under all conditions requisite to a fair sale.

**Material Alteration** When a note is changed unilaterally by the holder.

**Materialman** Person who supplies materials, equipment, etc., for construction projects. *See:* **Lien, Materialman's**. *Compare:* **Mechanic**.

**Maximum Guarantee Amount** The maximum amount that can be guaranteed by a VA loan.

**Maximum Mortgage Amount** The maximum amount that can be financed by an FHA loan.

**Mechanic** A person who performs work (construction, remodeling, repairs, or demolition) on real property. *See:* **Lien, Mechanic's**. *Compare:* **Materialman**.

**Member Banks** The 5,000+ commercial banks across the U.S. that are subject to the rules and policies implemented by the Fed.

**Minor** A person who has not yet reached the age of majority; in Ohio, a person under 18.

**Misrepresentation** A false or misleading statement. *See:* **Fraud**.

**Monetary Policy** Means by which the government exerts control over the supply and cost of money.

**Monthly Income** Income received on a monthly basis. *See:* **Income**.

**Moral Suasion** Trying to use persuasive influences on the public and financial markets so they will perceive credit in a specific way.

**Mortgage** An instrument that creates a voluntary lien on real property to secure repayment of a debt. The parties to a mortgage are the mortgagor (borrower) and mortgagee (lender).

**Mortgage, Adjustable Rate (ARM)** A mortgage that permits the lender to periodically adjust the interest rate so it reflects fluctuations in the cost of money.

**Mortgage, Bi-Weekly** A fixed rate mortgage, similar to a standard mortgage, but with payments made every two weeks instead of every month, thus making an extra payment each year.

**Mortgage, Blanket** 1. A mortgage that covers more than one parcel of real estate. 2. A mortgage that covers an entire building or development, rather than an individual unit or lot.

**Mortgage, Bridge** A mortgage that occurs between the termination of one mortgage and the beginning of another.

**Mortgage, Budget** Mortgage agreement where payments are set up to include principal and interest on the loan, plus 1/12 of the year's property taxes and hazard insurance premiums.

**Mortgage, Cash-Out** A mortgage that a borrower gives to lenders so that the borrower can get cash for the equity that has built up in property (e.g., a home equity loan taken out for a non-house purpose, or an investor trying to recoup money invested in fixing up a property).

**Mortgage, Construction** A temporary loan used to finance the construction of a building on land. Replaced with a takeout loan.

**Mortgage, Conventional** A loan that is not insured or guaranteed by a government entity.

**Mortgage, Equity Participation** A mortgage that lets the lender share part of the earnings, income, or profits from a real estate project.

**Mortgage, First** A security instrument with a first lien position, meaning the first mortgage holder is paid first from a foreclosure sale. One exception is a tax lien on the property, which always takes first lien positions.

**Mortgage, Graduated Payment (GPM)** Payment structure that allows the borrower to make smaller payments in early years of the mortgage, with payments increasing on a scheduled basis at a predetermined point until they are sufficient to fully amortize the loan over the remainder of its term.

**Mortgage, Hard Money** A mortgage where the borrower receives cash (e.g., cash-out mortgage).

**Mortgage, Hybrid ARM** Loans that offer fixed rates for a certain period then become adjustable. (e.g., 7/1 or 5/1).

**Mortgage, Junior** Any mortgage that has a lower lien position than another mortgage.

**Mortgage, Open-End** A mortgage where the borrower can request more funds from the lender, up to a certain pre-defined limit, even re-borrowing part of the debt that's been repaid (at lender's discretion) without having to renegotiate the loan. (*Note*: Most mortgage documents say *open-end* mortgage, but it's rare for lenders to loan more money without reassessing the borrower and renegotiating the loan. Borrowers usually need to get a line of credit because it has an adjustable interest rate.)

**Mortgage, Package** A mortgage where personal property (e.g., appliances) are included in a real estate sale and financed with one contract.

**Mortgage, Purchase Money** A mortgage where the seller finances all or part of the sale price of property for a buyer.

**Mortgage, Purchase Money Second** A purchase money mortgage in a second lien position.

**Mortgage, Refinance** A mortgage that a borrower gives a lender to redo or expand the loan on the property, usually to get a better interest rate or pay off other debts.

**Mortgage, Reverse** When a homeowner age 62 or over, with little or no outstanding liens, mortgages his or her home to a lender and, in return, receives a monthly check. *See:* **Term Loan, Split Term Loan, Tenure Loan.**

**Mortgage, Satisfaction of** The document a mortgagee gives the mortgagor when a mortgage debt has been paid in full, acknowledging that the debt has been paid and the mortgage is no longer a lien against the property.

**Mortgage, Second** A security instrument in a second lien position.

**Mortgage, Senior** A mortgage that has a higher lien position than another mortgage.

**Mortgage, Shared Appreciation (SAM)** A mortgage where the lender charges below-market interest rates in exchange for a share of the borrower's equity.

**Mortgage, Soft Money** A mortgage where the borrower receives credit instead of actual cash (e.g., a purchase money mortgage).

**Mortgage, Variable Balance (VBM)** A mortgage with an adjustable interest rate, but with payments that never change. Instead, as the rate goes up or down, the balance due on the mortgage changes.

**Mortgage, Wraparound** When an existing loan on a property is retained, while the lender (or seller) gives the buyer another, larger loan. Often the seller keeps existing mortgage, still pays on it, and gives the buyer another mortgage.

**Mortgage Banker** One who originates, sells, and services mortgage loans, and usually acts as the originator and servicer of loans on behalf of large investors, such as insurance companies, pension plans, or Fannie Mae.

**Mortgage Broker** One who, for a fee, places loans with investors, but typically does not service such loans.

**Mortgage Companies** Institutions that function as intermediaries between borrowers and lenders. Mortgage companies are resources of service and expertise more than sources of capital.

**Mortgage Insurance** Insurance offered by private companies (PMI) or the government through the FHA (MIP) to insure a lender against default on a loan by a borrower. *See:* **Private Mortgage Insurance (PMI)** and **Mortgage Insurance Premium (MIP)**.

**Mortgage Insurance Premium (MIP)** The fee charged for FHA mortgage insurance coverage. Initial premium can be financed, and there is a monthly premium. Also called **Upfront Mortgage Insurance Premium (UFMIP)**.

**Mortgagee** A lender who accepts a mortgage as security for repayment of the loan.

**Mortgagor** A person who borrows money and gives a mortgage to the lender as security.

**Mrs. Murphy Exemption** An exemption to the Federal Fair Housing Act, which holds that the rental of a unit or a room in an owner-occupied dwelling containing four units or less is exempt from the Fair Housing Law, provided rental ads are not discriminatory and a real estate agent is not used to locate tenants. **Ohio does NOT recognize this exemption.**

**Multiple Listing Service (MLS)** Listing service whereby local member brokers agree to share listings, and agree to share commissions on properties sold jointly.

**Mutual Mortgage Insurance Plan (MMIP)** Name of the FHA residential mortgage insurance program.

**Negative Amortization** When a loan balance grows because of deferred interest.

**Negotiable Instrument** Promissory note or other finance instrument that is freely transferable.

**Net Income** Income after expenses.

**Net to Seller** An estimate of the money a seller should receive from a real estate transaction, based on a certain selling price after all costs and expenses have been paid.

**Net Worth** The value of a person's assets, determined by subtracting liabilities from assets.

**No Document Loan**—A loan, which is no longer available, where a borrower had good credit, but trouble providing income documentation, so the loan was decided on other merits. (These loans may have been offered at a lower LTV, and lender may still have required tax returns.) Also called **Stated Doc**, **No Ratio**.

**Nominal Rate** The interest rate stated in a note. Also called **Coupon Rate** or **Note Rate**.

**Nonconforming Loans** Loans that do not meet Fannie Mae and Freddie Mac standards, and thus cannot be sold to them but can be sold to other secondary markets. *Compare:* **Conforming Loans**.

**Nontraditional Financing** When real estate is financed with terms or financing concessions other than those typical for loans.

**Nontraditional Financing Tools** Specific financing programs or methods, not used in financing, to help get a loan approved.

**Notary Public** An official whose primary function is to witness and certify the acknowledgment made by one signing a legal document.

**Note** A written, legally binding promise to repay a debt. Also called a **Promissory Note**.

**Note, Fully Amortized** A note that calls for regular payments of principal and interest, calculated to pay off the entire balance of the loan by the end of the loan term.

**Note, Installment** A note that calls for periodic payments of principal and/or interest during the term of the note. (In reality, a balloon payment is often required to pay the balance, but **on the state sales exam, always assume there is NO balloon associated with an Installment Note.**)

**Note, Partially Amortized** A note that calls for periodic payments of principal and/or interest during the loan term, with a balloon payment at the end of loan term to pay off balance due. Also called an **Installment Note with Balloon**.

**Note, Promissory** An instrument that is evidence of a promise to pay a specific debt.

**Note, Straight** A note that calls for payments of interest only during the term of the note with a balloon payment at the end of the loan term to pay off the principal amount.

**Note Rate** The interest rate stated in a note. Also called **Coupon Rate** or **Nominal Rate**.

**Offer** When one party proposes a contract to another; if the other party accepts the offer, a binding contract is formed. *See:* **Acceptance**.

**Offeree** A person who receives an offer or to whom an offer is made.

**Offeror** A person who makes an offer.

**Office of Thrift Supervision (OTS)** The government entity that regulates savings and loans in the same manner the Federal Reserve regulates commercial banks.

**Ohio Civil Rights Law** State law that prohibits housing discrimination on the basis of race, color, religion, sex, ancestry, national origin, disability, military status, and familial status.

**One-Time Premium** The initial fee paid for private mortgage insurance, with no renewal premium. *See:* **Private Mortgage Insurance**.

**Open Market Operations** When the Federal Reserve Board sells or buys government securities (bonds) as a means of controlling the supply of, and demand for, money. The Fed can also buy and sell U.S. dollars on the international market.

**Option** A contract giving one party the right to do something within a designated time period, without obligation to do so.

**Option Money** Cash consideration given for an option contract.

**Option to Purchase** A contract giving the optionee the right, but not the obligation, to buy property owned by the optionor at an agreed price during a specified period.

**Optionee** Person to whom an option is given.

**Optionor** Person who gives an option.

**Order of Execution** A court order directing a public officer (often the sheriff or marshal) to seize and/or sell property to regain possession for the owner and/or satisfy a debt. Also called an **Order of Attachment**.

**Origination** The process of making or initiating a new loan.

**Overtime** Money paid to someone for hours worked beyond their normal workday or week. Overtime may be counted as income only if it is consistent.

**Part-Time Earnings** Money paid to someone for a job that is not considered full time. Part-time earnings may be counted as income only if consistent.

**Partial Release, Satisfaction, or Conveyance Clause** A contract clause that obligates the creditor to release part of the property from lien and convey title to that part back to the debtor once certain provisions of the note or mortgage have been satisfied.

**Partially Amortized Loan** Loan where payments are applied to principal and interest, but the payments do not retire the debt when the agreed upon loan term expires, thus requiring a balloon payment at the end of the loan term.

**Partially Amortized Second Mortgage** A second mortgage that is a partially amortized loan. *See:* **Partially Amortized Loans**.

**Participation Plan** A loan for which the buyer and another investor (or seller, lender, etc.) enter into a partnership, with the buyer paying an equity share in a deal in lieu of interest. Also called a **Shared Equity Plan**.

**Pass-Through Securities** Mortgage-backed securities issued by Ginnie Mae, which are more common and pay interest and principal payments on a monthly basis.

**Payee** The one promised payment in a note.

**Pension Funds** Sources of large sums of capital for high return investments, which are now playing a bigger role in real estate finance via secondary markets and mortgage brokers.

**Pensions** Money paid to someone as part of their retirement benefits. Pensions may be counted as income only if consistent.

**Periodic Re-Amortization** When the payments on a loan are recalculated at a specific time based on the loan balance at that time, so the new payments will fully amortize the loan over the remaining loan term.

**Permanent Construction Loan** A special type of construction loan where there is only one loan and one closing, with no take-out loan.

**PITI** A typical mortgage payment that includes **p**rinciple, **i**nterest, **t**axes, and **i**nsurance.

**Points** One percent of the loan amount. Points are charged for any reason, but are often used for buydowns (where they may also be called **Discount Points**). Points are used to increase the lender's yield on a loan.

**Police Power** The constitutional power of state and local governments to enact and enforce laws that protect the public's health, safety, morals, and general welfare.

**Portfolio** The collection of mortgages and other securities held by a lender and not sold on the secondary market.

**Portfolio Lenders** Financial institutions that make real estate loans that they keep and service in house instead of selling them on the secondary markets.

**Power of Attorney** An instrument authorizing one person (called an attorney in fact) to act as another's agent, to the extent stated in the instrument.

**Power of Sale Clause** A clause that allows the trustee to sell trust deed property, without court supervision, when terms of the trust deed are not kept.

**Pre-Approval** Process by which a lender determines if potential borrowers can be financed through the lender, and for what amount of money.

**Pre-Qualification** Process of pre-determining how large a loan a potential homebuyer might be eligible to borrow. Pre-qualification is typically done by an agent or lender, but it doesn't guarantee approval.

**Prepayment Clause** A contract clause that gives a lender the right to charge the borrower a penalty for paying off a loan early.

**Prepayment Penalties** Additional money charged by a lender for the borrower paying a loan off early.

**Primary Mortgage Market Lenders** Lenders who make loans directly to borrowers (e.g., neighborhood banks).

**Primary Mortgage Markets** When lenders make mortgage loans directly to borrowers. This is also referred to simply as **Primary Markets**. *Compare:* **Secondary Mortgage Markets**.

**Prime Rate** The lowest interest rate that banks charge their best commercial customers.

**Principal** 1. With regard to a loan, the amount originally borrowed. *Compare:* **Interest**. 2. A person who grants another person (an agent) authority to represent him or her in dealing with third parties. 3. One of the parties to a transaction (such as the buyer or seller), as opposed to those who are involved as agents or employees (such as a broker or escrow agent).

**Prior Payment** When the maker of a note pays off the note, but does not have the note returned and the original holder sells it to someone else.

**Private Mortgage Insurance (PMI)** Insurance offered by private companies to insure a lender against default on a loan by a borrower.

**Profit** The difference between the money made from an investment and the money actually invested.

**Promisee** A person who has been promised something; a person who is supposed to receive the benefit of a legally binding contractual promise (e.g., with a promissory note).

**Promisor** A person who has made a contractual promise to another (e.g., in a promissory note).

**Promissory Note** An instrument that evidences a promise to pay a specific amount of money to a specific person within a specific time frame. A written, legally binding promise to repay a debt.

**Public Auction** An auction held at the courthouse where anyone can bid on property that is in foreclosure proceedings.

**Purchase Agreement** A contract in which a seller promises to convey title to real property to a buyer in exchange for the purchase price. Also called a **purchase and sale agreement**, a **purchase contract**, or an **earnest money agreement**.

**Purchase Money Second Mortgage** A purchase money mortgage that's in a second lien position. *See:* **Mortgage, Purchase Money**.

**Qualified Endorsement** When the holder of a note writes "without recourse" when signing a note, which means that if the maker of the note refuses to pay, the holder will not be liable for the amount.

**Qualifying** The process of determining whether or not a borrower is likely to default on a loan and that the property is worth enough to satisfy the debt if the borrower does default.

**Qualifying a Buyer** Evaluating a borrower's creditworthiness.

**Qualifying Standards** Guidelines used to measure the quality of a borrower and property.

**Quality (of Stable Monthly Income)** The dependability of a borrower's income. *See:* **Stable Income**.

**Quality Control** The secondary mortgage market's effort to standardize mortgages.

**Racial Discrimination** Treating people unequally because of their race, ancestry, or national origin in violation of civil rights law.

**Re-Amortization** When payments on a loan are recalculated so the new payment will fully amortize the loan over the remaining loan term.

**Real Estate Contract** 1. A purchase agreement. 2. A land contract. 3. Any contract having to do with real property.

**Real Estate Cycles** General swings in real estate activity, resulting in increasing or decreasing activity, and property values, during different phases of the cycle.

**Real Estate Investment Trust (REIT)** A real estate investment business with at least 100 investors, organized as a trust.

**Real Estate Owned (REO)** Property acquired by a lending institution through foreclosure and held in inventory.

**Real Estate Settlement Procedures Act (RESPA)** Federal law dealing with real estate closings that provides specific procedures and guidelines for the disclosure of settlement costs.

**Real Property** Physical land and everything attached to it, plus the rights of ownership (bundle of rights) in real estate. Also called **realty**.

**Realtist** A real estate licensee who is a member of National Association of Real Estate Brokers.

**REALTOR®** Any real estate licensee who is a member of the National Association of REALTORS® and their affiliate state and local boards. Only members may use the term REALTOR® because it's a registered trademark of the NAR.

**Redlining** When a lender refuses to make loans secured by property in a certain neighborhood because of the racial or ethnic composition of the neighborhood.

**Refinancing** A borrower redoes or expands the loan on a property, usually to get a better interest rate or to pay off other debts.

**Regulation** 1. A rule adopted by an administrative agency. 2. Any governmental order having the force of law.

**Regulation Z** Federal guidelines under the Truth in Lending Act that require full disclosure of all credit terms for consumer loans.

**Release** 1. A document in which one gives up a legal right. 2. To give up a legal right.

**Renewal Premium** Recurring fee to continue an insurance policy, such as PMI.

**Rent** Consideration paid by a tenant to a landlord in exchange for possession and use of property.

**Rent Credit** When part of a rent payment is applied against the purchase price of a property, especially with lease/purchase contracts.

**Rental Income** Money paid to someone for the right to use a property. Rental income may be counted as income only if it is consistent. Only the part of the rental income that is over and above expenses (net rental income) may be counted.

**Rescind** To take back or withdraw an offer or contract. *See:* **Right to Rescind**.

**Reserve Requirements** The percentage of customers' deposits that commercial banks are required to keep on deposit, on hand either at the bank or in a bank's own accounts. Money a bank can't lend to other people.

**Reserves** Cash on deposit or other highly liquid assets a borrower must have in order to cover two months of PITI mortgage payments, after they make the cash down payment and pay all closing costs.

**Residual Income** The income a borrower has left after subtracting taxes, housing expense, and all recurring debts and obligations (used for VA loan qualifying). Also called the **cash flow** analysis method.

**Restrictive Endorsement** When the holder of a note restricts future negotiation of the note by writing something such as "for deposit only" and then signs the note.

**Right to Rescind** The right of a consumer to rescind any credit transaction involving their principal residence as collateral, except a mortgage, involving their principal residence as collateral, up to midnight of the third business day.

**Roundtable Closing** A closing conducted with all parties present.

**Rural Development** A government agency under the Department of Agriculture that guarantees or makes loans to help buyers of homes and farms in rural areas or small towns. Formerly the Farmer's Home Administration (FmHA).

**Savings and Loan Associations (S & Ls)** Institutions that specialize in taking savings deposits and making mortgage loans.

**Scarcity** Physical characteristic of real property referring to the limited supply of real estate.

**Secondarily Liable** When a party is not completely released from liability on an obligation; thus, if the lender cannot recover the loan amount from the new party, the original party, who is secondarily liable, may still be pursued.

**Secondary Financing** When a buyer borrowers money from another source in addition to the primary lender to pay for part of the purchase price or closing costs.

**Secondary Mortgage Markets** The private investors and government agencies that buy and sell real estate mortgages. Also called **Secondary Markets**. *Compare:* **Primary Mortgage Markets**.

**Section 203(b) FHA Loan** The standard FHA-insured loan program. There are no income limits on this type of loan. The borrower must meet all FHA qualifying standards and the property cost must not exceed the maximum FHA mortgage amounts. Also called the **Standard FHA Loan Program**.

**Section 203(k) FHA Loan** The FHA-insured loan program that allows a buyer to buy property and borrow extra money to repair it. Borrower must meet all FHA qualifying standards and must spend at least $5,000 in rehab costs; property cannot exceed maximum FHA mortgage amounts and must be brought up to FHA standards. Also called **Rehabilitation Loan FHA Loan Program**.

**Section 234(c) FHA Loan** The FHA-insured loan program for condominiums, available only for FHA qualified, single-family condos. Borrower must meet all FHA qualifying standards and property cost must not exceed the maximum FHA mortgage amounts. Also called **Condominium FHA Loan Program**.

**Section 251 FHA Loan** An FHA-insured ARM loan with rate adjustments limited to 1% annually and 5% over the life of the loan. No negative amortization is permitted. Borrower must meet FHA qualifying standards and property cost cannot exceed maximum FHA mortgage amounts. The number of ARMs that may be insured by the FHA is limited to 10% of the total number of all Title II mortgages insured during the previous fiscal year. Also called **FHA ARM Loan Program**.

**Securities** Instruments that pledge assets as security for a debt (e.g., mortgages and trust deeds), or documents that serve as evidence of ownership (e.g., stocks and bonds).

**Securitization** Act of pooling mortgages, then selling them as mortgage-backed securities.

**Security Agreement** Instrument that creates a voluntary lien on property to secure repayment of a loan. *See:* **Security Instrument**.

**Security Instrument** An instrument that gives a creditor the right to sell collateral to satisfy a debt if the debtor fails to pay according to the terms of the agreement.

**Security Interest** The interest a creditor may acquire in the debtor's property to ensure that the debt will be paid.

**Self-Employment Income** Money someone earns working independently, either doing freelance work, as an independent contractor, or as the owner of a company (person owns at least 25% of the company). Self-employment income may count as income only if it is consistent. Tax returns are usually required proving consistency.

**Seller Financing** When a seller extends credit to a buyer to finance the purchase of the property, which can be instead of or in addition to the buyer obtaining a loan from a third party, such as an institutional lender.

**Seller-Paid Items** Closing costs paid by the seller instead of the buyer. This usually refers to items normally paid by the buyer, but in some instances are paid by the seller to help close the sale. Fannie Mae, Freddie Mac, FHA, and VA loans limit this.

**Seller's Market** Situation in the housing market where there are more buyers than sellers. This allows sellers to choose from a large number of buyers looking for property in a specific area. **Servicing** The process of collecting loan payments, keeping records, and handling defaults for loans.

**Settlement Statement** A document that presents detailed accounting for a real estate transaction, listing each party's debits and credits and the amount each will receive or be required to pay at closing. Also called a **closing statement**.

**Sheriff's Deed** A deed issued by the court to a purchaser of property from a foreclosure sale.

**Sheriff's Sale** A foreclosure sale held after a judicial foreclosure. Sometimes called an **execution** or an **execution sale**.

**Simple Interest** Interest calculated as a percentage of the principal only. *Compare:* **Compound Interest**.

**Social Security Income** Money one receives from the government under Social Security program. Social Security payments may be counted as income only if they are consistent.

**Special Endorsement** When the holder of a note writes, "pay to the order of" a newly named party when signing a note.

**Specific Tax Policies** Tax laws that encourage or discourage a particular behavior or activity.

**Speculation** Investing or optioning with the anticipation something will go up in value.

**Split-Term Loan** A type of reverse mortgage loan that provides for monthly advances to qualified senior citizens, which doesn't need to be repaid until the borrower moves, dies, or sells the house.

**Stable Income** Income expected to continue in the future.

**Steering** Illegal activity of channeling prospective buyers or tenants to particular neighborhoods based on their race, religion, national origin, or ancestry.

**Straight Note** A note that calls for payments of interest only during the term of the note, with a balloon payment at the end to pay off the principal balance.

**Subject To** When property is transferred to a buyer along with an existing mortgage or lien, but without the buyer accepting personal responsibility for the debt. The buyer must make the payments to keep the property, but loses his or her equity only in the event of default. *Compare:* **Assumption**.

**Subordination Clause** A contract clause that gives a mortgage recorded at a later date the right to take priority over an earlier recorded mortgage.

**Supply and Demand** Law of economics that says when supply exceeds demand for all products, goods, and services, prices will fall and when demand exceeds supply, prices will rise.

**Take-Out Loan** A loan used to pay off a construction loan when construction is complete.

**Tax, Property** An annual tax levied on the value of real property.

**Taxation** The process of a government levying a charge on people or things.

**Teaser Rates** A low initial rate on an ARM. The rate usually returns to normal at the first adjustment date.

**Tenant** Someone in lawful possession of real property; someone who is leasing property from the owner.

**Tenure Loan** A type of reverse mortgage that provides monthly advances to qualified senior citizens for as long as they occupy the house as principal residence. Monthly payments are less because there's no set repayment date.

**Term** A prescribed period; especially, the length of time a borrower has to pay off a loan, or the duration of a lease.

**Time is of the Essence** A contract clause that means performance on the exact dates specified is an essential element of the contract; failure to perform on time is a material breach.

**Title** Lawful ownership of real property. Also, in informal usage, the deed or other document that is evidence of ownership.

**Title, Equitable** An interest created in property upon the execution of a valid sales contract, whereby actual title will be transferred by deed at a closing. The buyer's interest in property under a land contract. Also called an **equitable interest**.

**Title VIII** Part of the Civil Rights Act of 1968; prohibits discrimination based on race, color, religion, sex, national origin, disability, or familial status. Also referred to as the **Federal Fair Housing Act**.

**Title Insurance** Insurance that indemnifies against losses resulting from undiscovered title defects and encumbrances.

**Title Theory States** States where a mortgagee holds actual title to property until the loan is repaid. *Compare:* **Lien Theory States**.

**Total Debt Service Ratio** The relationship of a borrower's total monthly debt to income, expressed as a percentage. Debt obligations include housing and long-term debts with more than ten payments remaining.

**Trust** A legal arrangement in which title to property or funds is vested in one or more trustees, who manage the property or invest the funds on behalf of the trust's beneficiaries, in accordance with instructions set forth in the document establishing the trust.

**Trust Deed** An instrument held by a third party as security for the payment of a note. Like a mortgage, it creates a voluntary lien on real property to secure repayment of a debt. Parties to a deed of trust are grantor or trustor (borrower), beneficiary (lender), and trustee (neutral third party). Unlike a mortgage, a trust deed has a power of sale, allowing trustee to foreclose non-judicially. Also called a **Deed of Trust**.

**Trustee** A person appointed to manage a trust on behalf of the beneficiaries; in a trust deed, an independent third party that holds the trust instrument.

**Trustor** The borrower in a trust deed.

**Truth In Lending Act (TILA)** Act that requires lenders to disclose credit costs in order to promote informed use of consumer credit.

**Underwriter** Individual who evaluates a loan application to determine its risk level for a lender or investor; final decision maker on a loan application.

**Underwriting Standards** The criteria an underwriter uses when determining if a borrower or property qualifies for a loan.

**Unemployment** Money paid to someone for support, compensation, or temporary income after losing a job. Unemployment compensation may be counted as income only if it's consistent.

**Unencumbered Property** Property for which the seller has clear title, free of mortgages or other liens.

**Uniform Commercial Code** A body of law that governs transactions involving personal property and sets requirements for negotiable instruments.

**Uniqueness** Characteristic of real property that says each piece of land, every building, and every house is said to be a different piece of real estate. Also called **non-homogeneity**.

**United States Treasury Department** The part of the executive branch of the federal government that's the fiscal manager of the nation. The U.S. Treasury is responsible for carrying out the nation's fiscal policy by doing the actual spending, taxing, and debt financing via an account it keeps with the Federal Reserve.

**Usury** Charging an interest rate that exceeds legal limits.

**VA Automatic Endorser** Lender authorized to underwrite their VA loan applications and who is responsible for the entire mortgage process through closing.

**VA Entitlement** The dollar amount of loan guarantee to which an eligible veteran is entitled.

**VA Guarantee** The dollar amount of loan that will be paid by the VA in the event of borrower default.

**Valid** The legal classification of a contract that is binding and enforceable in a court of law.

**Value** The amount of goods or services offered in the marketplace in exchange for something else.

**Vendee** A buyer or purchaser; particularly, someone buying property under a land contract.

**Vendor** A seller; particularly, someone selling property by means of a land contract.

**Verification of Deposit** A form sent by a lender directly to a bank verifying the borrower's accounts.

**Veterans Administration (VA)** Government agency, part of the U.S. Department of Veteran's Affairs, that guarantees mortgage loans for eligible veterans.

**Void** Having no legal force or effect.

**Voucher System** A disbursement plan for construction mortgage payouts whereby the contractor pays his or her own bills and then submits bills to the lender for reimbursement.

**Waiver** The voluntary relinquishment or surrender of a right.

**Warrant System** A disbursement plan for construction mortgage payouts whereby the lender directly pays bills presented by the various suppliers and laborers on the project.

**Welfare** Money paid to someone by the government for support. Welfare may be counted as income only if it's consistent or permanent.

**Wraparound Financing** When a seller keeps an existing loan and continues to pay on it, while giving the buyer another mortgage.

**Writ of Execution** A court order directing a public officer, often the sheriff or marshal, to seize and/or sell property to regain possession for the owner and/or satisfy a debt.

**Yield** The total amount of money that can be made from an investment.

**Yield, Lender's** The total amount of money that a lender can make from a loan. Also called *lender's return*.

# Index

2-1 Buydown  128

11th Federal Home Loan Bank
    (FHLB)  131

15-Year Mortgage  77

40-Year Mortgage  78

80% Conventional Loan  79

90% Conventional Loan  79

95% Conventional Loan  80

### A

Ability to Repay Rule  20

Acceleration Clause  49

Adjustable Rate Mortgage (ARM)
    55, 77, 129

Advertisement  17

Affiliated Business Arrangement
    Disclosure (AfBA)  33

Alienation Clause  49

American Recovery and
    Reinvestment Act of 2009  8

Amortization  87
  Negative  76

Amortized
  Installment Note  44
  Loan  76

Annual
  Escrow Statement  33
  Percentage Rate (APR)  16, 20,
    135

Application
  Completed  20
  Loan  157

ARM  55
  Option  56

ARM - Adjustable Rate Mortgage
    77, 129

Asset  158
  Liquid  176

Assumability of Loan  101

Assumption  143

Auction
  Public  47

Automated Underwriting  165

Average One-year Treasury
    Constant Maturity Index
    (TCM)  131

### B

Balloon Payment  44, 76, 86

B-C Loans or B-C Credit  67

BEACON  174

Bill Consolidation  175

Bi-weekly Mortgage  136

Blanket Mortgage  54

Board of Governors  9

Bond-type Security  71

Bridge Mortgage  54

Broker
  Mortgage  64

Budget Mortgage  54

Buydown  124, 125, 126
  2-1  128
  Permanent  127
  Temporary
    Calculating  128

Buyer's Market  2

### C

Calculating Cash to Close  20, 31

Calculation
  Loan  33

Cancellation  100

Cap  77, 133
  FHA/VA  133

Capital Gain  147

Cash Flow  170
  Analysis Method  181

Cash-Out Refinance Mortgage  53

Certificate
  of Eligibility (COE)  108
  of Reasonable Value (CRV)  112

CHARM  135

Clause
  Acceleration  49
  Alienation  49
  Conveyance  50
  Defeasance  50
  Due on Sale  49
  Prepayment  51
  Subordination  51

Closing  183
  Cost  125
  Disclosure  24
  Roundtable  184

Commercial Bank  62

Community
  Home Buyer Program  141
  Reinvestment Act (CRA)  78,
    140, 141

Comparison  145

Completed Application  20

Confirmation of Sale 47
Conforming Loan 78
Consideration 145
Construction Mortgage 56
Contract
 Installment Sales 57
 Land 57
 Land Installment 57
 Land Sales 57
 Purchase 146
 Real Estate 57
Conventional
 Financing 76
 Loan 76, 79, 81
  80% 79
  90% 79
  95% 80
Conveyance
 Clause 50
 Voluntary 48
Cost
 Closing 125
 Loan 19, 30
Cost of Funds Index of the 11th
 District Federal Home Loan
 Bank (COFI) 131
Coupon Rate 125
Covenant 51
CRA - Community Reinvestment
 Act 141
Credit
 History 176
 Union 64

D

DAP Program 140
DD-214 108
Dealer 148
Debt 158, 172
Deed
 in Lieu of Foreclosure 48
 of Trust 45
  Advantages and
   Disadvantages 46
 Sheriff's 47
 Trust 45
Defeasance Clause 50
Deficiency

Judgment 47
Deficit Spending 6
Demand Deposit 62
Department of Housing and
 Urban Development (HUD)
 10, 96
Deposit
 Demand 62
 Insurance Flexibility Act (Garn-
  St. Germain Act) 50
Depreciation 7
Desktop Underwriter® 166
Direct Endorser 96
Discharge Paper 108
Disclosure
 Closing 24
Discount 124
 Rate 11
  Federal 11
Disintermediation 63
D-O-R-M 10
Down Payment 79, 99
Due on Sale Clause 49
Durability 169

E

ECOA - Equal Credit Opportunity
 Act 14, 159, 173
Economic Base 4
EMPIRICA 174
Entitlement 112
Equal Credit Opportunity Act
 (ECOA) 14, 159, 173
Equifax 174
Equilibrium 2
Equitable
 Right of Redemption 48
 Title 57, 144
Equity 177
 Exchange 147
Escrow 183
 Annual
  Statement 33
 Closing 184
Estimate
 Loan 19, 24
Experian 174

F

Fair, Isaac, & Co. 174
Fannie Mae 70, 80, 90
Federal
 Advisory Council 9
 Budget Deficit 6
 Discount Rate 11
 Home Loan Bank Board 135
 Home Loan Mortgage
  Corporation 71
 Housing Administration (FHA)
  76, 96, 124
 Housing Enterprise Oversight
  (OFHEO) 10
 Housing Finance Agency (FHFA)
  10, 70, 71
 Housing Finance Board (FHFB)
  10
 National Mortgage Association
  70
 Open Market Committee
  (FOMC) 9, 11
 Reserve 135
  Bank 9
  Board 4, 8, 9
Fed Funds Rate 11
FHA
 Loan Guideline 96
 Loan Guidelines
  Property 97
 Loan Program 102
 Loan Regulation 98
 Regulation 102
 Section 251- ARM Loan 105
 Underwriting Standard 180
FHA - Federal Housing
 Administration 76
FHFA - Federal Housing Finance
 Agency 10, 70, 71
FHFB - Federal Housing Finance
 Board 10
FICO 174
Fidelity Savings and Loan v. De
 La Cuesta, et. al. 50
Financial
 Statement 178
Financing 100
 Conventional 76
 Secondary 85, 98
 Seller 67, 142
First Mortgage 52

First Time Home Buyer Loan 141

Fiscal Policy 5

Fixed Rate Loan 76

FOMC - Federal Open Market Committee 9, 11

Foreclosure
  Action 46
  Judicial 46

Form 26-1880 108

Forward Commitment Purchase Program 71

Freddie Mac 71, 80, 90, 129, 133

Freely Transferable 44

Fully Amortized Loan 76, 86

Fund
  Pension 66

### G

Garn-St. Germain Act 50

Ginnie Mae 70

GNND - Good Neighbor Next Door 105

Good Neighbor Next Door (GNND) 105

Government National Mortgage Association 70

Graduated Payment 128

Gross Base Income 169

### H

HAFA - Home Affordable Foreclosure Alternatives Program 48

HAMP - Home Mortgage Affordability Program 48

Hard Money Mortgage 53

HECM - Home Equity Conversion Mortgage 104

HELOC Loan 54

HERA - Housing and Economic Recovery Act of 2008 64

Home Affordable Foreclosure Alternatives Program (HAFA) 48

Homebuyer Assistance Program 125

HomeBuyer Assistance Program 140

Home Equity
  Conversion Mortgage (HECM) 55, 104
  Line of Credit 54
  Loan 54

Home Mortgage Affordability Program (HAMP) 48

Homeowners Protection Act of 1998 84

Housing and Economic Recovery Act of 2008 (HERA) 64, 124

Housing
  Cycles 2
  Expense Ratio 90, 167, 168

HUD - Department of Housing and Urban Development 10, 96

Hybrid ARM 105

Hypothecate 45

### I

Immediate Delivery Program 71

Income
  Durable Source of 169
  Gross Base 169
  Quality Source of 169
  Source 169
  Stable Monthly 167, 169

Indemnify 114

Index 130, 132

Initial Escrow Statement 33

Instrument 40
  Negotiable 44
  Security 45

Insurance
  Company 65
  Mortgage 99

Interest
  Rate Cap 133

Interest-Only Loan 88

Interim Loan 56

Internal Revenue Service (IRS) 6

Internet Lender 65

Investment 145

IRS - Internal Revenue Service 6

### J

Judgment
  Deficiency 47

Judicial Foreclosure 46

Jumbo Loan 78

Junior Mortgage 53

Junk Fee 101

### K

Kickback 34

### L

Land Contract 57
  Advantages and Disadvantages of 58

Law
  of Supply and Demand 5
  Revenue Generating 4
  Right to Regulate 4

Lease 144, 146

Lease/Purchase 146

Lender
  Internet 65
  Portfolio 65

Lending
  Predatory 67
  Private 67
  Subprime 67

Liability 158

Lien
  Priority 51
  Theory 45

Liquid Asset 176

Loan
  95% Conventional Loan 81
  Amortized 76
  Application 157
  Approval Process 155
  Assumability of 101, 114
  Calculation 33
  Conforming 78
  Conventional 76, 79
    80% 79
    90% 79
    95% 80
    Traditional 76

Cost  19, 30
Estimate  19, 24
FHA Guideline  96
   Property  97
FHA Program  102
FHA Regulation  98
First Time Home Buyer  141
Fixed Rate  76
Fully Amortized  76, 86
HELOC  54
Home Equity  54
Interest-Only  88
Interim  56
Jumbo  78
Long-term Real Estate  76
Lot  56
Nonconforming  78
Origination Fee  156
Partially Amortized  86
Permanent Construction  56
Pick a Payment  56
Section 251-FHA ARM  105
Service Fee  156
Subprime  125
Underwriting  166
VA Guideline  108
Loan Prospector®  166
Loan-to-Value Ratio (LTV)  79, 134
London InterBank Offering Rate
      (LIBOR)  131
Long-term Real Estate Loan  76
Lot Loan  56
LTV - Loan-to-Value Ratio  79, 134

**M**

Manufactured Home  106
Margin  130
Market
   Buyer's  2
   Function of Secondary  68
   Primary Mortgage  62
   Secondary  70
      Function of  68
      Quality Control  71
   Secondary Mortgage  68
   Seller's  2
Maximum Guarantee Amount
      112
Member Bank  10

Military Eligibility  108
MMIP - Mutual Mortgage
      Insurance Plan  96
Mobile Home  106
Modular Home  106
Monetary Policy  5, 8, 10
Moral Suasion  13
Mortgage  46
   15-Year  77
   40-Year  78
   Adjustable Rate, (ARM)  55
   Advantages and Disadvantages
      of  49
   Bi-Weekly  136
   Blanket  54
   Bridge  54
   Broker  64
   Budget  54
   Cash-Out Refinance  53
   Company  63
   Construction  56
   Disclosure Improvement Act  15
   First  52
   Fund
      Flow of  69
   Hard Money  53
   Home Equity Conversion  55
   Insurance  99
   Junior  53
   Package  54
   Purchase Money  53
   Refinance  53
   Reverse  55, 104
   Reverse Annuity  55
   Reverse Equity  55
   Second  53
   Senior  52
   Soft Money  53
   Subprime  139
   Wraparound  55
Mortgage-Backed Security  69
Mortgagee  46
Mortgagor  46
Mutual Mortgage Insurance Plan
      (MMIP)  96

**N**

National Housing Act of 1934  96
Negative Amortization  76

Negotiable Instrument  44
Net Worth  159
Nominal Rate  125
Nonconforming Loan  78
Non-Occupying Borrowers
      ("Kiddie Condo")  105
Note
   Amortized Installment  44
   Promissory  40
   Rate  125
   Straight  44
Notice
   of Default  46

**O**

OFHEO - Federal Housing
      Enterprise Oversight  10
Ohio
   Division of Real Estate  58
   Housing Finance Agency
      (OHFA)  141
   Mortgage Broker Act  64
   Senate Bill 185  64
One Time Close  57
Open Market Operation  11
Option  145
   ARM  56
   Money  145
Optionor  145
Order of Execution  47
Origination Charge  30

**P**

Package Mortgage  54
Partially Amortized Loan  86
Partial Release  50
Passive
   Losses  7
Pass-through Security  71
Payment
   Balloon  44, 76, 86
   Down  99
   Graduated  128
   Shock  133
P-E-G-S  3
Pension Fund  66

Permanent
  Buydown  127
  Construction Loan  56
Pick a Payment Loan  56
PITI  91, 167, 180
PMI - Private Mortgage Insurance
    81
Point  124
Policy
  Fiscal  5
  Monetary  5, 8, 10
Portfolio Lender  65
Pre-Approval  154
Predatory Lending Practice  67
Prepayment
  Clause  51
  Penalty  89, 101
Primary Mortgage Market  62
Prime Rate  130
Private
  Lending  67
  Mortgage Insurance (PMI)  81
Profit  145
Promissory Note  40
Property Guidelines for FHA Loan
    97
Public Auction  47
Purchase
  Contract  146
  Money Mortgage  53

Q

Qualifying  145
  a Buyer  166
  the Buyer  178
Quality  169

R

Rate
  Adjustment Period  77
  Annual Percentage (APR)  16
  Coupon  125
  Discount  11
    Federal  11
  Fed Funds  11
  Nominal  125
  Note  125

Prime  130
  Teaser  133
Real Estate
  Investment Trust Act of 1960
      (REIT)  66
  Mortgage Trust (REMT)  66
  Owned (REO)  65
  Settlement Procedures Act
      (RESPA)  18
Refinance  175
  Mortgage  53
Regulation Z  15, 135
REIT - Real Estate Investment
    Trust Act of 1960  66
REMT - Real Estate Mortgage Trust
    66
REO - Real Estate Owned  65
Repay
  Ability to, Rule  20
Report of Separation  108
Request for Verification of Deposit
    177
Rescind  16
Reserve  176
  Requirement  12
RESPA - Real Estate Settlement
    Procedures Act  18, 184
Revenue Generating Law  4
Reverse Mortgage  55, 104
Right of Redemption
  Equitable  48
Right to Regulate Law  4
Roundtable Closing  184

S

SAFE Act  64
Safe and Fair Enforcement
    Licensing Act (SAFE Act)  64
Sale
  Confirmation of  47
  Short  48
Satisfaction  50
Savings and Loan Associations
    (S&Ls)  62
Secondary
  Financing  85, 98
  Market  70
    Function of  68

Mortgage Market  68
  Quality Control  71
Second Mortgage  53
Section
  203(b)  103
  203(k)  103
  234(c)  104
  251-FHA ARM Loan  105
  1031  147
Securitization  70
Security Instrument  45
Self-Liquidating  76
Seller
  Contribution Limit  100
  Financing  67, 142
Seller's Market  2
Senior Mortgage  52
Servicing Transfer Statement  33
Settlement  183
Shared Equity Plan  148
Sheriff's Deed  47
Short Sale  48
Social Force  5
Soft Money Mortgage  53
Speculation  145
Stable Monthly Income  167, 169
Standard Form 180  108
Statement
  Annual Escrow  33
  Financial  178
  Initial Escrow  33
  Servicing Transfer  33
Straight Note  44
Streamlined 203(k) Loan  103
Subordination Clause  51
Subprime
  Lending  67
  Loan  125

T

Tax
  Reform Act of 1986  7
Taxation  6
Tax-Deferred Exchange  147
Tax-Free Exchange  147
Taxpayer Relief Act of 1997  7

*T-Bills 6*

*Teaser Rate 133*

*the Fed - Federal Reserve Board 8*

*TILA - Truth in Lending Act 15,
    135*

*Title*
  *Equitable 57, 144*

*Title V 64*

*Total Debt Service Ratio 91, 167,
    168, 181*

*Traditional Conventional Loan
    76*

*Transferable*
  *Freely 44*

*TransUnion 174*

*Treasury*
  *Bills 6*
  *Certificates 6*
  *Notes 6*

*Trust 66*

*Trust Deed 45*
  *Advantages and Disadvantages
      of 46*

*Trustee 45*

*Trustor 45*

*Truth in Lending Act (TILA) 15,
    17, 135*

## U

*Underwriter 165*

*United States Treasury
      Department 6*

## V

*VA - Veterans Administration 107*
  *Home Loan Program 107*
  *Loan Guideline 108*

*Voluntary Conveyance 48*

## W

*Worker, Homeownership and
      Business Assistance Act of
      2009 8*

*Wraparound Mortgage 55*